Women
in MASS COMMUNICATION

THIRD EDITION

Women
in MASS COMMUNICATION

THIRD EDITION

PAMELA J. CREEDON & JUDITH CRAMER

The University of Iowa   *St. John's University*

SAGE Publications
Thousand Oaks ▪ London ▪ New Delhi

For information:

Sage Publications, Inc.
2455 Teller Road
Thousand Oaks, California 9[13]
E-mail: order@sagepub.com

Sage Publications Ltd.
1 Oliver's Yard
55 City Road
London EC1Y 1SP
United Kingdom

Sage Publications India Pvt.
B-42, Panchsheel Enclave
Post Box 4109
New Delhi 110 017 India

Printed in the United States of America.

Library of Congress Cataloging-in-Publication Data

Women in mass communication / edited by Pamela J. Creedon, Judith Cramer.— 3rd ed.
    p. cm.
Includes bibliographical references and index.
ISBN 1-4129-3694-2 (cloth) — ISBN 1-4129-3695-0 (pbk.)
  1. Women in the mass media industry. I. Creedon, Pamela J.
II. Cramer, Judith. III. Title.
P94.5.W65W67 2007
302.23082—dc22

                              2006001906

This book is printed on acid-free paper.

06   07   08   09   10   10 9 8 7 6 5 4 3 2 1

Acquiring Editors:	Margaret H. Seawell/Todd R. Armstrong
Editorial Assistant:	Sarah K. Quesenberry
Project Editor:	Astrid Virding
Copyeditor:	Carla Freeman
Typesetter:	C&M Digitals (P) Ltd.
Indexer:	Kimberly Merchant

Contents

Acknowledgments

This edition would not have been possible without the exceptional effort of Judy Cramer. Without her coordinating, editing, consoling and cajoling, we would not have a third edition of *Women in Mass Communication.* Special thanks to my partner, Kelly Reid, who literally saved my life, and to all of the great women in this book, who continue to work for transformative change in mass communication. We will never stop believing in equity, equality and "r'evolution."

—PC

There are a number of people who've touched my life and have, in some way, contributed to this work. I would like to thank Pam Creedon for nearly 20 years of friendship, collaboration, and mentoring; Richard Weber for seeing the number of chapters I'd contributed to others' books and challenging me more than a decade ago to shepherd a book with my name on it; Kay Saucier for believing in me and taking me under her wing when I was an undergraduate; Roger Wetherington and Barbara Fowles for their ideas and editing; and my aunt, Mary Brogan, a woman way ahead of her time as a business owner working in a man's world, for her love and support. Finally, I am especially grateful to Lucille Tortorici for her strength, patience, and understanding.

—JC

We both owe special thanks to Margaret Seawell and Astrid Virding at Sage Publications. Their support of the project made the third edition a reality. Special thanks to Kim Merchant, University of Iowa journalism and mass communication master's student, who prepared the subject and author indexes.

The editors and Sage gratefully acknowledge the following reviewers: Debora Wenger, Virginia Commonwealth University; William Click,

Winthrop University; Lynn Klyde-Silverstein, University of Northern Colorado; Linda Lumsden, Western Kentucky University; Susanne Gubanc, Simpson College; Corless Smith, San Francisco State University; Michael Leslie, University of Florida; Candace White, University of Tennessee, Knoxville; and Sharon Bramlett-Solomon, Arizona State University.

PART I

Two Decades of Progress?

1

Introduction

We've Come a Long Way, Maybe . . .

Judith Cramer, St. John's University

Pamela J. Creedon, The University of Iowa

This should be a season of celebration. America has its first female in the Oval Office. Everywhere you look, there are women surgeons, police officials, hard-charging executives and even amazingly resourceful undercover operatives. So why aren't women across the country cheering? Well, perhaps because those role models—important as they are—are all fictional.

—Barbara Kantrowitz (2005)

They are all characters on the 2005–2006 season's prime-time television programs: *Commander in Chief, Grey's Anatomy,* and *Alias.* And, with few exceptions, these women do not model values different from those of their male TV character predecessors.

3

It has been 30 years since women began entering the workforce in significant numbers and 12 years since the previous edition of *Women in Mass Communication* was published, containing the hopeful writings of many feminist scholars and professionals. So much has changed . . . and yet, so little.

Play, Rewind, Fast Forward

Reformist Feminism

In 1989, George Herbert Walker Bush was president of the United States, the Tiananmen Square pro-democracy rally was held in China, and the Exxon *Valdez* spilled 11 million gallons of oil into Prince William Sound in Alaska. This is also the year *Women in Mass Communication: Challenging Gender Values* was first published. The book focused on the challenge of "re-visioning" gender values in mass communication.

In the first edition, we and 18 other feminist media scholars described issues and prescribed solutions to gender inequities in the mass communication professions. Our chapters reflected on "re-vision," a term borrowed from author Adrienne Rich (1979):

> Re-vision is the act of looking back, of seeing with fresh eyes, of entering a new text from a new critical direction. For women it is an act of survival because until we can understand the assumptions in which we are drenched, we cannot know ourselves. (p. 35)

Our treatment of gender embraced our understanding of "the other" in our assumptions about race, class, sexuality, and gender.

Many of the studies we reported about women in mass communication had never been amassed into one volume. While each author was knowledgeable about a specific media profession, such as newspapers, television, radio, magazines, public relations, or advertising, or a theory or a research niche, their findings had never before been assembled into the "big picture."

When we all viewed the big picture, it looked pretty dismal. We reported about the "glass ceiling" in promotions, the $1 million penalty for being a woman in public relations (that's the salary gap between men and women over a career), sexist images in advertising, and the paucity of female full professors in our discipline. It was not a pretty picture in 1989, but we believed that bringing the issues into the light would make a difference.

Play, Fast Forward, Rewind

Transformist Feminism

Five years later, in 1994, Bill Clinton was president, and the Whitewater scandal investigations had begun. Nelson Mandela was the first Black president of South Africa, and the first terrorist act against the World Trade Center had taken place. We thought it was time to take another look at the issues related to women in mass communication, in a second edition of the book, and document what changes had taken place.

The second volume expanded to 28 feminist media scholars and included new chapters covering research in mass communication and women of color in academia. Unexpectedly, the authors—some from the first edition and some new ones—while preparing their chapters for the updated edition found that nothing had really changed. Feminist mass communication research and the increased number of women in the field had had little effect on the practice. The traditional structure of mass communication education remained largely intact, with males still dominating the ranks of full professors. We decided that reformist feminism, which we had been advocating, had done nothing more than open Pandora's box.

As author Shana Alexander (1988) put it,

> When we decided to be equals, we meant, without thinking of it, equals in a man's world. We were still playing by their rules, or defining equality in their terms. We forgot that we are different from men; we are the other, we have different sensibilities. Today younger women across America are paying for our error. (p. 44)

When we realized what had happened, we argued in the second edition for *transformative change.* We wanted change that would address the basic issue: the gendered nature of the system. The second edition of the book updated the status of women in various media professions—but questioned the increased ghettoization of gender issues as "women's issues," an example of which would be the designation "Mommy Track," a term that reinforces the woman's role as primary caregiver.

Play, Fast Forward, Rewind

Twelve years later, in 2006, George Walker Bush is president, and terrorism has demolished the World Trade Center in New York and damaged the Pentagon. U.S. troops are in Iraq, Afghanistan, and beyond; a tsunami has devastated numerous developing Asian countries; and Hurricane Katrina has wiped out New Orleans as we knew it. Germany recently elected its first female chancellor, while the American people have lost one of only two U.S. Supreme Court seats held by women.

One Step Forward, Two Steps Back?

The third edition of *Women in Mass Communication (WMC3)* includes 24 feminist scholars—some from the first edition, some from the first and second editions, and some new. Several authors in this edition suggest that "maybe" we have come a long way over the past few decades, but nearly all agree that transformative change has not happened. Where change has taken place, it has occurred in baby steps, not in long strides and only in some locations, and not universally across the media professions.

The Third Edition

Women now constitute more than half of all college students and about 65% of all undergraduate and graduate student journalism and mass communication enrollments. In Part I of *WMC3*, "Two Decades of Progress?" Linda Steiner argues that after 30 years of feminism, today's journalism textbooks still address only relatively simple issues such as the use of sexist language and sexist stereotyping. She further asserts that texts are out of touch with changing definitions and methods of delivering news. They do not provide sufficient insight about newsroom culture, sexism in assignments, balancing professional and domestic responsibilities, and gender issues in hierarchical, exploitative relationships. According to Steiner, "No textbook seriously considers what male-ness means for journalism practice or the newsroom culture."

Maurine Beasley updates her 1988 and 1996 "New Majority" reports and finds that while women journalists today are much less likely to suffer from blatant discrimination, they still have not reached parity with men in the newsroom. According to Beasley, women may be leaving journalism at a faster rate than their male counterparts partially because newsrooms are not especially welcoming or supportive places for women.

Part II, "Update on the Professions," explores the status of women working in the traditional media professions of newspapers, magazines, radio, television, public relations, and advertising, while recognizing that there have been changes in technology and the breadth and depth of women's involvement in mass communication. June Nicholson, Judith Cramer, Jannette Dates, Elizabeth Toth and Carolyn Cline, and Nancy Mitchell find little or no growth in their respective media professions and that where there has been growth, women are working in lower-level and lower-paying positions and haven't earned salary parity with men. They conclude that the growth has not been as much as they had hoped 12 years ago. The lone exception to these conclusions is the magazine industry, which, Sammye Johnson finds, is still a good place for growth and stability for women despite the fact that salary parity has not been reached.

There is a mixed prognosis in the more specialized media professions of health communication, scholastic journalism, online journalism, and sports journalism, all new chapters in this third edition. Julie Andsager reports that women are playing an equal if not greater role than men in shaping the burgeoning field of health communication and promotion, but she cautions that because the field is so young, there are no data on women's job satisfaction, salaries, or managerial roles. Candace Perkins Bowen wonders "what is wrong with the picture" when women far outnumber men in scholastic media leadership positions and yet are extraordinarily underrepresented at the highest management-level positions in commercial media. Shayla Thiel Stern's research concludes that women online editors are leaving to find more rewarding careers and are being replaced by the White male "old guard." Pam Creedon and Roseanna Smith conclude in their chapter that despite more than two decades of Title IX, the overall hierarchy in sports coverage and sports beats has not changed. In rank order, major men's professional sports and men's collegiate football and basketball still come first—and "everything else," which may or may not include women's sports, comes after that.

As Part IV, "International Perspectives" reveals, women in journalism and mass communication have not fared much better overseas. Romy Fröhlich explores the status of Western European women journalists and finds they are working in lower industry positions and making less money than their male counterparts. She introduces us to the "friendliness trap," in which, sooner or later, the supposed highly prized feminine values, attributes, and behavior in women's journalism careers become associated with a lack of assertiveness, poor conflict management, and weak leadership skills. What was an apparent "head start" turns out to be what Fröhlich asserts is a "career killer."

Debra Mason examines the intersections of media, faith, and women across religions and concludes that women have been underrepresented or ignored in the coverage of religion since time in memoriam, despite the fact that women have long dominated religion journalism. She calls this area of research "fertile" ground and suggests that it could be an important tool in an effort to globally empower women of faith.

H. Leslie Steeves's research explores media and women in a global context and contends that the continuing absence and oppression of women in media content and women's economic disadvantages can be linked to the increasing power and concentration of multinational corporations and the associated values of global consumerism. She advocates for closer feminist scrutiny of this and the nation-state in its support of neoliberal economic dominance, growing militarization, and fundamentalism.

Part V of *WMC3*, "Building a Foundation for Further Study," attempts to do just that by examining racial and ethnic minority women and lesbians in relation to the construction and mediation of social reality in mass communication law, culture, language, and leadership. This section also explores the impact and contributions of feminist theory to the study and practice of mass communication. Diane Borden and Maria Marron examine court cases about free expression involving women's sexuality and social status that have largely reinforced cultural stereotypes and marginalized women. They argue that the current political climate and the changing composition of the U.S. Supreme Court may end up restricting the definition of equality and equity in First Amendment law, which will ensure the continuation of difference and dominance.

In constructing the concept of "Other," Carolyn Byerly finds that the media play a significant role in continuing the syndrome of "the Other." She suggests that this is accomplished through the production of images and messages of nationality, culture, religion, race, gender, and sexual dimensions. And through semiotic analysis, Meenakshi Gigi Durham demonstrates how girls arrive at definitions or understandings of what "beauty" is, which contributes to racial and cultural myths current in today's youth culture.

In her chapter about leadership, Linda Aldoory reports that research finds that women in mass communication leadership positions are described as "nurturing," "participative," and "supportive"—all characteristics consistent with transformational leadership. She believes that a "leadership-literate" audience of women and men in mass communication might break down barriers that are keeping more women from leadership positions.

Laura Wackwitz and Lana Rakow argue in "Got Theory?" that feminist communication theory does not just consider the images or absence of women in media content and the media professions but also provides a framework to examine difference, voice, and representation that can be used by anyone to build interpersonal and cultural coalitions and bridges for the purposes of change or transformation.

Twenty-four feminist scholars of varying races, cultures, and nationalities, spanning five decades in age, having lived and worked in a broad range of media positions in different parts of the United States and the world, have contributed to this third edition of *Women in Mass Communication*. And so, in the final chapter, we attempt to look ahead to offer a global perspective on the status, changes, and concerns for women entering the journalism and mass communication professions.

2

Sexed and Gendered Bodies in Journalism Textbooks

Linda Steiner, Rutgers University

I f classroom education is important, then textbooks are important. Textbooks articulate and celebrate a discipline's paradigms and procedures, declaring canonical standards of knowledge. Textbooks for professional groups not only describe key practices but also prescribe, albeit in ways that accommodate existing distributions of authority and power, how the profession ought to be practiced and who can practice it. Newswriting—now often called "media writing"—textbooks are particularly significant in defining what students learn about journalism, including who can report the news. Given their professional experiences and their explicit commitment to "realism," authors of reporting textbooks want to enforce standard newsroom procedures and socialize recruits into professional norms. For their part, newswriting instructors (sometimes former practitioners with little training in pedagogy, sometimes scholars with little interest in skills) typically assign textbooks.

Meanwhile, opportunities are relatively limited for students to read these textbooks "oppositionally" or subversively, even in journalism, where students are presumably discouraged from ingesting information uncritically. The fact that many textbook authors have been senior professors, deans, and well-known reporters or editors may confer an unusual degree of credibility and authority. According to a 2002 survey (available at http://www.poynter.org), approximately half of all full-time journalists in the United States (i.e., a figure including older journalists) majored in journalism or communication.[1] So, understanding these textbooks helps explain and even predict both classroom and newsroom practices and cultures. Furthermore, students in advertising, public relations, and other media professions often take the same introductory courses, so they read the same textbooks.

The textual analysis here of how 170 college-level newswriting and reporting textbooks published in the United States since 1890 have dealt with gender issues offers evidence of relative stability over time as well as remarkable consistencies within given time periods. Despite their fundamental conservatism and commitment to conventional practices, however, textbooks do get rewritten in the aftermath of paradigmatic revolutions. Since reporting textbooks rarely discuss outdated or discarded practices, students learn new understandings and new ways of doing things without realizing anything has changed. But careful comparative analysis suggests that controversies over gender and the meaning of social identity have inspired rewriting of journalism textbooks.

Comparing multiple editions of textbooks starkly dramatizes revisions of ideas about how and when gender matters to journalists. For example, the 1960 edition of *The Professional Journalist* noted that women reporters proved their professional competence during World War II; echoing claims often heard at the time, John Hohenberg explained that women left these jobs because home and motherhood were "stronger attractions." But Hohenberg's 1978 edition conceded that the women who kept newspapers going during the war "had great difficulty in maintaining their foothold once peace came" (p. 19). The 1983 edition eliminated all discussion of women reporters. Different shifts emerged in Fred Fedler's *Reporting for the Media,* first published in 1973. By 1989, Fedler discouraged sex stereotyping, as long as efforts to eliminate male bias were not overly awkward. He strongly endorsed hiring minority reporters, partly as a matter of social justice, yet he did not ask whether gender makes a difference. In his 1997 edition, Fedler and his coauthors continued to warn against "the cumbersome and repetitive 'he/she' . . . . The effort to rid the language of male bias should never become so strained that it distracts readers" (p. 42). The 1997 chapter on careers also briefly acknowledged that news organizations lag behind other industries in hiring and promoting women, especially in management. It suggested no solutions or strategies, however. The discussion in the 2005 edition by Fedler is shorter but in some sense more prescriptive: A subhead asserted, "The Industry Needs More Women and Minorities" (p. 628), and the text explains that although White men tend to hire and promote people like themselves, an all-White male staff cannot accurately reflect a community.

Method

This chapter first defines what textbooks features were emphasized and then, after a highly condensed overview of journalism education in the United States, proceeds more or less chronologically. The analysis and interpretation are grounded in close readings of 170 books about how to write and report news. It is worth noting, however, that the research began with a search for relevant terms in the indices and tables of contents of these textbooks. A dozen textbooks published before 1920 never referred to women. After 1920, *women* increasingly showed up in the indices, first, usually referring to "women's news" and, much later, in the context of apologetic discussions of women reporters' marginalization. Now, the terms *women, sexism,* and *gender* rarely appear. Melvin Mencher's 2003 edition is a notable exception: References to women in its index indicate discussions of, among other things, the economic costs of discrimination and sexual slavery.

The key feature is what textbooks said about who can succeed in journalism and what precludes success. Nearly every reporting textbook explicitly discussed careers. Carl Warren's *Modern News Reporting* (1951) was typical in asserting that reporting "can be mastered by any young man or woman with average brain capacity plus initiative, study, practice and experience" (p. 1). At least until the 1970s, however, textbooks held that women were not rough or tough enough for serious reporting.

Semantic choice is a second issue. Few authors defined their audience as clearly as George Knapp's (1939) *Boys' Book of Journalism.* Until the 1970s, however, authors routinely used masculine nouns and pronouns to describe the "newsman" and "his" qualifications. Their stylebooks often explicitly required using masculine pronouns whenever gender was irrelevant. Perhaps authors did not intend to exclude women, yet students, especially women, may not interpret references to "men" as including women. More important, the regularity with which textbooks first broadly discussed "reporters," then later specified precisely what women can and cannot do, calls into question whether authors' intentions were generic.

Third, the treatment of readers is relevant; textbooks long equated female readers with female reporters. The founding dean of the first university journalism school stated this formula succinctly: "Since [society] news largely concerns women and women's affairs, the position is generally held by a woman" (Williams & Martin, 1911, p. 253). A related question is the extent to which the concept of womanhood was universalized (i.e., erasing potential differences among women on the basis of race, class, ethnicity, education, occupation, or sexual orientation) and how the emerging notion of gender was attached to women. Thus, gender became a "woman's issue."

Finally, it is noteworthy that authors' journalistic or university affiliations and geographical location made no difference. Even in recent years, few women have coauthored, much less single authored, reporting textbooks— certainly fewer than the number of women in journalism schools and jobs would predict.

Early Journalism Education

From 1886 to 1900, Martha Louise Rayne, a poet, novelist, reporter, and editor, ran a journalism school for women. Rayne's 1893 *What Can a Woman Do?* included a chapter on journalism, which called for professional journalism training and promoted journalism as "agreeable, wide-awake work, with no more drudgery than there is in other occupations, and with many compensations" (1893/1974, p. 44). Occasionally, someone called for formal education, yet the apprentice approach to journalism training held sway into the 20th century. The primary instructional resources for would-be journalists before 1900 were short manuals. In the 1880s and 1890s, *The Journalist*, "A Weekly Publication Devoted to Newspaper Men and Publishers," published several "how-to's" as serials, which were then reprinted as booklets. The resistance to journalism schools and to hiring college graduates as reporters was, moreover, expressed in specifically sexual rhetoric: Book learning was disdained as effete and "womanish," thus irrelevant for work praised as lusty, vigorous, and "masculine."

Journalism education garnered support once journalists saw advantages for enhancing their status and sense of professionalism. This coincided with increasing pressure on universities to begin teaching practical subjects and with growth in the news industry itself. Once inaugurated, momentum grew quickly. The University of Illinois launched a 4-year curriculum in 1904; the University of Missouri, having intermittently taught journalism since 1878, opened the first full-fledged school in 1908. Columbia's journalism school opened in 1912. By 1920, students at 28 schools could major in journalism; by 1928, there were 56 separate schools or departments. Now there are about 460 journalism and mass communication programs in the United States.

In 1903, a long-time literary editor mused in his textbook, "Why any woman who can get $800 a year for teaching should wish to take up the harder work of newspaper reporting is difficult to understand" (Shuman, 1903, p. 157). Hard life that it entailed, reporters earned more money, status, and glamour than did nurses and schoolteachers. Despite discouraging words from textbooks and teachers, women applied to journalism schools, especially at the coeducational land grant schools. Since the 1970s, women have represented 55% to 65% of the journalism enrollments.

The First Generation of Textbooks

By the 1890s, newspapers began to change in particular ways, first, by incorporating the same trends toward specialization that were transforming other business enterprises. Furthermore, newly emerging department stores needed buyers, especially women; on the other hand, newspapers, which were increasingly reliant on department store advertising revenue, needed "pleasant" copy to attract women readers. The resulting demand for women as readers, and as writers for them, was acknowledged in textbooks in the context of society news. Even this produced a backlash, however. Edwin L. Shuman complained about an "ambitious feminine army" encroaching on journalism. In *The Art and Practice of Journalism* (1899), Shuman conceded that women's brains are as good as men's but, nonetheless, articles "from a woman's standpoint" are "naturally superficial and frothy" and insufficiently virile. Moreover, according to Shuman, newspaper work was de-feminizing: "[Women] will swiftly lose many of their high ideals and sweet and tender ways, as inevitably as if they had been run through a machine for the purpose. And what is the use?" (p. 156). He advised women determined to find jobs (i.e., despite these hazards) to write for children's or society pages or to concentrate on stories and verse: "The literary way is beset with fewer rocks and precipices for the feminine traveler" (p. 156). Shuman's often-cited 1903 textbook warned that yellow journalism was difficult, risky, and unpleasant, if not despicable: "The work of news-gathering, as a rule, is too rude and exacting for [women]" (p. 148). Likewise, Charles Olin (1906), explained that when women publish humorous sidebars,

> Her story is not supposed to add anything of importance to the report of her brother journalists, its whole value lying in the fact that it is written from a wholly feminine standpoint, in a bright feminine manner, with little touches of feminine sympathy, pathos and sentiment. (p. 51)

Don Seitz (1916) saw the only opportunities for women in fashion and society news and in clerical jobs. Women, he said, did much better on typewriters than men did.

Textbooks for Women

This newsroom sexual division of labor provoked debate over whether women students should take the same courses as men. One editor-scholar pair complained in 1935 about journalism schools "overflowing" with coeds, since, after all, women "almost invariably get married and quit about the time they have had enough experience to be of some real use around the office" (Porter & Luxon, 1935, p. 8). They explained,

> Newspaper work is so demanding physically that many women who can teach or do ordinary office work cannot stand up under it. Its general tempo—with the deadline-fighting element always present—is such as to bar many women because of nervous temperament. (p. 8)

The solution was for women to take a few electives in writing for women. These courses tracked (or rather, derailed) women in ways acceptable to men, indeed, in ways that mirrored the public/private distinction marking the larger social order—that is, away from the high-status arenas that men took to be their exclusive territory and toward domestic, consumption roles that remained lower status, despite women's attempts to glamorize them. By 1940, a dozen universities taught writing for women readers, courses seldom taken by males but often required for female majors (Beasley & Theus, 1988).

Men no more wanted to teach these electives or develop textbooks for them than they wanted to write news for women. Of the handful of journalism textbooks single-authored by women, the majority were published between 1926 and 1936, when courses specifically for women were developed. Genevieve Jackson Boughner (1926), who taught feature writing for women at Wisconsin and later at Minnesota, set the trend with her 348-page tome: *Women in Journalism* firmly directed women toward specializations where "they may capitalize on their tastes and instincts rather than oppose them, as they are called upon to do in many lines of newspaper writing in which they duplicate men's work" (p. viii). Boughner compared advice columnists, for example, to priests or ministers who nurtured the "protective, mother side" of women's nature (p. 176). Even beauty experts needed a "feminine love of beauty and daintiness" and scientific knowledge of physiology and hygiene.

Ethel Colson Brazelton's *Writing and Editing for Women* (1927) likewise celebrated women's writing as a noble calling and only indirectly hinted at the economic handicap of women's "specialness." Brazelton, who taught journalism for women at Medill, insisted,

> The fact of sex, the "woman's angle," is the woman writer's tool, but it must never be her weapon. . . . But being a woman, she is possessed of a real advantage in the business of doing, recording, interpreting women's interests, ways and work. (p. 8)

For example, covering clubs required the entire range of journalism skills, plus knowledge of sociology, philosophy, economics, art, hygiene, music, homemaking, civics, and politics. Brazelton downplayed sexism on the part of editors, insisting that "common sense, courtesy, persistence, courage and quiet cheerful determination make mightily for success" in finding and keeping jobs. Women earned at least a third less than men, she speculated, because of "continual turn-over due to feminine restlessness" and marriage (p. 207).

The Status of Society Editors and the Feminine Mystique

As the economic stakes and competition for jobs increased, textbook authors grew more adamant that women enjoyed a peculiar "fitness" for feature stories, club news, and certain forms of criticism. A couple of men proclaimed respect for society departments. More often, male authors openly disdained social news. Robert Neal (1939) ferociously attacked the "pretty little society editor" who created misery for the copy desk. Maybe as the only woman on the staff, she rationalized that rules did not apply to her, Neal speculated; her only other possible defense was that society news was "unbelievably monotonous" (p. 360). As late as 1943, Wolseley and Campbell, in the widely used *Exploring Journalism*, explained,

> [Editors] are men and prefer to hire men. Moreover, many of them are convinced that journalism is a man's profession and that the woman who doesn't believe her place to be in the home should choose an occupation sheltered from the ugly realities that journalists encounter. (p. 52)

The authors therefore warned women that wartime jobs would be temporary.

In sum, pre–World War II textbooks delivered contradictory reasons for women's unfitness: Newsroom behavior was too crude for the feminine sensibility, or the work was too exacting. Women lacked necessary knowledge and expertise, or male sources would not trust them. They were de-feminized by contact with men, or they wasted their training by marrying. They had no sense of humor, or they did not take work seriously. Despite women's "natural advantage" in "distaff writing," they apparently needed to be taught its basics. Many textbooks continued to provide highly detailed instructions for covering weddings and other social events. Certainly, those who bemoaned the slush and gush of society pages failed to acknowledge how journalists and journalism educators were perpetuating conventional attitudes.

After the war, to justify women's postwar eviction from newsrooms, most authors drew on the increasingly popular interest in psychology and the notion that women had a distinct psyche. Carl Warren (1951) confidently asserted, "You cannot hold a woman's interest long with abstractions, logic, inanimate things and processes" (p. 360). He encouraged women reporters to capitalize on their "natural inquisitiveness and ability to talk information out of men" (p. 8), as well as women's need for glamour. Meanwhile, like his fellow textbook authors, Warren justified editors' reluctance to hire women:

> A good many young women treat a job as a stopgap between school and marriage . . . whereas marriage and its economic responsibilities rivet a man more closely to his job. Some women who continue working after marriage often are absent because of illness at home, confinement periods or just for shopping. (p. 8)

Grant Hyde's 1952 textbook called the society desk "almost universally the first job for women"—and their last: "What holds them there is the pleasure they gain from acquaintance and cooperation with the most active and interesting women in the community" (p. 358). Even *Herald-Tribune* reporter India McIntosh, in her chapter for *Late City Edition* (Herzberg, 1947), advised "girls" to exploit their femininity and exploit the stories about women and babies that city editors saw as women's "natural" province. Siegfried Mandel said in 1962 that marriage and parenthood stabilized men and made them better workers; these same events—"the natural fulfillment of any girl"—made women a greater employment risk (pp. 275–276). Compared with some others, then, one author was forthright in warning women not to write society news "if it can be avoided" (Byerly, 1961, p. 133).

Paradigm Changes in the 1970s

The second wave of the women's movement exposed the ways that sexist language symbolized and reinforced contempt for women, and lobbied for significant changes in mass media. According to feminists, the same logic justifying creation of the racial/minority affairs beat applied to ethnicity, sexual orientation, and gender, although feminists were not using this to justify women's sections. Retooling in news media was slow. Textbooks were even slower to catch up to cultural transformations. The first and most consistent shift was the elimination of society news. Newspaper publishers' decisions to replace women's sections with lifestyle sections justified deleting discussions about female audiences from textbooks.

More important, the lag among textbooks was evident in authors' resistance to new stylebooks that called for equal treatment of women and men. The 1977 *Associated Press Stylebook* condemned sexist references, demeaning stereotypes, and condescending phrases about women, and it warned reporters not to imply an inconsistency between women's attractiveness and professionalism or to describe a woman's physical appearance or family relationships when they would not do so for a man. Accordingly, some textbooks adopted gender-neutral language, inserted examples or photographs of women reporters, or appended guides to nondiscriminatory communication. Ironically, a few authors failed to follow their own advice. For example, two experienced journalists violated their own admonitions about sex stereotyping when describing a police reporter, apparently a 36-year-old mother: "With her large frame and her brown hair swept haphazardly into a bun, [she] looks more like a fifth-grade music teacher than someone whose job is to chase fire engines and ambulances" (Porter & Ferris, 1988, p. 44).

Long after such changes were afoot, several authors aggressively protested linguistic change, defending use of the masculine "generic" as merely a graceful space- and time-saver. Their resistance seems to betray fear that concessions would cede authority to feminism. Both in 1977 and 1991, William Metz debated feminists, particularly on language issues. His chapter on sexism in news mocked feminists for getting "teed off on silly issues," such as the term "women's lib." Having quoted the *Washington Post Deskbook*'s apology for sexist language, Bruce Garrison (1990) added, "But some words and forms are so historically and culturally embedded they defy efforts to eradicate them. Moreover, awkward and self-conscious new forms can interfere with readers' comprehension" (p. 69). Ralph Izard (1982) critiqued coverage skewed by prejudice on the basis of race, sex, age, or physical ability and encouraged individuals and institutions to consider how "unconscious neglect" causes distortions. Nonetheless, resistance to change did not upset Izard: "Reporters cannot please everyone. The language cannot be restructured every time someone gets a new idea" (p. 334).

When textbooks characterized women's work prospects, it was to deny that women were disadvantaged. Occasionally, textbooks noted that about one third of the newspaper professionals were women and that as a result of sex discrimination lawsuits, more women were being hired in management, at larger newspapers, and in broadcast newsrooms. More often, however, 1980s-era textbooks confidently dismissed concerns about sex discrimination, saying "feminine" journalists who complained about promotions should realize promotions were slow for men, too.

1990s to the Present

In general, the issue of women reporters is now a nonissue. Textbooks suggest that no sex or gender issues remain in the context of internships, entry-level jobs, or work stressors. Perhaps the very commitment to gender-blind language inhibits authors from addressing whether a reporter's gender matters to sources or readers (and, in any case, authors imply that only women are gendered). If there is an issue, it is merely content marred by sex stereotyping and sexist language. Michael Ryan and James Tankard's *Writing for Print and Digital Media* (2005) explains how male pronouns and male suffixes marginalize and potentially exclude women. Moreover, their highly sophisticated and innovative chapter on evaluating career choices notes that media organizations may share the vested interests of most power brokers in supporting the status quo. The book credits news professionals with helping to give voice to the disenfranchised and offers guidelines for internalizing sensitivity to diversity and for thinking critically about racism, privilege, sexism, and powerlessness.

Brooks and his three (male) colleagues, Kennedy, Moen, and Ranly (1992), discuss in detail how to avoid phrasing that is derogatory or imprecise on the basis of stereotypes about race, ethnicity, sexual orientation, age, and physical impairment; they are highly specific about how to avoid sexism (drop feminine endings on words like *hero;* use generic terms like *firefighter;* drop sexist pronouns) and scrupulously operate according to their own advice. Stovall (2006) is less prescriptive regarding the "language sensitivities" of some audiences: "Although some people have gone to extremes in identifying supposedly offensive language, there are terms and attitudes in writing that should legitimately be questioned and changed" (p. 63). Whitaker, Ramsey, and Smith (2000) are similarly calm in reporting, "Although stereotypes impede information flow, audiences—as well as news organizations—have long used them in stories about race, gender, age, politics or international affairs" (p. 6). That said, the authors argue that noninclusive language alienates people and prevents effective communication.

The *Associated Press Stylebook* (2004), which remains the basis of the stylebooks included in many textbooks, now warns against courtesy titles (Miss, Mrs., Mr., or Ms.). Accordingly, a dozen or so journalism textbooks published since 2000 include examples of both women and men in this regard and either use gender-neutral terms or alternate between female and male pronouns. There are a few minor "relapses," including the use of courtesy titles for women. Perhaps predictably, in *Online Journalism* (2005), Richard Craig describes the cyberjournalist as a "he" (p. 263). Craig never suggests that women lack knowledge of the Internet, but neither does he address the question of whether women are discouraged from developing Internet knowledge as a medium and as an information resource.

Shifting Perspectives on Sex and Gender

The exception proving the rule, Nancy Mavity's 1930 reporting textbook integrated models of and for women reporters and was not intended for use in a women-only course. An *Oakland Tribune* writer, Mavity attributed gender differences to child-rearing practices but also admitted that certain acquired differences—like emotionalism—handicap women. She decried the notion that personal charm was women's route to success. More to the point, Mavity asked students to consider what women reporters should do when interviewing flirtatious or vulgar male sources. Threaten to call the police? Leave? Ken Metzler's 1986 book indirectly proposed answers. Metzler advised women to not date sources, to dress conservatively, and to ignore off-color remarks. After all, "social and business mores don't change overnight" (p. 295). Meanwhile, he encouraged women journalists to use feminine wiles and to exploit men's "natural propensity" to trust women. These two authors, however, were virtually unique in addressing the problem of sexual harassment, although neither of them used the term.

Writers of textbooks no longer say that sex disqualifies women from "real" reporting. Instead, they offer a vague, politically and theoretically evacuated notion of gender as an issue, along the lines of other "lifestyle," "multicultural," and "diversity" issues. While they are willing to condemn sexism in society, they state or imply that sexism no longer exists in the newsroom. No textbook seriously considers what male-ness means for journalism practice or the newsroom culture. No textbook considers whether sexism persists in newsroom promotion or assignment patterns, or warns students about the difficulties of managing conflicting work and domestic responsibilities. None addresses why few women break into top management. None tackles sex with respect to relationships with sources or colleagues. No textbook helps women students figure out the professional and ethical implications of being encouraged, or forced, to use their bodies to charm sources or attract audiences. Women reporters' memoirs and autobiographies are replete with recollections of being asked to dress provocatively (sexually) (Steiner, 1996), but textbooks do not help students resist the bosses who demand that they function as "cheesecake."

Over 115 years, women—and children—have remained low-status audiences. To the extent that textbooks steered women toward writing about and for women and children, it was because this was their safest entrance into newsrooms. Men can afford to refuse to write for or about women and children. For the last 25 years, women could refuse such assignments, too. But gender is still defined as a women's problem. Thus, a disembodied sort of masculinity is implicit and unproblematic, while a highly embodied (yet universalized) femininity looms as the dangerous exception. Textbooks have abandoned the pre-1980s tradition of treating the female as violating male physical, economic, cultural, and social space. Female-ness no longer dictates how and for whom women may write. Nearly all textbooks now on the market are scrupulous about carefully integrating women and men. Newer generations of authors, however, haven't decided what gender means, and they avoid the issue of sex. Their integration of women with men implies that no reporters have bodies or embodied experience—and therefore everyone should and can cover all topics identically and objectively. Ironically, recent textbooks profess sensitivity and respect for multiculturalism yet simultaneously warn reporters to transcend race, culture, and gender—to distance themselves from the cultural-social settings and life experiences affecting everyone else.

Women textbook authors have been no less pragmatic than men. They also want their students to get jobs. Women authors—a rare breed—appear to insist on slightly more examples of women journalists. Carole Rich (2005) devotes a chapter to multicultural sensitivity, mentioning that while women are doing well in newsrooms, in 2000, they made up 25% of broadcast news directors and only 9% of newspaper management. In general, however, like men, women authors now largely disregard gender, ignoring the ways sex and gender scripts matter with reference to benefits, assignments, and management structures.

Directions for Change

Textbooks do not stand apart from university life. They complement classroom discussions, lectures, homework, mentoring, internships, and career counseling as well as extracurricular activities. The emphasis here on university life is not meant to discount the impact of larger social ideologies. Journalists and journalism educators imported, rather than invented, the mechanisms for devaluing and limiting women writers and women's writings. Thus, further transformations in textbooks also require changes in journalistic practices, in mass communication pedagogy, in education generally, and in all social arenas: "Schools cannot teach what society does not know" (Spender, 1982, p. 3). Yet in suggesting that *standpoints* emerge in the complex layered experiences of historical agents, feminists have helpfully theorized both the political and epistemological consequences of people's social identities. Standpoint theorists argue that the structure and content of people's thoughts are tied to material conditions of their lives; different bodies, sexual preferences, physical abilities, race, and class all "matter" (Harding, 1991). Textbooks' explanations of the connections between social identity and professional behavior will be more useful when they attend to the various ways in which complex interactions of race and gender and class enter people's experiences, journalists included. Textbooks should help students anticipate how personal experiences affect one's judgments about whose problems are deemed newsworthy and one's decisions about how (or what) news is obtained and written.

Moreover, educators can no longer assume that students want to work for mainstream organizations that blindly insist on value-free rules and accept conventional dichotomies of private/public, female/male, and subjective/objective. Feminist theorizing offers models for rethinking hierarchical, sexualized, and potentially exploitive relationships between reporters and their sources. Feminist theory on the sex-gender system needs to be incorporated if educators are to meet their obligation to help students anticipate ethical and professional quandaries. New challenges concerning the definition of news, newsroom structure, and journalistic practices demand continuing changes in journalism education.

Note

1. This survey of 1,149 print and broadcast journalists, commissioned by the Knight Foundation and conducted by journalism scholars at Indiana University, also found that, consistent with results obtained in 1982 and 1992, about one third of all working journalists are female, although women are a majority of the graduates of journalism schools and of the new hires.

Questions for Discussion

1. Why are textbooks important to study and understand?

2. What do journalism textbooks tell us about journalism practice?

3. What claims were made in journalism textbooks in the 1890–1960 period about the potential of women to succeed as journalists?

4. How and to what extent were feminist criticisms of news media incorporated into the training of women journalists?

5. According to journalism textbooks now in use, how, if at all, does gender matter? What do they say about who can be a journalist and what is required to be a successful journalist?

Accessing Additional Information

International Women's Media Foundation: http://www.iwmf.org

Poynter Institute: http://www.poynter.org

Washington Press Club Oral History Project: http://www.press.org/wpforal

Women's Enews: http://www.womensenews.org

3

How to Stir Up a Hornets' Nest

Studying the Implications of Women Journalism Majors

Maurine H. Beasley, University of Maryland

Two decades ago, as the only tenured woman at the University of Maryland College of Journalism, I found myself reviled and humiliated, not so much by educators as by journalists, because I directed a study that looked at the shift in journalism enrollments from predominantly male to predominantly female. It was published under a ponderous title that hardly indicated its potential for controversy, *The New Majority: A Look at What the Preponderance of Women in Journalism Education Means to the Schools and to the Professions* (Beasley & Theus, 1988). Today, when newspapers are wondering why women reporters leave the newsroom and reports about pay differentials between male and female occupations are quite common, the uproar over the modest little project carried out by my colleague, Kathryn Theus, and me, seems almost laughable. It wasn't at the time.

In my naïveté, I endured painful criticism and was advised by a leading professor at another university to stop dealing with women's issues. If I hadn't had tenure coupled with a thick skin, I certainly would have left, or been thrown out of, journalism education. I learned from bitter experience that some people seem unable to deal rationally with the fact that gender differences have long had an impact on our field.

As an academic major, journalism education was dominated by male students until 1977, when the proportion of women students reached more than 50%, but little notice was taken of this development. Our Maryland study, financed by a $34,000 grant from the Gannett Foundation, was the first to draw national attention to the influx of women into journalism schools and to examine the impact of this development. We got interested in the question because the annual censuses of journalism enrollments by sequences showed that women, the "new majority," were less interested in traditional print journalism (mainly newspapers) than in advertising and public relations (Peterson, 1980). We surmised that newspapers had less appeal to women students than did other communications-related professions, particularly public relations and advertising, because of their predominantly male orientation. Nevertheless, we assumed large numbers of women students would seek careers in the traditional news field.

Our report said that as the new majority of graduates moved from school into the workplace, gender-related issues and gender socialization were likely to have an effect on news, but this was not our major concern. Discrimination in employment was. We did speculate, however, that the nature of news might change, at least somewhat, if women became the majority in newsrooms—unless they were restricted to the prevailing male model for advancement. We stopped short of saying that the new majority would change the news.

Our main conclusion, based on historical evidence, was that women graduates in journalism were likely to encounter lower salaries and less opportunity to advance than their male counterparts. We did say that journalism and related fields might become "pink-collar ghettos" on the lower levels, with salaries and status lower than those of male-dominated professions. We used the term, however, sparingly and cautiously, only five times in the whole report, which was 182 pages long (Beasley & Theus, 1988, pp. 5, 45, 98, 127, 140).

The "pink-collar" term usually is applied to traditionally low-paid female jobs, like beautician, waitress, and secretary (Hoffman, 1998, pp. 450–451). Applying it to journalism obviously was a mistake from the public relations point of view, since it turned some women journalists against the report, which called on journalism educators to mobilize themselves as advocates against gender discrimination. The report warned,

> If salary and status in journalism-related fields decline relatively [to those in other occupations] and those fields become less competitive, some of the most important work of a democratic society will become less attractive to students gifted in intellect, resourcefulness and general ability. (Beasley & Theus, 1988, p. 140)

This carried an implied message that educators and professionals should work together in an effort to raise starting pay and make journalism and related professions attractive to capable students whether male or female, but the report was not read in that light. Instead, a few women editors saw the statement as a personal attack on themselves.

By no means were we capable of dealing with all the ramifications of gender discrimination in our well-meaning but rather unsophisticated attempt. We were neither economists nor experts on social roles and cultural constraints. We did not have the funding or institutional support to conduct studies of other occupations to find out how they compared with journalism in terms of women's status and advancement. (For that matter, such studies still haven't been done, although they should be.) We had no crystal ball. We didn't foresee the invention of new technologies that have changed the communications landscape or the emergence of a global economy and massive consolidations in the structures of communications industries. We did not realize the extent to which newspapers would become increasingly squeezed by other media and find themselves a less powerful force than previously in society. Little did we know that what we were doing would be blown out of all proportion.

The first portion of our report examined the experiences of women students and faculty in journalism schools as well as in the field itself from a historical perspective. We did not need to look hard to find numerous examples of women being consigned to second-class status. Our study had 45 pages full of examples drawn both from journalism education and the occupation of journalism itself (Beasley & Theus, 1988, pp. 5–50). There could have been hundreds of examples.

The second portion was a statistical study of the journalism graduates of our own school, the University of Maryland at College Park, comparing the careers of male and females at 3-year intervals from the 1950s through the early 1980s. (We would have liked to compare their experiences with those of graduates of other institutions, but we lacked the resources to do so at the time.) Our survey found that males were more likely than females to be satisfied with their jobs, income, and chances for advancement. It also found that women were 13 times more likely than men to have career interruptions due to family responsibilities and seemed to have suffered substantial income loss as a result. In addition, men were more likely than women to have married and to have had larger families (Beasley & Theus, 1988, pp. 56–57).

We supplemented this research with a survey of the employers of University of Maryland journalism graduates. This survey found that male and females were evaluated rather evenly on job skills, although males were usually evaluated a percentage point or two better than females. Female employers, however, evaluated female employees significantly higher than did male employers in a variety of categories, including reporting, photography, and media relations (Beasley & Theus, 1988, p. 59).

After receiving the results of the surveys, we held two round-table discussions, one composed of successful women in journalism and mass communication and the other composed of entry-level graduates. Participants were asked to comment on the report and to identify issues for further exploration (Beasley & Theus, 1988, pp. 116–142). They concluded that journalism educators should prepare women journalism students for employment by attempting to make sure they had (a) strong basic writing skills, (b) suitable role models, (c) strategies to persuade employers of their worth so they would not be forced to settle for less than men, and (d) plans for combining family responsibilities with careers (if they wished to have families). There was an implied message that more women faculty should be hired and that students should be exposed to coursework dealing with gender issues.

Nothing revolutionary here, no attack on men or on industry. It was all rather dry, commonsense stuff, but that's not the way the study was perceived. From the negative response, mainly from a few editors and sensation-loving headline writers, you would have thought that we were undermining the very foundations of journalism itself. Well, maybe we were, because some feminists argue journalism is built on a model of conflict-laden values associated with male pursuits (Covert, 1981), but that wasn't our intent. We thought we were attacking discrimination, but our study was not received in the same spirit in which we had conceived it.

Our work first attracted attention on October 14, 1985, when the University of Maryland College of Journalism held a press conference at the National Press Club in Washington to unveil a 5-year plan for upgrading itself. Various faculty research projects were highlighted, including ours. A college press release, which I did not see until the conference began, caught the eyes of reporters, with its big headline: "Maryland Study Warns Against 'Pink-Collar Ghettos' of Lower Pay and Status in Journalism-Related Fields."

The press release began, "Journalism and related professional fields are becoming principally female, with a danger that they will be 'pink-collar ghettos' offering lower salaries and status than they would as largely male fields, a new University of Maryland study says." The release went on to say that "female-dominated fields such as teaching, social work, nursing and librarianship traditionally have been lower-income professions." It continued, "Although salaries in journalism-related fields (some of which already are noted for low pay) may not decline, there should be concern that they will not rise as they might if these fields remained predominantly male."

If I had written the press release myself, I would have been more pedantic, and that's probably why I was not asked to write it. Whoever did write it (and I still don't know) made the study sound more flamboyant than it actually was and apparently raised the specter of inferring that women were "ruining" journalism. Yet with the wisdom of hindsight, who can say that the press release turned out to be a totally false prophet?

Look at what has since happened to journalism graduates in terms of starting pay. At the time we started the study in 1983, women constituted about 60% of undergraduate journalism enrollment. By the time the study was published, they constituted two thirds of the graduates in the field (Dow Jones Newspaper Fund, 1988). The most recent figures show this has continued to be the case. Women make up 64.7% of undergraduate journalism students and 65.2% of journalism master's degree candidates (Becker, Vlad, Hennink-Kaminski, & Coffey, 2004). Unfortunately, journalism graduates, both male and female, are not likely to fare very well in the job market.

After conducting their annual survey of journalism graduates, Becker and Vlad reported in 2004 that "job offers were few. Unemployment rates were higher than the national average. Salaries were low and inadequate to compensate for increase in the costs of living" (p. 1). Furthermore, they said, "Only half of the journalism and mass communication bachelor's degree recipients in 2003 found work within the broad field of communication" (p. 1). While Becker and Vlad gave the average starting salary for bachelor's degree recipients as $26,000 dollars annually in 2003, the same as graduates earned in 2001, they noted this figure represented a decline of $1,600 in actual purchasing power since 2000 when adjusted for inflation. Even more depressing was the fact that liberal arts graduates in general were being offered higher starting salaries of $29,119 annually (Becker & Vlad, 2004, pp. 1, 5). Without doubt, a weak overall economy contributed to this picture, but it seems likely issues of gender were involved in the economic factors of supply and demand that sets pay scales in our field. Is there a field dominated by male graduates where the starting pay is so low?

Thinking back 20 years to the reception of our report at the press conference, I remember how carelessly some journalists engaged in blatant oversimplification. United Press International (UPI) sent out a dispatch beginning, "Women are quickly dominating the ranks of the news profession and their emergence threatens to keep both the money and the status of the industry low, a 2-year study by the University of Maryland says." The dispatch said that women constituted about 40% of the daily newsroom workforce (still true today). This led to headlines such as the following appearing across the United States: *St. Louis Post-Dispatch,* "Study: Women May Devalue Journalism" (October 15, 1986); *Easton Star-Democrat* (Maryland), "News Women Creating 'Pink-Collar Ghetto'"(October 15,

1985); *Deseret News* (Salt Lake City), "Women Are Taking Over Journalism" (October 16, 1985); and the *Miami News,* "Journalism Seen Turning 'Pink Collar'" (October 15, 1986).

Other newspapers handled the story more responsibly. The *Washington Post* headlined the story simply, "Women Predominate in J-Schools," and used a comprehensive lead:

> Women now make up 60 percent of all journalism students in the country and may soon outnumber men in communications, according to a University of Maryland study whose authors expressed fears that the shift will lower pay and the prestige of the field in comparison to male-dominated fields. (Arocha, 1985, p. 1)

The Evening Sun of Baltimore used a similar headline: "Women the 'New Majority' in Journalism Schools." This story began, "Women have taken over the classrooms of journalism and mass communications school around the country, but they still face discrimination when they graduate and look for work, a new University of Maryland study shows" (Dickman, 1985, p. D2).

Some of the news coverage drew an inflamed response. In a column in the *Trenton Times* (New Jersey), reprinted in part in *Editor & Publisher,* executive editor of the paper Linda Cunningham declared, "Not since conservative Patrick Buchanan's column, which said it was a woman's fault if she were raped, has anything in the newspapers raised my dander so much" (as quoted in Miller, 1985, p. 52). She quoted a statement attributed to me at the press conference and carried in the UPI report: "If journalism joins other devalued professions dominated by women, such as nursing and teaching, the watchdog role of the news media might become trivialized" (as quoted in Miller, 1985, p. 52).

Cunningham exclaimed,

> Hogwash. Spend 15 minutes in this newsroom *[Trenton Times]* and then tell me the women around there are less demanding or more inclined to believe unquestioningly what their sources tell them. Ask my bosses if I demure daintily when thwarted or sit quietly in a corner. (as quoted in Miller, 1985, p. 52)

Reacting to the implication that the nature of news might change if women predominate in the field, Cunningham retorted, "I'm often asked whether women editors approach the news differently from their male counterparts. My answer is, invariably, no. News is news; it has no sex" (as quoted in Miller, 1985, p. 52).

The excerpts from Cunningham's attack and other criticism of the Maryland study appeared in a column in *Editor & Publisher* written by Susan H. Miller, director of editorial development for Scripps Howard Newspapers. Miller quoted from a letter by Judith Clabes, editor of the *Covington Post* (Kentucky): "A seething anger is growing to a crescendo of outrage over the disservice the Maryland 'research' has done to a whole group of professional, hardworking and dedicated women journalists" (as quoted in Miller, 1985, pp. 32–33). Miller herself claimed the study "adopted unwarranted and unsubstantiated assertions about the professional performance of women" (pp. 32–33).

Forced to defend myself, I too wrote a column for *Editor & Publisher*, contending that the emotional response had obscured the point: Women were clustered in low-paid positions in journalism not because they wanted to be, but because of factors that historically had undervalued them economically. I wrote, "The community press, where large segments of women increasingly are concentrated at low salaries, may not be in an economic position to embrace the watchdog function"; and, I concluded, "Let's see 'seething anger' and 'a crescendo of outrage' over discrimination in general and over low salaries in particular—whether men or women are being victimized" (Beasley, 1985, pp. 44, 33).

Defending the report, Chuck Stone, writing in the *Philadelphia Daily News* in 1986, pointed out that women writers and journalists historically have not fared well at the hands of White males. He said, "But let the word go forth to Cunningham, women journalists . . . everywhere. Maybe you have come a long way, baby. But in 1986, male America is still dumping on you" (Stone, 1986, p. 36). Stone, an African American, said the issue was power for White males and weakness for "everybody else."

Nearly two decades later, looking at the angry exchange between Miller and me, Elmore said it was one illustration of the way the feminist movement was delegitimized in the press as a "catfight" or battleground that divided women (Elmore, 2003, p. 40). I agree, but I still think I had no choice except to answer the attack, which missed the point I had originally intended to make: that women faced difficulty in moving into a male-dominated area. Was I wrong? I do not think so.

Today, two decades later, far from taking over traditional journalism, women still have not achieved parity with men in newsrooms, in part because they leave at a faster rate than men. In a 2004 commentary for WOMENSENEWS, Michele Weldon, assistant professor of journalism at Northwestern University, pointed out that the number of women on the staffs of daily newspapers in 2003 had increased minutely, to 37.23% of newsroom employees, according to the American Society of Newspaper

Editors. Weldon wrote, "The meager improvement from 37.05% after a 2-year decline in numbers of women in newsrooms forces us to decode the writing on the wall and choose the appropriate cliché: Is it 'slow and steady wins the race?' Or 'quit while you still can?'" (Weldon, 2004).

Also, there is academic discussion of gender and news values that relates to some of the questions we raised regarding the status of journalists. The European scholar van Zoonen (1998) pointed out that the market-driven nature of news in the United States depends on elements with a gendered subtext, including "human interest" appeals, greater attention to audience needs and desires, and an emotional investment from news consumers. She wrote that these "relate exactly to the norms and values that many traditional news journalists, men and women alike, think are typical of female journalists" (van Zoonen, 1998, p. 41). She contended that these values have led to increased job opportunities for women in journalism in the broadcasting and magazine fields. Yet, she continued, political and intellectual elites view the status of market-driven journalism as lower than that of traditional journalism, wedded to its male ideal of objective and rational standards. She concluded, "It is not only the popularization of news that is on trial in these debates; implicitly it is women and femininity as crucial components of this popularization as well" (p. 46).

Van Zoonen raised an important point. Journalism in general, particularly local broadcast news, has lost stature as a field in recent years, certainly not as a direct result of more women, but as the outcome of a complicated interplay of issues, including competing technologies and market forces. Did we foresee this development in our study? Only in that the report predicted change, and change has come. Abundant evidence exists that women can cover traditional news as well as, if not better than, men, but that newsrooms are not especially hospitable places for women. At the same time, if one expands van Zoonen's theory, some women may appear to be utilized for their sex appeal by male-run news corporations in cynical pushes for high ratings and audience attention. It is possible that the presence of a larger number of women in mass communication as a whole may be viewed as part of the current erosion of the line between news and entertainment.

In 1996, Katherine McAdams, my colleague at the University of Maryland, and I set out to update a portion of the *New Majority* report. We surveyed our journalism graduates at 3-year intervals in the 1980s and early 1990s in an attempt to find out whether there still were clear differences in the career experiences of men and women graduates, with men faring better than women in pay and promotions. This time, we also surveyed graduates of the University of North Carolina at Chapel Hill. Unhappily, we had a relatively low response rate of 30%, giving us a total of only 475 responses.

This time, we found fewer differences between men and women graduates. Journalism degrees gave both of them background for employment versatility, with surprisingly few following the traditional news-editorial route. Only 13 described themselves as writers or reporters (McAdams, Beasley, & Zandberg, 2004, p. 320). Men and women graduates were equally likely to marry, have children, and experience some type of career interruption. For men, layoffs were given as the most frequent cause; for women, childbirth and child care were most common, but after interruptions, women were more likely than men to change careers totally, not just change jobs within journalism/mass communication (McAdams et al., 2004, p. 321).

While the data did not support a finding of inequality in the job market, women were significantly more likely than men to perceive that men are promoted more quickly and that the salaries of women are lower than those of men (McAdams et al., 2004, p. 322). Women were more likely than men to perceive age, gender, and racial discrimination in education classrooms, although this subject was not explored in depth. In open-ended comments on their education, respondents called for more (a) teaching of communication technology, (b) required internships, (c) hands-on experience, (d) business and marketing classes, and (e) mentoring programs. Negative comments from news-editorial graduates were the most pronounced, with low wages cited as the most frequent source of job dissatisfaction. Just over half said they would major in journalism again.

We were left with the impression that the "new majority" has benefited from journalism and mass communication education but that the major itself needs a comprehensive study. The "new majority" is much less likely today to suffer from the blatant discrimination of 20 years ago, but the entire field of journalism/mass communication is changing so rapidly that we fear journalism education may be left behind. Questions facing journalism graduates still involve pay, status, and career interruptions, as they did two decades ago, and educators still need to try to address these concerns. In doing so, we must face issues involving diversity, including gender, although I hope no other educator ever receives the public flailing given me in 1985.

Questions for Discussion

1. Why are gender-related issues likely to lead to emotional exchanges?

2. Should news staffs reflect the gender makeup of the population? Why or why not?

3. Should journalism educators take into account the gender of their students? Why or why not?

4. In your opinion, why it is that about 2 out of 3 journalism students are women, while only about 1 out of 3 newsroom staff members is female?

5. Is gender a factor in the marketing of news products?

Accessing Additional Information

American Society of Newspaper Editors: http://www.asne.org

Cox Center, Grady College, University of Georgia: http://www.grady.uga.edu/annual

Journalism and Women Symposium (JAWS): http://www.jaws.org

Media Report to Women: http://www.mediareporttowomen.com

Radio-Television News Directors Association: http://www.rtnda.org

Women's Institute for Freedom of the Press: http://www.wifp.org

PART II

Update on the Professions

4

Women in Newspaper Journalism (Since the 1990s)

June O. Nicholson,
Virginia Commonwealth University

Since the early 1990s and continuing a trend since the 1970s, women in newspapers have gained ground as more women have become top editors of newspapers and CEOs, presidents, and publishers. More women also have taken leading roles on opinion pages of U.S. newspapers, and are visible in the major industry organizations.

But in the early 21st century, women have not achieved power and influence that mirrors their numbers in newsrooms and companies. Women are underrepresented in management, where they hold a quarter of the jobs. At the very top, women hold fewer than a fifth of corporate jobs as CEOs, presidents, and publishers and are mostly absent on corporate boards (Arnold, Hendrickson, & Linton, 2003). Women of color as a group have fared poorly in newspapers (Arnold et al., 2003), and few women of color are news executives or editors.

According to research published in recent years, women in newspapers face barriers to advancement, work-family balance issues, and a lack of mentors, role models, and professional development opportunities. Many women expect to leave the news business entirely, some for careers they see as more rewarding. The lack of influence and opportunity for women in newspapers has major implications for the news industry and for society.

The Annenberg Public Policy Center, at the University of Pennsylvania, stressed in a report on the "glass ceiling" and other issues for women in corporations that communications companies have a responsibility to address diversity and discrimination, because of their function in society. "They [companies] communicate in subtle and often unconscious ways who and what is important and normal and who has status and power, and the media help tell us what our national agenda should be" (Falk & Grizard, 2003b, p. 7). The study, which examined 57 Fortune 500 companies categorized as printing, telecommunications, entertainment, and advertising, said people at the top of such companies "who make decisions about what kinds of news, information, and entertainment get produced have additional power" (p. 7).

More women in positions of authority could have a positive effect on the success of news companies. A report on a sample of Fortune 500 companies (Catalyst, 2004) found that those with more women in executive positions financially outperform companies with fewer women at the top. A number of other studies have tied the success of U.S. corporations to having a diverse workforce and senior leadership (Lockwood, 2005).

Recently published news industry research also has stressed the importance of gender diversity and diversity broadly to the success of newspaper companies. The companies in the best position to draw new readers and increase circulation "tend to have greater diversity in race and/or gender, both in the workforce generally and in positions of influence" (Readership Institute, 2004, p. 13). The findings suggest that diversity in those companies may help to ensure that news content is more relevant to readers and that companies have more innovative and adaptive cultures.

Moreover, leading researchers have emphasized that women in the 21st century are poised to take on even more leadership roles in corporations, government, nonprofits, and other sectors because of their democratic and collaborative leadership styles and characteristics (Arnold et al., 2003; Fisher, 1999).

Women in newsrooms and on the corporate side of companies will play a crucial role in the future of U.S. newspapers and the communications industry as it evolves in the 21st century. Will companies better position themselves for success by improving training and professional development opportunities for women, addressing work-family balance issues, and more aggressively recruiting women for the top jobs? Or will the status quo for women prevail in newsrooms and corporate executive suites, thus endangering the future of news companies? The answers will play out at a critical juncture for the U.S. newspaper industry, which faces circulation declines, credibility issues, increased competition, and a rapidly changing media marketplace.

"Glass Ceiling" Firmly in Place

As the new century began to unfold, more women were executives or editors of leading U.S. newspapers and news companies than probably at any time in history. In early 2005, just over one fifth, or 22, of the top editor positions at the nation's 100 largest newspapers were held by women; the number is roughly double the number of 13 from the late 1990s (Sullivan, 2005, p. 11). Women were in charge at the *Chicago Tribune,* the *Philadelphia Inquirer,* the *Oregonian* (Portland), the *Atlanta Journal-Constitution,* the *San Jose Mercury News,* the *Tampa Tribune,* and the *Akron Beacon Journal,* to name a few. Women became managing editors at influential newspapers such as the *New York Times, USA Today,* and the *Philadelphia Inquirer.* Women also moved into positions as CEOs or publishers or held other senior posts in the largest newspaper companies. The Associated Press, which has 1,500 member newspapers, named Kathleen Carroll as executive editor in 2002 and as a senior vice president in 2003.

As further evidence of the visibility of women at the top of the news industry, since 2000, two women have served as president of the American Society of Newspaper Editors (ASNE). Only four women have held that ASNE office in its history.

Nevertheless, progress for women has "slowed, after a spurt in the 80s" (Hemlinger & Linton, 2001, p 11), and while some women have moved into top positions, the gains for women in newspapers overall have been incremental; women have lost ground in some years. Women continue to lag far behind their male counterparts, particularly in the top ranks of the corporate side of news companies. The Media Management Center (MMC) at Northwestern University has conducted some of the major research in recent years about women in newspapers, in a three-part *Women in Newspapers (WIN)* study. The 2003 *WIN* study concluded that "73% of executive jobs and 82% of the top jobs in newspapers today are still held by men" (Arnold et al., 2003, p. 53). The study found that women made up less than one fifth, or 18%, of CEOs, publishers, and presidents, an increase from 14% in 2002. The *Women in Newspapers* research examined 137 newspapers with circulations of more than 85,000.

Women lost ground in the number of executive vice presidents/general managers, which dropped from 21% to 16% in 2002, and the number of women heading advertising divisions, which declined 7 percentage points, to 31% (Arnold et al., 2003). Women held 27% of executive jobs overall in 2003, a drop of 2% from the previous year, according to the 2003 *WIN* study.

Women were most underrepresented in boardrooms. In 2003, 22 women, or an average of 18% of board of directors of 15 of the nation's newspaper groups were female, up 3% over the previous year (Arnold et al., 2003). Susan Bischoff, associate editor of the *Houston Chronicle,* said the lack of women in top management, including corporate boards, where corporate policy is set, is particularly disappointing (personal communication, August 31, 2005). She said, "Women [in those positions] have not reached parity [but] are no less qualified." The pace of change is extremely slow, she emphasized.

Most of the female publishers were in just a few of the top newspaper groups (Arnold et al., 2003). Community Newspaper Holdings, Inc.; Gannett; and Lee Enterprises have the most female publishers at 7, 23 and 9, respectively. McClatchy, the Tribune Publishing Co., and Landmark had the highest percentages of women publishers at 55%, 40%, and 33%, respectively, according to the research.

Women at or above the rank of assistant vice president or higher hold a higher percentage of leadership positions at eight of the 21 corporations studied: Freedom Newspapers, the New York Times Co., Cox Newspapers, A. H. Belo, Gannett, Dow Jones & Company, Washington Post Co., and Knight Ridder (Arnold et al., 2003)

Women are most often found at the lower end of newspaper employment and in middle management (Hemlinger & Linton, 2002), and they have serious difficulty moving from managing editor to higher positions (Arnold et al., 2003). Female executives are found mostly in areas that are outside the usual lines of succession to top positions, such as personnel or community affairs, according to the 2003 study, which means women are not in prime position to move to the top in years to come.

Men and women have differing perceptions of the reasons for the lack of advancement of women in newspapers. CEOs of newspaper companies said women had not been in management pipeline long enough to reach the top and that it takes two decades for women to gain the experience necessary to be a CEO (Hemlinger & Linton, 2002). But women say the main reason they do not advance is that men prefer to promote other men who think and act like they do. They say women are excluded from formal and informal social networks (Hemlinger & Linton, 2002). Men say women need to be more decisive and assertive (Arnold et al., 2003). Many women say that "men for whom they worked misunderstood the advantages of their collaborative work styles" (Arnold et al., 2003, p. 54).

Women are about one third of full-time journalists at daily newspapers and are about the same percentage of women in all news media (Weaver Beam, Brownlee, Voakes, & Wilhoit, 2003a). As measured in the 2000 census, women are 47% of the U.S. civilian labor force and 52% of the nation's population. ASNE figures show that in 2005 (ASNE, 2005), some two thirds, or 65.2%, of newsroom supervisors were male and 34.8% were female, only a slight improvement for women since 1999 (ASNE, 1999).

The Career Confident and Career Conflicted

The Great Divide: Female Leadership in U.S. Newsrooms (2002), conducted for the American Press Institute (API) and (then) Pew Center for Civic Journalism (PCCJ) by Selzer & Company, underscored several important issues for the news industry, including a decades-old retention issue and the view held by women that male managers hinder their advancement. The study also indicated that the news industry is underutilizing a vast amount of female talent of women who work in newspapers. The study was released in 2002 in conjunction with the J. Montgomery Curtis seminar on newsroom leadership, which focused on women in newspaper management.

The women surveyed split into two categories: the "career confident," who were satisfied with their jobs and opportunities to advance, and the "career conflicted," who had doubts about advancement opportunities and were less pleased with their bosses and news content. The study surveyed 273 editors, or 40%, of top managers at dailies with circulations of more than 50,000. The main findings were as follows:

Forty-five percent of female editors said they expected to be offered a job at another newspaper or to leave the news business, compared with 33% of men.

Women were 4 times more likely than men to say they would leave newspapers and work in another field.

Sexism was the primary reason women said they did not expect to advance. Sixty-four percent of women who had doubts about their ability to advance said the main reason was that managers preferred to promote men. Six percent of male editors said sexism was an obstacle to advancement.

Many women did not feel supported in the workplace and said they lacked mentors as well as professional training and career-planning opportunities.

Only 20% of women said they definitely wanted to move up in the newspaper industry, considerably fewer than the 36% of men who said they definitely wanted to move up. Almost three quarters, or 72%, of the women said they would reconsider moving up if given the authority to make meaningful change. This finding suggests that women see the news industry as entrenched.

Career-conflicted women had different news agendas than women in news management in general. These women said that too few resources went to coverage of health and medicine and the interests of women and parents and that too many resources were used to cover crime and political news.

Loss of Female Talent and Perspectives

News organizations continue to have a substantial problem in retaining women. Companies are experiencing a loss of female talent that could jeopardize the ability of companies to draw new and diverse readers as well as to innovate and adapt in the rapidly changing world of media and be successful overall in the highly competitive modern megacorporate environment (API and PCCJ, 2002; Falk & Grizard, 2003b; Readership Institute, 2004). The industry risks losing differing perspectives about news content and agendas that women could bring to the workplace (API and PCCJ, 2002) and risks losing readers. Why do women leave newspapers?

In an interview, Pam Luecke, Donald Reynolds professor of business journalism at Washington and Lee University and former editor and senior vice president of the *Lexington Herald-Leader* (Kentucky), said for top editors today, the "sense of reward may have diminished because many editors find themselves spending more of their time worrying about the bottom line than good journalism" (personal communication, August 30, 2005). Luecke also said some women leave newspapers because they "have other things they wanted to accomplish in their lives" and many find it difficult to balance family and work. To counter that, she said, newspapers must "make the workplace more manageable for women and women's life cycles" and work on the "satisfaction issue." "The public's respect for what they [journalists] do has fallen, the hours are long and competition is round the clock," Luecke said. She added that the work at newspapers must be emotionally rewarding, and that element has been languishing.

Women as Sources

Too few women in newsrooms and in the top ranks of companies may mean that newspapers are not fully reflecting the role of women in society. A 2005 study of American news media found that women are used less than half as often as men as sources in newspapers (Project for Excellence in Journalism

[PEJ], 2005), though newspapers are more apt to include females as sources than are other media. "The numbers suggest that the representation of women as sources in the news has a significant distance to go towards reflecting their role in American society generally," according to the study (PEJ, 2005, p. 4). The study concluded that too few women in newsrooms may be partly responsible for the scarcity of female sources. This finding takes on significance as newspapers struggle to draw new and diverse readers, including women. The study continued,

> The findings [men are used more than twice as often as women as news sources] may strike some observers as ironic given the efforts of many news outlets to increase their audience by reaching out to women—and particularly to younger women, a group that generally is under represented as news consumers. (PEJ, 2005, p. 2)

Opinion Pages

The slow pace of change for women in newspapers is exemplified by the firestorm in 2005 over the dearth of women on opinion pages. Women in recent years became editorial page editors of major newspapers, including the *New York Times,* the *Atlanta Journal-Constitution,* and the *Boston Globe.* But those successes were blunted by the lack of female voices represented overall on op-ed pages. The percentage of female op-ed columnists for the largest syndicates is 24.4%, a .7% increase from 23.7% in 1999 (Astor, 2005a).

Some women columnists say women are not as willing to be hard-hitting and combative; but many female columnists argue that that op-ed pages are run largely by men who avoid change and risk (Astor, 2005a). Patrisia Gonzales, a Universal Press Syndicate columnist, said,

> Men make most of the decisions about who's hired as a columnist or who's accepted as having "authority" to write. There are untold numbers of women and people of color whose ideas are cutting edge and "outside of the box"; unfortunately, they rarely make it into the commentary pages on a regular basis. (Astor, 2005a)

Suzette Martinez, head of the National Society of Newspaper Columnists, said many experienced female columnists seek syndication: "They're knock, knock, knocking on heaven's door, but there's no answer from the guy in charge" (Astor, 2005a, p. 2). She said, "It's a . . . lack of courage and conviction to fully invest in half the population" (p. 2). Of 578 members of NSNC, 277 are female (Astor, 2005a).

Women of Color

Scant research has been done about women of color in newspapers and companies in recent years, which leaves a serious gap in understanding the experiences of minority females in contemporary newspapers. One encouraging sign is that minority women are 17.20% of all women in newsrooms, an increase over 14.28 in 2000 (ASNE, 2005). Minorities overall made up 13.42% of newsroom employees in 2004 (ASNE, 2005), which falls far short of the more than 31% of minorities in the U.S. population. Only 10.8% of supervisors were minorities (ASNE, 2004).

A 1999 study conducted by the International Women's Media Foundation (IWMF) found that women of color said their careers were "hampered by lingering racial stereotypes and subtle discrimination" (IWMF, 1999, p. 1, executive summary). The study surveyed newsroom managers and women journalists of color who were members of the four minority media groups: National Association of Black Journalists (NABJ), Asian American Journalists Association (AAJA), National Association of Hispanic Journalists (NAHJ), and Native American Journalists Association (NAJA). These women cited the chief causes for their lack of advancement as discrimination, lack of high-visibility assignments, and not having a mentor of the same racial or ethnic group (IWMF, 1999).

In that study, 17% of news managers said barriers to advancement were the main reason women of color leave journalism, while 54% of women journalists of color cited this as the cause (IWMF, 1999). Eighty-two percent of managers say they respect cultural diversity of employees, but only 32% of women of color say that managers do so, according to the research.

Women and New Technology

In the mid-1990s, the field of online journalism was considered an area of possible growth and promise for female journalists. Women, however, have not made significant progress in this field. Some evidence discussed in this book suggests that fewer women today are present in the field online than a decade ago. Many women who entered the online newspaper workforce have left, and the top editors of newspaper online operations presently are overwhelmingly male and follow the "gender hierarchies" (see Thiel Stern, Chapter 12, this volume) of newspaper management.

Nora Paul, director of the Institute for New Media Studies at the University of Minnesota, explained the reason in part is that a number of "potentially really good women journalists ran into male-dominated cultures that were not accommodating to women" (personal communication, August 31, 2005). The women who left were replaced largely by men, particularly as online became more established in newspapers, she said. As a result, "A new medium may be left looking very much like an old one" (Thiel Stern, Chapter 12, this volume). Paul said she sees some promise for women, however, once online "settles and the competitive advantages go to those who have the better content" (personal communication, August 31, 2005). She said that such an evolution "may drive more women back to online" as women see opportunities for serving communities, and that readers and citizen journalism and other initiatives that use technology to reach new "communities" provide additional new opportunities for women in newspapers (personal communication, August 31, 2005).

Salaries

Overall, women journalists continue to be paid less than men. In 2001, the median salary for female journalists in all news media was $37,731, or 81% of the $46,758 median salary for males (Weaver et al., 2003a). The percentage for women's salaries compared with men's salaries was unchanged since 1991. Among journalists in all media with 15 to 19 years of experience, men annually made $4,425 more than women journalists; and among those with 20 or more years of experience, men made $7,314 more than women. However, median salaries were roughly the same for men and women with less than 15 years of experience (Weaver et al., 2003a).

Conclusion

Building on the gains of the 1970s and 1980s, women have made strides in the newspaper profession in the past 15 years. But progress for women must accelerate if women are going to move into top positions of power and leadership in coming years in numbers that reflect their overall presence in the field. Diversity in newsrooms and companies and in senior leadership must be a higher priority of news organizations—and must be central to the planning and direction of companies. Aggressive efforts should be made to advance women of color.

Mary Arnold, an author of the Media Management Center's *Women in Newspapers* studies, predicted the pace of change for women is not likely to alter dramatically until the number of women editors and executives reaches a critical mass. Arnold said, however, "We do not really know whether that mass is one-fifth of top editors or where the critical mass is, but once the critical mass is reached things will happen a lot faster" (personal communication, September 7, 2005). She said the change may require a new generation of top corporate officers and editors who see diversity in leadership and in newsrooms as a higher priority and insist on accountability in diversifying companies and newsrooms.

Women are not likely to advance in greater numbers unless accountability for promoting women is a part of the performance system. The Annenberg study reported that most of the Fortune 500 companies studied "failed to make any efforts to recruit women for top jobs and tended not to rate top officers on their ability to create equal employment opportunities" (Falk & Grizard, 2003b, p. 9).

Arnold said news companies must place a high priority on advancing women as part of corporate policy for the pace of change to quicken (personal communication, September 7, 2005). Meanwhile, she added, a combination of the shrinking newspaper workforce (ASNE, 2004, 2005) and circulation declines may mean fewer opportunities for women to advance.

Coverage patterns need to change. Arnold noted that while attracting new and diverse readers, a driving force in the newspaper industry today, "some newspapers still are appealing to women readers through old filters" of food and fashion, for example, instead of through contemporary issues that women care about, such as health and family "and the role of women in business, religion, sports, and in society generally" (personal communication, September 7, 2005). She said that newspaper companies are worried about survival and are not always connecting the issues for women in journalism with solutions to readership and circulation.

Mae Cheng, an editor at *Newsday* and president of UNITY: Journalists of Color, Inc., said in an interview, "I am not sure the door has been swung wide open to make it possible for women [or men] of color to get a shot at the top jobs [in newspapers]." Those who recruit need to "think differently about how to fill positions, and work two or three times as hard to find [candidates] who bring something different to the table" (personal communication, November 10, 2005), she said. Newspapers need to "put a lot of money into recruitment, training and [hiring] bonuses [to attract diverse candidates]," Cheng added. "The message about diversity must come from the top—the CEO, and reach down through assignment editors." Cheng also said the newspaper industry "is not getting the message" that coverage of the thoughts and interests of a changing U.S. population "translates into dollars" at a time of industry soul-searching about its future. UNITY is an alliance of almost 10,000 members of AAJA, NABJ, NAHJ, and NAJA.

Each of the *WIN* studies included recommendations to the news industry that, if adopted, would redress some of the current problems. The 2003 recommendations would:

Advance more women, including women of color, in the newspaper profession and on boards of directors. At least one female would be included in every pool for top jobs.

Provide women with challenging opportunities. Often outside the line of succession to the top jobs, women should be given more opportunity to head departments that lead to the executive ranks.

Address the work-family balance issue by providing more flexible work schedules. The report noted, "This is the area where women exhibit the most uncertainty and conflict between the demands of an executive career and societal expectations for women" (Arnold et al., 2003, p. 57).

Develop industry-wide initiatives as part of good business practice that would provide women with career counseling development and training, as well as networking opportunities.

News managers must come to understand gender and culture differences as a means of improving the environment of newsrooms and companies and advancement opportunities for women. Dr. Nancy J. Adler, professor of organizational behavior at McGill University, in Montreal, Canada, who has studied women in business around the world, said in the 2003 *WIN* study that as executives, women tend to be change agents and to be collaborative, compassionate, visionary, and more inclusive and to have more participatory leadership styles (Arnold et al., 2003).

Men seek power and control, whereas women are motivated by a desire to improve society, Adler said in the same study. Adler and other researchers have said the leadership style and traits of women will be in more demand in the future as business becomes more global and more competitive and as the need for companies to innovate and adapt becomes greater (Arnold et al., 2003; Fisher, 1999).

Too few women in boardrooms and senior posts of news companies and also in newsrooms could leave newspaper companies at a competitive disadvantage compared with other companies and professions in which women have more opportunities for leadership, professional development, and rewarding careers.

The future of newspapers and of women in newspapers depends on whether companies are willing to make the necessary changes, modernize policies, and provide women with more opportunities for advancement and fulfilling careers. The momentum of the past several years could signal better times ahead for women (Arnold et al., 2003; Sullivan, 2005). Or change may have to wait for a new generation of men and women leaders—and a critical mass of women at the top—to move the newspaper industry more rapidly toward parity.

Questions for Discussion

1. What are the barriers to advancement for women, and how can women in the profession address those issues? How important is mentoring to women in the news industry? Why is it important for newspaper companies to have women in senior leadership?

2. What should the news industry do to be more accommodating to women in the news business and to recruit more women into the top managerial ranks?

3. What are the gender differences in how men and women think and lead? Why is an understanding of these differences important in the newsroom and in senior leadership?

4. How is news coverage affected by diversity issues in the newsroom and in management?

5. Why does the news industry have a serious retention problem regarding females, and what does the news industry lose when women leave the profession?

Accessing Additional Information

American Press Institute: http://www.americanpressinstitute.org

American Society of Newspaper Editors: http://www.asne.org

Freedom Forum: http://www.freedomforum.org

International Women's Media Foundation: http://www.iwmf.org

Media Management Center: http://www.mediamanagementcenter.org

5

Women's Salary and Status in the Magazine Industry

Sammye Johnson, Trinity University

W omen have been active in the magazine industry as readers, writers, editors, and publishers since 1784, when the first magazine to include women as an important part of the target audience was established. Earlier magazines had targeted male readers only. The farsighted publishers of the *Gentleman and Lady's Town and Country Magazine* recognized that women also wanted reading material (Johnson, 1995, p. 96). The New England area had the highest literacy rates for women, so it wasn't surprising that the Boston-based *Gentleman and Lady's Town and Country Magazine* had "only one major editorial policy in mind: definitely to appeal to feminine readers. For the first time in American magazine history this policy governed the title of a periodical" (Richardson, 1966, p. 228).

By 1828, women were editing their own magazines. Sarah Josepha Hale, who founded *Ladies' Magazine* in 1828, was one of the earliest great magazine editors; her "mission was to encourage and publish as many quality women writers as possible" (Cronin, 1995, p. 114). Hale merged her publication with Louis Godey's *Lady's Book* in 1837, creating *Godey's Lady's Book*, which became famous for its elegant essays and hand-colored fashion plates. Serving as editor for 50 years, Hale "defined and promoted a role for middle-class women in American society" at a time when options for women were very narrow (Cronin, 1995, p. 115).

Some of the most famous women in 19th-century American history owned, published, or edited women's magazines: Amelia Bloomer, Elizabeth Cady Stanton, Susan B. Anthony, Ida B. Wells, Jane Grey Swisshelm, and Rosa Sonneschein. Significant 20th-century editors included Margaret Sanger, Gertrude Battles Lane, Ruth Whitney, Frances Lear, Grace Mirabella, Myrna Blyth, Jean LemMon, Helen Gurley Brown, Marcia Ann Gillespie, Gloria Steinem, and Robin Morgan. Through the decades, then, magazine mastheads have listed notable women in top editorial positions.

Several women's magazines have successfully navigated more than 100 years of publication: *Town & Country, Harper's Bazaar, Ladies' Home Journal, Cosmopolitan, Good Housekeeping, Vogue,* and *Redbook.* Magazines dedicated to women uniformly appear in the top 10 magazines by total circulation year after year, according to the Audit Bureau of Circulations (Magazine Publishers of America [MPA], 2005). It's not surprising that women traditionally have dominated the magazine market as readers and subscribers, accounting for 52% of monthly subscriptions and 57% of single-copy purchases (MPA, 1997, p. 19). Approximately 89% of U.S. women age 18 years and older read an average of 13 different magazines a month (MPA, 1997, p. 46).

The Magazine Workplace

Readership and circulation provide solid data for magazine analysis and trend studies about audiences. However, studying the magazine workplace is a different—and difficult—situation. The magazine industry is constantly changing in terms of the numbers of titles and kinds of publications. For example, there is no way of knowing how many magazines celebrated the industry's 264th birthday in 2005, because no one knows for certain how many different magazines exist in the United States. It has never been easy to define magazines or to assign definitive figures to the workplace environment.

No central clearinghouse lists all the magazines that have been or currently are being published, nor is there agreement on how to count magazines. There are no standard classifications as to whether a publication should be identified as a consumer, specialized business-to-business, organization, association, public relations, or custom magazine.

Depending on which reference you choose, you can make an argument for using just about any set of magazine (also called periodical) numbers in the industry:

Ulrich's Periodicals Directory (2005): more than 186,100 publications worldwide

Standard Periodical Directory (2004): 26,669 U.S. and Canadian periodicals

National Directory of Magazines (2004): 21,266 U.S. and Canadian magazines

SRDS Business Publication Advertising Source (2004): more than 9,300 magazines

SRDS Consumer Magazine Advertising Source (2004): more than 2,700 magazines

The Magazine Publishers of America (MPA) represents more than 240 domestic publishing companies, with approximately 1,400 titles (MPA, 2004, p. 43). Although consumer magazines make up the bulk of the membership, some specialized business magazines also join MPA. The American Business Media (ABM), the primary association for specialized business-to-business or trade publications for a particular industry, profession, or service, has more than 250 member companies, publishing more than 1,750 magazines (ABM, 2004).

Whole groups of magazines, however, fall through the cracks in these lists: most public relations magazines, many custom publications, magazines that do not accept advertising, many small regional and city publications, and newly created magazines. Hundreds of magazines are started up every year—1,006 new magazines were launched in 2004 alone (Husni, 2005). No accounting has been done of public relations magazines; scholars and researchers estimate there could be as few as 10,000 or as many as 100,000 publications (Johnson & Prijatel, 2000, p. 20).

Government data do not clarify the magazine workplace, either. There are too many overlapping job titles and classifications in Bureau of Labor Statistics data. Newspapers, books, motion pictures, broadcasting, telecommunications, Internet service providers, software publishers, libraries, archives, and printing establishments, as well as consumer and trade periodicals, are lumped together under the "information industry," which employed more than 3.4 million people in 2004 (U.S. Bureau of Labor Statistics, 2004, Table 18). In the "publishing except newspapers and software" category for 2004, which includes magazines, books, and newsletters, women are listed as being 54% of the total 325,000 employees (U.S. Bureau of Labor Statistics, 2004, Table 18). Women make up 49% of the "editors and reporters" classification with its 280,000 jobs (U.S. Bureau of Labor Statistics, 2002, Table 11). Based on government statistics, the magazine industry doesn't appear to be skewed toward one gender or the other.

Interviews with women in the magazine industry over the past 20 years support the concept of gender balance in the industry. This is not a media field that is in danger of becoming feminized, nor do women reach a glass ceiling in terms of promotion because they are in a "pink ghetto." Women in the magazine industry believe the field is balanced and that women are making about the same amount of money as their male counterparts. They do not believe they have experienced discrimination. "I think we are paid proportionally to our experience here. I've never been under the impression that a male editor would make more than I would," said an editor of a food magazine recently (Thompson, 2004). "As far as I know, everyone is paid equally. We're all paid on performance levels," said a female publisher of 10 business-to-business magazines in 2004 (Thompson, 2004).

Despite this perception of equality, salary studies by *Folio: The Magazine for Magazine Management* indicate that men historically have tended to out-earn women in most editorial positions. However, the salary gap has narrowed over the years, resulting in the success of such high-powered women as Martha Stewart *(Martha Stewart Living)* and Oprah Winfrey *(O: The Oprah Magazine).*

Research About the Magazine Industry

Although numerous studies have been made of magazine covers, content, advertising, and readers, there is a paucity of scholarly research on the current status, structure, and roles of those employed at consumer or specialized business-to-business magazines. Although the MPA has conducted competitive compensation and performance surveys for more than 20 years, that information is proprietary and available to MPA members only.

Compounding the research dilemma is that the magazine industry is very volatile; the numbers of magazines fluctuate, as do the numbers of jobs and people employed. There is no consistency in job title and position description, making salary surveys difficult. A senior editor at one magazine may have the responsibilities of an associate editor at another; an advertising manager at one company may be the marketing director elsewhere. Though all magazines need four kinds of personnel—editorial, advertising sales, circulation, and production—this doesn't mean every magazine has four departments or even four employees (Johnson & Prijatel, 2000, p. 160). Other key factors in determining salary and status include the size of the magazine, particularly its circulation, as well as its location. Editors based in New York City are almost always paid the most.

The most accessible, ongoing source for information about salary and status at consumer and specialized business magazines is *Folio: The Magazine for Magazine Management. Folio* has conducted yearly salary surveys of top managerial positions in editorial, production, circulation, and advertising sales since 1985. However, because of space constraints, only editorial data will be discussed in this chapter.

The first survey in 1985 asked editors to report anonymously on their salaries in six positions: editorial management, editor, managing/executive editor, senior/associate editor, copy editor, and art director. *Folio* broke out salary averages by region, type of magazine, average number of editorial pages produced annually, number of editors on staff, magazine frequency, magazine circulation, number of magazines responsible for, years of experience, and gender. Using *Folio* data is frustrating because of the lack of consistency in the survey instrument. The universe changed from year to year, with categories being eliminated or modified and job descriptions being collapsed into varying titles.

The results of the 1985 survey were depressing: "Wide variations in salaries for people with same title; lower pay for women; general dissatisfaction with editorial compensation" (Love & Angelo, 1985, p. 69). When the average magazine salary for editorial management (editorial director, vice president/editorial, editor-in-chief, and editor/publisher) at both consumer and business magazines was indicated by gender, women's pay was 73% of men's pay, or $36,230 compared with $49,650. This same pattern existed at all job levels and at both consumer and trade magazines. Several women commented about the differences in salary: "I'm still waiting for equal pay for equal work," and "Men make about 25% more, even if they work on less prestigious and smaller circulation magazines."

An examination of *Folio* survey data over the next 15 years showed more and more women moving into top editorial positions and a slow-but-steady progress toward equal pay at both consumer and specialized business magazines. The salary gap remained greater in the top editorial positions of editorial director and editor-in-chief than in midmanagement levels of managing editor and senior editor. By 1992, interviews with women at consumer magazines and specialized business publications revealed that most believed there had not been overt discrimination against them and that, in general, women were paid about the same as men in similar positions. However, women editors acknowledged that they had to overachieve to make it to the top. A woman who had been a senior editor for 11 years at a high-tech business magazine said, "I believe management is more concerned about talent than gender. Employers are looking for people who can do the job regardless of sex. However, the women I know who work in editorial jobs have worked harder than the men" (Valys, 1992).

At the start of the 21st century, women weren't mentioning gender concerns or salary differences, although the 2000 *Folio* editorial survey still found wage disparity. The surveyed job titles had been collapsed into four categories: editorial director/editor-in-chief (previously called editorial management), editor/executive editor, managing editor, and senior editor. Men continued to outnumber women in the editorial director/editor-in-chief, editor/executive editor, and senior editor categories. Sixty percent of the editorial director/editor-in-chief jobs were held by men, and 40% were held by women; this ratio was an improvement for women (Moseley, 2000, p. 42). The percentage difference was closer in the editor/executive editor and senior editor slots, where it now averaged around 53% male to 47% female. Women continued to be dominant in the managing editor slot, averaging around 60% female to 40% male, which had been the case since 1995.

In the editorial director/editor-in-chief level at both consumer and specialized business magazines, women averaged 85% of men's salaries (Moseley, 2000, p. 42). At the editor/executive editor level, 99% salary parity existed, while at the managing editor level, women made 88% of men's salaries. At the senior editor level, women averaged 87% of men's salaries.

In 2001, for the first time, *Folio* reported estimated earnings for "marquee editors" at some of the top consumer and business-to-business magazines, stating,

> We chose to name names only for high-profile people—those well-known not only within media circles, but within the industries their magazines cover. For the less public positions, like managing editor and senior editor, we pinpointed the typical salary at a specific magazine. (*Folio* Staff, 2001, p. 34)

Although men still outearned women in all categories except for managing editor, in which women made $6,000 more, the average salary disparity remained at about the same percentages as previously reported (women making about 90% of men's salaries).

For 2001, *Folio* reported that editor-in-chief Anna Wintour of *Vogue* made an estimated $1.5 million, including a clothing allowance, luxury car, car service and driver, country club membership, and no-interest home loan (*Folio* Staff, 2001, pp. 34–35). Her male counterpart at *Vanity Fair,* also a Condé Nast publication, received the same salary and perks. Glenda Bailey, editor-in-chief at *Harper's Bazaar,* a Hearst magazine, was estimated to earn $1 million; her male counterpart at Hearst's *Esquire* received $650,000. The most highly paid magazine editor-in-chief, at an estimated $2 million, was Tina Brown, editor-in-chief of *Talk* (now defunct). This seemed to indicate that women were finally in the same salary league as men at the top editorial positions of editorial director/editor-in-chief for high-circulation magazines.

In the 2001 survey, salaries for specific magazines were identified, revealing a wide range of salaries for the same title (*Folio* Staff, 2001, pp. 36–38). Plus, by naming the magazine's salary for a particular job, *Folio* signaled that it did not matter whether the position was held by a male or a female. For example, an editor/executive editor at *Good Housekeeping* made

$250,000, while *Gear*'s editor made $80,000. On the specialized business side, an editor at *Computer World* made $125,000, while one at *Builder* made $68,000. In the managing editor category, examples ranged from $150,000 at *Self* to $31,000 at *Lift Equipment*. A senior editor at *ESPN The Magazine* earned $120,000, while one at *D Magazine* (Dallas) brought in $65,000 and another at *Affordable Housing Finance* made $50,000.

Also for the first time, *Folio* included lower-level editorial salaries for associate editors, assistant editors, and editorial assistants (*Folio* Staff, 2001, p. 39). Associate editor salaries ranged from a high of $50,000 at *Glamour* to a low of $26,000 at *Modern Salon*. Only two assistant editor salaries were identified: $28,000 at *Men's Journal* and $30,000 at *Redbook*. The entry-level editorial assistant position came in at $25,000 at *Builder,* $26,000 at *Cosmopolitan,* and $30,000 at *Intelligent Enterprise*. Previously, the only information about entry-level salaries was found in the annual survey of journalism and mass communication graduates made since 1997 by researchers at the University of Georgia. The 2003 Annual Survey of Journalism and Mass Communication Graduates reported that graduates starting at consumer magazines earned $25,000 and those at specialized business magazines began at $27,000 (Becker & Vlad, 2003).

The last *Folio* survey to include gender comparisons of salaries occurred in 2002. *Folio* stressed that the gender gap was closing, reporting for the first time that female editorial directors/editors-in-chief made more money than males, or 103% salary parity (*Folio* Staff, 2002, p. 40). At the editor/executive editor level, women achieved 98% salary parity. Males made slightly more than females in the managing editor category, with women reaching 96% of men's salaries. The largest gap occurred at the senior editor slot, with women earning 84% of men's salaries. Men continued to outnumber women by 65% to 35% in the editorial director/editor-in-chief and executive editor/editor categories. Women dominated the managing editor slot, 63% to men's 37%; at the senior edition position, the ratio was 54% male and 46% female. However, salary parity was the closest it had ever been, averaging 95%.

No survey was done in 2003. In the *Folio* 2004 survey, males still outnumbered women by 60% to 40% in the editorial director/editor-in-chief level (Borod, 2004, p. 22). Women now matched men 50% to 50% at the executive editor/editor level; they dominated by 62% to men's 38% at the managing editor slot; and they led by 55% to 45% at the senior editor position. However, salaries were no longer broken out by gender.

Salary ranges were provided, and, though interesting, this information merely reflected the problems in quantifying data about the magazine workplace. For example, in 2004, the range reported in *Folio* for editorial director/editor-in-chief was $35,000 to $185,000, for editor/executive editor $22,000 to $220,000, for managing editor $27,500 to $135,000, and for senior editor $29,000 to $143,000 (Borod, 2004, pp. 19–22). The extensive range between the lowest and highest salaries was affected by factors such as age, years worked in editorial, years worked at the present company, years in current position, number of people supervised, number of magazines responsible for, magazine circulation, bonus possibilities, and geographic location. *Folio* pointed out that most survey respondents worked at magazines with less than 100,000 circulation and less than $6 million in revenues.

"At companies such as Time Inc., Condé Nast, and Hearst, even editors-in-chief at smaller books get a base of $300,000 to $400,000 and a bonus can bump that up to $600,000," said an executive vice president of an executive search firm (Borod, 2004, p. 21). Other publishing houses, such as Rodale and Hachette Filipacchi, provided a base of $175,000 to $250,000, with bonuses of $50,000 to $75,000; business-to-business publishers such as Crain's, IDG, and Reed also paid that range. Small, independent publishers paid their top editors-in-chief the least, in the $125,000 to $200,000 range. Geography can significantly boost salary: An editor-in-chief in New York City earned an average of $108,000, compared with one based in the North Central states, where the average was $74,500.

A female business-to-business editor interviewed in 2004 pointed out that gender representation tends to be different at business-to-business magazines than at consumer magazines:

> I think consumer magazines are more dominated by female editors, due to the subject matter. For whatever reason, b-to-b magazines tend to appeal more to men, perhaps just due to the nature of the industries they represent. I guess you could trace this back to what males vs. females study in college. Some subjects and careers tend to appeal more to one gender than the other. (Thompson, 2004)

However, this editor said she hadn't personally experienced gender discrimination in her publishing company, adding, "I feel I have had the same opportunities as the men at this company." She said because her magazine represents a manufacturing industry, "I'm constantly in an environment where there are few, if any, women. I've been to industry meetings where I've been the only woman in a crowd of 50 to 60 people."

Women's Status at the Top

Although Oprah Winfrey and Martha Stewart are high-profile celebrities with successful magazines and even more successful media conglomerates, many top women publishers and editorial directors of magazines are relatively unknown to the public. But their impact in the magazine industry is significant. For example, Ann S. Moore oversees the world's leading magazine company as chairman and chief executive officer of Time Inc., whose 134 magazines (including *Time, Sports Illustrated, Fortune, People,* and *Entertainment Weekly*) reach a total audience of more than 300 million readers and account for nearly a quarter of the total advertising revenue of U.S. consumer magazines (Time Warner, 2005). Christie Hefner, daughter of *Playboy* founder Hugh Hefner, has been chief executive officer of Playboy Enterprises, Inc., since 1988. At *Playboy,*

> Nearly half of all employees are female: 28% of the executives and 44% of the managers are women. By comparison, about 16% of corporate officers at Fortune 500 companies are women, according to Catalyst, an organization that focuses on the advancement of female executives. (Posnock, 2004, p. 42)

Cathleen Black, president of Hearst Magazines, has been dubbed "The First Lady of American Magazines" and "one of the leading figures in American publishing over the past two decades" by the *Financial Times* (Hearst Corporation, 2005). Black oversees the financial performance and operations of 18 of the largest and most successful magazines in the industry, including *Cosmopolitan, Redbook, Esquire, Good Housekeeping, Seventeen, Harper's Bazaar, Marie Claire,* and *Popular Mechanics.* Reaching the top positions in any industry takes time. Black started in advertising sales at *Holiday* and *Travel & Leisure* in 1970 and was involved in the launch of *Ms.* magazine in 1972; she took the job at Hearst in 1996. Moore has been at Time, Inc., since 1978. She was named to her current position in 2002.

A 30-year veteran in the magazine industry, who has worked at six different consumer magazines in her climb to the top as a senior vice president and publisher of a major women's magazine, said recently,

> In the 1970s, most of the people in magazines were men, but there's been a gradual shift since then. In general, more men work in business books than women. Because of the content, more women work at women's consumer magazines. (Thompson, 2004)

According to a vice president and publisher on the business-to-business side of the magazine industry,

> Right now, we've got a full generation of women working at magazines, and there's going to be more. Women only really started working at magazines

20 years ago. So there are more women working every year, which helps. Eventually, everything will be equal. (Thompson, 2004)

Currently, the highest-paid editor in the magazine industry in 2005—possibly the highest-paid print journalist anywhere—is a woman: Bonnie Fuller, editorial director for American Media and the mastermind of a slick new look and attitude for *Star.* Fuller, who has held top editorial positions at *YM, Marie Claire, Cosmopolitan, Glamour,* and *Us Weekly,* is reported to have a $3 million yearly compensation package consisting of a $1.5 million salary, a $1.5 million equity stake, circulation incentives up to $900,000 per year, and perks such as car service and health club expenses (Washington, 2004).

Conclusion

Although an examination of 20 years of editorial salary data reveals fluctuating salaries and wage disparities, women working in the magazine industry dismiss the notion of gender discrimination. "I've never experienced any sort of discrimination or known someone who has," declared a managing editor of a shelter magazine in 2004 (Thompson, 2004). Women seem optimistic about their roles and salaries at consumer and specialized business magazines. They aren't complaining about their status, at least not to *Folio* and not in interviews. The magazine industry has a balanced ratio of men and women in a variety of editorial positions as well as in key slots in advertising sales, production, and circulation. The environment looks very good for women entering the magazine field and working their way to the top. In an industry based on the written word, women are just as likely as men to hold the pen.

Questions for Discussion

1. Why do women's magazines appear in the top 10 in terms of circulation year after year?

2. Why is it difficult to define magazines and to define the workplace environment?

3. Why do women in the magazine industry today believe they haven't experienced discrimination in terms of salary or status?

4. Why do you think editors-in-chief at such top consumer magazines as *Vogue, Vanity Fair, Harper's Bazaar,* and *Esquire* make so much money?

5. Is the success of Oprah Winfrey's *O: The Oprah Magazine* and Martha Stewart's *Martha Stewart Living* the result of their television personae, or are the magazines themselves delivering messages that women want to hear?

Accessing Additional Information

American Business Media: http://www.americanbusinessmedia.com

Magazine Publishers of America: http://www.magazine.org

6

Radio

The More Things Change . . .
The More They Stay the Same

Judith Cramer, St. John's University

- Radio reaches over 94% of consumers weekly.
- Car radio reaches four of five adults each week.
- About 1/3 of all adults turn to radio for their news in the morning.

—National Association of Broadcasters (NAB)
Radio Marketing Guide & Fact Book
for Advertisers, 2003–2004

In one way or another, radio touches us all. But significant events since 1993 have changed the radio industry markedly, and in unexpected ways. Continued deregulation, technological advances, and elimination of the Equal Employment Opportunity (EEO) rules by the Federal Communications Commission (FCC) have preserved the largely male face of the radio industry, something not predicted in the last edition of this book.

Waves of Change

Deregulation

Broadcasting has gone from being an industry with structural regulation to one of free-market deregulation (Chambers, 2003). The process began during the Reagan administration with the loosening of broadcast ownership restrictions and the elimination of the Fairness Doctrine, which required broadcasters to provide differing viewpoints on controversial issues. Free-market deregulation peaked in 1996 with passage of the Clinton-backed Telecommunications Act, which spawned numerous mergers and consolidation of the industry.

The Telecommunications Act of 1996 required the FCC to drop its rule limiting the number of AM and FM stations one entity could own or control (FCC, 2001, p. 1). Prior to the legislation, only minority or small businesses could own three AM and three FM stations. Following this legislation, anyone, any entity, or any company could own as many stations as they could afford.

As a result, while the number of commercial radio stations increased by 5.1% between 1996 and 2001, from 10,256 to 10,779, the number of separate commercial radio station owners dropped by 22%, from 4,887 to 4,006. Existing owners merged with others, increasing the size of the largest radio groups. For example, the two largest radio groups, Clear Channel and AMFM Radio, merged to form Clear Channel Communications; and by 2005, Clear Channel owned more than 1,200 stations across the country (Anderson, 2005; Journalism.org, 2005). "The top 50 radio group owners went from controlling a little less than 9% of the industry in 1995, to controlling more than one-quarter (27.5%) of it by 2000" (Fratrik, 2001, p. 42).

Finally, the Telecommunications Act of 1996 required that the FCC loosen its local ownership rules (FCC, 2001). As a result, a number of large corporations each bought several stations in the same market (Nellessen & Brady, 2000). The impact has been dramatic. Ownership and program diversity have declined at the local level (FCC, 2004). In small markets, for example, while the average number of radio stations increased from four in 1972 to nine in 1998, the average number of radio owners did not keep pace with the increase in the number of stations. The majority of these owners are highly educated White males, "several from Ivy League universities, schooled in business and law, not broadcasting, with annual salaries and compensation well into the millions" (Huntemann, 1999, p. 396).

Advances in Technology

Another force affecting the radio industry is technology. Advances in digital technology, such as computers, satellites, and the Internet, have facilitated and accelerated consolidation. Technology has allowed large radio groups to consolidate station operations, content development, and distribution. Many argue that the result is a loss of jobs and the homogenization of on-air programming (Huntemann, 1999). Owners connect their clusters of stations electronically so that music and news can originate from one location. By 1998, satellites, computers, and digital editing made it possible to provide local syndication programming, live radio programs made to "sound" local, to stations in entirely separate and distant markets (Huntemann, 1999). At radio stations with music formats, personnel no longer are needed to operate equipment such as the audio board, microphones, and CD players because they "voicetrack." Voicetracking allows stations to use computer-edited, prerecorded shows that sound live or to do "virtual remotes," live broadcasts that use a voicetracked DJ on computer for the in-studio voice (Huntemann, 1999).

The local focus of radio news programming has suffered from the effects of these technological advances. A news anchor can produce and deliver a generic newscast in just minutes, perhaps even a few seconds, before it is to air on one or more sister stations located many miles away from that central location. With advances in technology, one person can do what used to be the work of many (Nellessen & Brady, 2000). From the large-group owner's viewpoint, the use of this technology is more cost-effective.

Equal Employment Opportunity (EEO) Rules

These changes in regulations governing the broadcast workplace, coupled with the increasing use of technology, have had a negative impact on the employment of women and minorities in radio. In separate rulings, the U.S. Court of Appeals for the District of Columbia in 1998 and 1999 threw out the FCC's 30-year-old EEO rules. Stations are no longer required to make special efforts to recruit and hire minorities and women in proportion to the local population.

Commercial Radio

The Workforce

A woman's place in radio in the 1920s was in singing, acting, and giving household hints. It was also in research, off-air interviewing, and writing. It was not, however, in announcing and reading the news, nor was it in managing or owning a radio station. That has changed, but not as much as one might have thought or hoped. Although World War II, affirmative action, and the women's movement of the 1970s combined to open those doors of opportunity, the opportunity was largely unfulfilled.

Initially, women gradually improved their numbers and status in radio programming. In the 1950s, they worked as "script girls," interviewers, and coordinators of network radio programs. Yet it was routine for women's voices to be rubbed off the tape so that an on-mic male announcer could be heard asking the interview questions (Marzolf, 1977). But despite tremendous social change in the 1960s, the bias against women in radio newsrooms persisted: Women made up just 4.7% of radio and television newsroom staffs in the 1960s.

A 1971 survey done by the American Women in Radio and Television (AWRT) indicated that the radio workforce and industry had begun to change. The survey found that women had begun to move into larger radio markets, to receive higher salaries, and to hold more responsible and visible positions. Those surveyed were hopeful about the future (Marzolf, 1977).

In fact, women made great strides between 1972 and 1976. Stone (1976), for example, surveyed 330 commercial radio stations at a time when the women's movement was at full strength and found that the number of stations where newswomen were on the air had more than tripled from 15% in 1972 to 49% in 1976.

Women's radio collectives and women's program-formatted stations became somewhat prominent in the 1970s (Carter, 2005). The latter provided alternative ways for women to become engaged in radio's creative process, developing programming from a feminist perspective that their sisters would find interesting and necessary. None of these stations lasted beyond the 1980s. They failed for several reasons: (a) Alternative, non-revenue-producing programming was diminishing as fringe FM stations increased their market shares and became more profitable in the late 1970s; (b) the women's movement was nearing its end, and so feminist politics were fading by the late 1980s; and (c) broadcast deregulation in the 1980s caused the FCC to drop many news and public affairs program requirements, which eliminated the market for programming from women's radio collectives and eliminated the requirement to hire women broadcasters. The greatest contributing factor in the failure of women's radio collectives and women's program-formatted stations was the fact that their programming was labeled as *female* or *feminist,* which drove audiences away in the postfeminist 1980s (Carter, 2005). (See Table 6.1.)

Table 6.1   Percentage of Female Workforce in Radio News Markets, 1986–2003

	1986	1991	1999	2003
All radio	32.0%	29.4%	35.0%	22.4%

SOURCE: Data from "Recovering Lost Ground," by B. Papper, *RTNDA Communicator*, 2004, p. 26.

In terms of pure numbers, positions, and salaries, women in the 1980s did not continue to make the large gains in radio that they had during the previous decade. Parity between men and women in the newsroom did not occur at either the commercial network or the local level. The least impressive gains were at the radio networks, where the number of women managers increased just 3% between 1983 and 1986 ("Women in Broadcasting," 1987). According to *Variety*, CBS was the only radio network to employ women as general managers in 1983 and 1985. In 1987, however, no woman was a general manager at CBS—or, for that matter, anywhere! At the local level, improvement was gradual. Overall, the number of women employed by local commercial radio station news departments grew by 30% between 1972 and 1986 (Stone, 1987; Stone & Dell, 1972, p. 4). Most of the growth took place at locally owned stations in large markets, where, because the size of the news staff was larger, they were more likely to hire women.

The number of women in radio news dropped from about 6,800 in the mid-1980s to 5,000 in mid-1991 (Stone, 1992). During that same time period, 250 radio news departments ceased operation, resulting in the loss of 2,100 radio news jobs, many of which were held by women (Stone, 1992). In the mid-1990s, the percentage of women in radio news hovered around 30% before reaching 35% in 1999 (Papper & Gerhard, 2000). One year later, at the turn of the century, the percentage of women in radio news peaked at 37.4% (Papper & Gerhard, 2002).

According to Rebecca Fisher[1] of the FCC's Media Bureau, the FCC does not maintain statistics of the number of women in the overall radio workforce or in radio station management (personal communication, January 28, 2005). The Radio-Television News Directors Association (RTNDA), however, continues to track the status of women in radio news, and the results are not encouraging: Papper (2002, 2003, 2004) has reported that the percentage of women working in radio news declined 15%, to 22.4%, in 2003.

Table 6.2   Percentage of Female News Directors and General Managers
Workforce in Radio News Markets, 1986–2003

	1986	1991	1999	2003
Female news directors	24.0%	29.0%	20.0%	25.9%
Female general managers	—	—	13.0%	13.4%

SOURCE: Data for 1986 from "Women Gaining as News Directors," by V. A. Stone, 1988, *RTNDA Communicator*, p. 21; data for 1991 from "Women and Men as News Directors," by V. A. Stone, January 1992b, *RTNDA Communicator*, pp. 143–144; data for 1999 and 2003 from "2000 Women and Minorities Survey," by B. Papper, 2000, *RTNDA/F Research*, and "Recovering Lost Ground," by B. Papper, 2004, *RTNDA Communicator*, p. 26.

Management

Women seem to be moving into radio management positions at a snail's pace. In 1986, women made up 24% of all radio news directors (Stone, 1988). In almost 20 years, little has changed. In 2003, women held just 25.9% of those positions (Papper, 2004). (See Table 6.2.)

While there were few, if any, women occupying the position of radio station general manager in 1986, the number of women station general managers has improved and held relatively steady at about 13% from the late 1990s through 2004 (Papper, 2002, 2003, 2004; Papper & Gerhard, 2000; WomensRadio, 2005b). Jane E. Gerberding, president of Nassau Media Partners and Most Influential Women in Radio (MIW) group spokesperson, says only a handful of companies are demonstrating real progress in hiring women general managers (WomensRadio, 2005b). Among them are Clear Channel, Entercom, ABC, and Cox. According to the MIW group, which is made up of top-level radio women,

> Industry sources estimate that, since the early 80s, 54% of the people working in radio sales are women. This demonstrates that women have talents that are valuable and viable in the radio business. After 25 years, if all things were equal more than 1 out of 5 of them should have been capable of advancing to managerial positions. (WomensRadio, 2005b)

On the flip side, women can sell radio and are gaining in numbers. According to the Most Influential Women in Radio (MIW) 2003 composition analysis, the number of women moving into the advertising sales side of radio station management has steadily increased from 26% in 1995 to a little more than 31% (WomensRadio, 2005a).

Ownership

Twelve years ago, no figures were available on the number of female radio station owners. The FCC defines female ownership of a station as "ownership where women in the aggregate have a greater than 50% voting interest" (Noel Uri, personal communication, January 31, 2005). Today, those numbers are available, although rather difficult to find. According to Noel Uri of the Industry Analysis Division of the FCC's Media Bureau, as of September 30, 2004, the FCC unofficially put the total number of commercial FM radio stations at 6,217 and commercial AM stations at 4,770. Using responses from the 2003 FCC Form 323 filing, Uri indicated that women owned 357 commercial FM radio stations and 335 AM radio stations in the United States (personal communication, January 31, 2005). The percentage is revealing: Women owned 50% or more of only 6.2% of all FM and AM commercial radio stations in the United States in 2003. Yet in 1997, women owned 26.0% of all nonfarm businesses in the United States (U.S. Department of Labor, Women's Bureau, 2002, p. 1).

Public Radio

The introduction of National Public Radio (NPR) in 1971 brought with it increased opportunities for both male and female radio broadcasters. In 1972, a survey of public radio stations found that women were employed at 103 public radio stations, making up 14% of the management and 16% of all on-air positions (Butler & Paisley, 1980). Two years later, women held 26% (3,452) of all public radio jobs.

In 1974, Caroline Isber and Muriel Cantor conducted a survey of 245 public television and 159 public radio stations on behalf of the Corporation for Public Broadcasting. According to their Task Force on Women in Public Broadcasting report, male employees were found to make more money (in some cases, they had been in their present jobs longer than the women), and they received requested and unrequested promotions in greater numbers than did women (Isber & Cantor, 1975). The task force also examined 13 different kinds of adult public radio programs and found that men were much more likely to narrate/moderate discussions of business, economics, law, and government, with women most often leading general human interest discussions (Isber & Cantor, 1975).

Each year, the Corporation for Public Broadcasting (CPB) is required to submit a diversity report to Congress. The 2002 to 2003 report does not appear to contain information regarding the status of women in the public radio workforce. The filing does track the minority workforce and shows a

5.8% increase, to 19.0%. However, the report does not include a gender breakdown of those figures.

Theoretically, public radio should play a vital role in supporting diversity both in hiring and in programming because it lacks the many and varied influences of outside commercial interests. Yet today, according to Steve Rendall and Daniel Butterworth (2004) of Fairness and Accuracy in Reporting (FAIR), women continue to be underrepresented, at least on public radio. Their June 2004 report indicates that there has been little change in the representation of women on NPR over the past decade. Women now constitute only 21% of all NPR's story sources, an increase of just 2% from 1993.

What Now, What Next?

The contemporary women's movement, together with affirmative action, helped open the doors of opportunity in the 1970s for women interested in radio careers. Since then, industry deregulation, consolidation, increased competition from television and other technologies (such as the iPod for music), and the elimination of the EEO rules have partially closed those doors. In raw numbers at least, women have made few gains in radio since the publication of the last edition of this book. The number of women working in radio news has dropped 7% since 1991. According to enrollment statistics, more and more women are being educated and trained to work in the electronic media, but those advances have not translated into any real increase in the number of women working in radio on-air positions or in the types of on-air positions they hold.

Today, on-air work for women is primarily in supporting roles. According to Donna Vaughan, the 40-year-old news director at WALK-FM on Long Island, New York, the programming/on-air side is still dominated by men, especially during "morning drive," the most lucrative on-air daypart. She says that "because most of your morning hosts are male, a lot of stations have unofficially said that the person who does news needs to be a female to balance out the huge number of males" (Donna Vaughan, personal communication, December 7, 2004). Vaughan's perception echoes that of a female news director more than 10 years ago (Stone, 2000) that "in a profession that's still predominantly male, there's a desire for female 'voices' to offset or complement male coworkers."

According to Vaughan, this implied need for women in this area of radio has created more news job opportunities for them even though there are fewer overall news jobs because of consolidation. But, she says, a shortage of "good female talent" compounds the problem. Vaughn says there is nobody in the pipeline because everyone wants to work in television (personal communication, December 7, 2004).

Tonya Powers, 35, has worked in radio for 18 years and is currently the midday anchor and community service director at WREC News Radio 600, in Memphis, Tennessee. Powers does not think much has changed for women working on-air. She still considers it an "uphill battle" and points to the very powerful lure of television as one reason for this (personal communication, January 10, 2005).

Gendered Perceptions of News

Jo Ann Allen, 51, is an African American, 28-year veteran of radio news. She was the host of the local *All Things Considered* on public radio's WNYC in New York for 18 years before moving on to the Air America network in 2004, where she anchored the news for 1 year. She believes there are differences in the ways men and women view events and decide what is news. According to Allen, women look at situations "more humanely." She says, "We don't just want the facts, we want to know how the facts affect people" (personal communication, December 16, 2004). Powers agrees the differences are obvious in the ways she, as the only full-time female anchor and reporter at her station, and her male colleagues put together a newscast: "I will do more health and human interest stuff and the guys will do more hard news and they'll do more sports stuff" (personal communication, January 10, 2005). Both Allen and Powers believe that more women's perspectives on local, national, and world events would enrich the news being produced in what continues to be a White-male-dominated radio newsroom.

Salaries

In the early 1990s, the typical radio newswoman earned between $19,000 and $20,000 per year (Stone, 1991). Research conducted by Papper and Gerhard (2002) indicates that radio salaries increased significantly between 1996 and 2001 except for those of news reporters, whose wages, when accounting for inflation, actually fell 2.1% (p. 5). The most substantial growth in salaries occurred in small markets for news directors and for reporters in stations with three or more full-time news staff members. In addition, Papper and Gerhard reported that for the fourth straight year, "The number of stations in a group, and likely responsibility and workload—did not translate into higher pay" (p. 7). According to the *State of the News Media* (Journalism.org., 2005), individuals working in news at group-owned stations continue to earn lower salaries than those employed by independently owned stations.

Vaughan, an 18-year radio veteran, has spent the last 10 years as a news director and morning news anchor. Currently, she has one full-time reporter (male) working for her. She says her responsibilities have changed over the years to include anchoring two 3-minute newscasts an hour (newscasts that used to be 5 minutes). With consolidation has come more responsibility. For the past 3½ years, Vaughan also anchored two newscasts an hour on Clear Channel sister station WLTW/Lite FM in New York City, which were pre-fed just a few minutes before airtime.[2] Vaughan believes she has been "adequately, reasonably compensated" (personal communication, December 7, 2004).

In contrast, Powers says her experiences in the South lead her to believe there is disparity in commercial radio pay: "I know for a fact that I earned less in my position as my cohost doing the same job at the same time on the same show as a man" (personal communication, January 10, 2005). And Powers says that women are treated differently when they ask for raises: "I have female coworkers who have been promised raises and bonuses and when they point this out and ask for them, they're pacified and pushed to the background, never receiving them" (personal communication, February 2, 2005).

As was the case in the previous edition of this book, pay equity appears to be less of an issue in public radio. Allen says she was not aware of any differences and that public radio stations on the whole "pay pretty low." According to Allen, "The position usually determined what you got paid. I would be surprised if with all things being equal, a male producer or reporter or host had a higher salary than a woman with similar experience and duties" (personal communication, February 1, 2005).

Management

Powers has worked in both small- and large-market radio, first as a disc jockey, then as a morning news anchor and cohost. She is now a midday news anchor and station community service director. While women are still where they were 10 years ago on the air, Powers says she has seen a lot of positive changes on the corporate side of radio, especially in the area of sales, "where the money is." Powers worked for a woman general manager and says she was "very, very good" because

> She didn't forget that she had to be tough and at the same time, fair. She was able to tell you "no" and smile at the same time. She meant what she said and you knew she did. . . . At the same time, you knew that if you had a problem

or an issue you needed to talk with her about, you could. (personal communication, January 10, 2005)

Vaughan concurs with Powers that more and more women are moving into radio sales. She says that women are increasingly dominating this area of radio and the majority of general manager positions are filled by those coming from sales. She believes it stands to reason that the number of women general managers will increase.

Ownership

Although the FCC cannot provide data on women-owned stations by market size or group ownership, research does suggest that women owners tend to program their stations differently than do their male counterparts. According to Spitzer (1990), women (and minorities) may be more likely to sacrifice some profits to offer specialized programming that develops group identification, ethnic pride, or "psychological need to communicate with one's own community" (p. 32). The report by the National Telecommunications and Information Administration (NTIA) further stated,

> Ensuring a diversity of viewpoints is a cornerstone of our nation's broadcasting policy. The continuing and emerging trends in minority commercial radio and television are chipping away at a valuable, indeed essential, means of achieving this goal and over our nation's historic commitment to localism. (NTIA, 1998)

Back to the Future?

Since 1993, little new research has been conducted on the representation of women working in radio. With deregulation, consolidation, ever-changing new technologies, and audience numbers consuming the attention of the radio industry (management, ownership, and regulators), the research focus has clearly shifted to the business side of radio. As was suggested in 1993, it is possible that less attention is devoted to the status of women in radio because they are perceived to be integrally involved in the radio workforce. The numbers, however, present a more complex picture.

Since the last edition of this book, deregulation of the broadcast industry has spawned an increase in the number of broadcast radio stations. However, television has become increasingly appealing for women wanting to enter the broadcast or electronic media industry. The continuing trend toward consolidation has curtailed job and ownership opportunities, limiting the numbers of women working in broadcast radio. The one area of radio in which women clearly have made inroads is in sales, which, traditionally, has been a direct pipeline to management positions.

Consolidation of the broadcast radio industry is likely to increase, but improvements in technology can open other doors for women that deregulation has partially closed. These opportunities may be found on Web and satellite radio, which is in the early stages of development but holds much promise. Web-based WomensRadio is searching for women to host a variety of Web radio programs and has asked women who are interested and have some experience to submit their names and programming topics (WomensRadio, 2005c).

For a long time, the argument in commercial radio was that women, for the most part, did not have the audience appeal and advertising support necessary to sustain the programs they hosted and produced, including women's issue-oriented shows. Optimistically, we can hope for change with satellite radio and the more than 120 channels of niche programming that each of the two satellite networks, XM and Sirius, offers. Unlike local terrestrial radio, these satellite networks reach a national audience, are subscription based rather than advertiser driven, and have specialized receivers locking subscribers into a particular network, thus developing audience loyalty (Journalism.org., 2005). It is, therefore, conceivable that the opportunities for women to host and produce programming, with or without a female focus, can grow with the number of channels and female subscribers.

Creating more outlets and positions is no guarantee, however, that the radio industry will be more welcoming to women. Women and men of different races and ethnicities who are hired into various managerial positions must share a philosophy of change, of including "others" like themselves, and of giving "others" greater visibility. More important, they must make a real commitment to developing and implementing hiring policies and retention practices (e.g., mentoring programs, flextime, and day care benefits) that help foster diversity and thus enrich their employee ranks, programming, and audience. Sadly, the structural and technological face of radio has changed dramatically, without a commitment to diversity.

Notes

1. I made a conscious decision to use the first names of those in personal communications in an effort to make these women sources as visible as possible.

2. Donna Vaughan's additional anchoring responsibilities at Clear Channel sister station WLTW/Lite FM ended in May 2005, when that station hired a full-time morning news anchor (a female).

Questions for Discussion

1. What three significant events have happened to change the landscape of the radio industry?

2. What area of the radio industry has been especially welcoming to women, and why?

3. How does the representation of women working in commercial radio compare with women working in public radio?

4. Is it important for the radio industry to diversify its workforce, and if so, why?

5. Do you think steps should be taken to increase the number of women working in the radio industry, and if so, why?

Accessing Additional Information

American Women in Radio and Television (AWRT): http://www.awrt.org

Donna Halper, radio and management consultant and author: http://www.DonnaHalper.com

Most Influential Women in Radio (MIW): http://www.radiomiw.com

National Association of Broadcasters (NAB): http://www.nab.org

News for African American News Professionals: http://www.BlackJournalist.com

Radio-Television News Directors Association: http://www.rtnda.org

Women's Online Media and Education Network: http://www.WomensRadio.com

7

Women and Minorities in Commercial and Public Television News, 1994–2004

Jannette L. Dates, Howard University

In the United States, like newspapers and radio, television news operations have been sluggish in increasing the number of people of color among their workforces, particularly among the decision makers. They have more readily embraced women within their ranks.

This chapter focuses on increases in the percentages of women and minorities who have managed to position themselves in the workforces of some of the nation's commercial and public television news and information systems.

Commercial Television

In 1978, the American Society of Newspaper Editors (ASNE) set the "Year 2000 goal," challenging its newspaper affiliates to achieve minority representation in newsrooms equivalent to the overall population in the United States by the year 2000. Many electronic news operations, following this model, also designed plans for increasing the diversity of their workforces. By 1994, however, the national minority population was more than 20%, and the news industry (print and electronic) was nowhere near parity. Although some American newsrooms had become more diverse, it was clear that the newspaper industry would fall short of its goal. The decision makers at newspapers seemed to lack the will and the way to move their operations toward the minority diversity goals they had established.

Thus, in 1998, the ASNE revised its plan; it reaffirmed a commitment to diversity and urged everyone in journalism to join the quest for greater newsroom diversity (ASNE, 1998). The goal and plan of action by ASNE set a new precedent for the news industry. Commercial and public broadcasting systems also began to reset their measurable goals. Despite these goals and action plans, however, by 2004, none of them had made strides toward achieving their written diversity goals. As before, there seemed to be a resistance to the changes that needed to be made in order to effectively embrace diversity.

Research Reports: Women

According to data and analyses conducted by researchers over the years, the proportion of women in commercial television news operations tripled from 11% to 33% between 1971 and 1982, changing little after that period (Smith, Fredin, & Nardone, 1993, pp. 172–174) until the late 1990s and beyond, when it grew to 39% (Papper, 2004). Among television news directors, the percentage of women grew from 14% to 16% in 1990 (Smith et al., 1993) and then to 24% by 2003 (Papper, 2004).

Interestingly, the 1998 elimination of the Federal Communications Commission's (FCC) Equal Employment Opportunity (EEO) guidelines for increasing and documenting employment figures for women and minorities precipitated a decline in the number of minorities in the radio news workforce but did not adversely affect the number of women and minorities employed in the nation's television newsrooms. During this period, women actually continued to make impressive gains; by 2000, 99% of the network affiliated news staffs had women workers, while women made up 24% of the news directors and 41% of the newsroom workforce.

Research Reports: Minorities

By 2000, research indications showed that some progress had been made by minorities in commercial television's news operations. By then, 14.2% of the news directors and 21% of the workforce were minorities (see Figure 7.1).[1] In commercial television, all of the minority groups had increased their numbers, with the exception of Native Americans (Radio-Television News

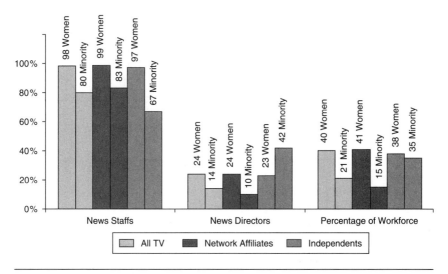

Figure 7.1   Women and Minorities in Local TV News, 2000

SOURCE: RTNDA Research (2000, pp. 1–4).

Directors Association [RTNDA] Research, 2000). By 2003, women had become 12.1% of all television broadcast news general managers, making the greatest strides in Designated Market Area (DMA) 151+ markets.

Most significantly, however, by 2000, television news operations were leading all other news operations on the diversity front. Minorities were faring better in television than they did in print journalism or in radio news operations. Radio news had 8.1% minority supervisors, whereas print had 9% and television news had 12.5. In addition, in network-affiliated television newsrooms, minority journalists made up 21.8% of the staffs (see Figure 7.2).

In the 2004 RTNDA/Ball State University Annual Survey Report, "Recovering Lost Ground: Minorities Gain Ground and Women Make Management Strides in Radio and TV Newsrooms," Papper noted that, discouragingly, although the minority population in the United States had grown by 5% between 1994 and 2004, in television newsrooms, the already-low numbers of minority workers had grown by only 3% during this 10-year span (see Figure 7.3).

Among broadcast news general managers (GMs), Whites and males continued to dominate. In the 2004 survey reported by Papper, for "All TV," 92.6% of news GMs were White, and only 7.4% were minorities; and

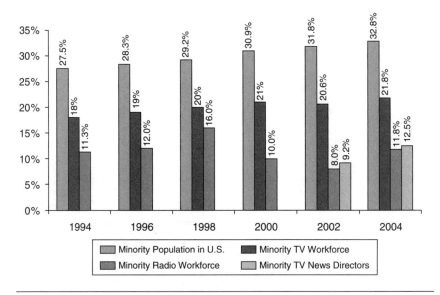

Figure 7.2   Minority Population and Minority Print and Broadcast Workforce, 1994–2004

SOURCE: Papper (2004, pp. 24–28); RTNDA Research (2000, p. 2).

87.9% of news GMs were male, with 12.1% females (see Figure 7.4). On a positive note, the report indicated that the percentage of minority television GMs had doubled from a year earlier, with the largest increase resulting from independent stations. The strong showing by Hispanic stations and the larger response rate contributed significantly to this jump.

Second in strength for both minorities and women were the smaller-sized markets (DMA 1–25), with the lowest-reported percentages, recorded for minorities, posted for the DMA 51- to 100-sized markets (see Figure 7.4).

Observations and Conclusions

Despite the more robust gains for women than for people of color as decision makers and as members of the workforce in television newsrooms, because of male domination, women were unable even by 2004 to wield significant power and influence. Consistently, for example, women were ignored as experts, being least likely to be cited as news sources, whether in newspapers, on the Web, or in television. "Women as people with authoritative views on the world are neither seen nor heard," according to a report by the Maynard Institute (Gibbons, 2005, pp 1–3).

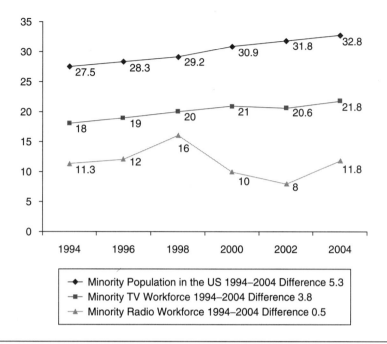

Figure 7.3   Minority Population and Minority Print and Broadcast Workforce, 1994–2004

SOURCE: Papper (2004, pp. 24, 28).

How important are this and similar findings? In the report, Gibbons (2005) noted that men, who cannot become pregnant, are the primary sources for stories about reproductive rights; and men are the ones consistently quoted and sought after to appear on television to share their views on all issues, even when women, by their job responsibilities, should be the invited experts. Gibbons also suggested that the persistent newsroom "coaching" on diversity may have fallen on deaf ears because to the persons "in charge of newsrooms, the majority of them men, [diversity] just doesn't matter" (p. 3). Until more women are in positions in which they can influence who gets called for an appearance and who is quoted as "the expert," many believe there will be a continuation of this consistent pattern, documented for many years.

In sum, between 1994 and 2004, women increased their percentage in commercial broadcast television news operations, making significant gains in employment over this 10-year period. They somewhat decreased the gap between their percentage in the populace and their percentage in the

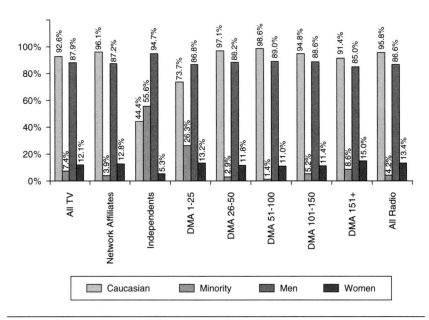

Figure 7.4   Broadcast News General Managers, 2004

SOURCE: Papper (2004, p. 28).

commercial television news industry as members of the workforce and as decision makers.

Between 1994 and 2004, however, minority participation in the commercial television news force had moved up only about 3 percentage points, and workers of color were concentrated at the lowest levels in ranks (Papper, 2004). Clearly, much more work needs to be done if minority participation in the workforce in television news operations is to move toward the goal of parity in the near future.

Moreover, despite the phenomenal growth of the minority population in the United States, the repeatedly espoused goals for newsroom diversity, and the huge expenditures by news organizations on diversity goal setting, according to Gonzalez and Torres (2004), of the National Association of Hispanic Journalists, "the pace of progress has been woefully slow" (p. 1). In 2004, journalists Gonzalez and Torres completed a well-respected report, released during the Unity Conference in August, that challenged journalists to a call to action. The report offered the following key conclusions:

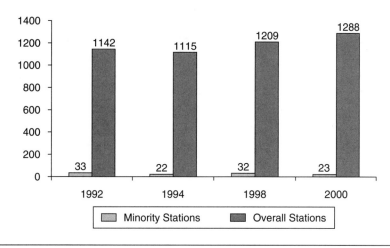

Figure 7.5   Minority Ownership of Commercial TV Stations, 1992–2000

SOURCE: Gonzalez and Torres (2004, p. 14).

- There have always been qualified people of color who sought to work as journalists but were excluded (and continue to be excluded). (p. 1)
- Such exclusion ensures that the press [will] routinely misrepresent, distort, and stereotype. (p. 2)
- American [taxpayers] subsidized the rise of various mass communication technologies with their taxes, but people of color have never enjoyed equal benefit from the . . . services those new media and companies were required to deliver in exchange. (p. 2)
- If the trend of media ownership concentration continues, where a handful of giant firms run almost exclusively by White male investors and managers dominate the market, minority media ownership will virtually disappear . . . and we will soon face a de facto apartheid media system. (p. 2)

Gonzalez and Torres view minority ownership as the key to the survival of democracy. Yet minority ownerships of television stations declined dramatically after 1998 (see Figure 7.5).

Without some definitive action by citizens who push the federal government, it seems likely that the trend toward consolidation and convergence will continue unabated.

Public Broadcasting

Designed to serve the needs and interests not met by the commercial radio and television industries, public broadcasting, a not-for-profit corporation that sells programs to member radio and television stations, was supposed to fill a void; and in some ways, between the mid-1960s and 2004, it gradually began to live up to that promise.

Through the decades since 1967, when it was launched, much of the programming on the various public broadcasting systems (PBS) provided news and cultural programming that the commercial systems were unable or unwilling to offer. Public broadcasting met many of the needs of the general populace, including women, who were generally pleased with PBS. Had it been otherwise, the periodic on-air requests for support from listeners and viewers would not have met with the great success PBS achieved through the years. Women were among the greatest supporters of public radio's programs, including *Fresh Air With Terry Gross* and *Prairie Home Companion With Garrison Keillor*. Women were also a major force behind the offerings on public television of children's programs, such as *Sesame Street* and *Arthur*.

Between 1994 and 2004, women made up a large proportion of staffers in key positions at PBS and the Corporation for Public Broadcasting (CPB), and public broadcasting program offerings reflected women's interests and concerns.

For minority groups, however, there was a mixture of satisfaction and dissatisfaction with public broadcasting. During most of its three decades as a viable alternative to commercial broadcasting, public broadcasters did not step up to embrace minority groups. People of color had to insist that public broadcasting meet some of their needs; eventually, public broadcasting began to offer a modest amount of news and information programming targeted with more regularity to these audiences.

By 2004, a report provided by PBS revealed that African American viewers of the largest television markets served by PBS ranged from 8.7% of the audience to 35.9% (see Figure 7.6).

Public Television

For minorities, after a rough start in the early years, by the 1990s PBS had begun to offer a variety of television programs targeted to or produced about African Americans and Africans.[2] With a few rare exceptions (such as the series *American Family*, about a Hispanic family, which aired on PBS, 2002–2004), most often other minority groups, such as Hispanics, Asians, and Native Americans, were left out. Hispanic groups also began to establish their Spanish language networks to address many needs, while Asian groups used newspapers written in their native languages to address many of their communication needs.

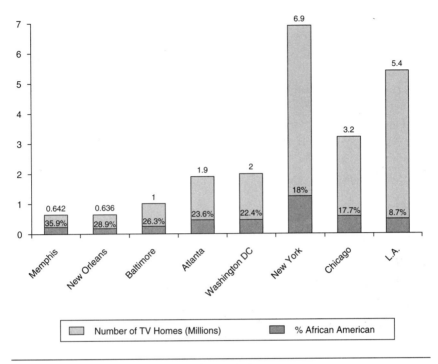

Figure 7.6   Public Television Markets, 2004

SOURCE: Cory Allen, Associate Director, PBS Research (personal communication, May 17, 2005).

Many minority producers, program developers, and other creative types still sought, in vain, the greater opportunities that were available to others to develop story ideas with the support of CPB, the funding arm of PBS. These opportunities remained elusive for minorities even into the 21st century. In addition, there were low numbers of African Americans in key positions at PBS and CPB. Although the diversity data seemed stronger in recent years, a closer look reveals that African Americans were clustered at the lowest ranks in public broadcasting.

More telling still, when Unity[3] was held in Washington, D.C., in 2004, more than 50 staffers from National Public Radio were among those who attended, but not one minority professional was hired as a result of the conference—and Unity represents the cream of the crop of minority journalists.

Still, during the period from 1994 to 2004, public television consistently offered more news and information programs addressing minority issues and concerns than did their commercial counterparts.

Conclusion

Women and people of color achieved some measures of success in the U.S. news and information operations between 1994 and 2004. The advances were much slower than most desired, however, and many have called for women and minorities to continue their partnerships to move the nation even more aggressively toward the inclusion of more voices and diverse perspectives. They see this as the only way that democracy can be buttressed and possibly "saved."

Notes

1. The figures in this chapter were designed by Nigel Martin, an undergraduate student in the John H. Johnson School of Communications at Howard University.

2. Between 1994 and 2004, PBS programs that targeted Black audiences included *News and Notes With Ed Gordon, Talk of the Nation, All Things Considered, The Tavis Smiley Show, The Derek McGinty Show, Crossroads,* and *Wade in the Water*. National Public Radio and Public Radio International programs with frequent topics and guests of interest to Black listeners included *Weekend Edition, Morning Edition, All Things Considered, Day to Day, Public Interest, The Diane Rehm Show, On the Media, Election Coverage, Fresh Air,* and *The Way* (Stone, 2005). Of course, this resourceful use of alternatives in no way released broadcast television from an obligation to serve all Americans.

3. Unity is the conference, held every 4 to 5 years, that includes journalists from the four national associations of minority journalists: National Association of Black Journalists, National Association of Hispanic Journalists, National Association of Asian Journalists, and National Association of Native American Journalists.

Questions for Discussion

1. Choose one of the figures in this chapter to review in more detail.

2. Describe something that you discovered on your own from your work on item 1.

3. Explain why it is important for women to be included as authoritative sources in news stories. Explain why minorities also need to be included.

4. Explain why the report by Gonzalez and Torres (2004) about the trend of concentration of media ownership into the hands of a few giant firms is of concern to modern generations.

5. Take the issue further to explore why minority groups may have had legitimate reasons for feeling left out of the public broadcasting system. List some reasons to explain why they might have begun to feel more included in recent years.

6. Find out more about public television's programs that were or are produced for and about minority groups and women. Watch and evaluate two such programs or series. Analyze the messages they send to viewers through their characters and plots.

Accessing Additional Information

CIIJE (Center for the Improvement of Journalism Education): http://www.ciije.sfsu.edu

Corporation for Public Broadcasting: http://www.cpb.org

Maynardije (Maynard Institute for Journalism Education): http://www.maynardije .org/columns/guests/050603_multimedia/

National Public Radio: http://www.npr.orgwww.npr.org

Poynter Institute–Romanesco: http://www.poynter.org

Project for Excellence in Journalism: http://www.pej.org

Public Broadcast Service: http://www.pbs.org

8

Women in Public Relations

Success Linked to Organizational and Societal Cultures

Elizabeth L. Toth, University of Maryland

Carolyn Garett Cline

A woman's place is no longer at home, but in a public relations department. However, even though women make up two thirds of all public relations professionals, they are paid less and promoted less than men. Women in public relations are the majority, yet they face barriers that subordinate their roles and their potential contributions to the profession.

Women make up 67%, or two thirds, of American public relations professionals (U.S. Bureau of Labor Statistics, 2005), whereas they make up only 48% of the U.S. workforce (U.S. Equal Employment Opportunity Commission, 2005). This gender imbalance happened relatively rapidly over the last 35 years, starting from a point at which the field was 70% men, in 1970, and dropping to about 30% men in 2005 (Toth, 2001), meaning a disproportionate increase in women compared with other occupations (Reskin & Roos, 1990).

Researchers have charted the increase in the percentage of women in public relations, starting in 1986, with the International Association of

Business Communicators (IABC) Research Foundation's *Velvet Ghetto* study (Cline et al., 1986). Other benchmark studies include *Beyond the Velvet Ghetto* (Toth & Cline, 1989) and three 5-year audits of the Public Relations Society of America (PRSA) members' perceptions of gender issues and public relations (Aldoory & Toth, 2002; Toth, Serini, Wright, & Emig, 1998; Wright, Grunig, Springston, & Toth, 1991).

These researchers found a real gender disparity between men and women on salaries and roles and negative perceptions of a female majority in public relations. In 2002, women public relations managers (grouped with advertising and marketing managers by the U.S. Bureau of Labor Statistics) earned 69.3% of what male managers made; and only 36% of public relations managers (grouped with advertising and marketing managers) were women. On the other hand, women represented 67% of the public relations specialists or technicians (U.S. Bureau of Labor Statistics, 2005). Public relations professionals reported that women throughout public relations received lower salaries; also, "they agreed that women in management positions get paid less than public relations men in their organizations and throughout public relations" (Aldoory & Toth, 2002, p. 115).

Women have been attracted to jobs in public relations for many reasons. Donato (1990) argued that women were a "better buy" than men because they were willing to work for less pay, whereas men could leave the field of public relations for more lucrative jobs. Women found public relations work, similar to banking, hospitals, and educational institutions, to have more flexible hours and fewer sexist barriers than the corporate world. Business and society considered public relations to be "emotional labor" and therefore more suitable for women (Donato, 1990, p. 139). Women found public relations to be a field that offered them better opportunities— "competitive if not more competitive than other accessible occupations" (Grunig, Toth, & Hon, 2001, p. 34).

Public relations, "the management of communication between an organization and its publics" (Grunig & Hunt, 1984, p. 6) involves many kinds of roles. Public relations people serve as organizational advocates in the court of public opinion. Public relations people carry out research to learn how their employers can meet the environmental, economic, social, and political changes that confront them. Public relations people promote products and services through campaigns, events, and mediated publicity. Public relations people advise organizational decision makers about internal and external communication demands. They are change agents to make their organizations more socially responsible. Public relations professionals set "social harmony" as their moral purpose (Seib & Fitzpatrick, 1995, p. 1).

Yet the gender imbalance in public relations salaries and roles suggests that the industry must first become supportive of its own gendered composition if it wishes to be credible to others.

Although studies have described the issues of the increasing numbers of women in public relations, there has been little theory building to explain the relationship between gender and public relations. Among scholars building gender theory was Rakow (1989b), who argued for the possibility that "a feminized public relations might alter relations of power between organizations and individuals, providing communal need rather than organizational greed, and creating a politics of egalitarian participation" (p. 296). The authors of the landmark "Excellence study" argued that "the role and status of communication is inexorably linked to the support and opportunities that organizations provide employees who are women" because they are the future of public relations (Dozier, Grunig, & Grunig, 1995, p. 152.) This chapter describes developing theory, explaining how organizational and societal culture helps or hinders success for women in public relations and for the field in general.

Feminist Theory

Scholars studying how gender influences public relations have used a feminist theory perspective. *Feminist theory* is a label, according to Littlejohn (1992), that represents a group of theories that explore the meaning of gender concepts (p. 239). Feminist scholars have argued that the term *gender* refers to a "scheme for categorizing people based on biological differences" (Powell, 1988, p. 44). Gender "involves predetermined physical traits, but gender develops also a cultural identity" (Grunig, Toth, & Hon, 2000, p. 51). Societies tend to stereotype these gender identities, using masculine and feminine labels and dichotomizing and pitting men and women against each other. For example, women who dress in certain ways may be accused of using their "feminine wiles." Women are welcome in the workplace as long as they meet the structural demands of an office workday from 9 a.m. to whenever the job gets done. Yet as Sha (2001) observed, "Women and men are sexual beings, yet we have created a workplace as if gender differences did not matter, when often in fact they do" (p. 159).

In contrast to gender, sex and sex role categories involve the characteristics of masculinity and femininity but are specifically a matter of social rather than biological difference (Grunig et al., 2000). We consider sex to be a dependent measure rather than an influencer of other characteristics:

"That is, sex is influenced by societal assumptions. We do not see sex as an independent variable, one that determines such factors as values, job aspirations, commitment to career or managerial role" (Grunig et al., 2000, p. 52).

There are many diverse perspectives on what constitutes feminist theory. Valdivia (1995) defined *feminism* as "the theoretical study of women's oppression and the strategic and political ways that all of us, building on that theoretical and historical knowledge can work to end that oppression" (p. 8). Aldoory and Toth (2003) argued that feminist theory concerns "gender constructions, stereotypes, and false expectations due to gender socialization" (p. 7). Feminist scholars have fought oppression of all people devalued by the dominant culture, "including but not limited to people of color, people with disabilities, people of different ages and socioeconomic classes, and lesbians and gay men" (Foss, Foss, & Griffin, 1999, p. 2).

Feminist theory has helped examine gender issues in public relations in three ways. First, feminist public relations scholars have exposed research findings that conclude that women are deficient according to the masculine norms of society. Examples include blaming the victim for not being "aggressive enough" or "unwilling to take risks." Feminist public relations researchers have asked the more pointed question: What are the realities that lie beneath the choices of men, women, and organizations when they define what public relations is and who should practice it?

Second, feminism exposes the gendered nature of social science research. Social science research has traditionally been valued for its rational constructions and "objectivity." All choices in social science research, however, carry values and preferences for some standards over others. Public relations feminists have argued for noncomparative approaches to research that would seek the causes of gender differences rather than merely demonstrating the differences between men and women. Third, feminist public relations scholars have called for the transformation and empowerment of women. Feminist scholars have challenged the status quo, the social norms of society that devalue women, by calling for actions that seek equality for women.

Theory Development in the Role of Societal and Organizational Cultures

Impact of Gender on Public Relations Excellence

Researchers have argued over whether organizations prefer men over women for leadership roles in public relations, whether women choose to stay in less influential and less well-paid technical roles, or whether organizational structures (the "glass ceiling") disadvantage women so that they don't advance into senior leadership positions.

The 1992 "Excellence study" considered the impact of gender on public relations excellence in a comprehensive investigation of how and to what extent public relations affects the achievement of organizational objectives (Grunig, Grunig, & Dozier, 2002). The Excellence study team tested the theory that women may have less opportunity than men to gain strategic experience to advance in public relations functions because of the time women spend in the technical roles, thus hindering women's achievement of public relations excellence in managerial activities (pp. 249–250). Also, they considered whether organizational communication structures influence women's opportunities to participate at the managerial level.

The Excellence study researchers surveyed public relations practitioners, CEOs, and organizational employees in 327 organizations in the United States, Canada, and the United Kingdom. The organizations included corporations, nonprofits, and government agencies and associations. Extensive quantitative surveys were answered by 4,600 participants. The researchers also conducted qualitative interviews in some of the participating organizations.

The survey questionnaire included items on the value of communication, contribution to strategic organizational functions, public relations roles, models of public relations, potential of the communication unit, activist pressure, and the status of women. Of the questions asked, 22 questions considered the perceptions of how well each organization enacted policies and programs to support women in their careers.

The Excellence study team found no significant differences in the extent to which male and female top communicators enact the manager role (Grunig et al., 2002, p. 249). The study also reported that women managers still played a dual manager-technician role, suggesting that women have less opportunity than men to gain valuable managerial expertise; however, "The gender of the top communicator does not help or hinder communication excellence" (p. 250). Female communicators may work harder, but when given the opportunity, they enact top communicator roles that provide "excellent public relations" to organizations.

The second finding of the Excellence study posited that organizational structures were influential in encouraging women communicators to participate in excellent public relations. This contradicts the assumption that all employees have the same opportunities in organizations—and suggests that organizational climate and culture through policies, structures, and functions create opportunities for, or barriers to, women employees.

Overall, the Excellence study reported that a supportive climate for women, including nondiscriminatory policies enacted to protect women, a supportive work climate encouraging women to take risks, and established formal mentoring and advancement programs, provides a context in which excellent public relations by women public relations practitioners can be found. Women communicators are in top public relations roles, performing them according to the best-practice criteria of excellent public relations and supported by organizational policies that recognize their needs.

Work-Life Integration

Since 1990, there have been three 5-year audits of PRSA member perceptions of gender and public relations. The findings from these studies continued to report gender discrepancies in hiring, salaries, and promotions. With the third audit in 2000, however, Aldoory and Toth (2002) sought to answer why these disparities were so enduring, "especially when the field is mostly women" (pp. 103–104). Rather than merely continue to document these differences, Aldoory and Toth argued that there needed to be more explanations for these differences that would help women advance the field of public relations.

Aldoory and Toth (2002) used three different theories from management, marketing, and sociology to give perspective to gender disparities in public relations: human capital theory, sex segregation, and organizational and social models. Human capital theory suggests that career opportunities are equally open to each of us. It is our effort or choice to invest, or not, in a college education, to obtain the necessary work experience, and to seek out professional development opportunities. If we choose to "take time off," that reduces our capital or career value. Some have argued from the human capital theory position that it is "just a matter of time" before women catch up with men in public relations, because they will have made the same investments in their careers.

Sex segregation looks at how occupations become all-female. According to Reskin and Roos (1990), women have entered some occupations, such as public relations, more rapidly than they have entered all job categories. Not all careers are open to women, so when an occupation does open, women "overoccupy" it, driving the status and salary down for the field. Reskin and Roos argued that women move into certain fields because men have found them less interesting or less lucrative or because women are assumed to have specific characteristics (stereotypes) that make them better at certain occupations.

Organizational and social models seek to explain gender differences in hiring, salaries, and promotion by pointing to the structural demands of society and of organizations on employees. Organizational and social structures create barriers for women workers, such as inflexible workplaces and hours, restrictions on leaves from work, and responsibilities for housework, parenting, and elder care.

The study by Aldoory and Toth (2002) included a quantitative survey of 864 members of PRSA and six focus groups held in Portland, Oregon; New York City; and Washington, D.C., with three all-male groups and three all-female groups in each city. Participants continued to report discrimination in salaries and promotions. Gender influenced salary even in a career in which the majority of workers were women, even when years of experience, job interruptions, age, and educational level were accounted for. The respondents rarely discussed human capital to explain gender differences. They did discuss sex segregation, because men were moving into management positions and women did the best they could in technical positions.

The participants addressed, more than other explanations for different treatment, the structural demands of organizations. Women spoke of being the primary caregivers and housekeepers and the organizational belief that those who leave work to have children will not return. Both men and women participants discussed the issues of work and family integration and the resulting conflicts they faced and how they found strategies to solve the conflicts.

To learn more about the impact of organizational and social structure on gender and public relations, Aldoory and Toth (2004b) analyzed focus group responses, also as all-male and all-female practitioner discussions, about work-life issues from their 2000 focus groups and from previous focus group data collected in 1995 (Toth, Serini, Wright, & Emig, 1995), from practitioners coming together in Washington, D.C.; Chicago; and Seattle, Washington. This research permitted an exploratory look at any possible trends on work-life perceptions.

Aldoory and Toth (2004b) found that although there were some similarities between what male focus groups and female focus groups reported about work-life integration, there were several distinct differences. In general, the male groups discussed work-family balance noticeably less than the female groups. In contrast, the women groups talked about work and family issues even when responding to questions about salary, promotion, and other professional issues. The responses/quotations in the discussion that follows were all taken from study participants, from 1995/2000.

Work-family balance is a women's issue. Both male and female participants of the focus groups agreed with this finding. One male participant remarked, "Juggling work and family needs is harder for women than men." A female participant said, "You've got your job at work and then you've got your job at home."

All of the focus groups talked about public relations practice creating its own opportunities and barriers to work-life balance. Client work and agency employment constrains a full family life because of the number of hours. One male participant said, "You are expected to be accessible all the time." A female participant remarked, "If you work with an agency, they demand that you work the hours whether you have kids or not." In comparing women in other industries with those in public relations, one woman said, "They don't have to worry about getting on a plane at the last minute and flying somewhere." Male participants stated that women benefited from having a choice to give up certain work aspects to be home with children, while they did not. One man said, "If somebody's going to be given a work-load, it may be the person without children who doesn't have commitments and the need to be home."

The men and women in the focus groups indicated that they placed different values on work and family. One man said, "Men want to play a bigger role in the household. They want to spend more time with the kids. They want to be able to do more around the house. They are demanding what women traditionally wanted." On the other hand, another male stated that although he and his wife were "very equal," their baby changed his perceptions about what he valued. He expected his wife to stay home, explaining, "I'm not saying that I'm not going to share in the child raising, but right now I may be very skewed in my perception." Whereas women want a job that contributes to society, one male participant argued, men find value in making money to support a family: "The desire to do good," he said, "creates the role conflict for women as they make less salary and do not get promoted." He concluded, "I probably care a lot less about the value of my job to society as a whole. I'm more concerned about the value of my job to my own satisfaction in being able to raise a family."

Women participants expressed a lot of role conflict, while male participants did not bring this up in their discussions. One female participant said, "We women, we refuse to shut ourselves off, we just can't, we won't. It's far easier for men to just come home after a full day outside the home and tune out. Women will go to work full-time, and they're still doing everything else."

Participants argued that personal control was key to making choices for greater salary and greater work productivity. One male participant said that "if women were having more trouble getting promoted, it is probably due to the fact that they have children living at home and they choose to devote a greater amount of their energies to family than they do to career." Another male participant said, "We've got three women in our office who work less than 40 hour weeks at their choice so they can have time to do other things, and they get paid less money, and they prefer it that way."

Female practitioners discussed women's lack of control when their family commitments detracted from their work environments. One woman, for example, described how her supervisor talked about client account selections: "You can take this account because you will be able to manage it." Another woman said that she would not get promoted anytime soon: She was getting less "plum" assignments because it was assumed that because she had kids, she would be distracted.

The conflicts between work and family and expressions of lack of control may be explained because of the number of hours practitioners must work. Most male participants believed that if men with children chose not to work "24/7," they would be less successful due to work expectations.

There were some resistance strategies expressed within the female groups. A common response was for a woman to start her own public relations company. Second, women described strategic transitioning over the course of their careers in different public relations industries during different times in their child rearing. One woman said, "I worked in universities for 9 years as my kids grew up. And then went to other things that pay better . . . and when I was working on the Hill, I didn't have any kids because there was no other way."

The practitioners of these focus groups gave different meaning to their organizational policies about family-friendly cultures. Some women said that they had taken advantage of "flextime" arrangements, although the men "were still getting face time in." Participants described instances of bias against women who took advantage of flexible hours and leave. One woman said, "Definitely, taking time off to have kids hinders your ability to progress and affects how much women make overall." Participants described organizational cultures that devalue employees who utilize family-friendly benefits, and, in addition, they blamed individual colleagues. In general, however, participants expressed a desire for organizational flexibility.

According to Aldoory and Toth's (2004b) analysis, between 1995 and 2000, there were changes in the male participants' discussion of work-life balance, but the female participants continued to discuss the same issues. Over the years, the male groups transitioned in their rhetoric on making meaning of work-life balance. They went from "blame" to "choice" for women, and from fearing repercussions to knowing several male colleagues who had taken leave. The male participants changed from predicting the impact of flexibility and technology in 1995 to seeing flexibility and technology as the norm in 2000.

Although these findings are not representative of the public relations industry, they do suggest that organizational and societal influences provide a framework in which to consider public relations and gender. We need to see more testing of how organizational policies encourage and prohibit public relations practitioners in their efforts to succeed personally and as communicators who reinforce these organizational and social expectations. Some concepts to consider further are (a) work-family balance as a woman's issue; (b) unique gendered aspects of public relations careers, such as "24/7" service; (c) perceived benefits of multiple work and family roles; and (d) role conflict, personal control, role strain, and resistance to organizational and social models. If practitioners reinforce gender discrimination by allowing women to bear more of the burden of integrating work and life responsibilities, women public relations practitioners may react by viewing themselves as lacking control and power and accepting that they have to change jobs or drop out of public relations for a time, or by starting their own companies.

The women of the public relations field may seem to be ahead of other female-intensive occupations in earnings and opportunity. Study findings suggest, however, that women public relations professionals are welcomed only into subordinated and less lucrative and influential roles. This causes a dilemma for public relations women who have leadership to give to their employers and society—but are kept from advancing by organizational barriers created through policies and preferences. Women's success is linked to how well they navigate organizational and societal cultures.

Questions for Discussion

1. Do you agree or disagree with the authors' contention that the public relations industry, an industry that seeks "social harmony," should be supportive of its own gendered composition if it wishes to be credible to others? Why or why not?

2. How do feminist scholars distinguish between "gender" and "sex or sex roles"? Why is this an important distinction?

3. The authors found from their research that women and men in public relations were not transforming their workplaces so as to respect differences in gender identity. Rather, women were leaving corporate and agency jobs and creating their own businesses or working part-time in public relations. Why aren't public relations women and/or men working to alter their organizations to adapt to gender differences?

4. How did you respond to the human capital, sex segregation, and organizational-structural explanations for women in public relations staying in subordinate, lower-paying technical positions?

5. Do you think that when women enter the public relations workplace, they must give up their gender identities in order to be professionally successful?

Accessing Additional Information

Institute for Public Relations: http://www.instituteforpr.com

International Association of Business Communicators: http://www.iabc.com

Public Relations Society of America: http://www.prsa.org

9

Advertising Women

Images, Audiences, and Advertisers

Nancy Mitchell, University of Nebraska

The year was 1963, some 115 years after Elizabeth Cady Stanton and Lucretia Motts organized the first Women's Rights Convention, when Betty Friedan published her book *The Feminine Mystique*. Friedan's work hit a cultural nerve by identifying "the problem that has no name" (Friedan, 1963/1997). The problem she recognized was the conflict between the 1950s image of the happy housewife and her dissatisfaction with a life unfulfilled. Friedan (1963/1997) proclaimed, "We can no longer ignore that voice within women that says: 'I want something more than my husband and my children and my home'" (p. 32). Furthermore, "A baked potato is not as big as the world, and vacuuming the living room floor—with or without makeup—is not work that takes enough thought or energy to challenge any woman's full capacity" (p. 67).

In the words of Anna Quindlen (1963/2001), the book "set off a social and political explosion," changing the consciousness of women's issues in the United States and abroad (p. xiii).

Friedan's work laid the groundwork for scores of scholars who built on her observations, investigating issues related to women and their place in American society. Offering a historical overview, this chapter considers Friedan's legacy as it relates to advertising and women. It reflects how portrayals of women in advertising have changed in the last half century, as well as the impact women have as audiences and as advertisers creating those images.

Friedan's groundbreaking work offered an analysis of a complicated social and cultural problem: portrayals of women that were inconsistent with their experienced realities. Friedan acknowledged the role of the media, and advertising specifically, in perpetuating the unhealthy, unrealistic image of the happy housewife. This theme permeates the book, as shown in the following passage:

> The public image, in the magazines and television commercials, is designed to sell washing machines, cake mixes, deodorants, detergents, rejuvenating face creams, hair tints. But the power of that image, on which companies spend millions of dollars for television time and ad space, comes from this: American women no longer know who they are. (Friedan, 1963/1997, p. 72)

Friedan's recognition of the important role advertising plays in conveying images of women spawned much scholarly activity on the subject.

Portrayals of Women in Advertising

In the 1960s, feminist groups formed, including the National Organization for Women (NOW), which elected Betty Friedan its first president (Berkeley, 1999). Through their consciousness-raising groups, feminists encouraged the elimination of gender stereotypes and the discovery of each woman's identity. One advertising scholar, Erving Goffman, did much to explain the stereotypical images depicted in advertising in *Gender Advertisements* (1979).

Underlying Goffman's work is an assumption that advertisements reveal much about our culture; they implicitly tell us who we should be. Goffman deconstructed advertisements by considering the gendered images that appear in them: the advertising model's relative size, the feminine touch, function ranking, family, ritualization of subordination (lowering oneself physically as a stereotype of deference), and licensed withdrawal (women drifting psychologically from the scene). His analysis of bits of behavior captured in advertisements revealed much about the social relationships they depicted. For examples, women were often shown as smaller than and subordinate to men. Men in their roles as executives and fathers were often depicted instructing and helping women. Women's poses could be interpreted as submissive and subordinate.

While Friedan focused on the portrayal of the housewife in society and noted that this image was communicated in part by the media, Goffman (1979) extended the examination of women beyond the housewife to reveal the kinds of stereotypes of women that appeared in advertising. He believed that the gender displays reflected what occurred in social situations.

Like Goffman, other scholars have confirmed feminists' claim that women are devalued in advertisements. Courtney and Whipple (1983; Whipple & Courtney, 1985), for example, summarized work conducted about gender in advertising and encouraged advertisers to use depictions that were more progressive than the traditional stereotyped portrayals showing that the woman's place is in the home.

Have portrayals of women changed from the images seen by Friedan, Goffman, Courtney and Whipple, and others? Some scholars indicate that old stereotypes have been replaced by more realistic portrayals (Miller, 1997), while others (e.g., Kilbourne, 1999; Wood, 1994) have suggested that women continue to be portrayed unrealistically. Women have been primarily portrayed as housewives and mothers in the last half century, although some advertising in the 1980s depicted females as career women and "supermoms" (Warner, 1997). Images of women in the 1990s changed as advertisements did a better job of depicting women in roles that were more than one-dimensional (Warner, 1997). A self-study of 1,000 women, aged 18 to 49, revealed that women were looking for individual solutions enabling them to balance work, family, and their own needs (Miller, 1997). Those images ought to be reflected in advertising, and although that may have occurred to some extent, several critics believe that covert messages culture sends women are still pernicious (Quindlen, 1963/2001, p. xii).

Author and lecturer Jean Kilbourne (1999) has vigorously criticized advertising. Like Friedan, Goffman, and so many other scholars of advertising (e.g., Leiss, Kline, & Jhally, 1990; Twitchell, 1996), Kilbourne recognized that advertising sells much more than the product. She argued that because advertising is so pervasive, it has an immense cultural impact, especially on women and girls. She said advertising creates problems because it "corrupts relationships and then offers us products, both as solace and as substitutes for the intimate human connection we all long for and need" (Kilbourne, 1999, p. 26). It objectifies people, turning them into *things*— things that we learn to love in place of people. She argued that women and girls are particularly vulnerable to the glamorized portrayals of cigarettes and alcohol and the addictive power of advertising.

Similar to Goffman, Kilbourne deconstructed advertisements to support her point. To illustrate their seductive power, for example, she discussed a 1995 Häagen-Daz ad that featured this copy: "Your fiancé agreed to have a big wedding. Have a Häagen-Dazs. He wants to have it in a sports bar. Have some more" (Kilbourne, 1999, p. 110). The message to women: If you're having a troubled relationship, you should eat something to make you feel better. The solution to your problems is food, not talking to your fiancé.

Equally disturbing, women and girls are shown images of ultrathin models. Kilbourne (1999) claimed that the advertisements contribute to eating disorders by normalizing and glamorizing unhealthy attitudes toward food. Kilbourne also criticized advertisements targeting adolescents for exploiting that market's insecurities, offering products as solutions: The right pair of jeans or perfume or beer offers status and concurrently confirms one's femininity or masculinity.

Friedan (1963/1997) recognized that advertisers exploit women's desires to buy products so they can be better housewives. Kilbourne added to Friedan's original ideas through her observations that women and girls—not their houses—have some inherent problem than needs fixing and the solution is not just a product for the house. They are not good enough as they are: They need a product, even if it is unhealthy, such as cigarettes or alcohol. Women and girls are, in Kilbourne's (1999) words, twice seduced: once by ads and once by products (p. 27).

Many advertising scholars have offered cultural critiques of advertising. Some of the emergent themes in their work investigate the beauty myth. Wolf (1991) argued that portrayed images of beauty present impossible standards for women to achieve. She claimed idealized beauty is unrealistic, just as Friedan found the image of the happy housewife. A study by Martin and Gentry (1997) argued that the beauty ideal portrayed in advertising targets adolescents, finding that adolescent girls compare themselves with models, which tends to adversely affect their self-perceptions and self-esteem.

Another aspect of the beauty myth provoked some writers (e.g., Cortese, 1999; Kilbourne, 1999; Wolf, 1991) to criticize advertising that portrayed the ultrathin, waiflike look of models, such as Kate Moss. Kilbourne noted in her work that, around 1979, fashion models weighed 8% less than the average female. Twenty years later, models weighed 23% less than the average female (Kilbourne, 1999, p. 125). As Kilbourne suggested, the underlying criticism with advertising messages and cosmetics products is that women are flawed when it comes to beauty and the solution is to buy a product.

People seem to think the products and advertising work. The cosmetics industry reached sales of $31.1 billion at the manufacturers' level in 2003 (Kline & Company, 2005). The diet industry earned an estimated $35 to $50 billion annually in 2002 (Oickle, 2005). However, the extent to which advertising causes women to want to emulate thin models is unclear, especially considering information reported by the American Obesity Association (2002) that for 1999 to 2000, more than half of adult women aged 20 to 72 in the United States were overweight (62%) and nearly half were obese (34%) or severely obese (6.3%).

Others have added different dimensions to the study of the portrayal of women. Three themes emerged from Wood's (1994) summary of gender studies and advertising. First, she claimed that women were underrepresented: Men appeared much more frequently in the media, which had the consequence, intended or not, of giving the impression that women were unimportant because they were virtually invisible. Second, Wood observed that women were portrayed stereotypically, often in ways that reinforced socially endorsed views of gender. The third theme that emerged was that depictions of relationships between men and women helped to maintain traditional roles and normalize violence against women. Concern about potentially detrimental effects of advertising normalizing violence against women has emerged in other scholars' work as well (Cortese, 1999; Kilbourne, 1999).

Twitchell's "AdCult" (1996) put a slightly different spin on the feminist critique of women in advertising. Although Twitchell did not find the feminist critique "entirely fair-minded," he admitted it has changed the industry. He observed that marketing products such as soap, deodorant, and mouthwash requires that gender be distinct from sex: "Sex is biological. Gender is cultural. Arguably the most lasting contribution of AdCult is the ongoing creation and maintenance of gender" (p. 147). Feminists would probably not dispute Twitchell's point.

Where feminists would differ is in the underlying power each side attributes to advertising. Some feminist critiques of advertising, notably by Kilbourne, have blamed advertising for the state of women in society and many of the problems that seem to be gender specific, such as eating disorders and poor self-esteem. Twitchell (1996) acknowledged that gender branding occurs, but he suggested that women are not victims of advertising and that they have power as an audience to reject advertising messages. Using a discussion of cosmetics as an example, Twitchell countered the argument proposed by Wolf and other feminists that advertising oppresses women, claiming that women are not duped by giant corporations into buying things they don't want. (He noted that women, ironically, have written some of the most memorable copy for cosmetics, although he did not acknowledge that perhaps those women have become part of the White, male constructed system.) Although Twitchell did not deny that some advertising to some extent reflects and shapes the image of beauty, he recognized that women as an audience have the power to reject messages promoting dangerous diets, breast implants, and the like. He pointed out that making oneself beautiful is not new. Emphasis on beauty is as old as the tales of Cinderella, Cleopatra, and Helen of Troy. It's part of culture and of biology.

Twitchell (1996) recognized that some advertising uses eroticism to sell jeans (Calvin Klein) or products that are harmful (Virginia Slims); however, he claimed such advertising is neither new nor oppressive. Even Friedan agreed, in the preface to the reprinting of *The Feminine Mystique* (1963/1997), that woman-as-victim is not the issue it once was: "But women are no longer the passive victims they once felt themselves to be" (p. xviii).

As scholars have continued to investigate women and advertising in the 21st century, they have focused their attention on a variety of areas that relate to other areas of diversity, such as studying the underrepresentation of older women, Black women, or gay and lesbian audiences (e.g., Cortese, 1999; Kern-Foxworth, 1994; Toth & Aldoory, 2001). Some authors have even noted that the problems with unrealistic portrayals are not limited to women, but affect men and boys as well (e.g., Cottle, 1998).

Interestingly, the work with portrayals of women in advertising has made its way into the classroom. Gender is one of many aspects studied under the umbrella of diversity (e.g., Cooper, 2003; Rios, 2003; Traudt, 2005; Wilson, Gutiérrez, & Chao, 2003). The textbook *Journalism Across Cultures* (Cropp, Frisby, & Mills, 2003), for example, features chapters on Latinos; women; gays, lesbians, bisexuals, and transgendered populations; older adults; Native Americans; Arabs and Arab Americans; religion; and people with disabilities. Books such as this emphasize a growing interest in diversity.

As the industry and academy recognized the need to understand their targets for marketing purposes, they stressed the importance of issues related to diversity and underrepresented groups. The Association for Education in Journalism and Mass Communications (AEJMC) and the accrediting body, the Accrediting Council on Education in Journalism and Mass Communications (ACEJMC), issued mandates to teach more perspectives than those of the dominant White male culture. Could it be that this growing emphasis on understanding diversity is evidence not only of shifting demographics in the United States but also of the far-reaching impact of Friedan's work?

Women as Audiences

Women wield power as audiences, and they can influence how they are portrayed in advertising. Friedan called for women to become aware that in the 1960s, large corporations valued women only because they were potential customers—and necessary for their economic lifeblood. She asked, "Why is it never said that the really crucial function, the really important role that women serve as housewives is *to buy more things for the house*" (Friedan, 1963/1997, p. 206, emphasis added). After all, by some estimates, women make 75% to 95% of all consumer purchases (Kern-Foxworth, 2003). Consciousness-raising by feminists resulted in women who expressed their emerging identities and sometimes rejected the traditional portrayals advertising presented, according to advertising historian Julienne Sivulka (1998). Sivulka observed that advertisers continued to show traditional stereotypes, however, because they believed those portrayals communicated to women. It was not until work by Goffman (1979), Courtney and Whipple (1983), and others that the industry finally began to listen to women's voices and alter the images portrayed (Sivulka, 1998).

Twitchell (1996) cautioned that gender differences are often confused with purchasing differences. He noted that advertisers cognizant of the audiences they target are careful not to offend those audiences. One example he offered is that women are not used as hood ornaments on cars, which women buy. Other scholars offer evidence supporting Twitchell's assertion. Frisby (2003) noted that Pantene features women belonging to a variety of races in its efforts to diversify its target market for hair care products. Similar efforts are made by advertisers to discover how they can best communicate to other audiences, including older women, lesbians and gays, young girls, Latinas, and global audiences.

Since the 1970s, advertising has evolved from a strategy that aimed at reaching the largest possible audience to one that advertises to specific audiences (Jamieson & Campbell, 2001). Another paradigm shift also occurred: Emphasis changed from messages focused solely on what the advertiser wanted to say to a focus on the audience and how to best communicate with that target. It would be comforting to think that this change has occurred because it is ethical to respect and consider typically underrepresented voices. But it is also good business to do so, and perhaps that is the ultimate motivation.

Women as Advertisers: The Profession

Given the chance, as participants in the advertising process, women can mold the images portrayed in the media. Friedan and other feminists recognized the link between opportunities in education and the job market, and the impact on society (Berkeley, 1999). In the 1960s, women were better educated and more socially and politically aware than they had been before.

They also represented about 30% of the workforce in the United States at that time (Berkeley, 1999). As women found themselves with expanded career choices, some of them entered the advertising industry. DDB, an advertising agency that was progressive in hiring women in the 1960s, employed creative talents such as Phyllis Robinson, Mary Wells, Paula Green, Judith Protas, Lore Parker, Rita Selden, and its first woman account executive, Marcella Rosen (Maxwell, 2003). Women also owned their own agencies by the late 1970s, including Shirley Polykoff, Paula Green, Faith Popcorn, and two African American·ad women, Joyce Hamer and Caroline R. Jones (Sivulka, 1998).

Despite the stellar careers some females achieved as early as the 1960s and 1970s, women currently represent only 15% of the staff in advertising agency creative departments and 22% of the Directors Guild of America, according to the Women's Image Network (Anderson, 2004). The low percentages suggest that the industry is missing opportunities to include women to help shape or revise images about women.

With some notable exceptions, such as Shelly Lazarus, chair and CEO of Ogilvy & Mather Worldwide, and Charlotte Beers, the first woman CEO of that corporation, women have been generally absent in leadership positions at agencies as well. The Annenberg Public Policy Center (2003) reported women's progress in reaching positions of leadership in communication companies. The underlying assumption for this study was a notion that changing corporate climate would be facilitated if women had a voice in leadership positions. The center studied board members, top executives, and women-friendly benefits at 57 Fortune 500 communications companies. The study included 25 telecom, 18 publishing and printing, 11 entertainment, and 3 advertising companies. Researchers found that the average percentage of women executives was 15%, while the average percentage of women board members was 12%. The advertising firms had the lowest average number of women executives: 3%. Although the 3 advertising companies may not represent the entire industry, it is surprising to note that the glass ceiling still exists—or, as suggested, "The glass ceiling is not glass after all; it consists of a very dense layer of White men" (Berkeley, 1999, p. 105).

What does the future of advertising look like in terms of employment of women? It appears that women are preparing for careers in advertising and other areas of mass communication. According to a national survey in the fall of 2003, 64.7% of students enrolled in undergraduate journalism and mass communication programs were women. The survey reported the percentages of women earning bachelor's (65.4%), master's (66.6%), and doctorate (55.2%) degrees were the highest recorded since World War II

(Becker, Vlad, Hennick-Kaminski, & Coffey, 2004). Women are poised to contribute their perspectives as well as their talents to the industry.

So much and too little have changed since the first publication of *The Feminine Mystique* (Quindlen, 1963/2001). Friedan's proclamation that "the world is larger than a baked potato" seems rather quaint in contemporary times. But the baked potato became a hot potato that forced advertisers to reexamine how they communicated with women. It started a revolution that is increasingly audience centered and includes not only women, but other underrepresented and unrealistically portrayed groups.

Questions for Discussion

1. Based on the material in this chapter and your own experience, do you believe that portrayals of women in advertising have improved since 1963? Do you think portrayals of different parts of the audience of women (e.g., women of color, older women, lesbians and gays, women with disabilities) have improved? Explain your answer.

2. This chapter looks at women in advertising from three perspectives: images of women, women as audiences, and women as professional advertisers. How can all three areas have an impact on women in society?

3. The content of this chapter is limited to a discussion of women in advertising in the United States. Consider other cultures. How are the issues similar to and different from other cultures?

4. How do you think the changing media environment, with the increase of product placement as a form of advertising in movies, television, and music, affects women in society?

5. Do you think that advertising causes women and adolescent girls to develop eating disorders?

Accessing Additional Information

Ad Council: http://www.adcouncil.org/

Advertising Age: http://www.adage.com/

Advertising Educational Foundation: http://www.aef.com/start.asp

Advertising Women of New York: http://www.awny.org/

American Advertising Federation: http://www.aaf.org/

American Association of Advertising Agencies: http://www.aaaa.org/

Annenburg Public Policy Center: Women and Leadership: http://www.annenberg
publicpolicycenter.org/04_info_society/women_leadership/WOMEN.HTM

Betty Friedan, National Women's Hall of Fame Web site: http://www.great
women.org/women.php?action=viewone&id=62

John W. Hartman Center for Sales, Advertising, and Marketing History, Duke
University: http://www.scriptorium.lib.duke.edu/adaccess/

New York Women in Communication Matrix Awards: http://www.nywici.org/
matrix.awards.html

PART III

Specializations . . .

10

The Power to Improve Lives

Women in Health Communication

Julie L. Andsager, The University of Iowa

Consumers today have a wealth of health information literally at their fingertips. Nearly every newspaper contains a health section; nearly every television news broadcast includes a health segment. The percentage of stories on personal health in seven major news venues increased about 500% from 1977 to 1997 (Project for Excellence in Journalism, 1998). Internet users can access a world of information on specialized Web sites, educating themselves or sharing their personal experiences with others. Even entertainment television programs, such as situation comedies and soap operas, incorporate information on healthy behaviors into story lines through what is known as "edutainment."[1]

The increased attention to health information in the last few decades can be attributed to several factors. First, technology and increased research funding have advanced medical knowledge at a more rapid pace than ever before. Second, feminist activism resulted in the expanded study of women's health issues, such as osteoporosis, breast cancer, and cancers and other diseases of the reproductive system, providing a broader range of health news. Third, the development of HIV/AIDS (and the resurgence of some diseases thought to be eradicated) increased the importance of health knowledge for the public. Finally, on a practical level, news media consumers tend to be mature audiences who need health information to prevent or combat conditions related to aging.

These developments have evolved in a synchronous relationship with the growing field of health communication. Health communication spans a wide range of activities, from the interpersonal communication between a doctor and her patient, to targeted campaigns designed to improve health behaviors, to the dissemination of medical news. The study of health communication generally comprises two distinct but interrelated fields: health promotion, in which the media are considered as conduits of information, either through edutainment or persuasion campaigns, and health care delivery, which focuses on decision making, the doctor-patient relationship, and other individuated topics (Kreps, Bonaguro, & Query, 1998). This chapter will examine the health promotion branch, due to its reliance on mediated communication. In general, health promotion "challenges the medicalization of health, stresses its social and economic aspects, and portrays health as central to a flourishing life" (Freimuth, Edgar, & Fitzpatrick, 1993, p. 510).

Compared with established media functions such as journalism, advertising, or public relations, the discipline of health communication is young. As in many developing fields, the majority of discussion and research to date has attempted to define the field and to determine the health communicator's role in bridging the gap between medicine and the public. Health promotion is too new, perhaps, for the profession's attention to shift to the practitioners themselves. Gender, therefore, has seldom been addressed within the health promotion field, although many studies have been conducted on gender issues in health care delivery. This chapter discusses how health communication fits within traditional gender roles for women, thus forecasting a female-oriented field, but explores as well how women play a substantial role in developing the discipline as researchers shaping knowledge about health communication.

Envisioning Women in Health Promotion

Gender roles and the participation of women in allied fields suggest that the profession of health promotion would inherently attract a strong female presence. Although men have traditionally dominated health care as physicians and medical researchers whereas women have been clustered in nursing, women have a long history as activists in promoting health reform. Notably, women (mostly in developed countries) have led temperance movements, fought for women's reproductive health, developed improved nutritional guidelines and hygienic practices, and crusaded for mental health reform in the late 19th century (see, for example, Sapiro, 1994). During the second wave of the women's movement in the United States, female activists formed the Boston Women's Health Book Collective (BWHBC) to produce the classic *Our Bodies, Ourselves* in 1970, a compendium of vital advice on women's common questions about reproductive and sexual health and other little discussed medical topics (Norsigian et al., 1999). For some women, the impetus for mobilizing to improve the quality of life through health was apparently the protection of children and younger women.

Feminist scholars, however, maintain that health care in the United States (and other Western countries) has long been unsatisfactory for women due to the hierarchical structure that reinforces social injustices and doctors' established habits of poor communication and impersonal treatment (e.g., Lorber & Moore, 2002). Thus, by creating a women's health movement, these BWHBC activists and others began to drag the medical establishment into a comparatively open era. Concurrently, the percentage of female medical students also increased, perhaps shifting the field a bit from the inside. As recently as 1990, however, female subjects continued to be omitted from most medical studies, ensuring that knowledge remained androcentric and women's health remained largely misunderstood (Willard, 2005). For example, one lingering result of such neglect is that doctors and the public have often failed to recognize the signs of heart attacks in women. Heart attack symptoms were derived from years of study of only male subjects, but women present differently, leading to a greater likelihood of death (Young & Kahana, 1993). The first Women's Health Equity Act passed the U.S. Congress in 1990, largely as a result of grassroots feminist activism, requiring that women be included in research studies and establishing the Office of Research on Women's Health within the National Institutes of Health.

As health promotion organizations gain a foothold in developing countries around the world, campaigners have discovered that, similar to the American and British women active in health movements of the past, women provide an excellent resource. In developing countries, women generally make up the majority of community health workers, including those promoting health through campaigns (Bhattacharyya, Winch, LeBan, & Tien, 2001; Kar, Pascual, & Chickering, 1999). Women's and mothers' "deep commitment to protect and promote the well-being of their children and families often serves as a motivating force for action" (Kar et al., 1999, p. 1452). The noble purpose of these women's involvement and the lack of employment opportunity elsewhere, unfortunately, may lead them to work for lesser wages than their contributions are worth, a situation all too familiar to female labor:

By seeking out women leaders to mentor other women and young women who are starting out, you can often identify talent in the field of communication that is available, reasonably priced, and personally committed to women's health issues. (Piotrow, Rimon, Merritt, & Saffitz, 2003, p. 36)

How to maximize resources? How to engage and activate the public? These are conundrums campaigners face frequently in attempting to improve health environments and structures in the third world. In these situations particularly, women's role in health promotion is crucial.

Feminist Values in Communication

Caring for others on a societal level has been ascribed to women's gender roles. Women have historically been the primary health information seekers and health care consumers for the family (Sapiro, 1994). It is not surprising that, when possible, many women have taken this role beyond their own households in attempts to better health policy and reduce likelihood of disease. Gilligan (1982) contended that caring, morality, and "experiences of attachment" have been socially constructed as feminine values and, as such, shape women's frames of reference. Combining elements of communication, caring, and quality of life, then, health communication and promotion can be viewed as gendered female, in terms of values if not numbers.

It would be a mistake, though, to discount the role that the feminist value of empowerment has played in health communication, at both the level of health promotion campaigns and doctor-patient communication. Women's health advocates instigated patient-empowering changes in the way that health care information is disseminated, considered, and put into practice. Willard (2005) argued that feminist activism has improved "how patients view themselves as agents of empowered agents of change, how medical personnel respond to patients as individual actors and decision-makers, and how the patient and the health care provider form a relationship of equality" (p. 144). Thus, health campaigns recommend behaviors that individuals can choose to practice (or not), and the plethora of health information in news media allows the lay public to be better consumers of medical care.

Research in Health Promotion

Traditional health communication research has largely ignored, or at best downplayed, the role of the media in our everyday lives (Seale, 2002). Thus, health communication is a relatively new discipline. In 1975, the first organizational recognition of the field occurred when the Health Communication Division was formed in the International Communication Association (Freimuth & Quinn, 2004). Scholars conducting health communication research continued to publish their work in established communication journals. Prior to the inception of journals specifically devoted to health communication, an early study found that less than one third of the articles discussing health communication published from 1983 to 1987 addressed health promotion, rather than health care delivery (Finnegan & Viswanath, 1990). This reinforces the notion that scholarship on health promotion came somewhat late to mediated communication, despite the recognition of general health communication as an area of study.

By 1989, interest was solid and widespread enough that *Health Communication* was founded, followed by the *Journal of Health Communication* in 1996 (Kreps et al., 1998). Within communication research, study of the topic began to take hold, such that a content analysis of 19 communication journals from 1989 to 2001 ($N = 5,506$ articles) found that 15% of the articles dealt with health communication (Beck et al., 2004). Still, the public health sector lagged behind, not developing a health communication division within its primary organization, American Public Health Association, until 1997, and health communication was only first included in the National Institutes of Health's "Healthy People" objectives for the year 2010 (Freimuth & Quinn, 2004).

The field of health promotion is broad. Practitioners may serve as "communication researcher, planner, implementer, evaluator, or trainer; as media advocacy specialist or public relations or marketing professional; as gatekeeper, negotiator, materials design expert, production specialist, or sometimes 'master of the dumb question'" (Clift, 1997, p. 67). Health promotion practitioners may work in academe, researching communication models and persuasive messages; they may serve as spokespeople for hospitals or clinics; and they often work for government-supported health institutions, such as the Centers for Disease Control or a state department of health. Another common area is the specialized nonprofit organization, developing information campaigns to educate the public, lobbying the legislature on policy issues, and raising funds to support research. Examples of health-related nonprofit organizations are the American Cancer Society and the Alzheimer's Association.

Today, health promotion is recognized as a growing field. In 2002, 44,536 people in the United States were employed in the industry, a number projected to increase by more than 20% by the year 2012 (Horrigan, 2004).

Despite the numerous roles health promoters may play, the unifying aspect of these is the need for education in the general communication field, either in public relations, journalism, or communication studies (Fowler, Celebuski, Edgar, Kroger, & Ratzan, 1999). Indeed, among the 72 health communication programs listed on the National Communication Association's HealthComm Web site as being affiliated with NCA, 81% are described as located within a communication program (HealthCOMM–Schools, n.d.). Thus, health promotion can arguably be considered a growing specialty area in mediated communication, much as public relations or advertising.

Of the traditional mediated communication fields, health promotion is perhaps most closely allied to public relations (PR). The professions share many of the same roles, such as spanning boundaries between organizations and the public, working with and through media, and planning campaigns. Feminist theory in public relations focuses on the belief that feminist values, such as sensitivity and justice, would benefit the profession because these kinds of values should ideally form the basis of PR (Grunig, Toth, & Hon, 2000). Like public relations, health promotion scholars have called for two-way communication, or an information exchange, rather than the traditional, top-down, one-way communication from medical community to individuals (Lee & Garvin, 2003). Supporting the contention that health promotion is related to PR is the finding that PR students in one survey perceived health, medical, and pharmaceutical PR as slightly more female oriented than male oriented (Andsager & Hust, 2005). In public relations, women do tend to be more likely than men to work in the health care, hospital, and social agency sectors (Toth & Grunig, 1993). Further evidence that health promotion is popular with women is the fact that about 90% of the graduates of one collaborative master's program in health communication over the past decade have been female (Edgar & Hyde, 2005). In one of the many organizations for health communicators, the National Association for Health Communicators, women make up 44.8% ($n = 205$) of the 458 members (A. Berg-Hammond, personal communication, July 18, 2005).

The Status of Women in Health Promotion

No systematic research has been conducted to determine the ratio of female-to-male health promotion practitioners, however. The lack of such a study is due, undoubtedly, to the scope of the task. In the United States and Canada alone, there are hundreds of health communication, education, and promotion associations, each with a slightly different mission. Some have their bases in public health or medicine, and fewer seem to have a predominantly mediated communication foundation. Hospitals label their communications specialists in a variety of ways as well. A second set of organizations to consider would be the plethora of disease- and condition-specific organizations that promote awareness and seek to raise research dollars to prevent or alleviate those ailments. In the future, research on health communication is likely to turn toward measuring gender, salary, and job satisfaction in the profession, but the field has not yet matured to that point.

To present a snapshot of whether health promotion is gendered female, I conducted an exploratory analysis of a broad branch of the discipline, scholars active in health communication education at the university level and their graduate students. These academics are likely to be the teachers of the majority of health promotion practitioners in the years to come. Their research arguably shapes the knowledge and practices that constitute the profession and its activities. Here, then, is a nonscientific picture of the state of health promotion scholarship in the last decade.

First, an attempt was made to determine approximately how many individuals in or affiliated with higher education define themselves as interested in health communication. Two of the major organizations for communication in higher education include divisions devoted to health communication: the International Communication Association (ICA) and the National Communication Association (NCA). (The Association for Education in Journalism and Mass Communication [AEJMC], another prominent mass communication organization, does not have a health communication division.) The membership lists of both ICA's and NCA's divisions, as of 2004 to 2005, were tallied. In each organization, women involved in the health communication division outnumbered men[2] (see Table 10.1.) For NCA, the disparity was great, with women constituting two thirds of the membership. In ICA, slightly more than half the membership was female. The ratio in ICA is likely more representative of health promotion, however, because much health communication research in NCA focuses on health care delivery issues. Assuming that professors (and those studying with them) are somewhat representative of the field, it appears that there are more women than men in the health promotion profession. Of course, it often takes years for the professoriate to catch up with a new career option.

Journals provide another indicator of where women stand in health promotion. Although researchers conducting studies on health promotion frequently publish in relevant medical journals, such as *Pediatrics* or the *Journal of Adolescent Health,* for example, *Health Communication* and the *Journal of Health Communication (JHC)* are the ones most closely associated with mediated communication research. These two are the only journals mentioned in reviews of health promotion history (Freimuth & Quinn, 2004; Kreps et al., 1998). I analyzed tables of contents and abstracts of all articles published in the two journals from 1996, when *JHC* was founded,

Table 10.1   Gender Composition of the Health Communication Divisions of ICA and NCA, 2004–2005

	Organization			
	ICA		NCA	
Member Gender	N	Percentage	N	Percentage[1]
Female	218	54.5	84	65.6
Male	166	41.5	41	32.0
Can't Tell	16	4.0	3	2.3
Total	400	100%	128	99.9%

SOURCE: Author.

1. Percentage does not add up to 100 due to rounding.

through 2004 to get an idea of how prominent women's work is in this field. First, an article's focus was categorized as *health promotion* or *health care delivery,* based on the population studied and the study's purpose. For health promotion articles only, the number of female authors and the number of male authors were simply counted.[3]

According to this nonscientific analysis, female researchers' work is prominently featured in health communication journals. Figure 10.1 displays the percentages of female and male authors by year in the two journals.[4] It is clear that women are publishing in health promotion at a rate about equal to, and often exceeding, their male counterparts. Overall, women constituted 53.4% ($N = 452$) of the authors of health promotion articles. This compares quite favorably to the gender ratio in other mediated communication journals, in which women authored less than 30% of articles from 1986 to 2000, with a high point of 49% (Blake, Bodle, & Adams, 2004). Thus, it appears that women slightly outnumber men in academic and associated health promotion fields, and their publication record is concordant.

Conclusion

We might expect that the medical community, given the inherent understanding of biological sex necessary for physicians to accurately diagnose and treat many conditions, would have long been sensitized to issues of sex and gender. Not so. It took the activism of women to raise awareness about their own special health needs for the federal government to allot more research funding to women's health at the end of the 20th century. Health and medicine have only lately begun to recognize the importance of gender

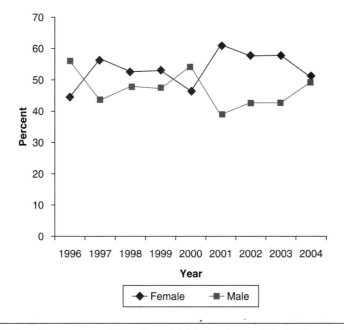

Figure 10.1   Percentages of Female and Male Authors of Health Promotion
Articles, 1996–2004

SOURCE: Author.

as a construct that must be addressed in order to successfully treat male and
female patients. Scholars have turned their attention to the matter of "how
disparately men and women encounter, relate to, and interact with the medical community is elucidating how pervasive gender differences are throughout health care, leading to the recent development of 'sex- and gender-based
medicine'" (Gesenway, 2001, p. 935). The growing proportions of women
in medical schools as researchers, students, and professors have unquestionably increased the salience of gender's role in health.

As health promotion became more sophisticated over the last half of the
20th century, women's roles expanded from the traditional social activism
of the past to move into formal campaign development and research.
Women are integral to the success of health promotion and education
around the world, whether as salaried professionals or volunteers. All available evidence indicates that their numbers are increasing in this field.
Although formal research has not yet been conducted on women's job satisfaction, salaries, or managerial roles in health promotion, women are playing an equal—if not greater—role than men in shaping this growing
profession.

Notes

1. For a comprehensive review of the increase in health information in media, see J. D. Brown & K. Walsh-Childers (2002), Effects of Media on Personal and Public Health. In J. Bryant and D. Zillmann (Eds.), *Media Effects: Advances in Theory and Research* (2nd ed., pp. 453–488). Mahwah, NJ: Lawrence Erlbaum.

2. Membership directories for each division were listed online, ICA's at its homepage, http://www.icahdq.org, and NCA's at the HealthCOMM site specifically for divisional members, http://www.sla.purdue.edu/HealthCOMM. Gender was determined on the basis of the author's knowledge of the individuals listed or their first names. If gender could not be identified by name, the Web site of the person's affiliation was searched for a photo or pronoun; if that failed, the name was searched on http://www.google.com. When gender could not be determined through these methods, the individual was placed into the *Can't tell* category.

3. Author gender was determined by the same procedure used for organizational membership. Percentages reflect only those authors identified by gender. Thus, the percentages used account for 95.2% ($N = 846$) of the authors.

4. Although percentages alone can be misleading, they are used here to control for changes in the number of articles published over time in the journals. Raw numbers for authors would also be misleading, as the *Journal of Health Communication* has occasionally published supplements to its regular volume. *JHC* also increased frequency of publication per volume in 2002. Most of the articles were coauthored by research teams. The numbers of authors per year ranged from 53 in 1997 to 207 in 2004.

Questions for Discussion

1. Examine news coverage of a current health issue. Do female and male reporters differ in their presentation of the issue? Are the sources used both male and female? Does the intended target audience appear to be female, male, or both?

2. In addition to the feminist values discussed in this chapter, are there other values inherent in health communication? What masculine values seem to be associated with health communication?

3. Think of your favorite television programs. Have you seen health messages included in the stories? What behaviors, diseases, or conditions do the messages discuss? Are the messages effective?

4. This chapter mentions a number of specific career paths that a health communicator might pursue. Are there other career options? How might health communication careers change in the next decade?

5. Identify a health communication campaign, such as promotion of safer sex, breast self-exams, or use of a designated driver. Find the campaign's site on the Internet. Can you identify the target audience, the persuasive message(s), and the media used to disseminate the message? What types of research have health communicators conducted to determine these strategies?

Accessing Additional Information

American Public Health Association: http://www.apha.org/

Coalition for Health Communication: http://www.healthcommunication.net/

National Association of Medical Communicators: http://www.ibiblio.org/namc/index.html

National Women's Health Resource Center: http://www.healthywomen.org/

11

Scholastic Media

Women in Quantity and Quality . . . But Is That Enough?

Candace Perkins Bowen, Kent State University

When the John S. and James L. Knight Foundation began a major initiative in the late 1990s to support high school journalism, teachers in the trenches and those running programs for them and their students through collegiate journalism schools said, "It's about time!" Research had long shown that those who choose media as careers—especially minorities—get their start working on strong publications in secondary schools. This field, also known as *scholastic media*, encourages critical thinking; civic concern; investigative research; clear, concise writing; and teamwork, to name a few valuable skills. Yet since its apparent beginning with the first-known high school class in Salina, Kansas, in 1912, the field's educators and publications advisers had little outside support (Dickey, 1996). Even its early organizations, led mostly by women, found little help outside their own ranks.

"It wasn't a group of 'founding fathers' who developed the forerunner of [today's largest organization for high school journalism teachers]. It was more accurately a group of 'founding mothers,'" wrote Molly Clemons (1999, pp. 1) on the 75th anniversary of the Journalism Education Association (JEA). In 1924, Rowena Harvey asked a handful of female teachers at a

Central Interscholastic Press Association meeting in Madison, Wisconsin, "Should teachers of journalism form a national organization?" When they answered "Yes," Harvey became its first president.

The group Harvey helped form changed names several times in the early years: the American Association of High School Teachers of Journalistic Writing (1925), the National Association of Supervisors and Teachers of High School Journalism (1928), the National Association of High School Teachers of Journalism (1929), the National Association of Journalism Advisers (1930), and, finally, the National Association of Journalism Directors (1939). During World War II, when a large percentage of men were serving in the military, Olive Allen was president, and Maude Staudenmayer was vice president. From the beginning, in 1924, until the group became the JEA, in 1963, eight different women served as president, and more women than men have served as officers (Clemons, 1999).

The preponderance of women in this early national organization is mirrored in today's ratio of females to males in the field. Female high school journalism educators outnumber their male counterparts more than 2 to 1. According to Jack Dvorak's 1991 survey, 71.5% were women, and 28.5% were men. When Dvorak replicated the survey in 1998, the numbers had changed little: 72.3% and 27.7%, respectively. Research by Mary Arnold (1996) showed the average journalism teacher was "a 41-year-old female, married and has children" (p. 10).

It is not surprising, then, that leaders in the scholastic media field have often been women. They teach journalism, mass communication, and photography courses. Traditionally, they have advised newspapers and yearbooks, but in recent years, high school media have grown to include broadcast and Web sites as well. Others have become directors of state, regional, and national press associations or elected officials in organizations.

Award-Winning High School Journalism Teachers

The Dow Jones Newspaper Fund began naming its National High School Journalism Teacher of the Year in 1960. From then until 2004, 21 of those were women, compared with 24 who were men. Since the early 1990s, the fund has offered these teachers a broader platform to spread the word about scholastic media to other organizations. They have been involved in the programs of groups such as the American Society of Newspaper Editors and the Association for Education in Journalism and Mass Communication. Gloria Grove Olman, the 1992 School Journalism Teacher of the Year, for example, made advocacy for student press rights her focus:

I was raised during the McCarthy era by parents with a minority viewpoint. They taught me to think independently and to stand up for First Amendment rights. I could see those rights being eroded and understood my responsibility to keep them alive. (personal communication, February 9, 2005)

Olman's leadership didn't diminish when she retired. She has been instrumental in the Michigan fight for a state law to protect student journalists from the impact of the U.S. Supreme Court case *Hazelwood v. Kuhlmeier* (1988), which principals often interpret as allowing them to censor what student media publish.

Olman's commitment to media isn't unusual for Dow Jones National High School Journalism Teachers of the Year. Opal Eckert, the 1963 winner from Maryville High School, in Missouri, was still writing a weekly column for her community newspaper at the age of 92. Likewise, the 1968 winner, Ruth Marie Griggs, of Broad Ripple High School, in Indianapolis, Indiana, was helping her retirement community put together a history to celebrate its 20th anniversary in 1999.

Scholastic Media Leadership Roles

Another indicator of the impact of women in the field is the number of presidents of the JEA who followed in Harvey's shoes. JEA members have elected 14 women and 17 men as president since 1924. Representative of these, Molly Clemons, president from 1975 to 1977, saw a need to "upgrade the communication process with members" (personal communication, December 21, 2004). During her term, she instituted postcard and call-in help services and a quarterly newsletter for all affiliates at the state and national levels. Another priority for Clemons was curriculum expansion.

Into the 21st century, JEA has had another leader, Ann Visser, who has encouraged curricular growth yet has been mindful of the increased time commitment for both journalism instructors and their association leaders. Providing more online resources has been a focus. Reelected president of JEA for another 2 years in 2005, she knows the struggles involved. "The countless women who have filled officer and director roles have made the commitment to serve, regardless of the fact that most of them were holding full-time jobs and raising families as well" (Ann Visser, personal communication, January 18, 2005).

Unlike the situation in JEA, women have not dominated the office of head of the Association for Education in Journalism and Mass Communication's division devoted to scholastic media. Under the name "Secondary Education

Division," the group had 13 men and 2 women as head from 1965 to 1991. Shortly afterward, the name changed to "Scholastic Journalism Division," and the 7 leaders since then have included 4 women and 3 men. Julie E. Dodd, head from 2001 to 2003, has noticed that men predominate in histories she has read about university-based scholastic journalism organizations. She thinks most women in these positions at universities "are in professional-track or service-focused positions" and not on a tenure track with an opportunity to be promoted to full professor (Julie E. Dodd, personal communication, November 25, 2004).

Columbia Scholastic Press Advisers Association honors "state or regional school press association officials who have distinguished themselves in the field" (Columbia Scholastic Press Association, 2005) with an award named for the late James Frederick Paschal, a former director of the Oklahoma Interscholastic Press Association and a former editor of the *CSPAA Bulletin*. Since the award began in 1987, 11 of those named were women, and 7 were men, although only 4 of those women were in tenure-track university positions: Dodd (1995), Elizabeth Dickey (1988), Mary Arnold (1991), and Laura Schaub (2002).

Leaders on the National Level

Lists overlook the human side of secondary school media. Although little is written in detail about the early pioneers like Harvey, more has been published about those since the 1960s and the changes and improvements they have brought to the field. Dorothy McPhillips and Sister Ann Christine Heintz represent two of these. Both were members of the Robert F. Kennedy Commission on High School Journalism, a series of forums and discussions to study the media after the Rodney King beating and subsequent riots in Los Angeles in 1991. Heintz and McPhillips offered insight and became voices in the dialogue that produced the 1994 book *Captive Voices: High School Journalism in America* (Nelson, 1974), a catalyst that helped, among other things, to bring about the creation of the Student Press Law Center. Notably, neither stopped her involvement in student media after the commission finished its work.

McPhillips was a "later bloomer," wrote Kenson Siver (1999), who followed her as JEA president. McPhillips, then recently widowed and mother of a 13-year-old, started college 17 years after she graduated from high school. In the 1960s, she taught in California, becoming active in JEA and the Southern California advisers' group. During that time, she and her administrators failed to see eye to eye as she encouraged her students to cover real-world topics that affected their lives. Eventually, she left Anaheim and settled in Washington state, continuing to teach journalism. During this time, she was JEA's first vice president, the organization's magazine editor for two terms, and the president for 4 years.

McPhillips's work and leadership didn't go unnoticed. In 1995, she received a $10,000 Free Spirit Award from The Freedom Forum. In her acceptance speech, McPhillips said she shared her honor with "many dedicated journalism teachers" who work in the profession. McPhillips, like Olman, spoke tirelessly about the value of student First Amendment rights. "A free and uncensored student press teaches all students about the rights and responsibilities that go with serving and preserving a free and open society," she said in her acceptance speech ("Former JEA President," 1995).

Heintz also had a long history of impact on students and their teachers, some of whom were not always comfortable with her:

> Her forthright manner and seemingly unbending stances—even on such important issues as minorities, accreditation and freedom of the press—often upset people aligned with more traditional approaches. In her later years she would often remark that she knew she wasn't good at playing political games with established groups and institutions. She didn't want to waste time on procedures or formalities because she saw tasks at hand that needed doing—now. (Dvorak, 1989, p. 12)

Heintz helped JEA form its first curriculum commission to study other media, classroom teaching methods, and trends. In 1976, Heintz also cofounded and advised *New Expression,* a citywide Chicago newspaper by and for teens, the prototype for similar successes in other cities, such as Los Angeles and Washington, D.C. She took young people she referred to as "street kids" and showed them how to have a voice in things that mattered to them. From this group came future editors and reporters for metropolitan newspapers around the country, many of them representing the diversity the media sought.

Representative Leaders on the State Level

Early pioneers at the national level, like McPhillips and Heintz, made a difference, but high school journalism teachers often lack the finances or time commitment necessary to participate at that level. Thus, state scholastic press associations often have had an even more direct impact on the lives of such teachers. As Arnold's research showed, and as she reported in *Quill & Scroll* magazine, the average journalism teacher is the only one with that job in her building and thus has no local peers for advice and support: "That must come from state and national journalism organizations to which she belongs" (Arnold, 1996, p. 10). Because, as Arnold's research also showed, the typical high school media adviser teaches at a public, rural high school, "much of her information comes in the form of journalism magazines and newsletters" (p. 10). Dvorak's findings showed that more than 27% of the advisers he surveyed in both 1998 and 1991 belonged to state scholastic press associations, compared with 21% or fewer belonging to the national groups—JEA, National Scholastic Press Association, or Columbia Scholastic Press Association.

Almost every state has a "heroine" who worked to build and maintain its association for student journalists and their teachers. One example is Mary Benedict. When Indiana's Benedict died in April 2004, those who knew her spoke of her vivaciousness, her ability to lead, her competence as a journalism educator, her deep love of family and friends, her power to influence people positively, and her love of golf and Scotch—not necessarily in that order (Dvorak, 2005, p. 1). Benedict taught at Washington and Arlington high schools in Indianapolis from 1950 to 1972, and the Dow Jones Newspaper Fund named her National High School Journalism Teacher of the Year in 1967. She served as director of the High School Journalism Institute in Indiana for 13 years, a period that saw attendance of 6,000 high school students at conferences. Elizabeth (Beth) Dickey, herself a leader in scholastic media, quoted Benedict when she gave the Honors Lecture to the Scholastic Journalism Division of the Association for Education in Journalism and Mass Communication in 2003: "I once asked Mary Benedict if the scholastic associations and workshops competed against each other and if the directors were adversaries. She said, 'There's enough missionary work for all of us'" (personal communication, January 11, 2005).

From High School Teaching to the Collegiate Level

Leaders in scholastic journalism often got their start as high school teachers and then moved to the collegiate level. This is not always an easy transition. Marilyn Weaver, who followed this route and became Journalism Department Chairwoman at Ball State University, said,

> Scholastic journalism must have higher recognition at universities. At some institutions there is little support for scholastic journalism. Faculty members are not always held with the same regard as their colleagues who are more focused on the typical professional areas. (personal communication, February 10, 2005)

Leaders such as Weaver, Cheryl Pell, Julie Dodd, Lillian Lodge Kopenhaver, Barbara Hines, and Linda Puntney owe at least some of their success to the ability to view scholastic journalism from two sides—and often helping one understand the other. Pell noted, "I think my job would definitely be more difficult if I had not taught high school and knew firsthand the challenges— and joys—that teachers/publication advisers face" (personal communication, December 29, 2004).

Weaver started her teaching career at Hartford City High School, in Indiana, and then moved to Muncie Southside, advising both the newspaper and the yearbook and teaching journalism and English. In 1977, she became sequence coordinator for journalism education at Ball State University, directing summer workshops and "J-Days" for high school and middle school students. She taught graduate-level workshops for in-service teachers, started the publication *J-communique,* conducted research in journalism licensing, and fought successfully to keep a journalism teaching license in Indiana. After becoming journalism department chairwoman in 1997, she continued to support scholastic media, receiving grants for the American Society of Newspaper Editors summer workshop for teachers and for "J-Ideas," an "institute for digital education, activities and scholarship." Weaver noted that her university and only a handful of others understand and support the importance of training teachers and serving scholastic journalism (personal communication, February 11, 2005).

Similarly, Lillian Lodge Kopenhaver spent 5 years teaching high school journalism and advising the student newspaper at Brick Township High School, in New Jersey, then started a journalism program and newspaper at a community college. She went to Florida International University (FIU), where she again launched a student newspaper. She was instrumental in founding what is today the School of Journalism and Mass Communication at FIU and is now its dean. A champion of student First Amendment rights, she has approached this issue through research, by conducting national studies, and through personal commitment as a long-time member of the Student Press Law Center board. Even her classroom projects have had an impact. Public school journalism teachers and advisers from Miami in a graduate class she taught at FIU studied the possibilities and drafted what became the Miami–Dade County, Florida, publications guidelines. Since 1981, Kopenhaver said, these have been a model, "fostering a vigorous free student press, influencing and being cited by scholastic groups across the country" (personal communication, January 8, 2005).

Barbara Hines became active in the Maryland Scholastic Press Advisers Association (MSPAA), which met in inner-city Baltimore, when she noticed her school did not have much diversity: "I sought opportunities for my students to meet and work with students 'not like themselves'" (personal communication, January 26, 2005). Her 1974 master's thesis, "A Promotional Campaign to Establish the University of Maryland Scholastic Press Association," was her way of bringing stability to MSPAA, which operated "out of teachers' closets and car trunks." This led to a position in the College of Journalism at the University of Maryland and a chance to create summer workshops, press days, and other support for scholastic media. Her 1984 move to Howard University allowed her to work with what was then called the Urban Journalism Workshop. She saw "there weren't opportunities for many of the District of Columbia public school students to meet some of the 'players' in the world of journalism," so she "expanded the network and brought people together who shared an interest in scholastic journalism and formed the Capital Area Youth Journalism Exchange" (Barbara Hines, personal communication, January 26, 2005). By the mid-1990s, when others began to discover scholastic journalism, Hines helped establish a citywide newspaper, *Young D.C.*, as part of the Youth Communication network that Sister Ann Christine Heintz had founded, and the Urban Journalism Workshop became the Howard University Youth Journalism Academy.

Mary Arnold, currently head of the Journalism and Mass Communication Department at South Dakota State University, shares part of her career path with these women. While in college, she was the city desk reporter and women's editor of the local newspaper. She then was a high school journalism teacher and newspaper and yearbook adviser in Minnesota and Iowa until she joined the faculty of the University of Iowa in 1986. While there, she earned her doctorate in mass communications and directed the Iowa High School Press Association and summer workshops. Later, she was a professor at Ball State University, in Muncie, Indiana, where she directed that school's American Society of Newspaper Editors' High School Journalism Institute. From 1989 to 2004, she was on the board of the Student Press Law Center, serving as president during a difficult but successful reorganization.

Arnold also represents another group of women: those who have supported scholastic media from positions in associations and foundations that offer a wide range of support to classroom journalism teachers and media advisers. From 1996 to 2001, Arnold managed youth and diversity programs for the Newspaper Association of America Foundation (NAAF), in Vienna, Virginia. There, she helped establish NAAF's student newspaper and youth editorial program, the latter being a group of teen and children's page editors who formed the Youth Editors Alliance under Arnold's guidance. After Arnold left that position, another former high school teacher,

Sandy Woodcock, stepped in and continued the valuable connections. Others who have supported scholastic media and encourage their organizations and businesses to do the same—those who really "get it"—include Diana Mitsu Klos and Connie Southard, of the American Society of Newspaper Editors; Barbara Cochran, Carol Knopes, and Carolyn Terry, of Radio and Television News Directors Association and Foundation; Linda Waller, of the Dow Jones Newspaper Fund; and some who have worn various hats over the years but have always kept scholastic media on their radar, including Roz Stark, Walterene Swantson, and Judy Hines.

The list of women omitted from this chapter is perhaps even longer than the list of those included. Hundreds have been honored with the National Scholastic Press Association Pioneer Award, the Columbia Scholastic Press Association Gold Key, the JEA Medal of Merit and Carl Towley Award, the Dow Jones Newspaper Fund National High School Journalism Teacher of the Year as well as its Distinguished and Special Recognition Advisers, and the JEA Yearbook Adviser of the Year. All across the country, whether she has received kudos or not, the typical high school journalism adviser puts in more than 78 hours at work a week, many of these being weekends and vacation days (Arnold, 1996). In 1998, Dvorak found the teachers spending a little less time advising and teaching, but spending more than half their days on journalism-related learning activities. Beyond normal class time, teachers spent 5.6 hours each week advising students in their publications or media work outside the school day. They also had hall duty, study hall, detention supervision, and time to fill out forms and prepare lessons, lectures, and tests.

The Future of Scholastic Media

Does this job satisfaction that both Dvorak and Arnold found in their research bode well for the future of women in scholastic media? Maybe, but maybe not. For one thing, student publications have become the victims of everything from censorship to financial crises to block scheduling. Problems in all aspects of education impact this field as well. Because women represent such a large percentage of the educators in this field, their futures are also in jeopardy. When, in 1997, the Columbia Scholastic Press Association conducted a publication adviser survey titled "The Future of Scholastic Journalism," adviser turnover was mentioned as a concern although no survey question quantified the situation. A 2005 study by the John S. and James L. Knight Foundation showed that 40% of the schools without student newspapers had dropped them in the past 5 years. The increased interest and support from professional journalists and their organizations may result in some successes. Weaver said,

> I believe there will be more emphasis on student media in the future. While we are going through a period of cutbacks in journalism in public schools, I believe the profession will finally understand the need to support and protect student journalists. (personal communication, February 10, 2005)

She added that a failure to do so could result in high schools that produce students unprepared to be responsible citizens.

Some signs in the membership are encouraging, but many are not. There are up-and-coming leaders in the ranks who could become press association officers and award winners. Monica Hill, University of North Carolina–Chapel Hill, is vice head of the Scholastic Journalism division of the Association for Education in Journalism and Mass Communication and will become head in August 2005. Ann Visser, current president of JEA, was reelected in 2005 for another 2-year term. Although Dvorak's study showed the sheer number of women in the field is high, finding those like Hill and Visser interested in leadership positions is often a hard sell. For the January 2005 JEA elections, nine women ran for the 15 elected positions, but six were unopposed. State organizations aren't faring much better. The Journalism Association of Ohio Schools had 13 board members in fall 2004, with seven females, but, of those, four had retired from classroom teaching.

Hope for scholastic media—with particular support from women—may benefit from the number of high school females involved in their newspapers, yearbooks, and a growing number of broadcast outlets. No one has researched this, but observing high school media offices and state and national workshops and conferences tells the tale. JEA Secretary Susan Hathaway Tantillo noted,

> When I look around at nearly 4,000 student delegates to a national high school journalism convention and see two-thirds of them are girls, it appears the future of women in scholastic journalism could be quite healthy. Our challenge as journalism educators is to tap this potential resource and infuse it with our own passion for teaching, for helping our students learn the value of the First Amendment and all the possibilities it holds. (personal communication, December 22, 2004)

Mark Goodman, executive director of the Student Press Law Center, points to the winners of the Courage in Student Journalism Awards, sponsored by the Newseum, the Student Press Law Center, and the National Scholastic Press Association. One of the two $5,000 awards recognizes a student journalist "who has shown determination, despite difficulty or resistance, in lawfully exercising his or her First Amendment press rights." Since 2001, 7 of the 10 students honored have been women. Goodman said,

> I think it's interesting that, despite the fact women are still underrepresented at the highest management levels in the commercial news media world, they probably outnumber men significantly in student media. And they are consistently demonstrating how courageous they can be as leaders by taking on fights against censorship and in pursuit of public records. (personal communication, February 10, 2005)

These teen journalists may not have their sights set on a career in education, but Linda Puntney, executive director of the JEA, thinks encouraging them to do so is an important goal for those already part of scholastic media. She said her greatest contribution to the field is

> the students who have decided to go into journalism education because they had the opportunity to discover the thrill of teaching through summer camps, national conventions or daylong workshops. I'd like to think part of the reason they decide to teach is because they discover how much fun it is, and they see that even after all these years, I really love what I do, and I believe unconditionally in its value. (personal communication, February 9, 2005)

Questions for Discussion

1. Why do you think Rowena Harvey wanted a national organization? Since several national organizations exist today, what should their focus be? Have the reasons for them changed?

2. Why do women dominate scholastic journalism? What strengths and weaknesses have they brought to the field?

3. What can scholastic journalism educators do to get more support from universities? From commercial media?

4. Pioneers in the field like Dorothy McPhillips and today's leaders like Lillian Lodge Kopenhaver have all been strong advocates of scholastic press rights. Why have they and others believed this is a necessary part of a strong scholastic media program?

5. What aspects of scholastic journalism education might entice—or discourage— women from entering the field? Can you suggest some ways to encourage more women to enter the field?

Accessing Additional Information

Columbia Scholastic Press Association: http://www.web.columbia.edu/cu/cspa

Dow Jones Newspaper Fund: http://www.DJNewspaperFund.dowjones.com

Journalism Education Association: http://www.jea.org

National Scholastic Press Association: http://www.studentpress.org/nspa

Quill & Scroll: http://www.uiowa.edu/~quill-sc

Student Press Law Center: http://www.splc.org

12

Increased Legitimacy, Fewer Women?

Analyzing Editorial Leadership and Gender in Online Journalism

Shayla Thiel Stern, DePaul University

Accarding to a recent extensive study of Americans and Internet use, 70 million American adults logged on to the Internet on a typical day in late 2004 in order to gain access to all kinds of information, communicate with one another, gamble, book travel reservations, and engage in countless other activities (Rainie & Horrigan, 2004). Seventy-two percent of these Internet users reported visiting the Web for general news (Rainie & Horrigan, 2005); 49% looked for political news and information; and 43% visited Web sites that provided sports scores and news (Rainie & Horrigan, 2004). Much of this kind of information can be found on the Web pages of the many U.S. national news organizations, whether they are produced by network television stations or by newspapers.

The online news sources receiving most of the traffic unsurprisingly represent the largest and most prestigious news organizations in the nation: USAToday.com, with 9.7 million unique users[1] per month; NYTimes.com, with around 12.7 million unique users per month; MSNBC, with nearly

25 million unique users per month; CNN.com, with about 20.7 million unique users per month; and washingtonpost.com, with more than 7.8 million unique users per month (Nielsen/NetRatings, 2005).

All of these online publications went online in the middle 1990s, and as they hit the 10-year mark, they have become adept at publishing rich content that draws both from their traditional newspaper and TV counterparts and their own additions, such as interactive chats, photo galleries, and multimedia components. By combining these, they have, in essence, revolutionized the online news industry.

Despite revolutionizing online news media, these organizations seem to have missed an opportunity to revolutionize newsroom organization and culture, particularly with regard to gender equity in leadership: None of the executive editors or editors-in-chief of these news sites are women, and only a handful of women belong to their top-level editorial teams as senior projects editors or managing editors. By looking at interviews with current and former women senior editors at national online news publications, this chapter examines the conflicting phenomenon that new media may function as a new paradigm and yet mirror gender disparities from the traditional newsroom, right up to its "glass ceiling."

Gender and Identity in the Newsroom

According to the annual newsroom demographic study by the ASNE for 2004 (which surveys only traditional newspaper newsrooms, rather than online newsrooms), 65.8% of the supervisory roles in newsrooms of all sizes are held by men (ASNE, 2004). Although there are no data available on the numbers of online editors, a quick glimpse at the mastheads of MSNBC .com, CNN.com, NYTimes.com, washingtonpost.com, and USAToday.com shows no women in the most senior rank of editor-in-chief or executive editor; in all, only a few employ women in positions such as managing editor or editor of special projects (Journalism.com, 2004).[2]

Now filling close to half of all professional roles in the workplace, women may produce power differentials based on gender both in the workplace and in the culture at large (Walby, 1997). Feminist inquiry into journalism holds that the culture of the profession often is gendered in masculine ways (Gilwald, 1994; Ross, 2001). Ross (2001) has stated that although journalism touts itself as a profession that embraces objectivity and neutrality, newsrooms often embrace a masculine culture that is for all practical purposes organized around a "man-as-norm and woman-as-interloper" structure (p. 535). Melin-Higgins and Djerf Pierre (1998) and Ross (2001) have noted that women often cope with this masculine newsroom culture by co-opting male norms and values into their own behavior. Studies have shown that women journalists often walk a fine line between embracing what van Zoonen (1998) has referred to as a "feminine news identity," which primarily entails a stronger identification with the audience, and falling in as "one of the boys," which entails fitting in with the status quo system of presenting the facts with less regard for the reader, as well as falling in with institutional newsroom norms (p. 31).

Revisiting Women Online Journalists: They're "Up or Out"

This chapter's research represents both a look at the present situation of upper-level women editors at online newspapers as well as an update to a research study that was conducted in 2001 and was published in 2004 in *Feminist Media Studies*. In the first study, I interviewed 13 women who were working in or had worked in online journalism—2 who had worked in online journalism for a number of years and decided to leave to work in academia and public relations. The remaining 11 held various positions at online news publications, including 2 who were upper-level editors within nationally known publications. Many of the women interviewed for the study said they viewed the online landscape not only as a space that facilitated experimentation and an opportunity to "pioneer" a new medium but also as a place where career advancement opportunities abound for women in journalism. Several had left "traditional" television and newspaper newsrooms when their publishing companies advertised new positions working for their Internet counterparts, and they felt they could not only enter at higher-level positions but also advance more quickly to even more senior levels.

In November 2004 through January 2005, I conducted short e-mail interviews with the women in the original study to get an update on their employment status. Of the 11 women who worked in online journalism at the time of the first study, only 4 had chosen to remain in online journalism, while the rest had opted out of this new form of journalism and its opportunities for reconfiguring the traditional newsroom.

The two who were senior editors at the time of the first study had maintained their positions or stayed at the same level as when they were first interviewed. June[3] was still a vice president at a national online entertainment site, where her job had remained essentially the same, though she had taken on a more public role for the site by participating in media panels on the topic of online journalism. Rachel had switched from her prestigious national online newspaper to another prestigious national online newspaper; as an executive producer instead of a managing editor, she was still considered to be among the top-level editors at her publication.

Of the other 11 women, 2 were in exactly the same positions as when they were interviewed 4 years before. Sheila was still on the online staff for a national trade publication dealing with education; she had attended graduate school while she continued to work full-time and was still in school at the time of the first study. Although she had finished her MA in 2004, she continued to work in the same position; a position above her had been filled some time ago by a man who worked in the offline part of the publication. Another woman, Maya, continued in her role as a content developer for a West Coast online newspaper; although she was happy with her position, advancement opportunities had not arisen in her 5 years there.

Others had moved on to different opportunities. Michelle and Karen had both been laid off from their large national news sites in the downturn of the economy in 2001; both had decided to work from home as freelance writers/editors and found steady work editing textbooks and publishing in hobby magazines. Karen also worked as an occasional freelance contributor and content developer for her former online news publication. Another woman, Susan, reported she'd been happy to leave the online journalism world when her first baby was born. She had had a second child the year before and found a part-time position as a copy editor for a local suburban newspaper 30 miles from her home in a large city. Elizabeth had left online journalism for a position in public relations, which she said was more lucrative and often entailed fewer hours than her position in online journalism. Patricia, another senior editor at a national publication, had received a fellowship earmarked specifically for journalists and had since become an adjunct professor at a large university. Wendy had been managing editor of a large national business publication until several months prior, when it was sold to a new company and underwent management reshuffling. She had decided "take a break" from journalism and the Web, but recently she had accepted a position overseeing online content and projects for a consumer-oriented Web publication; she admitted the position was less challenging and less supervisory than she had hoped when she'd accepted it, but she already planned to approach the upper-level management about taking on more responsibility.

It is important to locate particular times and circumstances in which women in lower-level positions (producers, content developers, section editors, and others) decide to exit the online journalism profession. For example, a number of the women in the 2001 study said they left because they were "burned out" with their former positions in online news. Others simply wished to devote more time to raising their families or to try different professions.

Rachel said in her recent interview that she felt many young women's defections from online news also may be attributed to the lack of senior, and even middle-management, positions within the newsroom. Often, she said, the young, talented producers will work for many years as producers or section editors, and they see no means for advancement to higher levels. They also leave online journalism all together for more lucrative careers in other industries or Internet companies that are not related to traditional journalistic publications. "There's no place for a talented young person to go up, so they go out," she said. "Obviously, we cannot afford to pay the huge salaries that they might get within private industry, so if there is not a vertical career move within, then it's out."

In this chapter, I explore the stories of women who opted to stay and progress within their careers in online journalism to the position of upper-level editor or to leave a traditional newsroom to join an online newsroom as an upper-level editor. Only one of the women from the initial study, Rachel, participated in the new round of interviews, which were with six women (including Rachel) at the level of managing editor, executive editor, or editor-in-chief in online news organizations that reach more than a million unique users per month and whose mastheads are recognized nationally. The interviews conducted for the current study were carried out by telephone and e-mail between September 2004 and January 2005.

Women Online Editors and Cultural Capital

To understand the experiences of several senior-level women editors in online journalism, it is crucial to listen to their stories. From these stories, one can then focus on the cultural narratives that manifest themselves in each, specifically looking for clues about how gender is played out within the workplace. Through narratives, people give meaning to their lives and construct themselves. Narratives are crucial to shaping personal and social identity and to understanding and constructing the identities of others, and this often plays out in gendered ways (McLaren, 1993; Walker, 2001).

Few women have held upper-level editor positions at the best-known national online publications since they were launched over the past decade or so, according to the women interviewed for this study and previous studies (Thiel, 2004). Because of the relative lack of senior-level leaders, I interviewed women who worked at the national publications and at well-known national trade publications as well as a senior editor at a regional online newspaper that receives 1 million unique users per month. Their narratives illuminate challenges and successes they have experienced as online editors.

In my initial study on women online journalists, a majority of the women interviewed said they left reporting and lower-level editing positions in traditional newsrooms in order to gain new technological skills that might propel their careers in different directions (Thiel, 2004). They also expressed hope for swifter promotion as a result of these skills. They felt the acquisition of technical savvy and the opportunity to demonstrate how these skills would shape a new medium for journalism would grant them cultural capital that would result (at least eventually) in respect, raises, and promotions (Thiel, 2004, p. 22–23).

McCall (1992) took a feminist perspective in understanding Pierre Bourdieu's (1973) concept of "cultural capital," the notion that each person holds value within a given culture or society through economic means, education, ethnicity, race, skills, political affiliation, gender, and other often-uncontrollable factors. McCall (1992) maintained that gender is one of the more potent embodied forms of cultural capital because it is often manifested physically (unlike economic capital) and it can be more of a detriment than other forms of cultural capital because gendered dispositions—for example, the cultural stereotype of men as strong and women as fragile—are rarely recognized as holding the same value as other forms of cultural capital (p. 842). In the workplace, women may attempt to offset the negative cultural capital associated with their gender by playing up other more valued types of cultural capital. For example, many women online journalists interviewed in the earlier research learned technical skills—skills that were often associated with the notion that men are more skilled technically and computer savvy—which they felt added to their cultural capital within the online newsroom (Thiel, 2004, p. 22).

However, it seems their attention to becoming more technically savvy by gaining computer-programming skills might not actually have given them the cultural capital necessary to compete for roles in upper-editorial management, evidenced by the fact that some of the women who mastered new technical skills were not promoted in the past several years. In fact, many of the women who did become upper-level editors at national publications said that while they had interest in the online world, they had little technical expertise going in to their editor roles. Instead, they were already senior-level editors in the traditional newsroom—sometimes for many years before moving to online. The women upper-level editors interviewed for this chapter carried a certain level of cultural capital among decision makers in their news organizations because of their experience in traditional news, not because of their experience with new media.

Furthermore, most did not apply formally for an open position as editor within the online newsroom. Instead, they often were approached by upper-level managers, generally on the traditional newspaper or television side, to help run the online news team. Technical skill was rarely a factor.

"I had started conversations with the assistant managing editor for [the Metro section of a national newspaper] about new opportunities, when a former colleague of mine asked whether I would be interested in working at the Web site," said Kimberly, who had worked as a reporter and then editor, for a total of more than 15 years, before being named the managing editor of one of the top national online newspapers.

Linda, a former executive editor of one of the top national online news-papers, said she had worked for more than 20 years as reporter and editor in a traditional newsroom at a large national newspaper before her man-agers asked whether she would be interested in a role with its fledgling online publication. "My bosses noticed I was showing more interest in the World Wide Web than my colleagues were back in 1995, when the Web was still new," she said. Her senior editors at the newspaper placed her on a spe-cial committee to oversee development of the newspaper's online service, which was already being published by a staff of editors and producers through a for-pay Internet service provider similar to AOL but was still being developed as a free publication for the World Wide Web. "When the newspaper's managing editor decided the newsroom needed a full-time liai-son to our fledgling Web site, he picked me. My role evolved from there [to taking over as executive editor several months later]."

Similarly, Wendy, who had worked as a reporter and editor for a large local newspaper for a decade, was asked by her publisher to create and over-see a Web site for the newspaper in 1996. After a number of increasingly more visible positions over the past 9 years, she was hired as managing edi-tor for one of the largest national online-business-oriented publications.

The women interviewed recently who achieved upper-level editor posi-tions often constructed narratives about being approached by members of the organization who already held a great deal of cultural capital and the decision being entirely in their own power. This contrasts with the women online journalists interviewed in 2001 who had applied for positions within the online newsrooms and hoped to be "entrepreneurs" or "pioneers"; many of them started as lower-level online producers or content developers in the new media, with the hope of eventually being promoted to the editor level (Thiel, 2004).

Other women online editors were overlooked for promotions both within new media and traditional media: Katharine, now the founding executive editor of an online publication that covers policy and issues facing women, realized that she might have to forge her own path early on. As the assistant managing editor of a well-known national trade publication in the mid-1980s, she developed programming for training reporters to use modems and upload their stories to an online bulletin board, which would eventually become an online news service for their publication. Still, she described the project as something she decided to instigate in order to make her own position more challenging and interesting, and she was never approached "officially" to become an online editor.

"On the very day that we launched the news service, we learned from an internal announcement that a guy had been hired as editor of the (trade publication's) online news service," Katharine said. "No one ever even asked me about whether I was interested." Although she continued her position as assistant managing editor there for a few years and then moved on to work as a reporter and editor for community newspapers for the next decade, she said she did not earn the upper-level editor position that she wanted until she founded her current publication.

At-Work Role Modeling: Cultural Capital or Detriment?

The women online editors often noted feeling strongly about their roles in "shaping" a new media and, in turn, making online newsrooms more progressive and cooperative than their traditional counterparts. They repeatedly referred to their positions as "role models" and "mentors," rather than simply "supervisors" and "editors," which is an important distinction because it draws less attention to the hierarchical (and often patriarchal) climate associated with traditional newsrooms.

"A lot of the section editors were grateful they finally had a woman manager," said Rachel. "They were thirsty to have a woman manager—in part because it offers a glimmer of hope of being able to ascend."

Kimberly said the producers who worked for her also seemed to appreciate the opportunity to be managed by her because of her willingness to mentor them and represent their needs to the higher management. "In senior management, you are a role model to many people. They trust you to represent them and to be their voice in leadership," she said. "Many of them turn to me when they need to talk through their own workplace challenges or career decisions."

The women interviewed view the online newsroom as a more "flexible" and "cooperative" environment than the traditional newsroom, adjectives that are often associated with feminine gender.

"Women are great at getting support and getting people to cooperate together, so this should be a perfect job for a woman," said Sylvia, who had worked as a senior editor at a large regional online newspaper publication since 1996. "I think of online as a more feminine thing to do. We don't have that paternalistic 'You can't do that' mentality."

"[The online newsroom] was a great place to be a female manager. . . . Web newsrooms tend to be less hidebound and rule dominated," said Linda. "Ours was much more open to new ways of doing things than the print newsroom was, and as a woman I really loved that aspect of Web journalism."

Katherine, whose newsroom was entirely staffed by women editors, said there is less aggression in her newsroom than she remembers at past traditional publications. "There is no place like this. The default is female," she said. "There is not a lot of shouting like there was in newsrooms where I used to work, and that doesn't mean that we don't have conflict and hold hands and work it out, but the screaming matches I recall—we just don't have anything like that."

This attention to mentoring, role modeling, and cooperation by women online editors certainly plays a significant part in shaping and improving newsroom cultures. It counters the earlier studies that paint the traditional newsroom as a masculine gendered space where women must behave as bullies or "one of the guys" to succeed (Ross, 2001; van Zoonen, 1998). It also provides evidence to section editors and producers that there is precedence for women in upper-level editor roles and shows that they can succeed in leadership roles by behaving civilly and cooperatively, and that the final product—a publication updated constantly and read by millions—often reflects the successful output of "feminine" skills.

Past studies, however, show that women demonstrating leadership through civility and cooperation is not always valued within a traditionally masculine-gendered workspace. Role modeling, instead, may be aligned with the patriarchal idea that women are naturally nurturing or giving in to an "ethic of care," which is defined as the way in which a majority of women attempt to solve problems by causing the least disruption in relationships among people and represents their "very strong sense of being responsible to the world" (Gilligan, 1982, p. 21). Role modeling might be seen as a type of mothering, and mothering is often culturally construed as natural and as a normalized identity for women (Ruddick, 1989, p. xi). Although care is valued culturally, it is overlooked politically and economically, especially considering the fact that women—culture's ascribed caregivers—are neither paid nor figured into the gross national product for caring for their families and homes (Tronto, 1993, p. 180).

In this view of care as a gendered ideal, these women editors may be marked as caregivers—and valued less for it—when they facilitate cooperation and act as mentors; a few women in the current study remarked that online newsrooms appear to employ even fewer top-level woman editors than they did 10 years ago, which makes this idea more troubling. In a field that has struggled to find legitimacy, particularly among its peers in traditional newsrooms (Singer, 2004), an ethic of care might be seen as a liability to professionalism among managers who embrace more masculine, traditional ideals.

Professionalism and Legitimacy in Online Journalism

In the time span between 1995 and 1998, women editors headed online publications such as washingtonpost.com, NYTimes.com, National Public Radio, Associated Press Online, and the *Chronicle of Higher Education*'s site. Today, the highest-level editors of all of these sites, as well as CNN.com, MSNBC.com, and LATimes.com, are men. And although the senior editing staffs of many of the best-known online publications employ women, they are the minority at this level. At washingtonpost.com, one senior editor is a woman. At USAToday.com, three women are part of the 11-person senior staff of editors (but the publisher, managing editor, and editor are men).

"I was just at the annual ONA [Online News Association] convention, and I was the only woman at my table of 10, which was really different from when I first started attending these conventions," said Sylvia.

Katherine added that she recently quit the ONA "in a huff" after several years of membership because none of the panels at the convention addressed women's issues nor did any of the keynote speakers reflect actual women online journalists (blogger/pundits Ariana Huffington and "Wonkette" Ana Marie Cox were the female keynote panelists).

Sylvia said she guesses that the increasing professionalism associated with online journalism may be the reason more men appear to be taking up positions of leadership in the online newsroom. "As it becomes more acceptable, stable, and prestigious, it attracts men who might not have done it 10 years ago."

Those practicing journalism online in the past were placed in the position of defending their jobs against those who think of the Web as a space where only nerds converge and where anyone can publish a Web page and call himself or herself a reporter. Online journalists have increasingly strived to be taken as seriously as their counterparts at traditional newspapers and radio and television stations; they may do so by hiring only persons with advanced college degrees in journalism or crafting codes of ethics that apply specifically to the new media (Singer, 2004). The drive for professionalism must be working: Online newspapers even win Pulitzers now. Linda said many people from the traditional newsroom at her national newspaper recently applied for the open executive editor position at its dot-com counterpart, which a decade ago was difficult to fill. "One reason might be that as the Web came of age, it gained more respectability and prestige, which made it more competitive," Linda said. "Men who once turned up their noses at leading a Web publication today actually consider some of those jobs to be plums."

Implications for the Future of Women in Online Journalism

Despite the hope of many women online journalists for a new paradigm with less gender disparities (Thiel, 2004), traditional news editors find new homes in the new media and often bring along old habits and notions of how newsrooms work. Although some of the ensuing clashes might be a result of gender inequalities, the majority of the women interviewed for this chapter said they did not think the lack of women in upper-level leadership roles was related to sexism or discrimination. Still, they acknowledged the low representation of women was problematic.

"Since I've been at the site, we've always had one woman in upper management in the newsroom. . . . That said, at times, I have been critical of what I've seen as a lack of female voices in key newsroom positions," said Kimberly. "During different cycles of management, the tenor has sometimes felt very much like that of old-school journalism—unabashedly combative and therefore restrictive. That style was very intimidating to some of the women in the newsroom, and with a lack of women in senior management, many felt locked out of the conversation. Let me be clear that not all of the men managed that way or embraced that style, but I heard from many producers who felt voiceless."

Kimberly said conflict and lack of empowerment might have to do with traditional journalists infiltrating a space once inhabited mostly by young idealists. "I suppose that because of the dynamics in new media—many times newsroom leaders are veterans of traditional media while the producers are much younger, with little or no real experience—that atmosphere can be more of a problem than in traditional newsrooms where the gap isn't as large," she said.

Wendy said she believes there just aren't enough good positions to go around. She wrote in an e-mail, "I've seen a lot of male friends lose their jobs, so I wouldn't say it was a male-versus-female thing. I think the question 'Is it a viable, sustainable career for anyone?' is what we should be asking. I think the top jobs are so few and hard to come by that I would say there isn't enough pie to share."

However, women online journalists might already be predisposed to wanting to carve their own niches—"pioneer" their own futures. Those who have left their positions as online editors at high-circulation national publications often have gone to jobs that seemed more rewarding, despite how many fewer eyes see their work. Moreover, they each admitted to being exhausted by online journalism, with its constant development and 24-hour news cycle, as well as challenges with corporate management.

Linda left her position as executive editor to become a reporter and columnist. "As for why I moved back to print journalism, I was a tad tired of the management challenges, which were formidable during the Internet's go-go years," she said. "And I had always wanted to end up writing again anyway—it was a long-time goal."

Wendy said, "I feel like I've been fighting a war all these years." She said she was often made to feel inadequate for her lack of management background and "not having an MBA," especially from the men around her (who were often younger and lacking any experience in the journalism field) who had them.

Pauline, one of the founding editors of one of the largest national online newspapers in the early 1990s, was now a publisher of a local online newspaper in a small city. "I'm happy to be back in newspapers, especially at a small, independent family-owned newspaper where I don't have to deal with corporate crap all the time," she said.

Perhaps online journalism finally appears to hold all the professionalism and legitimacy as its offline counterparts, but as it mirrors the gendered hierarchies of these predecessors, one must ask how much is actually new in this new media. As women online editors leave to find more rewarding careers and are replaced by the old guard of the newsroom, a new medium may be left looking very much like an old one.

Notes

1. *Unique user* is the standard term used to measure the number of individual persons who visit a Web site. It differs from *hits,* which counts how many times a person clicks on pages within a Web site but also counts downloaded images and other files embedded on a Web page, making it a very high number. It also differs from *page views,* which counts how many pages are actually viewed in total from a given Web site. For example, one "unique user" may generate 25 page views every time he or she visits a site.

2. It should be noted that a number of the sites, however, including washington-post.com and Tribune Interactive, recently hired women in general manager and publishing roles, which demonstrates a significant advancement for women media managers (fewer than 20% are publishers of newspapers, according to ASNE's 2004 numbers), but this study is concerned primarily with those who directly oversee the

editorial content and direction of their Web sites. Because of their focus on business and advertising, general managers and publishers are often disconnected from the day-to-day operations of the newsroom and major editorial decisions.

3. Although a number of the women interviewed in the research studies said they would not mind being identified by their real names and publications, the university internal review board mandated it potentially could be less harmful to their future employability and reputations if no identifying characteristics were included in this chapter.

Questions for Discussion

1. Why do you feel online newsrooms are currently more prevalently run by men at the major online newspapers discussed in this chapter? Why do you feel this is a change from the earlier years of online journalism?

2. How might the online journalism industry as a whole make its newsrooms more equitable in terms of race and gender? Might the solutions be different from the traditional news industry and, if so, why?

3. Do you feel that the lack of women upper-level editors at the major online newspapers has more to do with embedded sexism in the industry, or is it a matter of newsroom climate and the fact that it is potentially an even more frustrating culture to work in than traditional media? Why?

4. How might online newsrooms retain women at the level of section editors or producers so that they would continue to work in online journalism and progress up through the ranks?

5. How might the leadership style, newsroom culture, and final journalistic product be different with a woman executive editor in charge of the online newsroom?

Accessing Additional Information

American Society of Newspaper Editors: http://www.asne.org/

Cyberjournalist.net (from the Online News Association): http://www.cyberjourn alist.net/

Journalism.org: *The State of the News Media 2005 Annual Report:* http://www .stateofthenewsmedia.org/2005/index.asp

Online Journalism Review: http://www.ojr.org/

Poynter Institute's Section on Online Journalism: http://www.poynter.org/subject .asp?id=26

13

Women Journalists in Toyland and in the Locker Room

It's All About the Money

Pamela J. Creedon, The University of Iowa

Roseanna M. Smith, The University of Iowa

I'm sure I should be more upset about the pink décor in the visitors' dressing room at Iowa. But as it happens, my violent knee-jerk reaction is that it's merely funny. If the armies of feminism want to change my thinking on that, they're going to have to slap electrodes to my pretty little forehead until I stop giggling.

—Sally Jenkins (2005)

Female participation in sports in the United States has increased dramatically since the first edition of this book in 1989.[1] At the professional level, the Women's National Basketball Association (WNBA) is entering its 10th season and continues to be televised. The ladies' golf and tennis tours appear to be thriving. The ladies' tennis finals in Grand Slam events routinely draw a larger U.S. television audience than the men's finals.

Title IX, the 1972 landmark federal legislation in the United States, mandated that schools receiving federal funds must provide equitable opportunities for men and women in sport. By 1997, a fourfold increase in female participation in sport[2] at the collegiate and scholastic levels was attributed to Title IX (Valentin, 1997). Recent participation figures for the United States show almost 3 million high school girls and 150,000 college women (Hardin, 2005). Approximately, 4,000 women participated in the most recent summer Olympic competition in Greece. Of those, 257 were from the United States, and they medaled in more than 40 events (Shevin & Erickson, 2002).

Yet this dramatic increase in U.S. female participation in competitive sports due to Title IX is under threat as this book goes to press. On March 17, 2005, the U.S. Department of Education issued a clarification to its intercollegiate athletic policy (Sabo & Grant, 2005). The clarification endorsed the use of an online survey as the sole method for assessing student interest in sports and compliance with Title IX. The new guidelines call for a census, whereby all eligible students are contacted and asked to complete a questionnaire. The lack of response can be construed as lack of interest (Sabo & Grant, p. 5).

Despite increased participation of women athletes at all levels, media coverage of men's and women's sports continues to differ significantly. Research on coverage continues to find underrepresentation, "symbolic annihilation" and marginalization, heterosexism, gender stereotyping, and trivialization (Birrell & Theberge, 1994; Duncan & Messner, 1998; Duncan, Messner, & Williams, 1991; Hardin, 2005; Kinnick, 1998; Pedersen, 2002; Salwen & Wood, 1994; Shifflett & Revelle, 1994).

"Eat the Elephant: One Bite at a Time"[3]

For more than three decades, media coverage of women's sports has been a significant area of study. We have counted the number of articles, measured column inches, looked at covers and photographs, timed sports newscasts, and completed semiotic analyses. We have interviewed sports reporters, their bosses, and members of the audience. Reportedly, some studies have even used galvanic response tests. We have presented and published our findings.

What have we found? Below is a concise update on the major, occasionally overlapping, themes of feminist research on media coverage of women's sports.

Underrepresentation: Quality, Not Quantity?

Some progress in the amount of women's sports coverage is being reported by various studies (Bernstein, 2002; Messner, Duncan, & Cooky, 2003). One recent study found that while college newspapers covered men's sports more often than women's, the "quality" of coverage of women's sports was comparable to that of men's (Huffman, Tuggle, & Rosengard, 2004). In terms of quantity, the study found that men's basketball received 5 times the amount of coverage compared with women's basketball, and baseball received twice the coverage of softball.

Another study compared coverage in the *New York Times* and the *Indianapolis Star* in 1989 and 1999 (George, 2002). During the decade reviewed, the *Star*'s coverage of women's sports increased from 2.7% to 8.6%, and the *Times* coverage increased from 2.2% to 6.7% (Kaufman, 2003).

If this rate of increase stays consistent, women's sports can expect equal coverage in only 70 years at the *Star* and in about a century at the *Times*.

Marginalization and "Symbolic Annihilation": Below the Fold

Newspaper editors put important stories "above the fold" to attract customers and to sell papers at newsstands.[4] Studies continue to show that women's sports coverage is not only "below the fold" but is also more than likely "symbolically annihilated" (Tuchman, 1978), which means it is not covered at all or is marginalized by inconsistent coverage. The Houston Comets won the WNBA title from the inception of the league, in 1997, through 2000. The team's experience with the sports media, however, was on the margins. Former WNBA Houston Comets star Cynthia Cooper captured her personal experience with media marginalization as follows:

> I'm a pro athlete. . . . Why should we have to beg and plead for attention? I am so tired of ignorant journalists interviewing me. I'm so tired of being [mistaken for teammate] Sheryl Swoopes. How many NBA players have to deal with that? We're not getting a fair shake. (as quoted in Kaufman, 2003, p. 237)

In addition to being female, Swoopes and Cooper are African American, so Cooper's frustration with the sports media also may include racial discrimination, which has been documented in both men's and women's sports coverage. The Women's Sports Foundation's study *Title IX and Race in Intercollegiate Sport* (2003) documented a dramatic—955% from 1971 to

2000—increase in National Collegiate Athletic Association (NCAA) sports participation for female athletes of color. Yet in the U.S. sports media, women of color receive considerably less coverage than their White female counterparts and are often depicted in a racially stereotypical manner (Leath & Lumpkin, 1992).

Cooper retired after the 2000 season, and there is research to support her frustration. The Project for Excellence in Journalism and the Princeton Survey Research Associates[5] released a study titled *Box Scores and Bylines* in August 2005. The study examined more than 2,000 sports section fronts from 16 papers over 28 randomly selected dates in 2004. Findings posted on their Web site (http://www.journalism.org) show how little overall progress has been made in increasing the coverage of women's sports.

The study first looked at stories on individual athletes. These included stories on athletes as performers as well as personal profiles. Both were disproportionately male dominated. Overall, 35% of all stories on athletes were devoted to men, and just 5% covered women. The study also examined stories on men's and women's sports teams, and the gap in coverage between the two is striking. Whereas a third (33%) of the stories we looked at covered men's teams, a mere 3% dealt with women's teams. The light coverage of female athletes varied little across the different circulation categories. Regardless of circulation size, men consistently dominated.

Heterosexism: Sheryl Swoopes Is a Lesbian

The push for female athletes to emphasize the feminine is not new. The Ladies Professional Golf Association (LPGA) has long been the model. According to Mariah Burton Nelson (1994),

> Sponsors, LPGA staff, and players attempt to eradicate what they delicately call their "image problem" by publicly denying the existence of lesbians on the tour. To this end they play up marriages and mothers, and employ an "image consultant" to serve as hairstylist and makeup artist. (p. 139)

In October 2005, three-time WNBA league Most Valuable Player, four-time league champion with the Houston Comets, and three-time Olympic gold medalist Sheryl Swoopes "came out." She did so in an article for *ESPN The Magazine* (Granderson, 2005). According to the article, she (and her partner) had booked a cruise with Olivia Cruise Lines, which markets to lesbian vacation travelers, made contact with Olivia CEO Amy Errett, and was asked to "be the face of Olivia."

Swoopes's declaration was news, but she wasn't the first female athlete to reveal her sexual orientation. Billie Jean King, Martina Navratilova, and Rosie Jones had declared their sexual orientations years before (Creedon, 1994a).

Although she may be the best-known African American female athlete to "come out," Swoopes's declaration has met with some derision from the gay community: "Just once I'd like to see a gay woman athlete come out WITH-OUT an Olivia endorsement deal on the table" (Robinson, 2005).

Gender Stereotyping: Stop Throwing Like a Girl and Learn How to Dunk

Media coverage of women's sports is stereotyped from the start. The leagues and teams have gender identifiers, for example, the Women's NBA, the Ladies' PGA or Hawkeye Women's Basketball team, but the men's teams do not.

In media coverage of competition, women are implicitly or explicitly compared with male athletes (Dowling, 2000). Study after study continues to find that sports broadcasters describe female athletes differently, and the differences can be traced to gender markings (Billings & Eastman, 2002; Billings, Halone, & Denham, 2002; Eastman & Billings, 2001).

Trivialization: Marketing the Blond, Russian "Ova's"

Anna Kournikova, whose overall tennis record is 186 losses and 124 wins (combining her doubles and singles records), has a winning percentage of 60%. Her highest ranking in singles was eighth, in 2000. Russian-born Kournikova, who has appeared in the *Sports Illustrated* swimsuit issue and on the cover of *Maxim,* has a Web site that boasts naked pictures (http://www .kournikova.com).

Eighteen-year-old Russian-born tennis star Maria Sharapova has combined her beauty with talent. She was the highest-paid female athlete in 2004, with earnings of $23 million (Scott, 2005). She was ranked as the world's #1 female tennis player in 2005. A search for her official Web site (http://www.mariaworld.net) on various search engines resulted in up to 52,000 hits. Sharapova is fast becoming a commodity, however: Sharapova screensavers, Sharapova wallpaper, and Macy's own Sharapova perfume are available for purchase online.[6]

Where Is the Audience?

Coupling tennis with beauty has audience appeal. Kournikova and Sharapova have reinforced it. They have brought in fans and have marketing power. The age-old argument by sports editors is that the readers, the viewers, the fans, and the audience for media coverage of women's sports are missing (Cramer, 1994; Eskenazi, 2003). For media, audience means advertising revenue, and advertising revenue means profit (Coakley, 1990; McKay, Messner, & Sabo, 2000; Pedersen, 2002).

A comprehensive study in Ohio found that although editors at larger papers were better able to predict reader interest, they overestimated interest in five areas, including local sports (Bernt, Gifford, Fee, & Stempel, 2003). The researchers concluded that "news selection driven only by what is interesting is not acceptable, yet what is worse is news decisions justified by 'that's what the public wants' when there is little evidence editors know what the public wants" (p. 10).

Some editors never measure audience interest, but rely on community feedback. In one study (Etling, 2002), less than 10% of editors actually used formal measurement, but these same editors expressed confidence in their perceived knowledge of their audiences. Cramer (1994), who personally interviewed 20 sports editors, also found that they made news selections based on the assumption that they knew their audiences.

Hardin (2005) surveyed editors in the southeastern United States to determine how audience and work routines influenced their coverage decisions. Nearly 64% of editors agreed that coverage of women's sports was important. Yet a substantial percentage held the belief that their women readers were uninterested in women's sports coverage. In study after study, researchers have found that editors believe sports page readers want men's sports news (Salwen & Wood, 1994), so coverage remains the same—reinforcing stereotypes and the status quo (Vincent, Imwold, Johnson, & Massey, 2003). Former *Cleveland Plain Dealer* sports editor Tracy Dodds[7] has said that it is not her job to promote women's sports. Sports editors make decisions based on what's interesting to readers (Skwar, 1999).

Employment: Women in Toyland

For many years, the sports departments of newspapers or broadcast stations were derided by other reporters as "Toyland" or the "toy department" because sports stories and the sports section were viewed as "soft news" or entertainment.

Various studies profiling sports editors continue to describe the sports editor as male, college educated, Protestant, White, with 14 to 15 years of reporting experience (Brookes, 2002; Coakley, 1990; Craft & Wanta, 2004; Cramer, 1994; Garrison & Sabljak, 1993; Hardin, 2005; Nelson, 1994; Pedersen, Whisenant, & Schneider, 2003; Skwar, 1999; Theberge & Cronk, 1986; Vincent et al., 2003). The Associated Press Sports Editors' membership roster clearly shows male domination in sports editing jobs

(Eichenberger, 2004). Most women break into sports reporting by covering boy's high school athletics (Kane & Greendorfer, 1994; Pedersen et al., 2003).

Perhaps even more concerning is the fact that 47% of editors in one survey resented Title IX and indicated that Title IX had damaged men's sports (Hardin, 2005). Overall, studies have shown that gender is a liability for women in sports departments (Ordman & Zillmann, 1994; van Zoonen, 1994).

In 1987, U.S. women in sports journalism decided to form their own organization. They founded the Association for Women in Sports Media (AWSM) in 1987 with 115 members (Cramer, 1994). At the time, only 3% of the nation's 10,000 print and broadcast sports journalists were female. Christine Brennan, then of the *Washington Post,* served a 2-year term as the first AWSM president (Creedon, 1994a). The group's initial focus was threefold: sexual harassment of women sports reporters, salary disparity, and providing scholarship support for young women interested in sports journalism.

Sexual harassment was high on the initial AWSM agenda because of the long history of various locker-room incidents involving female sports reporters. For reporters to be competitive, locker-room access to athletes for interviews after games is critical.

The issue of women sports reporters in the locker room gained visibility when executives at *Sports Illustrated* filed a discrimination suit against Major League Baseball, the American League, and the New York Yankees in 1978 for denying reporter Melissa Ludke access to the locker room during the 1977 World Series (Creedon, 1994a, p. 87; Ricchiardi, 1991). Ludke gained access, but she was defamed and vilified by her male sports journalism colleagues.[8] Her story was followed by a litany of recorded confrontations and unpleasant incidents for other female pioneers in sports journalism.

Most locker rooms are now open to female sports reporters for postgame interviews. Their intrusion upsets the gender order to some extent, but female sports reporters appear to be doing a good job of keeping their eyes above the waist.[9] In off-the-record conversations, however, some have said they would prefer an interview room where both male and female reporters wait until after the athletes have showered, but competition for the "scoop" still prevails.[10]

AWSM now has more than 600 members from all media and public relations organizations (Kaufman, 2003). Over the past 17 years, AWSM has evolved as female sports reporters have risen through the ranks. Joanne Gerstner, a sports writer at the *Detroit News,* is serving her second term as president. She even has a special e-mail address: AWSMprez@aol.com. At the 2005 AWSM convention in San Diego, sessions included the following topics:

1. Performance-Enhancing Drugs and Sports

2. When Sports Goes Off-the-Field: How sports-related stories are handled when they blur the traditional lines of sports news

3. Sports Media Online: How the rise of the Internet has changed sports media

4. Investigative-Reporting Techniques: Using investigative tools to improve reporting skills

5. Freelancing as a Career: Embracing the positive aspects of being your own boss

6. Going X-Treme: The impact of action sports in the media

7. Producing coverage that reflects demographics while attracting younger readers

8. Athletes and Their Causes: Looking beyond the X's and O's for good story ideas

9. The Changing Face of High School Sports: Tackling the evolution and future of high school sports as an industry

10. Breaking Into the Business/Sportswriting 101: Suggestions aimed at getting your foot in the door

11. The Delicate Balance: Juggling life in and out of the office

12. Trends in Broadcasting: Addressing hiring/assigning practices and their effect on sports and sports journalism

13. Copy Desk Coexistence: Working together to overcome the obstacles of producing a daily section

14. Building a Better Public Relations Machine: Forging better connections in a business that is all about relationships

Two sessions dealt specifically with coverage and current issues in women's sport:

1. Title IX Today: 33 years after the landmark legislation was enacted, Title IX remains a hot-button issue. Panelists listed on the program included Scott Reid, moderator, the *Orange County Register* investigative reporter; Steve Butcher, USA Gymnastics junior national team coach; Jen Daniels, San Diego State assistant compliance director; Tracy Dodds, *Indianapolis Star*

enterprise reporter; Judy Sweet, NCAA vice president and former UC–San Diego athletic director; and Lindy Vivas, former Fresno State women's volleyball coach.

2. The Rise and Fall of Women's Sports Leagues: Survival comes easier for some in the world of women's professional sports. Panelists on the program included Linda Reid, moderator, former media relations director for USC athletics, the West Coast Conference, and the American Basketball League's Long Beach Stingrays; David Carter, The Sports Business Group, founder and consultant; Raquel Giscafre, Promotion Sports, Inc., Acura Classic tournament promoter; Aaron Heifetz, U.S. women's national soccer team press officer/former director of communications and player personnel for the Women's United Soccer Association; and Laura Neal, LPGA manager of communications (see http://www.awsmonline.org/).

The mission statement of AWSM adopted in February 2005 reads as follows:

> The Association for Women in Sports Media has the following objectives: to serve as a positive advocate for women in sports media, through support services, networking and national visibility; to mentor and assist young women entering into sports media, through scholarships, internships and contact with experienced members; to serve as a watchdog, promoting fair portrayal of female professionals in sports media, encouraging diversity, positive workplace environments and equal access to opportunities. (ASWM Online, 2005)

The AWSM mission is explicit. The agenda is to help women in Toyland succeed in Toyland. It's about "promoting fair portrayal of female professionals in sports media." It is not to work for equity in media coverage of women's sports.

Perhaps AWSM members have taken Frank Deford's words of advice, which he offered to AWSM members at their 1990 convention:

> I know you struggle . . . and the reason you have to is we men are pigs. It's nothing to be proud of, but that's us. We [men] think we need you for procreation and recreation but we don't need you for sports. We're trying to keep you out and we're going to make it tough on you. (as quoted in Nelson, 1994, p. 238)

So, Deford argues that male sports reporters are pigs. And female sports reporters view "the armies of feminism" as something to distance themselves from, overcome, or ignore if they want successful careers. Where do we go from here?

Acknowledging It's All About Money

The opening quote in this chapter about the pink locker room for visiting football teams in Iowa's Kinnich stadium comes from Sally Jenkins, a columnist for the *Washington Post,* occasional ESPN commentator, and former senior writer for *Sports Illustrated.* It illustrates a sad truth.

In 1996, Jenkins wrote a book titled *Men Will Be Boys: The Modern Woman Explains Football and Other Amusing Male Rituals.* In this "humorous handbook," she argued that women need to stop comparing themselves to men and forget about their concerns when a major university spends $120,000 to change the wood paneling in the office of a head football coach from oak to mahogany. A decade later, she has reinforced the same position on the "pink-locker-room issue" at The University of Iowa.

The pink-locker-room controversy is part of an $88 million renovation of the university's football stadium—yes, 88 million dollars (some unconfirmed estimates run as high as $120 million). Add to this the fact that The University of Iowa football coach has an annual salary of $1.2 million dollars—with endorsement deals, it may run as high as $2 million during a winning season. Contrast this with the salary of the president of The University of Iowa, who is a both an engineer and an MD and earns less than $300,000.

Jenkins knows the score; she doesn't need electrodes glued to her head as she suggested in the opening quote. That's why her comments are especially damaging as she supports the status quo in her national column by trivializing the locker room controversy (a Google search for "pink locker room" on November 25, 2005, resulted in more than 340,000 hits).[11] She has argued that the women's sports movement doesn't know what it wants: "Perfect equality? Separate equality? Virtual equality? Mostly, it seems like what we want is a Sort of Equality But Strictly on Our Own Terms" (Jenkins, 1996, p. 205).

Slightly more than three decades after Title IX, the varnish is off, and the tide has turned. With a few notable exceptions, ideas about equity in sport as well as equality in media coverage of women in sports are part of a bygone era.

The relationship between media and sport is a business deal. Unfortunately, it appears that women, who have fought their way in and up, understand the equation all too well: It's all about the money.

The conclusion is clear. Media coverage of women's sports is about as good as it is going to be for a long time to come unless something changes. And fans, parents, administrators, teachers, faculty—and some male athletes—are joining with feminists who are concerned about the role, cost, and value of sport in modern society. This coalition may have the potential to change the equation.

Notes

1. This chapter focuses on the status of women in U.S. sports journalism. It also does not specifically address gender and race as separate categories. In fact, very little has been done on this intersection. It is ripe for further study.

2. The term *sport* is used in this chapter to refer to the sociocultural institution. The term *sports* refers to activities or games that are components of the institution (Creedon, 1994b).

3. This quote was attributed to Bill Bowlsby, athletic director at the University of Iowa, in a *New York Times* article about reforming NCAA Division I-A sports. The story focused on reactions to a resolution passed by the faculty, which formed a Steering Committee of the Coalition on Intercollegiate Athletics (see http://www.uiowa.edu/facsen/Athletics/Coalition.htm).

4. The phrase "above the fold" is now being used by some to describe the top part of a Web page.

5. From the Web site: "The Project for Excellence in Journalism was created in September 1996 to develop initiatives that would clarify ways journalists could better do their job. It received initial funding from the Pew Charitable Trusts for 3 years in June 1997 and a second round of funding from the Trusts for 3 more years in March 2000. The Project administers the Committee of Concerned Journalists from its offices in Washington. Its affiliate, NewsLab, received its initial funding from the Park Foundation."

6. As of November 2005, Dodds is a sports enterprise reporter at the *Indianapolis Star*.

7. Let's not forget the other Russian tennis "ova's," Martina Navratilova and now, Svetlana Kuznetsova. Svetlana, who won five doubles titles with partner Martina in 2003, was the 2004 U.S. Open Champion, but then became embroiled in a drug controversy when she tested positive for ephedrine (Lyon, 2005). Described as "stocky" in some media reports, she bemoans the fact that Russian President Vladimir Putin didn't call to congratulate her when she won the U.S. Open title though he had called Sharapova after her Wimbledon victory!

8. A partial chronology of locker-room incidents from 1975 to 1992 involving female sports reporters can be found in *Women, Media, and Sport* (Creedon, 1994a).

9. A Web site (http://www.sensations4women.com/fem/Reporters/) shows graphic images of female sports reporters in locker rooms, along with some links to stories written by female college sportswriters recounting their experience in the male locker room. The host or sponsor of the site cannot be documented.

10. Ironically, as long as covering women's sports continues to be less important for the sports page, the women's locker room has not created an equal firestorm.

11. The visitor's locker room at Iowa had been painted pink since 1979. Coach Hayden Fry claimed that pink was a pacifying color and that a passive team might be a losing team. However, Fry indicated in his autobiography, *High Porch Picnic*

(Fry & Wine, 1999), that he did think pink was a "sissy" color often found in girls' bedrooms.

Questions for Discussion

1. How would you assess the media coverage of women's sports in your area?
2. Should media coverage of men's and women's teams be equal? Why or why not?
3. Should women sports reporters be active in promoting the coverage of women's sports?
4. Do you think the recent clarification of Title IX issues by the U.S. Department of Education will help or hurt women's sports?
5. How would you assess the media coverage of the pink-locker-room controversy at the University of Iowa?

Accessing Additional Information

Associated Press Sports Editors: (http://www.apse.com)

Association for Women in Sports Journalism: http://www.awsmonline.org/

Center for Research on Physical Activity, Sport, and Health: http://www.dyc.edu/crpash/history.html

Center for Sports Journalism at Penn State: http://www.psu.edu/dept/comm/sports/index.html

Project for Excellence in Journalism and Princeton Survey Research Associates: http://www.journalism.org/resources/research/reports/sports/ www.womenssportsnet.com

Title IX history: http://www.bailiwick.lib.uiowa.edu/ge/aboutRE.html

University of Minnesota Tucker Center for Research on Women and Girls in Sport: http://www.education.umn.edu/tuckercenter/

Women's Sports Foundation: http://www.womenssportsfoundation.org

PART IV

International Perspectives

14

Three Steps Forward and Two Back?

Women Journalists in the Western World Between Progress, Standstill, and Retreat

Romy Fröhlich, Ludwig-Maximilians-University Munich

M edia have a defining power, whether we like it or not. Thus, the people who make decisions about media content, may it be news or entertainment, have defining power. In democracies, the participation of (all) different social groups in this power may be seen as an important criterion for the democratic character of their media. Hence, a lack of women in media should be seen as a serious problem for modern democratic media around the world. What can current surveys from different countries concretely tell us about the professional situation of female journalists? Does the individual perception of women journalists as it is represented in the International Women's Media Foundation (IWMF) surveys really correspond with the "empirical" reality? Can we identify differences between countries? I will try to answer these questions by presenting relevant empirical data and statistics from different Western countries. The limitation of this international comparison to only Western countries is necessary because there are completely different journalistic traditions, media markets, and political systems (including totalitarian ones) around the world. Those differences make international comparisons difficult. Thus, one should compare countries with, to some extent, similar political systems (democracies with a free press), similar journalistic traditions, and similar media markets.

Against this formal background, a comparative overview about Western countries in North America and Europe makes the most sense. Thus, this contribution deals with the following West European countries: Austria, Finland, France, Germany, Italy, The Netherlands, and the United Kingdom. Wherever it makes sense, the situations in these countries are compared with facts and data for Canada and the United States. Due to the fact that in Israel, respective research and statistics are available for the first time now, I included this country in my selection—all the more considering that Israel is a member of the so-called first world but at the same time is a country "in between": "in between" different cultures and cultural traditions, "in between" continents, and "in between" an ongoing struggle between modern and traditional values. All together, the selection in this contribution is somewhat narrow in the sense that it focuses on women journalists in Western nations plus Israel, yet it is also broad because it covers nations on three continents and draws on different traditions of dealing with the topic.

Whereas the United States and Canada have since the mid-1970s investigated the development and the status quo of the situation of female journalists in their countries, respective research with original and reliable data is still not available for a lot of European countries. This is true above all for countries in Southern, Central, and Eastern Europe and means another limitation to the choices to report on for this chapter. In the majority of countries, including, for example, Germany, the National/Federal/Central Bureaus of Statistics do not classify a distinct occupational category of "journalists." Thus, the knowledge about this professional group stems from union statistics or individual surveys by communication researchers. In most countries, the latest surveys and research data available stem from the 1990s. This decade seems to be the period of time in which the question of women in journalism was most prominent. Thus, while some European countries have not yet discovered the topic as a relevant one, other countries seem to already be losing interest in the issue, a strange situation. Furthermore, the research on female journalists in Europe does not address issues of diversity such as race, ethnicity, sexual orientation, and disability. Perhaps it is due to the extremely low number of female immigrant journalists in Europe that this topic has not yet been discovered as relevant in the "Old World."

What Surveys Tell Us: General Findings

In the market economies of Western Europe and North America and after the democratization in Eastern Europe, the communications sector has substantially increased. This development had been expedited through the fundamental deregulation of the European broadcasting market since the early 1980s. Women seem to have benefited from this rapid development, since in the respective countries, the share of female journalists and media professionals did steadily increase (Fröhlich & Lafky, in press; Gallagher, 1992, 1995a). According to international studies of the IWMF (1996, 1998, 2001), however, an overwhelming majority of women journalists worldwide agreed that women journalists face professional barriers that their male colleagues do not and that the top obstacle for women in management is continually proving their abilities to colleagues and supervisors. What makes this even more of a challenge, respondents said, is that their male colleagues do not believe this to be true. At the same time, the majority is convinced that women in media make a difference and that the news would be different if more women held leadership positions in media companies.

While on one hand, women seem to have benefited from the rapid development of the media market, it has been also been argued that

> New technologies, the Single European Market, unemployment and changing work patterns have all influenced some of the radical changes occurring in the media industry in the European Union, often with negative consequences for women. Among these changes are: a large increase in the importance of commercial broadcasting companies more responsive to the market than to public scrutiny; a rise in the share of independent production companies; steadily decreasing permanent, full-time staff and a growing number of short-term or freelance contracts, often hired directly by individual units so that no centralized personnel records of these workers are held; and major restructuring within public broadcasting companies, thus making equal opportunity issues a low priority. (International Labour Office, 2004, p. 81)

When American researchers and professionals at the end of the 1980s predicted that in the United States in less than a decade, the mass media and related communication fields such as public relations would be predominantly female, the European field had just begun to gather data and facts. Against the backdrop of the substantial amount of research she has conducted around the world during a couple of decades, Margaret Gallagher has spoken of an "undeniable fact" when showing that in many Western countries (Western and Northern Europe and North America)[1] increasing numbers of women have entered the journalistic professions. She has described this development as the "apparently logical result of the gradual influx of women into higher education, training, and the professions in general, and into journalism in particular" (Gallagher, in press). But she has indicated that certain structural and market-determined factors are responsible for the increasing share of female journalists in media around the world and, among others, has especially identified the search for new (female) audiences as an important aspect. Relating to the latter and referring to van Zoonen's (1991) "tyranny of intimacy," she has observed a general trend of the media to expand their feature-length documentary content and to "humanize" or to "femininize" the news through a more personalized, "intimate" style of journalism. This may influence young women with their decisions to become journalists, and it also might lead chief executives to hire more women. Gallagher has warned of taking this development as good news. For her, it is not the "happy ending" to the struggle for more gender equality in journalism and the media, but rather more of a "temporary confluence of factors within a dynamic and fluid profession that, in terms of decision-making and managerial power, is still largely dominated by men" (Gallagher, in press).

Meanwhile, in the United States, women are no longer progressing in journalism. The latest study (Weaver, Beam, Brownlee, Voakes, & Wilhoit, 2003b) found the share of women even decreasing, from 34% to 33% in all areas of journalism in the United States. This means a standstill since 1982, despite the fact that in the United States, more women than ever are graduating from journalism schools and entering the profession. Is this the result of the media crisis that has brought more international competition among global media players, decreasing revenues from advertising, the decline of independent media organizations, declining circulation, an aging readership, the increasing influence on journalistic skills of technology, and the outsourcing of journalists? We don't know yet.

While in the United States, the traditional journalists are getting older (Weaver et al., 2003b), the journalistic population worldwide is still experiencing a rejuvenation, and this is true in particular for female journalists. In every country of my compilation, female journalists are younger than male journalists, and almost everywhere, 50% or more of the under-25 age group of journalists are women. In Finland, which has one of the highest proportion of female journalists worldwide (51%), women represent 65% of journalists age 20 to 29 years old. With increasing age, this figure decreases steadily, however, and in the 60- to 65-year-old age group, women represent 44% of the Finnish journalists. Still, this is probably the greatest share of women journalists in this age group worldwide. In general, however, the pattern is always the same: The younger the journalists and the shorter the

Table 14.1   Overall Share of Women in the Respective National Journalism Workforces

Country	Overall Share of Women Journalists (%)		
Republic of Austria	26		
Canada	33		
Finland	51		
France	39		
Federal Republic of Germany[1]	West: 25	East I: 30	East II: 36
Israel	37		
Italy	28		
The Netherlands	33		
United Kingdom	30		
United States	33		

SOURCE: Author's compilation from Fröhlich and Lafky (in press).

1. East I: Place of residence before reunification in West Germany; East II: Place of residence before reunification in the former German Democratic Republic.

respective time of experience in the field, the greater the share of women among them.

In the majority of Western countries, journalism continues to be a male-dominated profession.[2] In addition, women still have little decision-making power inside media organizations. According to a survey of the International Federation of Journalists (IFJ), the average percentage of women journalists in general around the world was 27% in 1990. Ten years later, a replication of this study found that about 38% of journalists were women (IFJ, 2001). The percentage of female editors, heads of departments, and media owners, however, was only 0.6%. According to the same study, in Europe, the share of women journalists was about 40%. Of these, only 3% were in decision-making positions. Forty percent as an average for Europe doesn't sound too bad—however, this average figure hides the striking differences between countries (see Table 14.1).

Finland has by far the highest share of female journalists (51%) in Europe and abroad (United States and Canada). In Finland, the equal share of women in journalism was exceeded for the first time in 1996. Finnish researchers explain this interesting exception to the rule with the relatively strong position of women in Finnish society in general. This position and the balanced representation of women in Finnish society and politics, however, is not the result of feminist action. Classical feminism is not a strong movement in Finland, nor has feminism been part of the mainstream debates in society. Instead, the exceptional situation of women in Finnish society is, rather, the result of confidence in a long-lasting official equality policy, the so-called state feminism, which led to the integration of women into the public sphere (Zilliacus-Tikkanen, in press).

At the end of the ranking list are Germany and Austria. Germany seems to be a particularly negative example: Here, the percentage of female journalists only increased from 17% in the early 1980s (Neverla & Kanzleiter, 1984) to 25% in the early 1990s (Schneider, Schönbach, & Stürzebecher, 1993). At the same time, the proportion of female journalism students and journalism trainees increased much more, to between 47% and 61%, depending on the respective educational model and the media type (Fröhlich & Holtz-Bacha, in press).

Average percentages, however, hide considerable differences among different media. Those media-related differences can be found in all countries. However, the patterns are not always the same. Table 14.2 illustrates the shares of women journalists in different types of media. Unfortunately, respective data are not available for each country. Furthermore, the data in the respective countries have not always been gathered in the same pattern. For example, some do not differentiate within the print sector between dailies and special interest magazines, others do not differentiate within the TV sector between public and private broadcasting, and so on. Thus, a direct comparison of data is again difficult but nevertheless gives an interesting impression.

Educational Situation and Overall Share of Female Journalists

As early as 1989, UNESCO's (United Nations Educational, Scientific, and Cultural Organization) first World Communication Report showed that the proportion of female journalism students was much higher then the share of female journalists in the professional field itself. In her work for UNESCO, Gallagher (1995b) showed that in most industrialized countries, the predominance of female students in mass communication courses stretches back to at least 1980. Splichal and Sparks (1994) found in their study, carried out in 26 countries, that the average percentage of female students of journalism was about 40% during the mid-1990s. In some countries, women accounted for up to 70% of the journalism students (United States, Bulgaria, Mexico). With the exception of France and Italy, where men and women share equal proportions on the educational level, women outnumber men in mass communication classrooms and also in some on-the-job training programs. In Israel, for example, women currently make up 80% of communication students and 60% of trainees at on-the-job training programs (Lachover, in press). Moreover, the international comparison shows not only that the proportion

Table 14.2   Share of Women Journalists in Different Types of Media

Country	Share of Women (%)						
	Public Broadcasting	Private TV	Private Radio	Newspapers	Magazines	News Agencies	Media Services
Austria[1]	26		18	26			
Canada	37			28			
Finland	40*	40*					
France	33			33[2]	50		
Germany[3]	28	38	41	27	42	25	44
Israel[4]				39			
Italy	"Strongly underrepresented"			19	40	"Strongly under-represented"	
The Netherlands	35	49					
United Kingdom	36	35		22[5]			
United States	37[6]	22		33	44[7]	20	

SOURCE: Author's compilation from Fröhlich & Lafky (in press).
*TV presenters only (Lynggard, 2002).

1. So far, Austria has no own private TV stations. The major private programs from Germany are available for the audience in Austria.

2. Parisian dailies only. At regional dailies, the ratio is 4.6 men to 1 woman (Neveu, in press).

3. Figures stem from Weischenberg et al. (1994).

4. Only a small number of women are working at Israeli television and radio stations (Lachover, in press).

5. With big differences among the respective dailies. The shares range from 13% at the *Daily Mail* to 36% at the *Independent* and the *Sunday Telegraph* (Christmas, in press).

6. The percentage of women on television news staff is even higher: 40% (Papper, 2003).

7. Newsmagazines only. Share of women journalists at weekly newspapers: 37% (Weaver et al., 2003b).

of female journalists with a university degree is much higher than that of males but also that female journalists have better grades than their male counterparts. In addition, the proportion of male journalists with no formal education is higher than that of female journalists.

With respect to this, the situation in the German public broadcasting sector seems to be particularly negative: Here, the gender switch among practical trainees took place as early as 1986 (Hessischer Rundfunk, 1987–2004). Since then, the proportion of female trainees continuously increased, from 52% in 1986 to 65% in 2004 (Fröhlich & Holtz-Bacha, in press). In contrast to this, women still represent only 28% of journalists at German public broadcasting stations (Weischenberg, Keuneke, Löffelholz, & Scholl, 1994, p. 19). The situation is even more astonishing when we take into consideration that public broadcasters are the only media organizations with affirmative action and equal opportunity plans. In Germany, those action plans are adopted by private companies only on a voluntary basis.

Today, we know that we cannot count on causal relations between the development in the educational/training sector, on one hand, and the circumstances in the professional field, on the other. The prognosis that women's share of jobs in journalism would gradually increase due to the very high numbers of women at the educational level has not come true. Instead, worldwide, the extent of this increase is far behind what was expected.

Hierarchy, Beats, Autonomy, and Equal Pay

The relatively inferior status of women is reflected in the significant difference in the jobs they hold compared with male journalists. The international comparison of studies from the different countries clearly shows that everywhere, women are more likely to cover and edit beats that are considered "soft" (e.g., lifestyle, health, education) and men are more likely to cover and edit beats considered to be "hard" (e.g., politics, business, economics, etc.). None of the countries compiled here is an exception to this rule, not even Finland. Needless to say, the salaries paid for "soft beats" are well below those paid for "hard beats"—and below even the average journalist's salary.

As for the hierarchical position, we again have the same picture everywhere: The majority of women are found in lower positions. In Austria, for example, 16% of the editors-in-chief, 20% of the leading editors, and 23% of the heads of department are female (Karmasin, 1996). For Germany, we have the most detailed data on the basis of types of media (see Figure 14.1).

What Milly Buonanno (in press) has written with respect to Italian women journalists is also true for the other countries:

> The distribution of editorial power between men and women shows proof of a sharp, although discontinuous, mismatch. This is shown by the low female proportions at the highest levels of career and power. . . . Plus, it is worth noting here that this sexual difference related to career access has not been subject to a significant change since the mid-nineties. In other words, even though numerous, visible and lastly appreciated [in Italy], women journalists are still widely excluded from the allocation of resources of authority and power. We could, therefore, say that in the imbalance between high visibility on the one

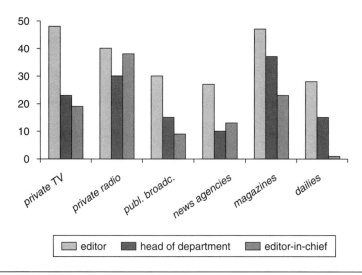

Figure 14.1   Share of Women Among German Heads of Department and Editors-in-Chief (Percentage)

SOURCE: Weischenberg et al. (1994).

hand, and low power on the other lies the key to understanding the present conditions of women in [Italian] journalism.

Another "pattern" is also proved internationally: As a result of attitudes of male decision makers and of women's minority status, which makes them "special" and permanent "standouts," female journalists experience greater control through their supervisors and colleagues (Lavie, 2004; Löfgren Nilsson, 1993). This, too, can be a career obstacle for women in the field and derogates their professional autonomy as journalists. Einat Lachover (in press) examined these circumstances in detail for Israel and found interesting results: Women were more likely than men (68% to 59%) to say they have less freedom in selecting their stories; and women were less likely than men (53% to 58%) to say their stories undergo little or no editing. In addition, more female than male editors (39% to 25%) responded that their work is subjected to further editing.

In Europe, virtually all countries have laws on equal pay, as do the United States (the Equal Pay Act and the Civil Rights Act) and Canada. However, it is easy for employers to circumvent such laws by simply giving men and women different working descriptions or titles even though they are doing the same work. This allows for different salaries (IFJ, 2001, p. 9), No wonder, then, that in practically every Western country for which data are available, female journalists suffer from salary inequalities (Gallagher 1995a; International Labour Office, 1996; Robinson & Saint-Jean 1997; Schneider et al., 1993; Weaver & Wilhoit, 1996). Some national studies show that salary inequalities between male and female journalists in Europe cannot be fully explained by age differences, differences in total working hours, or factors such as professional experience and hierarchical levels (Lealand, 1994; Zilliacus-Tikkanen, in press). A German study (Schneider et al., 1993, p. 17) found that the difference in salary increases even more when statistically considering variables such as women's shorter periods of permanent or uninterrupted employment, hierarchical positions, and age.

Despite the fact that Finland has the highest share of female journalists, it is not an exception to the rule concerning the salary gap. At present, female journalists' salaries in Finland, on average, are still only 86% of the men's, with the press being the sector with the smallest salary gap (89%) and the commercial TV sector having the biggest gap (85%). Finnish studies also show that differences in salary do not disappear with more working experience. To the contrary, those differences are small during the first 5 years in the field, but they increase with growing experience. Even women who have been in the field for more than 20 years earn significantly less money than men with comparable experience. Finnish studies have also proved that there is no salary difference between women with children and those without and that gender in general is the most explanatory variable for salary gaps (Zilliacus-Tikkanen, in press).

The average salary gaps in European countries are comparatively similar and range from 18% in France (Neveu, in press) to 12% in the United Kingdom (Christmas, in press). When comparing this with figures for North America (20% in Canada) and Israel (20%), women journalists in Europe seem to suffer less from big salary gaps. The really bad news, however, is that in Europe, the average income gap between female and male journalists is increasing rather than decreasing. This is especially the case for Sweden and the United Kingdom (International Labour Office, 1996) as well as for Austria (Dorer, in press). One reason for this negative development might be the deregulation of the broadcasting market during the mid- and late 1980s and, with it, the growing global competition as well as the still ongoing media crisis. The growing global competition might have resulted in decreasing salaries for journalists in general, which became most relevant for the younger generation and thus for the women who long since have been the majority among entrants. In addition, what might affect the growing salary gap is the fact that young female journalists were and still are more willing than male entrants to work within the growing fields of human interest and soft news. Both sectors are known as beats with low professional status, low image, and low salaries.

As a result of deregulation and growing competition, many European broadcasting companies reduced their workforces during the 1990s, especially public broadcasters. This downsizing probably was to the disadvantage of the women in the market, especially young women. Because they are young, because they are female, and because they have not yet worked a long time in the media, they are forced to newly negotiate their permanent employment and salaries with their employers. And they are the first to be fired. Due to the fact that almost everywhere in Europe, women journalists are the majority at the entry-level positions or at least represent half of the young working journalists with up to 5 years of experience, this new market situation might have had an important effect on the growing salary gap between (young) women and (older) men. There is evidence for this explanation from the recent study of the International Labour Office (2004, p. 84): While the ongoing media crisis in Europe makes things even worse for female journalists today, compared with women, men tend to remain more fully self-employed in media and entertainment.

Equal Opportunities and Affirmative Action Policy

When it comes to equal opportunity, the interesting question is whether special policy and action plans are effective. Looking at different countries, the answer is not easy. In Germany, for example, affirmative action plans were established by law at the end of the 1980s; however, they apply only to the public service media sector. Nevertheless, in Germany, we can look back to a certain time of translating these plans into action. However, comparing the present proportion of female journalists at public broadcasting stations with the percentage of women at private media organizations, where equality policies are still rare, one must decide that affirmative action and equal opportunity plans in Germany not only did not help with the problem, but seemingly even hindered progress: The public broadcasters have the lowest share of female journalists. With the exception of dailies (27%) and news agencies (25%), all private media in Germany have a much higher proportion of female journalists than do public broadcasters (28%).[3] This corresponds with women's share among editors-in-chief and senior editors: Again, with the exception of dailies (1%), public broadcasters in Germany have the lowest share of women among editors-in-chief (9%),[4] and with the exception of news agencies (10%), they together with dailies have the lowest share of female senior editors (15%).[5] From the German perspective, affirmative action seems to be problematic. Wetterer (1994) wrote that those plans and programs "make the 'women's question' nothing more than a troublesome, annoying administrative affair, which gets on all persons' nerves, swallows time and money and at the same time everything stands as it was" (p. 93).

There are, however, also positive examples that allow for the conclusion that action and equality plans might actually be effective: Gallagher (1995b) identified Belgium, Denmark, Italy, Luxembourg, Portugal, and the United Kingdom as countries where respective laws had a positive impact on the improvement of the professional situation of female journalists. Characteristic of the action and equality plans or laws in those countries is that they also apply to private commercial broadcasters. For example, the Broadcasting Act of 1990 in the United Kingdom requires that the commercial channels provide an annual statement to the Independent Television Commission of action taken to support equal opportunities. This requirement is a condition of their licenses. However, the Broadcasting Act in the United Kingdom, like most other comparable action plans, does not apply to the constantly growing independent suppliers of licensed media organizations.

Meanwhile, the IFJ noticed the worldwide standstill in equality plans and recently launched an international action plan aimed at challenging policies and practices that are contrary to gender equity within mass media, arguing,

> In all areas of media—including within the associations and unions that represent women—there needs to be a cultural shift that will put women into the picture. It is vital that the twenty-first century media challenge the practices and outdated social traditions that restrict the rights of girls and women to play an equal role at work and in society. (IFJ, 2004)

This argument tries to tie up to the presumption that a higher share of female journalists will not only change media content but also enhance the professional situations of women, hamper discrimination, and thus contribute to more equality between men and women. As the Finnish example clearly exemplifies, however, there is no correlation between a high or even more-than-balanced representation of female journalists in the field, on one hand, and professional equality between men and women, on the other.

Explaining Disappearance and Discrimination: The "Friendliness Trap"

The results from international surveys as well as national ones, as briefly described, summarized, and compared in this chapter, suggest that we cannot take the mere increase of women in Western media as a sign of progress and of more gender equality in Western journalism (see also Gallagher, 2002, pp. 6–7). In contrast, it seems that opportunities for advancement have not improved for female journalists around the world and over the course of time. For example, comparing the high shares of women at all institutions of journalism education in different countries with the still-missing gender switch among journalists around the world, an open question remains: Where do all the women go? And what exactly are the reasons for the obstinate "glass ceiling" effect in journalism worldwide? At first glance, the reasons behind women's "disappearing act" in communications professions don't seem much different from well-known reasons that hinder women in the professional world in general: starting a family and the associated responsibilities of raising children, "double shifts" in career and home, and lack of support from home (cf. Gallagher, 1981; Grunig, 1989; Lafky, 1991; Rakow, 1989a; van Zoonen, 1994).

These well-known reasons, however, are not the only ones. For example, they do not apply to women without families and without children. In addition, we know that not having "double shifts" in career and home doesn't really help with the problem. Thus, I would like to direct attention to another possible cause and argue that in the course of their careers, women in communications professions, such as journalism and public relations, more and more become victims of a "friendliness trap." I will now explain what I mean by this. Against the backdrop of already-mentioned market-driven aspects within the media market, women "content producers" have become most wanted. One could say feminine skills and values have been legitimized and women have been praised as the "better communicators." Within this context, supposedly feminine characteristics and behaviors such as honesty, fairness, morality, empathy, thoughtfulness, "natural" intuition, and a special talent for dealing with people are considered to be ideal qualifications that obviously cannot be learned.[6] With respect to the changing concept of journalism and because of the very special gender role expectations linked to this concept, young women frequently and increasingly choose the profession, which is deemed "appropriate" for their sex.

As a result of the thesis that women are better communicators, however, more importance will be attached to gender as a social category and it will once again be linked to strict, culturally determined stereotypes, which more than likely determine women's professional behavior as journalists. This could manifest as, for example, women journalists being assigned to subjects and beats that are "appropriate" for their gender and being expected to remain within the confines of these prescribed roles. In addition, one should not forget that those "exceptional" female communication skills are nothing more than the (not always fully conscious) learned use of particular behaviors and strategies. These strategies help women to maintain a harmonious atmosphere during the communication process in order to achieve personal goals and prosper within the given system. Research conducted by behavioral scientists refers to such behavior as "conciliatory gestures" (Alfermann, 1996, p. 140). Thus, women's cooperative behavior (= "better communicator") is the result of their limited social power, while the hierarchical and direct behavior of men is a result of their greater dominance and status (Henley, 1977).

Attempts to deviate from these prescribed gender-related behavioral patterns will, in all probability, be sanctioned. Thus, the vicious circle emerges involving the "better communicator": The concept of the new market-driven journalism allows women more access to communication professions at the entry level because of the very "feminine" skills they possess. For example, media owners and employers, in the struggle for higher circulation and larger audiences, began to shape their products toward more human interest and thus discovered the female audience. They might be more interested than ever in the so-called female view, which they believe can be best mirrored by female journalists. However, women's "feminine" skills obviously do not have a significant influence on how long women remain in the profession or how far they will be able to advance. Instead, women still drop out of media careers. This is because, in all probability, sooner or later in women's journalism careers, the supposed feminine values, attributes, and behaviors will be associated with a lack of assertiveness, poor conflict management, and weak leadership skills. And suddenly, the apparent head start turns out to be a "career killer." I call the whole process a "friendliness trap" (Fröhlich, 2004).

The international comparison of data and facts on the professional situation of female journalists gives a lot of examples that allow for a pessimistic rather than an optimistic prognosis. Thus, it remains a mystery that according to the latest survey of the IWMF (2001), the majority of international respondents (84%) said that despite the obstacles they described, they were optimistic about women's contributions to the future of the media and the resulting positive changes that women in the media will bring to society. I hope this book will inform the profession that the "feminization of journalism" is a myth: While making three steps forward in the 1980s, female journalists throughout the world have taken two steps backward since the mid 1990s.

Notes

1. This refers to Western and North Europe and North America. According to Gallagher, the situation in Central and Eastern Europe as well as in Africa, Asia, and in much of Latin America is still very different.

2. The only exception to the rule is TV presenters (Spears & Seydegart, 2001). According to Gallagher (1995b), in almost every one of the 91 European broadcasting organizations studied between 1990 and 1995, women were overrepresented as presenters and announcers (overall share of jobs, 38%; share of female presenters and announcers, 44%).

3. Private radio, 38%; private TV, 41%; magazines, 42%; local magazines, 48%; media services, 44%; news agencies, 25% (Weischenberg et al., 1994).

4. Private radio, 38%; private TV, 19%; magazines, 23%; local magazines, 31%; media services, 29%; news agencies, 13% (Weischenberg et al., 1994).

5. Private radio: 30%; private TV: 23%; magazines: 37%; local magazines: 20%; media services: 55% (Weischenberg et al., 1994).

6. See Aldoory and Toth (2001). With respect to the communication profession "public relations," Aldoory (1998) outlined her "feminist model of leadership" in public relations. Grunig, Toth, and Hon (2000) referred to a "revolution of the heart."

Questions for Discussion

1. Why does the success of affirmative action plans vary from country to country, and what is the secret of successful affirmative action?

2. What makes media professions so attractive to young women? What influences their decisions (in comparison with young males) to become journalist practitioners?

3. What would be an empirical verification/falsification of the theory of the "friendliness trap"?

4. What are the effects of the ongoing deregulation of the broadcasting market in Europe, the growing global competition, and the ongoing media crisis for the situation of female (compared with male) media professions?

5. What are the reasons for the still existing and in some countries even growing salary gap between female and male journalists, and what can/must be done to close this gap?

Accessing Additional Information

Association for Women in Sports Media: http://www.awsmonline.org/

Association for Women Journalists: http://www.awjdfw.org/ and http://www.awjchicago.org/

German Association of Gay and Lesbian Journalists (German version only): http://www.blsj.de/

German Women Journalists Association (English version): http://www.journalistinnen.de/wir/english/index.html

Girls, Women + Media Project: http://www.mediaandwomen.org/

International Women's Media Foundation (IWMF): http://www.iwmf.org/

Journalism & Women Symposium (JAWS): http://www.jaws.org/

Library of Congress Online-Exhibition: http://www.loc.gov/exhibits/wcf/

WomenAction: http://www.womenaction.org

Women's Institute for Freedom of the Press (WIFP): http://www.wifp.org/

15

Bewitched, Bedeviled, and Left Behind

Women and Mass Communication in a World of Faith

Debra L. Mason, Religion Newswriters Association

When Pope John Paul II died on April 3, 2005, the online database Nexis archived 552 stories announcing the pontiff's death.[1] Many of the stories recorded with precision the names of everyone who was in the room when he died, with the exception of three nuns. Of the world's 1.1 billion Roman Catholics, these Polish sisters were perhaps the closest to being family for the pontiff, having served as his personal assistants for much of his papacy. Their superior, Sister Tobiana Sobadka, also present at his death, was named in 4 of the 552 stories.

Who were these anonymous women who had shared John Paul II's most intimate circle? How did they interact with the pope and what, if any, influence did they have in church matters? How did they express grief and pain at their loss? It's doubtful we will ever know.

"Left behind"[2] aptly describes the characterization of women in faith and values news across the globe. Although women make up half the world's population—and with religion at the center of many world crises and practiced by about 85% of the earth's inhabitants—analysis of themes about women, media, and religion are difficult to find and are lacking in sufficient academic heft to create a meaningful body of research.

The reliance of mass media on political officials for most of its news sources is well documented. Religion news is similarly focused on officialdom. Just as government posts are dominated by men, so too is the leadership of all major world religions—either by decree, as in the case of the Roman Catholic Church, Orthodox Christianity, Orthodox Judaism, and most of Islam, or in practice, as in the case of most other faith communities, with the exception of goddess religions, paganism, and Native American spirituality.[3]

With women prohibited from ordination or other significant leadership roles in organized religious institutions, the possibilities for prominence and public visibility of women are rare in current power structures. In addition, religious imagery in documentaries and photographs is limited by gender separation that occurs as a part of religious observance. This is particularly true in mosques and in Orthodox Jewish synagogues. In both cases, women are generally seated separately from men, either on the side or in the rear. As a result, imagery focusing on religious leaders may omit women attending religious observances, diminishing their visible presence as either practitioners or participants.

While there has been much work done on media and culture, and religion and culture, both theoretical groundings and research have rarely progressed to what Hoover and Lundby (1997) called a "triangulation" of theories, in which media, religion, and culture are considered an interrelated web within society. The inclusion of a gender component to such an integrated theoretical framework further complicates the existence of already-limited work.

For example, in religious contexts, as in political ones, women (like men) are held hostage to existing power structures. But in religious contexts, unlike politically focused challenges to male hegemony, women's quest for eternity, some ultimate peace, and obedience to God are the prizes risked by radicalism. In such a worldview, where emotions and psychology play a role, information, the media, or communication are not necessarily the missing keys to empowering women. Even new information communication technologies (ICTs) are of less value than in other contexts in advancing a cause of increased participation by the world's women of faith in their religious communities. But a dearth of research into the topic makes such conclusions tepid at best.

God, Gender, and Islam

The only topic receiving much scholarship on women and religion in an international context is that examining the coverage of Islam.[4] Research suggests that news reports about Islamic women often focus on dress or domestic rights.[5] Another theme is analysis of stereotyping as it applies to female Arab Americans and Muslims.[6] Scholarship has also looked at the rhetoric used when describing female terrorists versus their male counterparts. Western media coverage of women bombers uses different explanations for their participation than the adoption of ideological statements used by men.[7]

The most detailed quantitative study of Muslim women to date is not about their presence in the Middle East, but rather how Muslim women are represented in the British Press. Elizabeth Poole (2002) found that women were marginalized and rarely presented as authority figures. Male Christians were more likely than female Muslims to appear in press articles on British Islam, Poole found. "What is clear . . . is that even when discussing customary female roles and topics, women are marginalized to the traditional, private sphere in the coverage of British Muslim." (Poole, 2002, p. 92). That marginalization of women—to feature articles, stories on relationships, and topics of private matters—holds consistent with women of other faiths as well. Poole left it unresolved as to whether this was a reflection of Muslim values and hierarchy, Western journalistic values, press framing of Islam, or some combination of these factors.

Asia: Religious Persecution and Benign Neglect

Media, religion, and gender issues as manifest in Asian countries are unexplored. One likely reason is because communism in several Asian countries, including China and North Korea, makes the practice of religion illegal. While restrictions have eased as China, particularly, embraces a more capitalist economic model, the government still represses individualism and takes a hard line on maintaining public order. Thus, not surprisingly, most of the coverage of religion from China focuses on human rights violations, including the torture or arrest of women. In August 2005, Agence France Presse reported on the arrest of five U.S. church leaders and the torture of villagers, including women (Agence France Presse, 2005). A May 2005 report on human rights violations indicated that Chinese women in detention included large numbers of Falun Gong[8] practitioners who were at risk for torture and rape (Inbaraj, 2005). Such reports are easily found, although no formal analysis exists that pertains to women and media coverage.

The other recent religion story from China—a growing effort to promulgate Christianity, including Catholicism—similarly highlights a male-dominated clergy adopting the model of religious power already in use by the Western world.[9]

In contrast, religion has been a major story in India, where Hindu nationalism rose to control Indian's central government in 1998, only to fall in 2004 to the secular Congress Party. However, religious freedom in India, where 80% of the population is Hindu, remains tenuous, and members of minority faiths such as Christianity and Islam report abuse.[10] Although the media have reported abuses of women generally, the relationship of gender to religious persecution remains largely unstudied.

Japan presents an interesting religiosity in which 84% of the country's 127 million people say they are both Shinto, an indigenous traditional philosophy with no diety or holy scripture, and Buddhist. Although Japanese society is highly secular in appearance, Soka Gakkai, a lay Buddhist organization, owns Japan's third-largest newspaper, *Seikyo Shimbun*. A study comparing Buddhist tenants with gender-related content creation in that newspaper is an interesting study waiting to be done.

The Divine Feminine in Central and South American Cultures

In Central and South America (and many Hispanic neighborhoods in the United States), the cult of the Virgin of Guadalupe serves as a reminder of the "feminine impulse" embedded amidst what Elizondo (2005) has called the "desert religions" of Judaism, Islam, and Christianity, and especially found in Latin and South American.[11] Each year, the media write dozens of stories about the divine feminine, including the Virgin of Guadalupe. The following, from a December 2004 article in the *Denver Post,* is one such example of how news reports of the divine feminine are framed:

> La Virgen is now a cultural icon whose popularity has exploded over the past decade. . . . She's morphed into a transnational symbol that effortlessly navigates border crossings of race, gender, religion and politics. . . . Her new popularity stems from the same trends that turned *The Da Vinci Code* and *The Secret Life of Bees* into major best sellers: the divine feminine and the Black Madonna.
>
> These trends are rooted in the pre-Christian goddesses such as Isis, whom scholars claim is the source of the Black Madonna. Found in cultures around the world, dark virgins like Our Lady of Guadalupe—known as la Virgencita Morena, "the little dark virgin"—are revered as ancient earth mothers. (O'Connor, 2004, p. L-1)

Research into the divine feminine in nonmedia disciplines is extensive and could serve as a useful theoretical and methodological framework. Such media reports have not been analyzed from a feminist studies perspective, however.

Under Development:
Africa, AIDS, and Women of Faith

The Western media interpret the vast majority of international religious news within a political framework. Thus, suggestions of stories to report in *Religion on the International News Agenda* (Silk, 2000) focused on political unrest and political unity, only rarely noting the potential for a feminist or women-focused story peg. Hackett (2000) noted the AIDS crisis in Africa as one underreported topic with potential for a gender component. Women's roles in treatment efforts, their roles in tribal-based spiritual systems, and their roles as educators are possible angles (Hackett, 2000)[12] for scholasticism and reporting.

An old theme cutting across every major faith and nation is that of modernists versus traditionalists. Most recently, this has been the focus of analyses regarding Islamic nations, in which one subtext is how those tensions affect women and their personal freedoms within and outside of the faith (Arjomand, 2000). This is true of every country or region in which Islam informs the political and legal systems, including a number of African nations, Iran, Iraq, Afghanistan, Saudi Arabia, Pakistan, and Indonesia.

Framing Stories of Women and
Faith: Inclusivity and False Prophets

Because the framing of religion shapes public opinion about a faith (Stout & Buddenbaum, 2003) and because no institution requires such sensitive handling in the media as does religion (Silk, 1995), analysis of those frames as they relate to women's issues is critical. Attempts to find some neat packaging of frames as they apply to faith and values in the media, however, is hampered by both the sheer diversity of faith and its relative infrequency as a stand-alone story.

A number of framing studies of religion news adapt what Silk (1995) has called moral formulas, or "topoi." Although not called frames, these topoi serve essentially the same function. According to Silk, most religion news fits into one of seven frames: good works, tolerance, hypocrisy, false prophecy, inclusion, supernatural belief, and spiritual decline. Whereas these topoi are useful for religion reports of all sorts, women's issues predominantly fall into Silk's topoi of inclusion and false prophecy. Certainly, inclusion serves as the framework for the vast majority of media attention to gender issues in religious contexts, appearing in stories about the ordination of women, achievements of women as religious leaders (e.g., "first woman bishop" stories), and reports about inclusive language in worship and scriptures.

Witches, Goddesses, and Heretics

In addition to the frame of inclusivity, women are frequently presented as radicals or heretics in stories about religion, a version of Silk's topoi of false prophecy. An emphasis on lesser-known and perhaps unusual rituals some- times recasts stories of inclusivity into stories of heresy or the bizarre (McCloud, 2004). This is perhaps best illustrated by the coverage of the 1993 Reimagining Conference.

Theologians had argued in the 1960s and 1970s, decades before the 1993 Reimagining Conference, that an increase in the number of religious groups ordaining women needed to be accompanied by reappraisal of their theol- ogy. A *Los Angeles Times* article by John Dart (1970) challenging the mas- culine image of God was among the first of such stories to appear in the mainstream media. More than 20 years later, journalists were still writing the story.[13]

But in 1993, reports of a women's gathering in Minneapolis shifted the focus in stories about women and faith from themes of inclusivity to the false-prophecy frame. The mostly Mainline Protestant women attending the Reimagining Conference said they were celebrating the femininity of their faith, but some members in denominations that helped pay for the con- ference claimed they went too far. An analysis of the event shows how media coverage fueled views of the event as radical and schismatic. Clark and Hoover (1997) noted,

> News media interested in controversy—in this case, on the topics of feminine images of God and female sexuality expressed in worship—serve to give a pub- lic airing to otherwise marginally supported views and interests, thus allowing them to achieve a wider hearing. The publicizing of these views then resulted in the mobilization of both supporters and detractors of the views expressed. In this way, the media played an important role in contributing to the devel- opment of an alternative religious movement while exacerbating the increasing polarization between liberal and conservative factions of religious expression in the United States. (p. 310)

Culture Wars, Faith, and Feminism

Understanding a story from the framework of women as radicals or heretics is closely related to the broad theme of *culture wars,* the ideologically driven confrontations of public culture and politics that emerged in the 1980s after the creation of Jerry Falwell's Moral Majority.[14] Women's issues that are framed for their relationship to culture wars include abortion and lesbian/ gay clergy. There is likely no story more divisive in public life and no better example of the culture wars theme today than abortion.

Abortion is one of the unifying issues of the U.S. Religious Right. If there is one belief uniting everyone from celibate Roman Catholic priests to Mormon mothers, it is that abortion is wrong on every level. Fortified with biblical admonitions against killing or for protecting children, some Evangelicals, Roman Catholics, and others continue steadfast, intense efforts to overturn *Roe v. Wade* (1973) and to make inroads with state restrictions. But curiously, while most mainstream media have framed abortion battles as part of the culture wars, they have not framed them as a religious story per se. Thus, while clergy are identified in acts of protest or support, relatively few stories of this type are written by religious specialists. Abortion stories are instead framed as political conflict, with citations from the major advocacy groups and politicians. It is rare for such stories to include the perspectives of women—ordinary or not—on either side, and rarer yet for the faith "angle" to be included.

One exception was a front-page story in the *New York Times* in fall 2005 (Leland, 2005). Reporter John Leland wrote a profile of women receiving abortions at a Little Rock, Arkansas, abortion clinic. Despite the story's focus on ordinary women, fewer than 150 of the story's 3,194 words focused on the women's faith, even though several said their religious views interpreted abortion as a sin.

One reason for the absence of faith and values in coverage of moral issues such as abortion is that "explaining beliefs and exploring meanings takes more space and time than covering people and events, or even issues for which the journalist can consult a few well-placed official sources," according to Buddenbaum (1998, p. 122). Including the religion angle is not as simple as calling the local parish priest or Presbyterian minister. Balance in a religious context is more complex because of the breadth of religious diversity, in which Christian denominations alone number more than 30,000 (Adherents.com, 2005).

Abortion is one key culture war story. The coverage of homosexuality and its treatment primarily within Christian organizations is the other. Today, the ordination of celibate or noncelibate gays and lesbians serves as a catalyst for dissenting groups to split off, similar in ways to the role women's ordination played among Protestant religious groups as early as the 1880s.[15] Women have been at the center of most religious trials of homosexuals seeking to serve in the pastorate. For the past two decades, the lesbian and gay clergy debate has been the single biggest controversy among many Protestant faiths and is still not resolved. One scholar has suggested that the media take a bigger role in helping bring an end to this component in culture wars (Earnest, 2002).

Politics and faith have become major themes in the U.S. culture since the first election of President George W. Bush in 2000. But for the most part, there has been little attention to women's political roles either within the religious institutions themselves or as it pertains to women's votes. Political scientist John Green and religion scholar Mark Silk (2004) have given one of the few analyses connecting the gender and religion gaps in political attitudes. According to Green and Silk, both groups "appear to be products of value conflicts that arose in the 1960s" (p. 11). Reportage of this angle was rare, however, during the 2004 presidential election. Rather, the woman's vote was most frequently analyzed in respect to views of abortion.

Religious Journalism and the Empowerment of Women

In the world of faith, empowerment of ordinary folk started with Johannes Gutenberg's first printing press, whereby new Bibles in the vernacular meant clergy educated in Latin were no longer the only ones who could read scriptures. Women in the New World apparently recognized as much and were active as publishers and printers of religious tracts (Brown, 2004; Nord, 2004; Sloan, 2000). Women began developing leadership skills and influence as they established social reform organizations such as the Women's Christian Temperance Union and the Anti-Saloon League, along with other moral societies that spoke against slavery and for women's suffrage (Marty, 1986). These organizations helped create the precursors to a vast religious publishing empire that by the 21st century was a multi-billion-dollar industry—and one in which women have always held positions of influence and power (Brown, 2004).[16]

James Gordon Bennett and the newspapers of the Penny Press era are credited with the start of covering religion as an objective topic, much the way city hall was covered (Brown, 2004; Buddenbaum, 1987). Eventually, however, the proximity of "church pages" to women's news pages may well have contributed to a ghettoization of both types of media (Mason, 1995; Nordin, 1975).

At the same time that most U.S. newspapers were establishing dedicated space for religion news in their Monday, Friday, or Saturday pages, women were also at the center of some interesting religious movements that emerged around the beginning of the 20th century. In 1879, Mary Baker Eddy founded the First Church of Christ, Scientist, in Boston. In Los Angeles, Aimee Semple McPherson was a contemporary of Billy Sunday and just as flamboyant a revivalist as Sunday.[17] In the early 1920s, McPherson was among the first to use and own a radio station to evangelize. That, along with news reports of her revivals and exploits, helped her become a national media curiosity (Campbell, 1997). But part of the media's fascination with these women was their role outside of mainstream Christianity—again reinforcing the media's framing of women in religion as heretical or false prophets.

Religion news became increasingly legitimized in the 20th century, leading to the establishment of the beat at both the Associated Press (AP) and United Press in 1951 (Cornell, 1990).[18] Even so, a 1995 content study showed that while most stories carried no bylines, of those articles with bylines, men's bylines outnumbered women's by about 2 to 1 (Mason, 1996).

Women also were among the earliest members of the professional association for secular religion journalists, the Religion Newswriters Association, founded in 1949. There was the "blunt, peppery Margaret Vance of the *Newark News;* the jolly, pungent Jo Ann Price of the *Milwaukee Journal* and later the *New York Herald Tribune,* who always gleefully conveyed the insider religious gossip," according to longtime AP Religion Reporter George Cornell (1990, p. 25). One of the longest-tenured women religion specialists was Lillian Block, the second editor of Religion News Service, who ran the national news service for 37 years, from 1958 to 1979 (Wright, 1993).

Today, some of the best religion specialists in the country are women. *Washington Monthly* Editor Amy Sullivan has built a reputation writing her shrewd analyses of faith and politics inside the Beltway. Gayle White was the only religion specialist assigned to cover the 2004 presidential election full-time, reporting for the *Atlanta Journal-Constitution.* From 2002 until 2006, Laurie Goodstein has been the sole national religion specialist at the *New York Times*—a task not only admirable but nearly impossible. And Cecile S. Holmes, now on the faculty of the University of South Carolina, was nominated for Pulitzers repeatedly during her 13 years as religion editor for the *Houston Chronicle.*

In broadcast and online news media, women have dominated as religion specialists. Sylvia Poggioli routinely covers the Vatican as National Public

Radio's (NPR) senior European correspondent. Linda Gradstein has been NPR's Israeli correspondent since 1990, and although most of her reports are political, she does include faith and values as a component of her stories. Lynn Neary was appointed NPR's first full-time domestic religion reporter in 1994. In 2005, another woman, Barbara Bradley Haggerty, was on the beat. CNN's first faith and values specialist, hired in 2005, was former Vatican correspondent Delia Gallagher. Michel Martin on occasion reports on religion for *Nightline,* and independent film producer Kate Olson spent 15 years as the religion specialist for the *McNeil-Lehrer Hour.* The nightly network news had only one prominent religion reporter, Peggy Wehmeyer, who was handpicked by former *ABC Nightly News* anchor Peter Jennings, in 1993 (Shepard, 1995). She was on the beat for 7 years before being laid off. Among Internet-only media, Deborah Caldwell in 2005 was named managing editor of Beliefnet, the second-largest online religion site, with more than 1 million visitors daily (Meacham, 2004). Caldwell, who was a founding member of the Beliefnet team, has been the major producer of the site's news content. Why women have dominated in the broadcast industry is unclear and awaiting further research.

Although this chapter has focused on the news media, presentations of religion in the entertainment media have received significant scholarly consideration. A fascinating ethnographic study is *From Angels to Aliens: Teenagers, the Media, and the Supernatural* (Clark, 2003). Although not specifically a gender study—it is more accurately a study of teens and their fascination with the supernatural as embodied in popular media—the book includes significant discussion of gendered portrayals of angels and witches, and television shows such as *Buffy the Vampire Slayer* and *Joan of Arcadia.*

In the area of documentaries, Harvard's Pluralism Project in April 2005 released *Acting on Faith: Women's New Religious Activism in America,* produced and directed by Rachel Antell.[19] The film features the lives of women such as Laila Al-Marayati, of the Muslim Women's League, and Mushim Ikeda-Nash, a peace activist and diversity facilitator at the San Francisco Zen Center.

New Religious Movements

Mass media continue to negatively characterize new religious movements (sometimes called "cults"), and within such coverage, men generally dominate as leaders and masters over women. This hegemony extends to these faiths' interpretations of sexuality, which sometimes includes polygamy, free sex, sex with children, or abstinence. For example, like media coverage of many new religious movements, stories about Satanism often portray women as helpless victims of satanic sexual violence, with little control over their lives (Foushee, 2002).

Future Research

For journalists and scholars here and abroad, the intersection of women, faith, and media is a fertile area for future research, particularly because so little has been done thus far. In recognition of the void, the coeditors of *Feminist Media Studies* called for special submissions to the March 2006 issue on the theme of *Gender, Media, and Religion.* The journal's editors suggested fruitful areas of inquiry, including gender politics of religion; religious nationalism; religious communities as constituted in and through media; women as subjects of the discourse of religion, nation, and community; feminist perspectives on questions involving religion, media, and imagined communities; and religion and media contributions to feminist activism in relation to the global media.

Technological and societal changes fuel the birth of new media. Not so in religion, in which traditions and adherence are codified in ancient holy books and time-honored rituals. In matters of religion, it is obedience and servitude that are rewarded; change requires risk and commitment to reform. Increasing research on media and faith, including an open-eyed view of how women are portrayed as "bedeviled and bewitched" in those contexts, could be a vital tool in efforts to empower women of faith globally to ensure they are no longer "left behind."

Notes

1. These numbers reflect a search of the terms *Pope* and *dead* for the dates April 3 and April 4, 2005, in English language media archived at the most complete electronic database of newspapers, http://www.nexis.com. The subset of 552 stories was then searched separately for the terms *nuns* and *Sobodka*.

2. The phrase "left behind" alludes to the popular book of the same name and a series by evangelicals Tim LaHaye and Jerry Jenkins. See T. LaHaye, and J. B. Jenkin (1995), *Left Behind: A Novel of the Earth's Last Days*, Carol Stream, IL: Tyndale House.

3. Among Christians, Roman Catholicism and Orthodox Christianity expressly forbid women clergy. In Islam, there are some women prayer leaders, or imams, but they are rare and generally not allowed to lead prayers at which men are also present. Although women rabbis exist in the Reform and Conservative

movements of American Judaism, there are no female Orthodox Jewish rabbis. Buddhists have both monks and nuns, but the Dali Lama is traditionally a male. Gods and goddesses do share roles in Hindu theology. Mainline Protestant groups allow women to be ordained and serve as bishops, although most of the largest denominations have never had a woman as head bishop or leader. A large number of Evangelical groups, including the 16-million-member Southern Baptist Convention, prohibit the ordination of women. In the Mormon Church, all prophets are men (see http://www.adherents.com, 2005) To see a historical timeline of when denominations, mostly Christian, began ordaining women, see B. A. Robinson (1996–2005) at Ontario Consultation on Religious Tolerance, http://www.religiontolerance.org/femclrg13.htm.

4. See discussions of media coverage of the veil in essays by A. Sreberny (2002), "Seeing Through the Veil: Regimes of Representation," *Feminist Media Studies, 2*(2), 155–169; and K. Wilkins (1995), "Middle Eastern Women in Western Eyes: A Study of U.S. Press Photographs of Middle Eastern women." In Y. Kamilipour (Ed.), *The U.S. Media and The Middle East: Image and Perception* (pp. 50–61), Westport, CT: Greenwood.

5. The veil, in particular, is a focus of fascination among Western media and has been the center of several legal freedom-of-religion battles in both the United States and France.

6. See, for example, M. A. Weston (2003, Winter), "Post 9/11 Arab American Coverage Avoids Stereotypes," *Newspaper Research Journal, 24*(1), 92–106; and a similar article, M. A. Weston and M. Dunsky (2002 Spring/Summer), "One Culture, Two Frameworks: U.S. Media Coverage of Arabs at Home and Abroad," *Journal of Islamic Law and Culture, 7*(9), 132–133.

7. See T. T. Patkin (2005), "Explosive Baggage: Female Palestinian Suicide Bombers and the Rhetoric of Emotion," *Women and Language, 27*(2), 79–88; and R. Handley and S. Struckman (2005, August), *Conflicting Images: Representations of Women Terrorists in U.S. Newspapers,* unpublished paper presented at the AEJMC Annual Convention, San Antonio, TX. The authors found that women terrorists are presented as an aberration more frequently than are male terrorists, with implications of their femininity or masculinity. Edward W. Said's *Covering Islam: How the Media and the Experts Determine How We See the Rest of the World* (1997) is a classic work, yet it includes little analysis of how Muslim women are portrayed.

8. Falun Gong is a spiritual movement that blends practices from Buddhism and Taoism. The Chinese government, alarmed at Falun Gong's ability to organize large public demonstrations in the late 1990s, began a brutal crackdown on the movement in the 1990s.

9. China apparently has about 50,000 Roman Catholics, who operate somewhat more openly than members of the growing Evangelical Protestantism (Associated Press, 2005).

10. See International Christian Concern (2004).

11. In these desert religions, the faiths' history was "oft repeated by old men to boys, got told through stories of battles and crusades, sultans and emperors" (Rodriguez, 2005, p. 209).

12. The means and methods of communication play a role, along with politics and faith, in dealing with the issues of developing nations, such as some in Africa. Thus, it is easy to understand why the World Association of Christian Communication sponsored a Global Media Monitoring Project after a 1994 international conference on women and communication.

13. By saying stories are framed by their relationships to culture wars, we mean that these stories are generally written in a way so as to portend improvement or further conflict between the factions on either side of these issues.

14. A more complete reporting of data related to the religion and gender gaps can be found in the January 2005 publication *Religion & Public Life: A Faith-Based Partisan Divide*, from the Pew Forum on Religion and Public Life.

15. Brown recounted stories of women such as Elizabeth Prentiss, whose mission was to write books with religious content to counter the popular literature. She wrote 31 book-length volumes, and publishers at the time said they sold over 200,000 copies of her works. Brown reported that as many as 90 specialized women's periodicals were published from 1850 to 1886, many with unordained women editors (Brown, 2004).

16. Religious journalism, meanwhile, was a source of empowerment for women, including African American women. Ransaw and Borchard (2005) found that representations and contributions of African American women in the publications of the African Methodist Episcopal Church (AME) between 1854 and 1913 contrasted with the contemporary portrayals of African American women. AME publications showed them as cultured, outspoken, educated, and political. In addition, the publications gave African American women important opportunities to learn journalism.

17. For an analysis of McPherson's rhetorical style as a front-runner to modern-day female televangelists, see S. Pullem (1993, September), "Sisters of the Spirit: The Rhetorical Methods of the Female Faith Healer Aimee Semple McPherson," Katheryn Kuhlman; and Gloria Copeland, *Journal of Communication and Religion*, *16*(2), 111–126.

18. Men held the religion beat at both United Press (later, UPI) and Associated Press (AP) from the beat's creation in 1951 until the 1990s, when AP hired Julia Lieblich as its first female religion reporter. A woman has been one of AP's two domestic religion specialists ever since.

19. See http://www.pluralism.org/events/women/index.php. The Pluralism Project is headed by Diana Eck and housed at Harvard University.

Questions for Discussion

1. Why is religion a fertile area for mass communication researchers looking at gender issues?

2. What are some reasons that explain why grasping relationships among faith, media, and gender is difficult?

3. How might a theory of "triangulation" look, and how would it be different when feminist considerations are incorporated?

4. What similarities are there between gender studies in faith and media and other disciplines? What differences are there?

Accessing Additional Information

Religion News Service: http://www.religionnews.com

Religion Newswriters Association: http://www.religionwriters.com

Religion Scholars: http://www.religionsource.com

Women and Religion: http://www.hirr.hartsem.edu/research/research_women_religion.html

Women and Religion: http://www.nd.edu/~archives/lau_bib.html

16

The Global Context of Women in Communication

H. Leslie Steeves, University of Oregon

The post–World War II decades of the 20th century were marked by political and ideological tensions between advocates of modernization and advocates of balance and resistance. The former argued that capital-intensive modernization projects would reduce poverty via a "trickle-down effect" and increase free flows of global information. Opponents cited considerable evidence of failures in modernization and argued that an unfettered "free flow" harms cultural diversity and indigenous values.

These polarizations faded in the 1980s and 1990s, as debt-plagued developing countries were forced into structural adjustment agreements, and the forces of modernization, Westernization, and globalization became dominant. At the same time, other pressing issues—terrorism, genocide, war, environment, and AIDS—became salient on national and global agendas.

Mass media and communication have been at the center of these issues. Women have remained on the margins, though women have often suffered as the result of actions by others and despite increased feminist activism and scholarship in all fields.

Feminist media activists, professionals, and scholars have recognized the urgent predicament of women globally and the ways in which communication may further harm them or possibly facilitate change. Specifically, women are poorer than men, and a vast literature of gender and development (GAD) shows that modernization has worsened women's situations by favoring males at all levels of the process. Relatedly, global problems of poverty, illiteracy, overpopulation, environment, and AIDS have affected women disproportionately. And while women have not been the instigators of genocide, terrorism, or war, women have been victims of violent acts, including rape and domestic abuse, which often accompany other forms of violence.

To the extent that mass media, telecommunications, and information and communication technologies (ICTs) have spread globally, they can help set activist agendas, and they can reinforce—or possibly resist—ideologies of women's secondary status. Women's access to media and ICTs is obviously crucial for their personal empowerment. Also, women need access for the networking and information sharing required to organize and create strategies for change.

Hence, "women and media" was a major topic at the conferences of the 1975–1985 Decade for Women and was one of 12 critical areas of concern addressed at the 1995 Beijing women's conference (United Nations, 1995, 1996) and subsequent Beijing +5 and +10 conferences. The Women's Environment and Development Organization (WEDO) was created in 1990 to increase women's power as policymakers, in part by monitoring each nation's progress in implementing United Nations agreements, including the Beijing document.[1] The Global Media Monitoring Project, an outcome of a 1994 conference on "Women Empowering Communication," has continued to work with activists to monitor news on radio, televisions, and newspapers (Gallagher, 1999, 2001; MediaWatch, 1995).[2] Other media-monitoring and activist organizations have been formed on every continent (Gallagher, 2001). Many conferences and organizations have emerged with a focus on promoting gender equality in and through media.[3]

This chapter briefly identifies, conceptualizes, and discusses global problems that are salient for continued feminist activism and scholarship in communication studies. I assume that scholarship can be useful to the extent that it responds to recognized problems and has relevance for practitioners and activists in suggesting explanations and actions that may lead to change. Furthermore, I assume that no one theory is sufficient for understanding gender and media problems globally. Taken together, however, available feminist and social theories may be helpful in understanding shared patterns of oppression and resistance. The frameworks particularly relevant are drawn from political economy theory and feminist cultural studies, including postcolonial studies. Much more conceptual work is needed, however, especially to understand collective resistance.

Ownership and Concentration

Political economic theory seeks to understand how capitalist societies and organizations function to maintain and produce material resources. A primary concern is how structures of ownership and control have historically created inequitable relations of power that are manifest in economic classes. Political economists analyze contradictions that sustain unequal power relations and suggest strategies for resistance. A related concern is the balance between capitalist enterprises and public intervention. Political economy "goes beyond technical issues of efficiency to engage with basic moral questions of justice, equity, and the public good" (Golding & Murdock, 1991, p. 18).

Political economic analyses include structures and policies of communication industries and their relations with other economic sectors, modes of cultural production and consumption under capitalism, and media as capitalist commodities (e.g., Smythe, 1960; Wasko, 2000). Of particular concern has been capitalist expansionism in global communications (e.g., Schiller, 1971) and media concentration (e.g., Bagdikian, 2004; Herman & Chomsky, 1988). As corporations expand, they receive assistance from national governments (e.g., via industrial policies) and from international banks and aid agencies, which target developing countries for sales. All of these relationships are topics for critique.

For many years, Marxian feminists have recognized that the market system is grounded in the dualistic and hierarchical assumptions of the Enlightenment related to class, gender, and nation. They have especially focused on links between class and gender, an artifact of capitalism's history in moving men out of the home to become capitalists or workers. Hence, men of both classes gained control over the capital for their families (Engels, 1884/1985). As women have entered the workforce, they have remained at the bottom tiers, and their labor and capital are still controlled by elite men.[4]

Political economic theory has been increasingly embraced by feminists concerned with the impact of male-dominated ownership and concentration on women, recognizing that women are all but excluded as CEOs and board members (Falk & Grizard, 2003a) and exploited by organizational marketing practices and products. Media concentration intensifies this effect, reducing the ability of small companies to survive, particularly in developing countries. It limits their sources of technologies and capital assistance, making it harder to resist financial absorption. In fact, 9 of the top 10 media and communications conglomerates have purchased telecommunications, TV networks, publishing houses, and/or other media in developing countries on at least two continents outside North America, Europe, and Australia.[5]

Although it is possible that men in top corporate positions could promote women and share their wealth more equitably, research shows that they seldom do so. According to Kathleen Hall-Jamieson, "Companies that have fewer women in top positions also tend to have less women-friendly human resource policies. That creates a self-generating cycle, making it less likely that women will be able to move their way up" (Annenberg Public Policy Center, 2004).

Women in developing countries, who constitute two thirds of the world's women, benefit least and experience the most harm as a result of patriarchal ownership and control and increased concentration. There are many ways this can happen. Technologies are developed and adopted that the poor cannot afford, further widening gaps in media access. Though new technologies, such as Integrated Services Digital Network (IDSN), may increase efficiency for large organizations, they may greatly increase costs for small users, who have less complex needs. In addition, the acquisition of expensive technologies may reduce finances available for cheaper technologies, such as radio, that benefit the rural poor (e.g., Heath, 1992). The trend toward media privatization in developing countries has exacerbated this problem.

In addition, increased technological complexity combined with globalization can mean simultaneous increases in skilled opportunities for men, who monopolize new technologies, and in unskilled, labor-intensive factory jobs for women in developing countries. The latter include jobs in electronics industries that have been outsourced by companies, such as Dell, IBM, and Hewlett-Packard (Catholic Agency for Overseas Development [CAFOD], 2004). The gendered effects of increased mechanization and the export of technological assembly are complex and need to be understood in each context (Beneria, 2003). In outsourced factories, young women under the age of 25 constitute the overwhelming majority of the workforce because of the belief that they are compliant and have great manual dexterity (CAFOD, 2004; White, 2005). Hence, most human rights abuses in these factories are suffered by women. Labor standards in computer manufacturing are often worse than other sectors, such as clothing and shoes, because they have thus far escaped scrutiny (CAFOD, 2004). While the jobs may offer some economic and other rewards, they subject women to new forms of exploitation: The jobs are low paying and unstable and have health risks related to stress, eyesight, hearing, and exposure to dangerous chemicals (Bales, 1999; CAFOD, 2004; Lim, 1981; White, 2005).

Finally, much communications research and development carried out by multinational corporations is funded for military purposes, as communication and information technologies are crucial to weapons, intelligence, and propaganda systems (Schiller, 1981, p. xiii). Military systems around the world are almost universally male (Seager, 2003, pp. 100–101), and their technologies, according to many feminists, are not gender neutral. Elise Boulding (e.g., 1981) was among the early scholars to point out that a goal of technological research has been the ability to control by force and that men have been the leaders in this project. Military expenditures, which continue to escalate, therefore contribute to other factors that subvert women's efforts to obtain more economic power. Feminist critiques of war and militarization have increased in recent years (e.g., WEDO, 2005). However, these critiques have had little impact on the rising development and use of tools for war, including communications tools.

Representations

Given the exclusion and oppression of women by corporations that make and sell communications products, the next area to examine is how this power translates into media representations. To address these issues, in the 1980s, the United Nations Educational, Scientific, and Cultural Organization (UNESCO) commissioned two reviews of the literature on women and media globally (Gallagher, 1981; UNESCO, 1985). More recently, the Global Media Monitoring Project, sponsored by the World Association for Christian Communication (WACC), has provided valuable information. Several bibliographies, edited collections, and journals contain resources: for example, Lent's (1999) international annotated bibliography, Valdivia's (1995) and Ross and Byerly's (2004) collections, and the journal *Feminist Media Studies*. Newsletters such as *Media Report to Women*,[6] *Women's International Network (WIN) News*,[7] *IWMFWire*,[8] and MediaWatch[9] provide updated news and data. The International Women's Tribune Centre and the United Nations Development Fund for Women (UNIFEM), based in New York City, are helpful.[10] Conferences of organizations such as the International Association for Media Communication Research, the International Communication Association, and the Association for Education in Journalism and Mass Communication have sessions for research on women's representations and roles in media internationally.

Many studies continue to critique the absence from and oppression of women in media content, as reviewed in the earlier edition of this book (Steeves, 1993). The neglect and distortion of women's and feminist issues in news has been an ongoing focus of study (e.g., Gallagher, 2000). Advertising remains an area of concern because of the power of multinational advertising agencies, which emphasize Western values (including conventions of gender representations) and target women as consumers. Advertising, in turn, affects media entertainment and editorial content, which usually reflect consistent values, often are imported from a wealthier country, and have proven appealing for a large urban audience. Because advertising content may be particularly offensive, it has been a frequent focus of activism via product boycotts and other strategies.[11]

As the material values of the multinational economy play a major role in shaping media content, it seems reasonable that political economy theory would contribute to the analyses of media representations. In fact, political economy has been criticized for its neglect of ideology and the ways in which representations shape meaning and allow for resistance.[12] In response, political economists have gone beyond studies of ownership to consider relationships between political economy and cultural studies and therefore include questions about texts, audiences, and consumption (Meehan & Riordan, 2002).

There have been difficulties in reconciling political economy and cultural studies (e.g., Steeves & Wasko, 2002). Two characteristics of cultural studies scholarship are significant: the assumption that material realities are meaningless until given meaning via discourse; and the rejection of grand theoretical narratives, including narratives of the Enlightenment and of Marxism. The latter characteristic reflects the influence of postmodern, poststructural, and postcolonial thought, including the works of international feminists (e.g., Amos & Parmar, 1984; Mohanty, 1988) who have argued that the foundational theories on which Western perspectives are based, including political economy theory and Western feminisms, are not relevant to women globally. In fact, great variations in women's lives argue against any generalizable explanation for patriarchy. Many feminists agree with postcolonial feminist thought (e.g., Spivak, 1988, 1999), which is concerned with the experiences, consequences, and discourses of colonization, including neocolonization that continues in the form of globalization. Postcolonial feminism favors shifting an emphasis from grand narratives to local events and from elites to the subaltern. It also uses poststructuralism to critique colonial narratives and roles of subaltern groups therein.

Analyses of gendered content and audience responses in global contexts increasingly draw on a mix of cultural studies and postcolonial theory to address questions about relations between local and global, cultural hybridity, and Euro-American influence.[13] Some studies additionally incorporate a Marxian critique of Western hegemony and consumer culture.[14] Radhika Parameswaran's research (2002, 2004, e.g., on discourses of "global culture" in *National Geographic* and of beauty pageants in postcolonial India) is noteworthy in this regard.

Continued scholarly research, theory development and analysis, as well as media monitoring may contribute to change. Many other strategies are also important.

Feminist Resistance

One way in which global representations could improve for women is by using the media for development. The limited research on this question indicates that, here also, Western commercial values often prevail over women's needs, especially when aid agencies work with the private sector to develop persuasive strategies. This can happen as the result of an emphasis on persuading individuals to adopt new practices or products versus addressing structural inequities (Wilkins, 1999) and also as a result of marketing conventions simply failing to consider women's needs (Luthra, 1991). In entertainment-education strategies, such as television serial dramas, research shows that education components may be subordinated to entertainment components and that gender, class, and urban biases may be evident (Matthews, 2004).

Another possible strategy to improve representations has been to increase the number of women working in media, particularly at the higher levels of decision making. Few, however, would argue that this is a sufficient condition for change. In fact, research shows that media content does not change with the simple addition of women (e.g., van Zoonen, 1994). Patriarchal political-economic power structures are so entrenched in all aspects of society that other kinds of change also are needed. As Gallagher (2001) concluded,

> Women's representation in the media will not be improved by increasing the number of women journalists, or by getting rid of the worst excesses of sexism in advertising. What it actually requires is a wide-scale social and political transformation, in which women's rights—and women's right to communicate—are truly understood, respected and implemented both in society and at large by the media. (pp. 7–8)

Additional modes of resistance include organizing and publicizing events and conferences, as well as follow-up analyses of media coverage. Media literacy projects to educate consumers can also play a role (e.g., Lemish, Liebes, & Seidman, 2001). Political activism and policy change and the creation of alternative media may be particularly worthwhile.

Legal and Policy Change

Feminist political economic theory assumes that law and policy constitute a powerful site for legitimating or resisting hegemonic patriarchy (Meehan & Riordan, 2002). While nation-states often face challenges from commercial organizations with global interests, most agree that states do have the power to pass laws regulating media within their borders.[15] "For many, the state remains the best hope for harnessing market-driven media globalization" (Waisbord & Morris, 2001, p. xi).

Some countries have taken specific actions to limit the activities of multinational corporations, actions that may help women and other marginalized groups (Mattelart, Delcourt, & Mattelart, 1984, pp. 65–66; Morris & Waisbord, 2001). These actions include requiring the use of the national language in advertising; requiring advertising to be created within the country and to utilize local talent; limiting advertising activities in certain sectors, such as pharmaceuticals and food; and fixing quotas on imports of foreign films and publications.

Laws that explicitly protect disadvantaged groups from media oppression are rare. These include policies on acceptable representations of women and on women's employment in and ownership of media and information industries. In preparation for the 1985 United Nations Decade for Women Conference in Nairobi, a questionnaire was distributed to all member states (UNESCO, 1985, p. 30). One section addressed media policies, including "policies and guidelines requiring media to promote the advancement of women" (p. 33). Just a few of the 95 responding countries (e.g., Sweden and Denmark) reported having policies on portrayals of women in media (p. 34). While many countries did appear to have laws or policies against unequal pay and gender discrimination, many of these laws were vague, and in most cases, it appeared that their effectiveness was not evaluated. Hence, the policies had little impact. Also, numerous obstacles to the successful enforcement of law and policy were reported in the questionnaires (see Steeves, 1993).

Since 1985, relatively little has changed globally regarding media policy for women. According to Gallagher (2001, p. 35) and a review by Isis International of Asian countries (Isis International, 1999, p. 18), the few existing policies are overly general and ambiguous and focus primarily on indecency and morality rather than gender equality. Also, public broadcasters appear more amenable to codes than commercial broadcasters (Gallagher, 2001, pp. 35–36). Gallagher observed that political activism for policy change is time-consuming and difficult but may pay off when allies can be found within media. She cited examples of promising developments, for instance, in Israel, Sri Lanka, Jamaica, and Korea (pp. 39–42).

Canada's Radio-Television and Telecommunications Commission (CRTC) remains notable for its 1986 adoption of regulatory codes on representations of women, following a 2-year trial period (1982–1984) of self-regulation.[16] As self-regulation was only partially successful, CRTC decided to make broadcasters' licenses renewal contingent on following the guidelines. Additional research was carried out in 1988 (CRTC, 1990), and the guidelines were updated in 1990 and 1992.[17] However, violations of the codes have occurred, and feminist monitoring groups such as MediaWatch have faced stiff opposition from commercial media interests (Gallagher, 2001, pp. 43–44).

Canada has also taken a progressive role in employment equity. In 1992, the CRTC announced an employment equity policy that would affect decisions about granting and renewing licenses. Protected groups include women, aboriginal peoples, and persons with disabilities and visible minorities. In 1997, CRTC announced a complementary policy regarding on-air presence, requiring broadcasters to provide information about the same four groups when applying for or renewing licenses.[18]

Alternative Media

Another important strategy of resistance is to establish and strengthen feminist organizations and networks. While alternative media obviously help provide information not found in the mainstream, communications are also central to feminist movements organized for other reasons, such as gender violence, labor, environment, health, and peace. As many such movements exist and take initiatives on varied issues, more theoretical work is needed to understand this reality, including the role of the media and communication (Smith, 1993; Steeves, 2004; Waterman, 1993).

Key alternative feminist media organizations include Isis International, a nongovernmental organization (NGO) formed in 1974 to support women's information needs and activism by networking, research, and media projects. Isis now has three independent offices: Manila, Philippines; Kampala, Uganda; and Santiago, Chile. A recent project has been the creation of a Beijing+10 Women's Media Pool to support the efforts of all practitioners, activists, and women's networking organizations in disseminating information about women's achievements and progress regarding the Beijing Platform for Action.[19] The New Delhi–based Women's Feature Service (WFS) remains the only international women's news/features agency, with writers based in 40 countries and media clients globally.[20] Also, the Institute for Global Communications (IGC) is noteworthy for facilitating Internet communications for women's groups via WomensNet.[21]

Table 16.1   Periodicals for Women, 2005

Number of Periodicals	Countries
> 100	United States (289)
> 20	United Kingdom (30); Canada (30)
5–9	Chile, Mexico, Korea (9); Netherlands (7); Australia (6); Spain, Philippines, Germany, Brazil, South Africa (5)
2–4	Argentina (4); Switzerland, India, Peru, Cuba, Japan, Kenya, Zimbabwe (3); Austria, Norway, Croatia, Italy, Belgium, New Zealand, Uruguay, Guatemala, Thailand, Pakistan, Nigeria, Sudan (2)
1	Portugal, Bulgaria, Turkey, Palestine, New Caledonia, Bolivia, Nicaragua, Trinidad & Tobago, Paraguay, Panama, Costa Rica, Venezuela, Nepal, Vietnam, Uganda, Ethiopia, Senegal, Egypt, Namibia

SOURCE: Women's Institute for Freedom of the Press (2005).

The best current resource for information on international media and media-related groups, organizations, and events for women is the *Directory of Women's Media,* published by the Women's Institute for Freedom of the Press, previously noted. The *Directory* is updated continuously and is available both online and in print.[22] It provides lists and descriptions in the categories of print periodicals, Internet periodicals, publishers, media organizations, news services, radio groups, film and video groups, music groups and Web sites, theater and art groups, media Web sites, media directories, bookstores, and listservs. Table 16.1 summarizes information from this publication on women's print and Internet periodicals.[23] The United States lists over 250 alternative publications for women, with the United Kingdom and Canada listing far fewer. Many publications and other media based in the United States, Canada, and Europe have international circulations, and some deal specifically with issues facing women in developing countries.[24] However, their actual diversity of circulation and availability to women internationally requires research.

Data on other women's media and publication activities indicate a similar trend. The United States predominates; Canada, Europe, and Australia follow, and developing countries show less, though increased, activity. Again, some of the North American, European, and Australian activity is international in nature. For example, the Canada-based news service WINGS (Women's International Newsgathering Services) is an all-woman independent radio company that produces and distributes programs about women to stations around the world.[25]

It is important to recognize that alternative media can easily be compromised by advertising or other political-economic pressures that affect their content. Some have managed to resist such pressures. For instance, the Manushi collective in New Delhi, India, has published a successful magazine that offers features and fiction confronting the oppression of women in Indian society (Kishwar & Vanita, 1984).[26] Thanks to subscriptions and donations, Manushi has not accepted advertising depicting women in oppressive roles. Other alternative media projects, however, have succumbed to financial and other pressures. Whenever commercial interests intervene, the line between "alternative" and "mainstream" becomes difficult to distinguish and women's interests are usually compromised.

Global Networking via New Technologies

The Internet, cell phones, and other technologies have exponentially increased opportunities for women to seek and share information. Feminists have lauded the Internet in particular for its potential to democratize communication and support activist agendas.[27] In addition, the Internet is extending the local to the global for women's radio, music, art and other media (Mitchell, 2004). The many women's Internet periodicals, listservs, Web sites, news services, radio groups, and music and video groups in the *Directory of Women's Media* and elsewhere support this optimistic view. UNESCO funded a major project in the 1990s to investigate and encourage women's networking (Harcourt, 1999). In fact, the vast majority of women's organizations globally now use the Internet. As Arizpe (1999) stated, "Feminism has created a global room of our own" (p. xiv).

While the Internet has been embraced as a powerful tool for supporting women's interests, the challenges are also greater than ever in part because of the Internet. As noted earlier, the Internet and other technologies support trends that are not in women's best interests: the increased dominance of a multinational economy, escalating militarization, and rising fundamentalism (WEDO, 2005). Relatedly, the Internet has opened up new opportunities to exploit women through advertising, pornography, and sex trafficking.

Hamada (1999) argued that the Internet is intensifying the expansion of Western consumer culture. Siew and Kim (1996) observed that in Malaysia, the cost of developing new technologies has been borne by the government and business sectors. As women's status and roles have been marginalized in these sectors, their access to the Internet and other technologies has been likewise limited. Lee (2004) pointed out the irony of believing that women can use new technologies to rescue themselves from poverty and oppression, whereas, in fact, they are simultaneously "reinforcing the economic domination of transnational telecommunications and information and communication technology corporations" (pp. 533–534). Issues of capitalist-patriarchal ownership must also be addressed.

In addition, the distribution and availability of the Internet and other technologies globally show great disparities, as indicated in annual reports of the United Nations Development Programme (UNDP, 2001).[28] They are largely restricted to literate and privileged women, resulting in a widening of information gaps. Poverty obviously affects access, as cybercafes and cell phones require discretionary resources. Throughout the world, but especially in developing countries, women remain poorer than men (Seager, 2003, pp. 86–87; UNDP, 2004, pp. 229–232). As literacy is essential for using the Internet, extending women's access requires continued improvements in literacy rates. Presently, 38% of countries with available data have a lower literacy rate for girls than boys. The countries with the greatest disparities are in sub-Saharan Africa and South Asia, and current rates of improvement suggest little progress within the next 10 years (UNDP, 2004, 226–228; United Nations Development Fund for Women [UNIFEM], 2002, p. 21).

In sum, clearly the Internet and other new technologies have facilitated the ability of women to network, share information, and publicize their agendas. Women's NGOs in developing countries in particular have benefited from them. Nonetheless, it is unclear whether these benefits have been outweighed by competing patriarchal agendas. In addition, women's poverty, literacy, and education remain problems that need to be addressed to extend access.

Conclusion

The increased power and concentration of multinational corporations require feminist analyses, as the absence and oppression of women in media content plus women's economic disadvantages can be linked to these conglomerates and associated values of global consumerism. A combination of insights from feminist political economy theory and cultural studies, including poststructuralist and postcolonial studies, may be helpful in understanding the behaviors of multinational corporations, their material and ideological products, and audience reception. The role of the nation-state in supporting neoliberal economic dominance, growing militarization, and fundamentalism also require feminist scrutiny. Beyond scholarship, resistance by women includes policymaking, alternative media, global networking, and media-monitoring projects. Much more research is needed to understand: collective global movements; motivations and strategies for collaboration across barriers of race, religion, nation, language, and sexual orientation; and contextual factors that may facilitate success.

Notes

1. See http://www.wedo.org.

2. The 1994 "Women Empowering Communication" conference was organized by the World Association for Christian Communication (WACC). The first Global Media Monitoring Project (GMMP) in 1995 was organized by MediaWatch Canada, and results were presented at the Beijing conference. WACC coordinated the second and third GMMP studies, in February 2000 and 2004. See http://www.wacc .org.uk/wacc/our_work/projects/gender/global_media_monitoring_project_2005

3. One example is the Gender and Media Summit in Johannesburg, September 2004, which led to the launching of the Gender and Media Network of Southern Africa (Joseph, 2004).

4. For example, see Barrett (1980, 1992), Eisenstein (1979), and Walby (1986).

5. These are AOL/Time Warner, AT&T, General Electric, News Corporation (Murdock), Viacom, Inc., Walt Disney Company, Vivendi Universal, Liberty Media Corporation, and Sony. Only Bertelsmann appears to restrict its range of ownership to the United States and Europe (Miller, 2002).

6. *Media Report to Women* is a quarterly newsletter published by the Women's Institute for Freedom of the Press (http://www.wifp.org/), with reports of research, conferences, and political and legal activity related to women and media around the world. For information, go to the WIFP Web site or write to Communication Research Associates, Inc., 38091 Beach Road, P.O. Box 180, Colton's Point, MD 20626-0180.

7. *WIN News* is published quarterly and includes information on women's activities worldwide, with considerable emphasis on developing countries. Most issues have a section on "Women and Media," with information on recent publications and events. For information, write to Fran P. Hosken, 107 Grant St., Lexington, MA 02420-2126. See also http://www.feminist.com/win.htm

8. *IWMFWire* is the newsletter of the International Women's Media Foundation, based in Washington, D.C. The IWMF seeks to develop projects and programs that will support the success of women journalists globally. For information, the newsletter and other publications, see http://www.iwmf.org/

9. MediaWatch is a volunteer activist group that began in 1984 and aims to challenge abusive and biased media images by distributing educational videos, media literacy information, and newsletters. See http://www.medi awatch.com/welcome.html

10. The International Women's Tribune Centre (IWTC) was founded following the 1975 United Nations Decade for Women conference in Mexico City. The IWTC provides information, education, and organizational support to women's organizations and other groups working to improve the lives of women in developing countries, including regular online reports. For information, see http://www.iwtc.org/ or write to IWTC, 777 United Nations Plaza, New York, NY 10017. UNIFEM provides financial and technical assistance for programs and strategies that benefit and empower women. For information on UNIFEM and to download publications, see http://www.unifem.org/

11. The organization Adbusters, based in Vancouver, Canada, has used a variety of creative strategies to expose and resist offensive and oppressive advertising images of women and other groups. See http://www.adbusters.org/home/

12. See, for example, "Colloquy," on the debate between cultural studies and political economy in *Critical Studies in Mass Communication, 12,* pp. 60–100 (1995), with an introduction by Oscar Gandy Jr., and articles by Nicholas Garnham, Lawrence Grossberg, James Carey, and Graham Murdock. See also Meehan and Riordan (2002).

13. The August 2002 (Vol. 12, No. 3) issue of *Communication Theory* provides a helpful introduction to postcolonial theory and scholarship.

14. Drawing on the arguments of Fraser and Nicholson (1990), among others, I have argued elsewhere that some feminists have gone too far in rejecting all grand narratives in favor of an absolute focus on local, time-specific situation. Effective feminist criticism requires some reference to large narratives, such as political economy, about social organization and its impact on ideology (Steeves, 2004).

15. For examples of laws and policies passed as a result of women organizing, see Seager (2003, pp. 102–103).

16. This research, on the portrayal of sex roles in Canadian television programming and advertising and radio programming and advertising, is presented in four volumes, by the Canadian Radio-Television and Telecommunications Commission (CRTC, 1990).

17. Policy statements issued thus far by the CRTC include "Sex-Role Stereotyping in the Broadcast Media: Policy Statement" (CRTC Public Notice 1986-351); "Industry Guidelines for Sex-Role Portrayal" (CRTC Public Notice 1990-99); and "1992 Policy on Gender Portrayal" (CRTC Public Notice 1992-58). See the CRTC Web site, http://www.crtc.gc.ca/eng/welcome.htm

18. The policy is titled "Implementation of an Employment Equity Policy" (CRTC Public Notice 1992-59). See http://www.crtc.gc.ca/eng/INFO_SHT/b310 .htm

19. For information, see http://www.isiswomen.org/index.html

20. See Byerly (1995). For current and archived features and other information on WFS, see: http://www.wfsnews.org/

21. The IGC's network WomensNet, formed in 1995, is an online community of individual and groups who use computer technology to advance feminist causes. IGC

manages Internet communications for several other groups with progressive agendas. See http://www.igc.org/index.html/

22. See the WIFP publications Web site, http://www.wifp.org/publications.html

23. Readers examining Table 16.1 in comparison to the 1993 edition of this book will note discrepancies, for example, the large apparent decrease in U.S. publications for women (609 to 289), a decline in publications from Canada and the United Kingdom, and a small number of publications reported from Europe, with some countries (e.g., France) missing altogether. I note that the *Directory of Women's Media* was published by the Women's Institute for Freedom of the Press from 1979–1985, followed by a 12-year gap until the 2002 edition was published. The 1992 edition of the *Directory,* on which the data for the 1993 table was based, was published by the National Council for Research on Women and included a number of "unindexed periodicals," for which no information was available at the time of publication. Since taking over the *Directory* again in 2002, the volunteer-staffed WIFP has relied primarily on networking and Internet searchers to rebuild and update the list. It will take time to fully develop a network for information (Martha Leslie Allen, personal communication, March 21, 2005). It likely that future editions of the *Directory* will provide increasingly accurate listings, especially of publications outside the United States.

24. The 2005 *Directory of Women's Media* lists many North American– and European-based print and Internet publications that have international content and circulations outside the United States. Some examples are *Media Report to Women* (previously noted); *Women's International Network (WIN) News* (previously noted); the *Tribune*, publication of the previously noted International Women's Tribune Centre; *SEEDS*, published by the Population Council in New York; and *AVIVA*, a free London-based "webzine," which publishes news of interest to women globally. Examples of U.S.-based academic journals listed in the *Directory* that have substantial international content are *Health Care for Women International; Race, Gender, & Class: An Interdisciplinary and Multicultural Journal; Signs: Journal of Women in Culture and Society; Violence Against Women;* and *WID Working Papers.* The United Kindgom–based *Feminist Media Studies* is notable in its efforts to include articles about gender and media issues globally.

25. WINGS was based in the United States until 2002, when its producer, Frieda Werden, moved to Canada. See http://www.wings.org

26. For information on *Manushi* and to browse past issues, see http://free.freespeech.org/manushi/about.html

27. Donna Allen (e.g., 1989, 1998), founder of the Women's Institute for Freedom of the Press, was among the most optimistic about the power of the Internet to facilitate change

28. UNDP (2001) introduced a new development indicator for comparing countries, the "technology achievement index," which joined two other frequently cited UNDP indices, the "human development index" and the "gender-related development index."

Questions for Discussion

1. Why have feminists globally critiqued theoretical frameworks developed in the United States and Europe? Give examples.

2. In view of the above, which theoretical perspective or combination of perspectives may be most helpful in understanding women's absence from and oppression in global media representations? Defend your response.

3. Why is economic class such an important consideration when examining women's oppression in media globally? Give examples of your points.

4. List at least five strategies that may help improve women's status in media globally. Which strategy do you think is most effective? Least effective? Explain your reasoning.

5. In what ways may the Internet help or harm women's interests regarding media representation and participation?

Accessing Additional Information

Global Media Monitoring Project 2005: http://www.wacc.org.uk/wacc/our_work/projects/gender/global_media_monitorinproject_2005

International Communication Association, Feminist Scholarship Division: http://www.icahdq.org/divisions/feminist/

International Women's Media Foundation: http://www.iwmf.org/

International Women's Tribute Center: http://www.iwtc.org/

MediaWatch: http://www.mediawatch.com/welcome.html

Network of Women in Media–India: http://www.nwmindia.org/

UNIFEM: http://www.unifem.org/

WIN News: http://www.feminist.com/win.htm

WINGS: http://www.wings.org

Women's Feature Service: http://www.wfsnews.org/

Women's Forum Against Fundamentalism in Iran: http://www.wfafi.org

Women's Institute for Freedom of the Press: http://www.wifp.org/

PART V

Building a Foundation
for Further Study

17

On the Margins

Examining the Intersection of Women and the Law of Mass Communication

Diane L. Borden, San Diego State University

Maria B. Marron, Central Michigan University

The law in the United States, as in other countries, is a concatenation of abstract principles, theories, precedents, types (constitutional, common, and statutory; federal and state; trial and appellate, among them), and the individual philosophies and dispositions of members of the judiciary, influenced by the political climate and social norms.

A review of the scholarly literature on feminist jurisprudence suggests that despite its fluidity, the law has been constant over time in constructing woman as "different," as "less than," and as living in a world where, according to Simone de Beauvoir (1989), "Men compel her to assume the status of the Other" (p. xxxv).

Through the prism of male, gendered law, woman is determined by her difference, a matter that "has had implications in regard to the way in which women are understood as objects and subjects of law" (Fineman, 1992, p. 1). For years regarded as man's property, woman did not even possess herself. Rape, for example, "was first regarded as a violation of the property rights of fathers and husbands" (Baer, 2002, p. 255).

The concept of a natural order based on biological differences between man and woman is embedded in constitutional decisions about gender. In the earliest U.S. Supreme Court case based on sex discrimination, the Court upheld a statute denying women the right to practice law (*Bradwell v. Illinois,* 1873).

Later court decisions upheld laws barring women from working more than 10 hours a day in the factory (*Muller v. Oregon,* 1908) and placing women on jury lists only if they made a special request (*Hoyt v. Florida,* 1961). All of these laws assumed that women have inferior capabilities and were aimed at limiting women to their traditional place in the home to discharge their wifely and maternal functions. It wasn't until 1971 that the Supreme Court held, for the first time, that sex discrimination violates the equal-protection clause of the Fourteenth Amendment (*Reed v. Reed,* 1971).

Feminist scholars in a variety of fields, including political science, history, sociology, and law, have worked toward defining difference and dominance and their implications through feminist jurisprudence. There is still no consensus on what constitutes feminist legal theory, however. Feminist legal thought seems caught between the extremes of a "grand theory" of male-originated abstract thought and narratives of "unique experience" (Schwarzenbach & Smith, 2003, p. 2).

Matsuda (1989), cognizant of the need for law to consider variables other than gender, such as race, has called for "a theory of multiple consciousness" (p. 9). Harris (1990) has argued that some feminist legal theorists rely on "gender essentialism—the notion that a unitary, 'essential' women's experience can be isolated and described independently of race, class, sexual orientation, and other realities of experience" (p. 585).

Minow has examined inequalities in the law, noting a pattern of judicial passivity and an ignorance of people's different situations in a study of how the Supreme Court has handled a variety of cases that excluded individuals and groups (Minow, 1987).

Both the law and feminist jurisprudence continue to evolve, but relatively little feminist scholarship has examined issues related directly to the First Amendment. Feminist jurisprudence, for the most part, has explored reproductive rights, sexuality and the family, equal employment opportunity, educational equity, and violence against women. With specific reference to mass communication, feminist jurisprudence has concerned itself almost exclusively with obscenity and pornography, although in recent years, some feminist scholars have begun to examine speech liability issues such as defamation, right of publicity, and intentional infliction of emotional distress.

Mass Communication Law

Women are largely invisible in mass communication law. When women's lives have intersected with the First Amendment, the courts historically have tended to replicate and reinforce cultural stereotypes, which construct women as sexual beings confined to the private sphere of the home to the exclusion of other parts of their identities—their intellectual capacities, their artistic impulses, their athletic tendencies, their compassion, or their "metaphysics of mind . . . approach to ethics, and concept of social action" (MacKinnon, 1987, p. 206). Sexuality and marginalized social status appear to be at the root of most freedom-of-expression cases involving female plaintiffs.

Mass communication law encompasses a broad palette of topics, including access to document governments, fair coverage of trials, and copyright. This chapter spotlights a few other categories of law whereby women have come before the courts to claim their First Amendment rights or to seek remedy from those whose words have brought them harm. The categories include defamation, invasion of privacy and right of publicity, intentional infliction of emotional distress, pornography, and cyber-expression.

Defamation

Legal protection against harm to one's reputation is of ancient origin; the Greeks and the Romans both authorized laws against slandering fellow citizens. But since citizens were defined as wealthy men, neither slaves nor women were so protected. Defamation law in the United States developed from English common (judge-made) law, and, early on, libel law in England was used as a judicial replacement for the duel—another means of protecting a man's honor (Forer, 1987, p. 52).

As traditionally defined, *defamation,* which includes the twin torts of libel and slander, is a false communication that "tends so to harm the reputation of another as to lower him in the estimation of the community or to deter third persons from associating or dealing with him" (Keeton, 1984, p. 774). In 1964, the U.S. Supreme Court ruled that the First Amendment protects false defamatory statements about public officials as long as the defendant does not publish them with "actual malice," defined by the Court as knowledge of falsity or reckless disregard for the truth (*New York Times v. Sullivan,* 1964). Over the next decade, the Court extended the actual-malice standard to include public figures as well as public officials. In many states, even private individuals must show actual malice in order to receive punitive damages (*Gertz v. Robert Welch, Inc.,* 1974).

Until recently, the literature has suggested that women have been under-represented in defamation law. One study notes, for example, that only 11% of libel plaintiffs in the mid-20th century were women (Bezanson, Cranberg, & Soloski 1987, p. 7). The overwhelming majority of libel plaintiffs are men engaged in corporate or public life who boast relatively elite standing in their communities (Bezanson et. al., 1987, p. 10).

In the last decade, however, feminist scholars have begun to examine defamation actions brought by female plaintiffs. One researcher found that the basis for most defamation actions brought by female plaintiffs involved statements about their sexual conduct (Borden, 1997, pp. 126–127). The same study suggested that even when women were successful in showing harm to their reputations, their damage awards were likely to be less than half those won by male plaintiffs (pp. 134–136). "This finding suggests that even a women's most 'valuable' socially constructed possession—her private chastity—is worth less than the male equivalent—his public honor" (p. 136).

Another study indicated that state defamation statutes historically have treated women and men differently, reinforcing the notion that women's reputations are generally tied to their sexual virtue while men's reputations are cast in terms of honor (Borden, 1998). One researcher argued that early-19th-century courts viewed the slandered reputations of women as a form of property, which required proof of "special damages" in order to be worthy of judicial redress (Pruitt, 2003).

In perhaps the only defamation action brought by a female plaintiff ever to reach the U.S. Supreme Court, Mary Alice Firestone, the third wife of the heir to the Firestone tire fortune, won a lawsuit against *Time* magazine for incorrectly reporting that her divorce was granted on grounds of her adulterous conduct (*Time v. Firestone,* 1976). Interestingly, even though she was very prominent in Palm Beach society and invited media attention during her divorce trial, the Court held that Firestone was not a public figure and therefore should not be required to meet the tough actual-malice standard set down a dozen years earlier in *New York Times v. Sullivan.* Yet it could be argued that by doing so, the Court simultaneously reinforced the cultural values that caused the reputational harm in the first place: that a woman's social self, her reputation, is attached to the twin doctrines of virtue and domesticity (Borden, 1997, pp. 112–115).

Invasion of Privacy

When an individual's interest in privacy has clashed with the interests of maintaining a press free from government interference, the courts have struck a balance in favor of the protections awarded the press in the First Amendment. Privacy law can be traced to a 19th-century *Harvard Law Review* article, in which the authors concluded that private individuals have an inherent right to be let alone and to be protected from unauthorized publicity in essentially private affairs (Brandeis & Warren, 1890, p. 193).

The public outcries against the publication of embarrassing facts or articles that intruded into the private sphere came during the era of Yellow Journalism, a time of stiff competition among newspapers, which relied on sensationalism to gain circulation. It was against this historical and social background that a common-law right to privacy developed, although turn-of-the-century courts at first rejected the privacy theory enunciated by Brandeis and Warren. The first such case to be decided involved Abigail Roberson, who sued a flour company and a company that made boxes for reproducing her likeness on their advertising posters without her permission (*Roberson v. Rochester Folding Box Co.,* 1902). The New York court denied her any right to protection against such conduct.

As the courts rejected such claims for invasion of privacy, however, the public embraced the doctrine, forcing the enactment of state statutes that clearly recognized a right to be let alone. In 1903, New York became the first state to enact legislation that allowed individuals to bring actions against those who invaded their privacy (N.Y. Sess. Laws, 1903, ch. 132, §§ 1–2). The privacy tort now encompasses four distinct kinds of privacy: unreasonable intrusion upon seclusion, improper appropriation of the name or likeness of another, public disclosure of private facts, and communication that places one in a false light.

Feminist scholar Jane Gaines has examined the intersection of invasion of privacy with intellectual property, an area of law known as the "right to publicity." She analyzed, among others, a lawsuit brought by Jacqueline Onassis against clothing designer Christian Dior in 1983. Onassis claimed that Dior appropriated her image without her consent for use in a sportswear advertisement, which appeared in several magazines, including the *New Yorker, Time,* and *Harper's Bazaar.* Although the person in the ad looked like Onassis, however, she was not; the photo was actually of Barbara Reynolds, an Onassis "look-alike," who was paid to appear in the ad. Whose image did Dior appropriate, that of the look-alike or that of the real Jackie Onassis?

The judge in the case decided in favor of Onassis, advancing the position that "the facial image had superseded the name, which was once thought to be personhood's nugget of value" (Gaines, 1989, p. 474). In the Onassis case, the image was more protectable as commercial (intellectual) property than as a claim to privacy.

Intentional Infliction of Emotional Distress

Like invasion of privacy, intentional infliction of emotional distress was not recognized as an independent cause of action until the late 19th century. The reluctance resulted primarily from concerns about fictitious claims and a torrent of new cases, as well as the fear that damages would prove difficult to measure (Keeton, 1984, p. 55). In addition, judges in early cases, many of which involved women who had suffered physical as well as emotional harm, scoffed at such lawsuits because such claims ran counter to what they considered reasoned jurisprudence. The prevailing view was that when it came to coping with the trials and tribulations of daily living, "a certain toughening of the mental hide is a better protection than the law could ever be" (Magruder, 1936, p. 1033).

Indicative of the early cases were causes of action brought by women under the following circumstances: a train nearly struck a women's buggy and she became ill (*Victorian Railways Commissioners v. Coultas*, 1888); a practical joker falsely reported to a woman that her husband had been seriously injured in an accident, and she went into shock (*Wilkinson v. Downton*, 1897); and a runaway team of horses stopped just short of a woman, and she suffered a miscarriage (*Mitchell v. Rochester Ry. Co.*, 1896). Only in *Wilkinson v. Downton* did the plaintiff recover damages for emotional distress and only then because the harm was deemed intentional.

Gradually, however, the courts have extended the protection and have come to define the emotional distress tort as comprising four elements: The plaintiff must show that the defendant's conduct was intentional or reckless, that the conduct was extreme and outrageous, that the conduct caused the plaintiff's emotional distress, and that the emotional distress was severe (Restatement, 1965).

Most of the emotional distress actions against the media have been brought in the last 30 years, and, because of the tough demands of the tort's outrageousness standard, the media have prevailed (Dreschel, 1985, pp. 346–347). In 1988, the U.S. Supreme Court first addressed the issue of whether actions against the media for emotional distress should enjoy the same high level of constitutional protection as defamation cases (*Hustler Magazine v. Falwell*, 1988). In the Falwell case, the Court held that the First Amendment protected an advertising "parody" published in the pornographic magazine, which depicted fundamentalist preacher Jerry Falwell as a drunk, a hypocrite, and foulmouthed and having engaged in an incestuous rendezvous with his mother in an outhouse in his hometown of Lynchburg, Virginia ("Jerry Falwell Talks," 1983, p. 20).

The Court reasoned that the First Amendment protected the *Hustler* ad because it was opinion, not fact; because Falwell was a public figure subject to the highest standard of proof of reputational harm (actual malice, as defined in defamation law); and because the statements in the ad were of public concern. What the Court failed to take account of, however, was the other person represented in the magazine's message: Helen Falwell, the minister's mother, a private person. One study points out that "the law would not have allowed recovery for harm to Helen Falwell's reputation because she died five years before publication of the ad-parody" (Borden, 1999, p. 292). Nevertheless, the harm to the reputation and the emotional tranquility of the symbolic Helen Falwell could be viewed as every woman's harm:

> For women, *Hustler* magazine's salacious and repugnant parody was born of centuries-old sexism, the manifestations of which are buried deep within the collective memories of the female psyche. As evidence of the depths of the sexism involved, one need only read the opinion in the Falwell case: Not once is Helen Falwell's name mentioned; not once is harm to her reputation seriously considered. (Borden, 1999, p. 315)

Pornography

As noted earlier, only a few feminist legal scholars have focused their research on freedom of expression, and when they have explored First Amendment issues, they have tended to write about pornography. MacKinnon argued that it is through a dearth of legal remedies regarding obscenity and pornography that First Amendment absolutism has come to be forged. "I take it seriously," she wrote, "when Justice Douglas speaking on pornography and others preaching absolutism say that pornography has to be protected speech or else free expression will not mean what it has always meant in this country" (MacKinnon, 1987, pp. 208–209)—in other words, women are excluded from exercising their rights of free speech.

Pornography is given First Amendment protection; obscenity is not, although the test for determining whether an expression is obscene is terribly murky. Neville (1995) made the point when he wrote,

> Obscenity would probably be the most viable First Amendment exception under which to analyze pornography, although certainly much pornography is not "obscene" under the legal definition and a great deal of obscenity is not pornographic. (p. 7)

In 1973, the U.S. Supreme Court broadened the protection for obscenity, holding that for a work to be deemed legally obscene, it must be patently offensive by community standards, appeal to prurient interests, and be without serious social, literary, artistic, political, or scientific value (*Miller v. California*, 1973). Trager and Obata (2004) agreed that the current definition of *obscenity* in the United States is far from clear and that the goal is to prevent the public "from being exposed to highly offensive erotic depictions" (p. 7). Pornography may be regulated only when it satisfies strict scrutiny or is similar to other proscribed categories of speech. Some argue that pornography is harmful in and of itself and that it should be regulated as a separate category of speech beyond First Amendment protection, much like obscenity, fighting words, or libel (Neville, 1995). Others regard pornography or erotic expression as contributing to the marketplace of ideas, "allowing people to explore a variety of views as part of a search for truth" (Trager & Obata, 2004, p. 13).

In 1984, feminist legal scholars Andrea Dworkin and Catharine MacKinnon crafted an ordinance for the City of Indianapolis, which provided a civil remedy for anyone harmed by conduct or content involving the "graphic sexually explicit subordination of women" (Indianapolis General Ordinance, 1984). The ordinance regarded pornography as a form of sex discrimination, subordinating women and denying them equality (MacKinnon, 1985, p. 22). It did not constitute a criminal law, but provided for compensatory remedies after the fact and on proof that the plaintiff had been harmed.

The federal courts struck down the Indianapolis ordinance (*American Booksellers Ass'n v. Hudnut*, 1984, 1986), arguing that to have done otherwise would have been to leave the government in control of all the institutions of culture, "the great censor and director of which thoughts are good for us" (*American Booksellers Ass'n v. Hudnut*, 1986, pp. 329–330).

First Amendment absolutist Nadine Strossen of the American Civil Liberties Union (ACLU) has argued that censoring hate speech or pornography would be as dangerous for equality rights as for free speech rights, noting that free speech is especially important to people who have traditionally suffered from discrimination; censorship has especially victimized members of politically powerless groups, including racial minorities and women; censorship of sexual expression has particularly harmed women and women's rights advocates; and restricting sexual expression undermines human rights more broadly (Strossen, 1996, pp. 7–13).

Heyman (2003), among others, has taken the opposing view, noting that "a strong argument can be made that violent pornography is wrongful in that it violates the right to recognition of women in general" (p. 21).

Cyber-Expression

Hate speech, privacy, and "cybersmut" (Burke, 1996) are among the key concerns of feminist jurisprudence as it examines issues involving the Internet and cyberspace. As early as 1996, Ditthavong (1996) wrote, "The Information Superhighway has apparently been evolving into a hostile environment for women; sexually explicit pictures, and, at times, hard-core pornography freely traverse the global superhighway, and chauvinistic bulletin boards and chat lines abound" (p. 1). The law is hard-pressed to keep pace with technological change, in part because "the government, hindered by its bureaucracy, does not have the resources to regulate the rapid changes in technology" (Ditthavong, 1996, p. 2). Furthermore, given its combination of elements of the print media, broadcasting, and interpersonal communication, it is unclear how the Internet can be regulated in keeping with "established First Amendment doctrine" (Leets, 2001, p. 4). Given the lack of geographical boundaries in cyberspace, the question of legal jurisdiction is also problematic.

The number of Internet users has doubled every year since 1993, and the number of hate speech Web sites has exploded since 1995 (Cronan, 2002, pp. 1, 2), making cyberspace a vast forum for hateful messages. Given the Internet's ability to provide speech that may incite violence, some scholars have called for a standard that meets the new demands of the Internet and yet preserves free speech (Cronan, 2002, p. 18) or a standard that places "very limited restrictions on some hate expression" (Leets, 2001, p. 1). The Supreme Court established the prevailing incitement standard in *Brandenburg v. Ohio* (1969). In that case, the Court held that a state could not forbid or proscribe advocacy of the use of force or of law violation except where such advocacy is likely to incite imminent lawless action.

Obscenity/indecency became the target of Congress in 1996, when it passed the Communications Decency Act (CDA), regulating obscenity/indecency for adults on the Internet. A year later, however, the Supreme Court ruled that two sections of the CDA were unconstitutional (*Reno v. ACLU,* 1997). Leets (2001) noted, "Congress and the Court disagreed on the medium-specific constitutional speech standard suitable for the World Wide Web" (p. 4).

Bartow (2000) has called for a property right to private, personal data on the Web, arguing that women, "reportedly the fastest-growing audience on the Web" (p. 2), are the subjects of personal data collection or "intelligence" that invades their privacy and makes them the targets of advertisers. Unlike European law, with strict and broad laws protecting personal information, "the only recent data protection law enacted in the United States protects only children" (Bartow, 2000, p. 10). That law was the Children's Online Privacy Protection Act, passed by Congress in October 1998, which requires Web sites or online services directed to children "to obtain verifiable parental consent prior to collecting individually identifiable personal information from children under the age of thirteen" (Bartow, 2000, p. 10).

Allen (2000) has argued that cyberspace offers to women who want it a level of privacy and anonymity "never before available for women who interact on a regular basis with numerous others" (p. 5). Conversely, Calvert and Brown (2000) have highlighted the dangers, mostly to women, of "peeping Toms" in cyberspace, calling for the legal system to act on "two emerging new social and technological trends—video voyeurism and the posting of voyeuristic images on the World Wide Web" (p. 49), both of which have implications for privacy, free speech, and commerce.

Conclusion

There is considerable scope for feminist scholarship of First Amendment jurisprudence. Opportunities abound for quantitative and qualitative work on the First Amendment and female protagonists in cases involving libel, privacy, emotional distress, obscenity and pornography, high school and college press, cameras in the courtroom, prior restraint, contempt issues, fair trial/free press, and more.

First Amendment jurisprudence in relation to women is relatively static. Cases involving free expression have involved women's sexuality and inferior social status, reinforcing cultural stereotypes and associating women with the private sphere and marginalizing them. As the composition of the Supreme Court changes with the retirement of Justice Sandra Day O'Connor, in January 2006, and the death of Chief Justice William Rehnquist, in September 2005, at a time when conservatives control both houses of Congress, the law may become even more divisive and even more gendered. If Supreme Court and federal appellate court vacancies are filled by Originalists, judges who "don't like interpreting the Constitution in light of present-day social developments and are generally skeptical of constitutional rights—like the right to have an abortion—that don't appear explicitly in the text of the Constitution" (Rosen, 2005, p. 44), future First Amendment cases may be subject to strict constructionism. Such an approach could restrict the influence of feminism on First Amendment jurisprudence and ensure the perpetuation of difference and dominance.

Questions for Discussion

1. Given past trends and contemporary political values and social mores, what predictions can you make for future First Amendment cases involving women?

2. Invasion-of-privacy suits have often involved women. Why do there seem to be more invasion-of-privacy cases involving women than there are libel cases?

3. Obscenity and pornography differ in First Amendment protection. Is the definition of *obscenity* plausible? Could the same definition apply to *pornography?* Is the market for pornography likely to affect its status under the First Amendment? Should pornography be regulated?

4. How are women both protected and imperiled in cyberspace?

5. Are women likely to interpret the law differently than men do? Why or why not? Please document your response with examples involving the Supreme Court's decisions in First Amendment cases, comparing the opinions of Justices Sandra Day O'Connor and Ruth Bader Ginsberg with those of their male colleagues.

Accessing Additional Information

Anita Allen-Castellitto, School of Law, University of Pennsylvania: http://www.law.upenn.edu/cf/faculty/aallen/

Ann Bartow, School of Law, University of South Carolina: http://www.law.sc.edu/bartow/

Diane L. Borden, School of Communication, San Diego State University: http://www.rohan.sdsu.edu/dept/schlcoom/facultybios/borden.htm

Catharine A. MacKinnon, School of Law, University of Michigan: http://cgi2.www.law.umich.edu/FacultyBioPage/facultybiopagenew.asp?ID=219

Lisa R. Pruitt, School of Law, University of California at Davis: http://www.law.ucdavis.edu/Facultyinfo.asp?PROFNAME=LisaRPruitt&bhcp=1

18

Situating "the Other"

Women, Racial, and Sexual Minorities in the Media

Carolyn M. Byerly, Howard University

I will no longer be made to feel ashamed of existing. I will have my voice: Indian, Spanish, white. I will have my serpent's tongue—my woman's voice, my sexual voice, my poet's voice. I will overcome the tradition of silence.

—Gloria Anzaldúa (1999)

The concept of "the Other," long entangled with an understanding of the self in Western culture, is the focus of this chapter.[1] The discussion reveals a journey by which the Other moved from the social and intellectual margins of 19th-century Europe into the cultural and academic mainstream of today, becoming increasingly politicized in the process. We will be particularly concerned with more recent developments in definition and application of the Other concept, which have expanded considerably by way of postcolonial, feminist, critical race, and queer theorists studying the media. These theorists recognize that the mainstream commercial media possess the potential both to act as a hegemonic force that reproduces the hierarchies of social power and a liberatory force that helps to bring about a more egalitarian society. The media industries and the visual and written products they produce are thus a significant and enduring site of struggle between the most and least powerful in society. For this reason, the chapter ends with an overview of how media activism has engaged problematic media representations, policy, and structural concerns.

A Short History of the Other

Nineteenth- and early-20th-century intellectual interest in the concept of self was related to a preoccupation with the individual and individualism. Austrian philosopher and theologian Martin Buber (1923/1958) described what he called the "I-Thou" relationship between the self and the eternal source of the world (or God). Austrian physician Sigmund Freud, who founded the field of psychology, spent much of his life conceptualizing the components of the self (id-ego-superego) and their significance in personal and social development. Freud believed that one's understanding of oneself operated at a subliminal level, what he called the "unconscious" (Hall, Held, & McGrew, 1992). Twentieth-century French psychoanalyst Jacques Lacan extended Freud's work by focusing on what he called the "mirror phase" of development in early childhood. We have no concept of ourselves, Lacan theorized, until we differentiate the self from the look (and face) of the Other, usually a parent. Lacan departed from Freud's theory of self as an internal (psychological-emotional) process by theorizing that the self is developed in relation to others, that is, through a process of social construction. Lacan believed that the formation of self in the look of the Other opened the infant to symbolic systems outside the self, with those systems including language, culture, and sexual difference (Hall et al., 1992, p. 287).

Who/What Is the Other?

Politicization of the "self-and-other" occurred by way of postcolonial writers, who moved the duality outside its Eurocentric, androcentric[2] origins and into international and academic discourses. Algerian writer Albert Memmi's (1965)[3] self-and-other preoccupation, as the title of his pathbreaking book *Colonizer and the Colonized* suggests, was with "the relationship of one group of people and another" (p. 38) at every level—psychological, economic, political, and cultural. Memmi recognized that "racism sums up and symbolizes the fundamental relation which unites colonialist and colonized" and that racism is built on ideological grounds that establish superiority of the colonizers at each of these levels (pp. 70-71). In the colonial process, Memmi said, the colonizer succeeds in depersonalizing the colonized, reducing individuality to "an anonymous collectivity" (p. 85). His critique of colonialism in North Africa factored economic, racial, and political dimensions into an understanding of self-and-other. Memmi also addressed liberation from oppression, a process that would require refusal (to assimilate) and self-renewal (through self-acceptance) (p. 136).

Even after such a rising up of the oppressed self to rid itself of colonial oppressors (the Other), however, the liberated self would be not be completely free, but rather a hybrid of colonized and colonizer, an ambiguous identity borne of membership in two cultures and the critical consciousness that emerged from understanding the complex relationship. By the early 20th century, the Other concept had already incorporated themes of ambiguity and double-consciousness, as expressed in postcolonial writings. Gloria Anzaldúa (1999) articulated a contemporary understanding of double-consciousness in *Borderlands,* in which she noted that the *mestiza,* formed by Mexican, Indian, and American cultures, "learns to juggle cultures . . . she has a plural personality" (p. 101).

The complexity of the racialized colonizer-colonized relationship was expressed by Martinique psychologist Frantz Fanon, who examined the impact of French colonization on Black people, both men and women. In *Black Skin, White Masks,* Fanon (1967) wrote, "The Antilleans have no inherent values of their own, they are always contingent on the presence of The Other" (p. 211). Emancipation for the Black people of Martinique had not erased the colonial relationship, Fanon argued, but rather reinscribed it so that Blacks remained reliant on their White superiors for their identities and self-worth. Concerned about colonialism's lasting impact on women, Fanon told the story of Mayotte Capécia, the laundress, in whom Fanon saw that "life was difficult for a woman of color" trying to achieve her dreams in the colonies (p. 45). Memmi's and Fanon's contributions to the self-and-other duality added political, racial, gender, and national dimensions, even though their basic parameters were still very close to Lacan's view of the self's development in relation to another entity, with the primary emphasis on the self.

The Marginalized Other

> *Je est un autre [I is other].*
>
> —Arthur Rimbaud (19th-century gay poet)

Palestinian scholar Edward Said's celebrated book *Orientalism* (1978) and its sequel, *Covering Islam* (1981), formulated yet another aspect of the

Other concept, the notion of marginalization. Said's Other was not the colonizer, but rather its opposite, the Middle-Eastern (Muslim) Arab, a generalized and racialized Other constructed through centuries of European paintings, drawings, photos, stories, and, more recently, the news media. The last of these focused on Muslims' exotic and mysterious religion, opaque language, strange dress, and anti-Western behavior. Said's criticisms addressed the news coverage of Muslims during various international crises in the 1970s, for example, the Iranian revolution that brought a theocratic state and the taking of the U.S. Embassy in Teheran and the hostage situation that occurred soon after.[4] Postcolonial writers like Said conceptualized the colonized Other as the third-world Other, the subaltern, the outsider, the less significant, the inferior, the silent, the less powerful, and so forth. How (and whether) the subaltern could speak[5] (i.e., communicate in order to articulate an analysis of his or her subjugation) would become a familiar question also posed by feminist, race, and queer theorists.

Differentiating "Samed" and "Othered"

Andermahr, Lovell, and Wolkowitz (2000) have suggested that if we are to differentiate self from Other, we should begin by asking who or what may be "samed" or "othered" (p. 192). As we have just seen, the postcolonial scholars introduced the notion of unequal power relations into their conceptualizations of the Other, and they implicated the media in disseminating an ideology of difference that served to reinforce the authority of those in positions of power. What is sought here briefly is an understanding of that more powerful side of the equation, the entity that is "samed."

In critical scholarship, the Powerful manifest themselves through the media in both subtle and overt ways today. At the macrolevel of ownership and finance, the Powerful extended its dominance through implementation of neoliberal policies[6] in the 1980s, both in the United States and throughout most of the world. Those policies permitted waves of mergers and acquisitions in all industries, but especially in telecommunication industries. That process concentrated ever more wealth and power in the hands of a few wealthy White men in the United States and Europe, a fact that has had consequences for those with less power and position (Byerly, 2004b; Gandy, 1998; McChesney, 1999).

Media and the Raced Other

Media scholars across theoretical perspectives see a causal relationship between media representation and real-life social relations, exemplified, for example, by the economic and political status of women, people of color, and sexual minorities, among others. Oscar Gandy (1998) cited cognitive (social science) research showing that the media contribute to an understanding and an appreciation of difference and that audiences integrate the beliefs and opinions generated by the media into their cognitive structures (p. 155). Gandy's own work on the cultural indicators project (with colleagues George Gerbner and others at University of Pennsylvania) for more than two decades revealed that women and young people in television programs, as well as non-Whites and the poor, were victimized more often than other groups. They concluded that these trends influenced, or cultivated, perceptions of society by frequent television viewers. Jack Glascock's (2003) content analysis of prime-time programs on cable stations UPN, Fox, and WB, which seek minority and youth audiences, found that Blacks and women are stereotyped, with Black men being more verbally aggressive than White men and Black women more provocatively (i.e., sexually) dressed than White women. Using social learning theory, Glascock concluded that these depictions would reinforce audience understandings of women and racial minorities.

Looking at representation historically, Jane Rhodes (1995) found that race figured into American media discourse as early as the 17th century in ways that helped to maintain the White-supremacist social order. For example, "The political discourse of early newspapers rendered [Blacks] invisible except as commodities," while publications both before and after the Revolutionary War "relied heavily on advertisements for the sale of slaves, or for the return of runaway slaves, as a source of revenue" (Rhodes, 1995, p. 35). Ward Churchill (1992) identified the U.S. media as major contributors to the degradation of Native Americans. Churchill's critique found that the media fail to show the underlying causes of most indigenous people's modern reality, including alcoholism, drug addition, poverty, family violence, high rates of teen suicide, and general despair (p. 8). In addition, the media create a profound invisibility of Native American culture and history, a misrepresentation of native beliefs and values (e.g., by lumping distinct tribal identities into a homogenous whole), and the enduring stereotype of the inferior Native (as opposed to the superior White European). These tendencies, Churchill said, "symbolically demolish" the achievements and humanity of a whole people (pp. 233–236).

The Gendered Other

Language, advertising, and other forms of communication are the vehicles through which men exert dominance over women's sexuality, according to

French feminist Luce Irigaray (1993). Irigaray theorized that women's identity formation, and hence women's behavior in the world, is based on "centuries of socio-cultural values to be rethought, to be transformed" (p. 11). Women, she said, have been deprived of images and meanings to affirm their own pursuits, to differentiate themselves from time-honored maternal scripts, or to be more masculine if they so choose. Feminist media scholarship since the 1970s has understood women's marginalization and stereotyping in news, television, and other media to be the result of a patriarchal media system that has manifested male biases in neglecting and undervaluing women's experiences, meanings, ongoing daily contributions, and imagery (Dines & Humez, 1995, p. xix). Women thus have been treated as the Other, marginalized in mainstream media representation by the powerful men who control media industries, with media content helping to systematically reproduce that unequal gendered social relationship.

Feminist journalist Betty Friedan (1963), an early critic of women's absence and stereotyping in serious U.S. news, magazine, and television content, was among the second-wave feminists who stimulated the birth of feminist media scholarship in the 1970s. That scholarship laid down a baseline of empirical research documenting women's omission from the media, what sociologist Gaye Tuchman (1978) called the media's "symbolic annihilation of women."[7] Tuchman said that the paucity of women's images on television means that "women don't matter much in American society" (p. 11). Feminist activists and researchers alike also called attention to the enduring stereotypes of the hypersexualized, male-dependent, basically unintelligent female. Woman as the Other thus has formed a central concern of both this early feminist literature and the more recent work by feminist media scholars.

Ellen Riordan (2004) focused her political-economic critique of the popular film *Crouching Tiger, Hidden Dragon* on the way that feminist themes and strong women's roles were undermined in the interest of profit. Riordan said the film "offers us a way to examine how global entertainment corporations naturalize patriarchal and capitalist ideology" (p. 87) by constructing and commodifying feminism in ways that undermine the political meaning of women's real self-determination. The film is visually stunning, financially successful, and features a number of accomplished female martial artists, but its story first stigmatizes (i.e., "Otherizes") and then kills off the strongest of these women, the only female who had not sought male approval.

Radhika Parameswaran's (2002) critique of *Crouching Tiger* also observed that the film's star, Malaysian actress Michelle Yeoh, is used to "narrate a story of sexuality for the consumption of the [Western] male gaze" (p. 296). Parameswaran also analyzed the widely circulating *National*

Geographic, finding that the magazine "uses women as indices of national tradition or global modernity" (pp. 292–293) without providing a clear indication that they are elevating the West, capitalism, Whiteness, and patriarchy in the process. The magazine has had a long history of Otherizing women from non-Western cultures, she said, by portraying them as naked, primitive, exotic, and devoid of history, social organization, traditions, values, or intelligence.

In *Black Sexual Politics,* Patricia Hill Collins (2004) analyzed the ways that mediated images of African Americans' masculinity and femininity contribute to their marginalization, something she has called the "new racism." The new racism is a system of de facto segregation by social class in urban areas, closed doors of opportunity in employment and education, and new gender stereotypes in the media. The last of these include deviant depictions, for example, the strong, angry, hypersexualized Black men portrayed as rappers and aggressive athletes; the compliant Black lady exemplified in the character of "Clare Huxtable"; the Jezebel (temptress) seen in the barely clad young Black women hip-hop performers; and the enduring welfare queen with too many children and a million ways to scam the system. Collins (2004) recognized the economic dimension of the new racism, in which "Mass media marketing of thug life to African American youth diverts attention away from social policies that deny Black youth education and jobs," leaving thug life in hip-hop as one of the "few places Black poor and working-class men can share their view of the world in public" (p. 159). Black men are particularly warned against stepping out of their tough guises lest they be branded *punks, sissies,* or *faggots,* all derogatory terms for homosexual men. Collins observed that "this Black gender ideology" constructs its thesis of weak men and strong women by drawing on heterosexism for meaning (p. 179).

The Sexualized (Queer) Other

Larry Gross (1995) has asserted that nonrepresentation in the mass media maintains the powerless status of groups that do not possess significant material or political bases of power (p. 62). Like Tuchman, Gross has found the term "symbolic annihilation" (which he and his colleague George Gerbner first coined) useful for problematizing the invisibility of gay, lesbian, bisexual, and transgendered (GLBT) minorities. To render them invisible is the first and most obvious way that news, entertainment television, and movies have historically Otherized GLBT (i.e., queer) citizens. Of all social groups, Gross said, lesbians and gay men are the least "permitted to speak for ourselves in the mass media" (p. 63). GLBT members have also been Otherized through their depictions, the most prevalent patterns being either to normalize gay and lesbian characters using standards for masculine and feminine heterosexuality or to stereotype them as campy, peculiar, or some other brand of deviant. Film scholar Vito Russo (1987) found that historically, mainstream films show gay characters (and their lives) as sterile in the areas of love and sexuality, and as silly or corrupt. Such depictions, he said, make gay people both nonthreatening and irrelevant.

Gross (1994) said that the current trend in television and film of "colonizing the straight gay" bows to a heterosexual normativity. Applying Gross's analysis, we see examples in network sitcoms like the award-winning *Will and Grace,* with Will's character devoid of sexual passion or a gay political consciousness. Some progress might be seen in the just-concluded police drama *NYPD Blue,* in the character "John Irwin" (played by Bill Brochtrup), who was occasionally allowed to have nonsexual dates with men. John's character was initially the butt of office jokes, but over time, he garnered both the respect and affection of his colleagues. Still, his character was constructed as the stereotypic sissy right up to a bouffant hairdo and a breathless, high-pitched voice, traits quite unlike Brochtrup's real-life persona. Program makers seem especially unwilling to represent lesbians, rendering invisible women's desire for other women and thereby avoiding any threat to heterosexuality or to the heterosexist male role of definer and center of female relationships (Hantzis & Lehr, 1994, p. 119). Not only are there few lesbian characters on television, but those who are present are seen through the lens of heterosexual normativity. Examples may be seen in the character of "Carrie," in the mainstream U.S. series *ER* (WB), and even "Buffy," of the eponymous *Buffy the Vampire Slayer* (UPN), whose romantic lives are mostly alluded to within the story rather than fully developed in story lines or explicit sexual scenes.

Liberating the Other

In tracing the development of the Other through both academic and political movements, as well as its contemporary manifestation in a range of critical literatures, we have intentionally focused on the problematic side of the situation in order to emphasize the relationship to real-life marginalized, colonized, and unjustly treated whole groups of people. We have also tried to bring some breadth to the discussion by considering nationality, culture, religion, race, gender, and sexual dimensions of the Other. In all instances, the media occupy a central role in perpetuating the syndrome of the Other through their images and messages. In developing the Other's journey, we have also had to explain its opposite, the Powerful interests against whom the Other is inevitably defined and measured and who, naturally, control the media systems that purvey the images and messages of the Other.

To let the problem side of the equation stand alone, however, would be to paint an incomplete picture and grant it the force of inevitability. A more accurate and empowering reflection would be to acknowledge that no hegemonic system is without its contradictions—indeed, these open the spaces for those in positions of less power to critique and to exert their agency in order to address the injustice. This denotes a dialectical process, an ongoing struggle between ideas, values, and control for legitimacy and authority among the parties involved. The dialectical process, however, is also understood as one that is both uneven in its progress and unpredictable in its outcome (Byerly, 1999). The foregoing examples have focused on the persistence of stereotypes and other marginalization.

Media activism by women, racial minorities, and gay and lesbian and other groups constituting the Other, undertaken since the 1970s, has also generated changes. As we bring a number of examples to light, we note that all modern social movements in the world have made media coverage and representation of their members and issues part of their political agendas. Change goals have (and do) include macrolevel reform through calls for public policy that would expand citizen access or limit ownership; mesolevel reforms, such as industry-level policies to promote greater diversity in employment; and microlevel changes involving areas like standards for more diverse (and honest) representations in content. Within my own nation, the United States, advocacy groups like National Organization for Women (NOW), National Association for the Advancement of Colored People (NAACP), Gay and Lesbian Alliance Against Defamation (GLAAD), National Lesbian and Gay Journalists' Association (NLGJA), and the range of minority journalist groups—national associations of Black, Asian, and Hispanic journalists—among many others, have used a range of tactics to gain media access and improve representation. Most of these groups give annual awards for specific improvements, for example, the NAACP Image Awards to the film and television industry, and they also lobby to prevent harm, for example, GLAAD's unsuccessful campaign in the late 1990s to stop gay singer Elton John from performing with White rapper Eminem, whose misogynist and homophobic lyrics had raised public protest.

Advocacy groups have also sought to train journalists, for example, NOW's use of press kits on specific feminist issues and political reforms (dating from the early 1970s), and GLAAD's reporter's manual with historical material and guide to GLBT terminology (Byerly, 2004a, 2004b). We also note the current presence of a number of excellent PBS television public affairs programs, for example, the weekly *In the Life,* on GLBT experience; the nightly *Tavis Smiley Show,* hosted by African American journalist Tavis Smiley; and the weekly *Now,* formerly with veteran progressive journalist Bill Moyers and his junior colleague David Brancaccio (and since January 2005, only with Brancaccio). Additional longtime players in expanding the voices of the Other are the range of media established within marginalized communities: *off our backs* (feminist newsjournal), *Ms.* (feminist magazine), *Essence* and *Ebony* (African American magazines), the *Washington Blade* newspaper, and *Advocate* (GLBT magazine), among thousands of others.

Another aspect of the struggle now emerges in the form of a broad, effective citizens' movement that is, among other things, challenging recent ownership rulings by the U.S. Federal Communication Commission (FCC). One significant outcome was a stay issued by the Third Circuit Court of Appeals in Philadelphia on September 3, 2003, stopping the implementation of the FCC's deregulation rules issued in June of that same year. The lawsuit was brought by the Media Access Project on behalf of the Philadelphia-based Prometheus Radio Project, started by a group of young people who establish and promote the use of low-powered radio in the United States and developing nations. The ruling, upheld by the U.S. Supreme Court in June 2005, noted that further consolidation in the telecommunications industry would harm Prometheus's ability to operate its projects, which have always specifically represented poor, minority, and women's interests. A longer-range political agenda for national media reform has been fomented through two conferences organized by the nonprofit organization Free Press. The first was held in November 2003, in Madison, Wisconsin, and drew nearly 2,000 people; the second, in St. Louis, Missouri, in May 2005, drew more than 2,500 (FreePress.org, 2005; McChesney, 2004), with the goals being to train grassroots media activists as well as to examine federal law and propose specific changes.

Space prevents a full review of the history and impact of media activism that strives to give those on the social margins access to mainstream media. However, it bears noting that such activism, while essential, should not be understood as necessarily harmonious in its undertaking. Problems are bound to arise, for instance, when any group of people or community tries to agree on what is authentic representation. Jigna (2004) observed, in relation to representation of people in South Asian diaspora films, that it is unlikely that all will ever fully agree that any representation is complete or "right" in seeking to "project the representation of all" (p. 210). Even as we celebrate the emergence of more diverse images of women, people of color, queer citizens, and others signifying the Other, media scholars will continue to be faced with the task of scrutinizing these images, the structural contexts within which they arise, and the struggle over who is in charge of speaking for whom. Scholarship thus becomes inevitably intertwined in the dialectical process through which the Other seeks recognition, voice, presence, and the right to exert itself in society.

Notes

1. In this article, I use the term the *other* in lower case when I refer to its position in the self-other duality, and I capitalize it, the *Other*, when designating it as a construct central to theory, such as that employed by various critical scholars over the last few decades.
2. Masculinist.
3. Originally published in the French in 1957.
4. Written more than two decades ago, Said's analysis is still fresh and relevant to contemporary stereotypic depictions of Arabs, particularly in relation to U.S. media accounts associated with the September 11, 2001, attacks and President George W. Bush's war on terrorism. For a fuller discussion of the research associated with media coverage of September 11 and U.S.-led wars against both Afghanistan and Iraq, see Byerly (2005), "After September 11: The Formation of an Oppositional Discourse," in *Feminist Media Studies*.
5. The reference here is to Gayatri Chakravorty Spivak's (1988) well-known article "Can the Subaltern Speak?"
6. Neoliberal policies stem from a philosophy that favors corporatism and seeks to weaken labor and other social movements that oppose it. For a fuller discussion of neoliberalism in relation to media industries, see McChesney (1999, 2004); for discussion more specifically related to women and media, see Byerly (2004b).
7. Tuchman borrowed the phrase from its originator George Gerbner (1972).

Questions for Discussion

1. What was the contribution of psychology to the definition of the Other?

2. How did postcolonial writers politicize the definition of the Other?

3. In what ways have feminist scholars found the concept of the Other useful in their analyses of women's subjugation?

4. Why might the media be understood as a central force in any study of the Other?

5. Describe the dialectical process associated when those representing the Other struggle to achieve greater self-determination. How are the media associated with this process?

Accessing Additional Information

Media Portrayals of Gays and Lesbians: http://www.media-awareness.ca/english/issues/stereotyping/gays_and_lesbians/index.cfm

MediaWatch: http://www.mediawatch.com/welcome.html

UN Chronicle|Marginalization of Women in the Media: http://www.un.org/Pubs/chronicle/2003/issue4/0403p38.asp-16k

19

Myths of Race and Beauty in Teen Magazines

A Semiotic Analysis

Meenakshi Gigi Durham, The University of Iowa

That the field of representation remains a place of struggle is most evident when we critically examine contemporary representations of blackness and black people. I was painfully reminded of this fact recently when visiting friends on a once colonized black island. Their little girl is just reaching that stage of preadolescent life where we become obsessed with our image. Her skin is dark. Her hair chemically straightened. Not only is she fundamentally convinced that straightened hair is more beautiful than curly, kinky, natural hair, she believes that lighter skin makes one more worthy, more valuable in the eyes of others.

—bell hooks (1993)

I n a recent article in the *New York Times Magazine,* writer Mary Tannen (2004, p. 60) reflects on the ideal American beauty; invoking such icons as Isabel Archer and Katharine Hepburn, she rhapsodizes over the way "the

American beauty is sexy" and the fact that her allure lies in "the courage of her intellect" and "her willingness to ignore boundaries." Yet the writer seems oblivious to the fact that her interpretation of "ideal American beauty" is unabashedly and unquestionably White. No women of color intrude on her construction of the closed and lily-white sphere of "American beauty," nor does she note this omission.

The absence of racial diversity in this article underscores the point that it is impossible to conceptualize beauty in Western society apart from considerations of race. The apparently racially unmarked figures of Marilyn Monroe and Katharine Hepburn and Jackie Kennedy that populate Tannen's essay are in fact unmistakably marked by Whiteness—what Dyer (1997) calls "the default" race. A long-standing literature on race and beauty examines the deep and complex articulations of these seemingly discrete concepts, reminding us that beauty is not only a social construction, but an ideological one that is bound to axes of power including race, class, and gender.

As Davis (1997) has pointed out,

> There is a racial hierarchy among women in terms of appearance. Women with white skin, blonde and straight hair, blue eyes and small noses are at the top, and women with dark skin, black and curly hair, and big noses are at the bottom. . . . Women who conform to the ideal, or come close to conforming, can feel superior to other women simply because of their racial characteristics. (p. 92)

Over the years, representations of beauty in the media and popular culture have reflected and reasserted these racialized social hierarchies. Even when non-White women have been portrayed as objects of beauty, their features and phenotypes are close to the Western Caucasian ideal; as Lakoff and Scherr (1984) observe, their "features [are] close enough to white not to shock the sensibilities of mainstream Americans" (p. 91). As feminist scholars point out, this narrow conception of beauty has had material consequences for women: The consistent societal exaltation of women who conform to the conventions of beauty conversely marginalizes and devalues women who do not.

In an effort to correct for some of these problems, magazines launched in recent years have declared goals of diversity in representation. At the forefront of this trend are teen fashion and beauty magazines. In 1997, *Women's Wear Daily* noted that teenage girls are "totally accepting of ethnic and cultural diversity" ("Free to Be Me," 1997, p. 10). That premise underpins the editorial philosophy of many new magazines aimed at adolescent girls. For example, "*Teen Vogue* has successfully differentiated itself editorially from the rest of the teen titles, reaching out to a more sophisticated, discerning, multicultural teen girl," asserts Condé Nast executive Carol Pais (Deeken, 2004, p. 22). Similarly, former editor-in-chief of *Seventeen* magazine declares, "We're very much aware that our readers live in a multicultural world, and we reflect that on the pages and on the cover" (Parr, 1997, p. 36).

The terms *multicultural* and *diversity* are easily bandied about by media managers eager to position their products at the cutting edge of the industry. But what do these terms mean in operational terms? How do they play out in the magazines themselves?

Teen Magazines and Their Readers

While teen fashion and beauty magazines may appear to be a frivolous and unimportant pop culture genre, in fact, these publications are tremendously influential in girls' lives and have been the subject of some 20 years of serious academic scholarship.

Textual analysis of this genre has yielded fairly consistent results indicating that these magazines' representations of ideal femininity, sexuality, and gender roles for girls are typically restricted, unhealthy, unrealistic, and supportive of a patriarchal power structure (Driscoll, 2002; Duffy & Gotcher, 1995; Durham, 1999; Garner, Sterk, & Adams, 1998 ; McRobbie, 1983; Peirce, 1990, 1993). On the other hand, audience work with the young readers of these publications indicates that they are not the passive cultural dupes one might imagine; many girls recognize the unrealistic and even harmful nature of much of the imagery in the magazines yet are ultimately illequipped to resist the rhetorical visions of these cultural forms (Currie, 1998; Duke & Kreshel, 1998; Durham, 1999; Frazer, 1987). In addition, the ways in which the magazines are read are contingent on girls' race and socioeconomic class. Duke (2000) found African American girls to be far more resistant to the dominant ideologies of femininity in these magazines than White girls, because "African Americans girls are largely excluded from the dominant discourse on feminine beauty" (p. 384).

Duke (2000) points out that "American teen magazines are lagging behind girls' desires to see new, more inclusive images of femininity" (p. 386). This observation runs counter to the vaunted statements of the editors and other executives quoted in the trade press, who assert that the "new and improved" versions of teen magazines are in fact responsive to the racial diversity and open-mindedness of their readers.

In an effort to interrogate their claims and investigate the representations of racial diversity in these magazines, in this chapter, I undertake a semiotic analysis of teen magazine texts and images. In tackling this topic, this study seeks to do three things:

Empirically analyze a representative teen magazine image in terms of the identity politics that mark contemporary female youth culture

Use these data to interpret representations of race in their relationship to beauty and sexuality

Employ these findings as a heuristic device for developing new research questions that can offer nuanced and socially conscious information about adolescent girls and the media in today's racial and gendered climate

Semiotics as Feminist Method

Semiotics, or *semiology,*[1] is an approach to the analysis of culture that is singularly suited to feminist critique because of its inherent questioning of the "taken for granted" dimensions of social life. Defined by one of its pioneers, Charles Saussure (1974), as "the study of the life of signs within society" (p. 16), semiotics, like feminism, interrogates the construction of social meanings in their historical, political, and cultural contexts, with a view to recognizing and actively critiquing their philosophical underpinnings and material implications.

"The appeal of semiotics is that it is basically iconoclastic," writes Danesi (1999, p. 197). Semiotics challenges the worldviews transmitted almost imperceptibly through everyday sign systems. Through its attention to the ideological themes and myths inscribed by means of various symbolic forms, including language, images, music, fashions, and other cultural products, semiotics offers us a way to understand the role of communication and culture in the shaping of the social environment and the location of people within it. Hierarchies of power based on signifiers such as race, gender, class, or physical ability can most effectively be understood and then deciphered as semiotic effects. This is a perspective that is closely aligned with the feminist conception of gender as a social construct rather than a biologically deter-mined essentialism (see, for example, Bem, 1993; Brownmiller, 1984; Butler, 1999; de Beauvoir, 1952; Devor, 1989; Fausto-Sterling, 1985; Millett, 1969; Money, 1995; Ortner, 1996). A great deal of feminist scholarship is con-cerned with the ways in which discourses of gender are generated by and function within a patriarchal system—what bell hooks (1997) describes as a "white supremacist capitalist patriarchy"—in order to sustain inequities that subjugate women. Because the focus of semiotics is the creation, circulation, and interpretation of such discourses in the form of social "signs," it provides a useful tool for feminist media scholarship.

The very premise of semiotic study—that social meanings and their attendant power formations can be uncovered through the analysis of texts—has been challenged in various ways. The poststructuralist critique of semiotics is based on the complaint that textual analysis fails to allow for the agency of people in a society to decode signs in a variety of ways. Signs, in the poststructuralist view, are polysemic (that is, they have many possible meanings); the deep structures of a society cannot determine the multiplicity of possible readings of a sign. Yet I would argue from a feminist and critical position that texts, and media texts in particular, are deliberately and carefully constructed in order to function successfully in a system of commodity capitalism. The very fact that media texts need to generate profits, not only for the entities that produce them, but for the media industries (notably advertisers) that support them, means that the texts are in fact encoded with ideological themes designed to create niche audiences and to encourage specific types of consumption and spending by those audiences. As Moores (1993) points out, there are "constraints imposed on polysemy at the moment of textual production" (p. 29).

Teen magazines' revenues are generated in large part by the advertisers who buy space in their pages, and these advertisers represent the billion-dollar cosmetics, fashion, diet, and fitness industries. As Smythe (2000) famously declared, the principle function of the mass media is to deliver audiences to advertisers, and "the work which audience members perform for the advertiser to whom they have been sold is learning to buy goods and to spend their income accordingly" (p. 266). Media content is thus intentionally designed to motivate spending on advertisers' products. In consuming media, audiences also consume the ideologies advanced by the magazines in support of their commercial interests. These ideologies are often the "common sense" of a society, by means of which power hierarchies are maintained, manifesting themselves in media texts. Of course, there is always the possibility that audience members can negotiate or resist the dominant ideological messages in the texts, as Hall (1980) suggested. Yet even Hall's well-known encoding/decoding model is cautious about the possibility of free-ranging interpretations of multiple meanings in texts, known in semiotics as polysemy:

> Polysemy must not . . . be confused with pluralism. Connotative codes are *not* equal among themselves. Any society/culture tends, with varying degrees of closure, to impose its classifications of the social and cultural and political world. These constitute a dominant cultural order, though it is neither univocal nor uncontested. (Hall, 1980, p. 134, emphasis in original)

The capital bases of the media industries, coupled with the ways in which hierarchies of power function to construct a "dominant cultural order," indicate that far from being disconnected from the material realities of the world, semiotic analysis is in fact highly attuned to the material consequences of ideological sign systems. Signs are "the products of human beings in particular material circumstances" (Seiter, 1993, p. 63), yet in media production, they are also institutional and societal products motivated by capital. Semiotic analysis is designed to uncover the ideological themes embedded in the signs, with the goal of addressing and rectifying the material injustices and social oppressions they sustain.

Basics of Semiotic Analysis

A *sign* constitutes the basic unit in semiotic analysis. Although semiotic analysis began with the study of language, and words constituted the signs under scrutiny, the term has expanded in contemporary semiotics to refer to any entity that conveys meaning in a society. Thus, a sign could be linguistic, visual, aural, or even tactile; a photograph, a building, an item of clothing, a word, a billboard, or a film can be defined as a sign. In semiotic analysis, signs are understood to have meanings that are determined by social convention. Signs may at some level refer to real-world objects, but each sign must be interpreted in the context of a particular society, culture, and moment in time. Umberto Eco (1976) emphasizes that a sign has no connection with its referent outside of social consensus. This point is crucially important in the semiotic analysis of media communication, especially in the case of teen magazines, in which images and texts may appear to represent a "real" referent but in fact are greatly manipulated prior to their appearance in print. It is important to note that the meanings conveyed by symbols are not only socially derived but also culturally and historically situated; symbols do not necessarily convey the same meanings at different points in time or across cultures. Thus, in semiotic analysis, meaning making is understood to be historicized, culture specific, and socially constituted.

In semiotic analysis, signs are closely examined to determine the specific strategies they employ in order to convey and fix meaning. The patterns or codes into which various types of signs are organized are studied to reveal how linkages among signs work to construct meanings. The ways in which meanings intersect with the cultural context of the signs are also studied. A sophisticated dimension of this contextual reading is myth analysis, which is predicated on the notion that signs have various levels of meaning or "orders of signification" through which certain cultural values and ideologies are inscribed or reinforced (Barthes, 1972). First-order significations are literal meanings; second-order significations are connotations or implied meanings created through social consenus. For Barthes, there is a level of meaning beyond connotation, which is *myth,* a third term that refers to widespread beliefs that make up the "common sense" of a society, although they are also constructions. As Barthes (1972) points out in his landmark book *Mythologies,* "There is no fixity in mythical concepts: They can come into being, alter, disintegrate, disappear completely. And it is precisely because they are historical that history can very easily suppress them" (p. 120). Myths, in Barthes's definition, are semiological systems that naturalize socially constructed concepts, making them seem innocent and unmotivated— when in fact they tend to operate in the service of dominant power.

Method

To interrogate the sign systems in teen magazines for their ideological content vis-à-vis multiculturalism, here I provide an example of a semiotic analysis of a magazine cover with, on the face of it, multicultural content. I use semiotic terms and concepts to analyze the sign systems at work in the cover art and the ideologies they convey via the codes of signification. For the analysis, I have selected the cover of the April 2005 issue of *Seventeen* magazine, for several reasons, the first being that the dominant cover photograph of Grammy-award-winning singer Alicia Keys offers a manifestation of multiculturalism that seems to conform to the ideas of the media executives quoted earlier in this article. Keys is African American, and thus the use of her image in a prominent position on the cover seems to vindicate the editors' claims that they are sensitive to diversity. Moreover, Keys's photograph is part of a photographic collage on the cover that features a number of young female celebrities and also seems to present a racially diverse range of people.

Seventeen was selected for this analysis because of its documented significance in adolescent girls' culture. It is a giant in the world of teen magazines—it outsells its nearest competitor *(Teen People)* by almost 2 to 1, with a circulation of 2,431,943 (*Bacon's Magazine Directory,* 2003). In addition, *Seventeen* has long been "a perennial leader" in the teen market, is in "every school library in the U.S." (and so has a pass-along readership far higher than its base circulation figures), and enjoys a general reputation for excellence (Rubin, 1993, p. 48).

Although specific circulation breakdowns by race are difficult to ascertain, there is evidence that *Seventeen* reaches a significant number of non-White readers:

Seventeen reaches 44% of "ethnic females 12 to 19" (defined as African American, "other" race, or from a Spanish speaking household); *Teen* and *YM* each reach 34% of these same girls. African American girls ages 12 to 19 make up the single largest nonwhite group of readers—they comprise, on average, about 12% of the readership for each of the three major teen titles. (Duke, 2000, p. 368)

By comparison, recent data indicate that almost 20% of *Teen People's* subscribers are non-White, of which 14.2% are Black and 5.5% are "other" (MRI Teenmark, 1999).

Thus, *Seventeen*'s readers are racially diverse, and its editors have claimed to represent that diversity in the magazine's editorial content. But a semiotic interrogation of an apparently multicultural image reveals a less sanguine picture.

Analysis

McCracken (1993) offers us a useful rubric for the semiotic analysis of magazine covers. She describes magazine covers as "complex semiotic systems, communicating primary and secondary meanings through language, photographs, images, color and placement" (p. 13). In semiotic analysis, it is important to see these elements of sign systems as operating via intricate interrelationships with one another as they are organized by means of design rules or codes. The codes through which signs are organized serve to stabilize their meanings and limit the possibility of polysemic readings (i.e., multiple interpretations) of the texts. Codes are, in effect, the mechanisms of ideology.

As McCracken (1993) points out, "The principal image on every cover is a nonverbal one, a photograph that we see before or while reading the verbal messages" (p. 22). In the case of the April 2005 *Seventeen* cover, the principal photographic image is a close-up of Alicia Keys's face. She has light-brown skin, and her dark hair, clearly below shoulder length, is straightened and blow-dried to curl away from her face. She wears makeup in soft, rosy colors that complement the colors used in the text on the page, and the dominant shades of pink and orange are culturally connected to a rather intense femininity (see Picariello, Greenberg, & Pillemer, 1990, who note the widespread association of pink with the female gender in American culture, and whose experimental research found that young children predict gender and gender behavior based on clothing color). Her orange lipstick complements the brilliant orange text in which her name, "Alicia Keys," is superimposed on her left cheek; this color, in turn, corresponds to the orange of the magazine's nameplate and the cover line, "Find your perfect hairstyle," on the left side of the page.

Thus, through the deployment of color and the arrangement of photograph, nameplate, and cover line, Keys is chromatically and symbolically linked both to the archetypal *Seventeen* reader and to the "perfect hairstyle" promised by the text. The placement of text and image works within a design code that is the equivalent of a grammar or syntax; its elements are arranged in a conventional pattern created to relate the words to the photograph in order to attach a specific meaning to the image. The relationship of these images effectively compels the connotation of the cover image. McCracken (1993) calls this a "montage" effect, calling on Eisenstein's cinematic theory of montage, in which two successive and separate images, "A" and "B," form a third cell, "C," in the viewer's consciousness, which produces a meaning that exceeds the two individual images. Similarly, on its own, the photograph of Keys might be read in various ways; but in combination with the colors and texts of the cover, it takes on a specific meaning linked with the concepts of ideal youth and beauty the magazine wants to convey. In Barthes's terms, the colors and texts "anchor" the meaning of the image so that other possible readings are less likely. Keys's looks are fixed as representing ideal youth and beauty.

For the purposes of this chapter, the cover must be interrogated more rigorously to apprehend how those ideals of youth and beauty are constituted through the use of Keys's image. Keys's skin color, long straight hair, and fine features are close to the Caucasian norm identified by Davis (1997). Thus, although the magazine does feature an African American woman on its cover, its editors have selected one whose looks do not vary much from the Caucasian models they typically use as cover girls. Hill (2002) finds that women's skin color is correlated with perceived attractiveness among African Americans: In his study, African American respondents assigned higher attractiveness ratings to women with lighter skin tones. Similarly, Russell, Wilson, and Hall (1993) posit a link between light skin and perceived femininity for African American women. So, what Bates (1994) has dubbed "colorism" is employed to reinforce societal hierarchies of beauty based on skin color and hair texture.

In semiotic terms, the paradigmatic selection of Keys from the range of African American women available to be featured on the cover reinforces the privileging of light skin, long hair, and small features in defining "beauty."

Syntagmatically—that is, looking at the image of Keys in relation to the combination of elements on the page—the main cover photograph is part of a series of photographs of female celebrities that border the page. Six smaller "mug shots" on the cover feature the singers and actresses Hilary Duff,

Lindsay Lohan, Beyoncé Knowles, Christina Aguilera, Cameron Diaz, Jessica Simpson, and Ashlee Simpson. Almost all are blond; and most striking is the fact that the two "women of color" (Knowles and Aguilera, who are, respectively, African American and Latina) sport blond tresses and have blue eyes. Thus, the "multiculturalism" of the cover images is again defined in terms of Caucasian phenotypes. These images are labeled with cover lines that read, "The best (& worst) looks," "Hot new MTV shows," and "Star beauty secrets," with red arrows pointing to photographs of two beauty products: Pavé hairstyling mousse and Physicians Formula mascara.

The need for similarity among models speaks to a construction of beauty predicated on sameness within an apparent discourse of difference. This homogenization works to co-opt and smooth over difference, subsuming it within a larger discourse of congruity that erases and elides any social, cultural, political, or class difference related to race (as well as any trace of individuality on the part of the girls), in a world where physical markers of racial difference are in fact still the cause of discrimination and systemic oppressions.

This theme of sameness resonates with one of Barthes's (1972) characterizations of the rhetoric of myth, which he calls "identification." He notes,

> The petit-bourgeois is a man unable to imagine the Other. If he comes face to face with him, he blinds himself, ignores and denies him, or *transforms him into himself.* In the petit-bourgeois universe . . . any otherness is reduced to sameness. The spectacle or tribunal, which are both places where the Other threatens to appear in full view, become mirrors. This is because the Other is a scandal which threatens his essence. (p. 151, italics added)

A confrontation with racial difference would jeopardize the seamless gratification of consumerism that is one of the magazine's primary roles; yet difference could not be completely ignored without the creation of a disjuncture between the magazine and the "real world" of diversity, as well as with the dominant ideology of multiculturalism its young readers have grown up with. Difference, therefore, must be incorporated and transformed, and the construction of beauty from a single paradigm effectively neutralizes any problems associated with racial difference.

The presence of the beauty products on the page conveys the message that the "beauty" of the cover models can be achieved through the purchase and use of the products. As McCracken (1993) points out, the magazine cover is a "covert advertisement" that "leads readers into the consumerist ideology that permeates the magazine as whole" (p. 15). According to Barthes (1972), these signs perform a relay function that refers to other texts inside the magazine, notably the ads that generate most of the magazine's profits.

Thus, the semiotic codes of the cover work to create a powerful myth: that beauty is defined in specific terms associated with a narrow range of phenotypical features—light skin, straight (preferably blond) hair, fine features, youth, and slenderness—and that such beauty can be purchased. Multiculturalism functions only within this paradigm. Any variance from these representational codes would threaten the consumer ideology that underpins the magazine's commercial basis, wherein beauty and hair products, fashions, and diet aids are touted in the advertising pages that financially sustain the magazine. As Mattelart (1986) has noted, "The ideology professed by a magazine is invariably the result of its commercial situation" (p. 75).

Conclusion

Myth analysis is a branch of semiology that strives to uncover the symbolic meanings of texts, with the understanding that these meanings are constituted and constrained by their cultural, historical, and social contexts. Myth analysis is always a social and political act: "Meanings are never just textual; they are always socio-political, and it is upon this dimension that the mythologist focuses" (Fiske, 1993, p. 108). The goal of myth analysis is demythologizing: uncovering and making transparent the ideological formations that are obscured by the naturalizing and normalizing effects of myths in our culture. As Macdonald (1995) put it, "The Barthian model claims that the diverse and multifaceted qualities of reality are flattened into routine ways of thinking and talking" (p. 1). Representations of racialized beauty in magazine texts offer a conception of racial diversity that is fraught with serious sociopolitical implications.

In conducting a semiotic myth analysis of the data texts, I sought to discern how sign systems were deployed to construct and frame racialized beauty. My analysis revealed that race was deployed ingenuously to signal superficial diversity that overlays a rhetoric of sameness, creating a myth of racial equivalence rather than equality. As it was used on this magazine cover, race functioned to support a dominant ideology of assimilation, whereby difference was minimized and marginalized in a beauty culture defined primarily by conformity to a hegemonic ideal.

This myth evaded any engagement with contemporary politics of difference. The myriad configurations developing from the rapid-fire cross-cultural and multiracial transactions that are part of contemporary youth culture are invisible in this *Seventeen* magazine cover's discourses of beauty. On the cover, racialized identity is not fluid, dynamic, or dialectical. Racial difference means only an incremental change in hair, skin, or eye color achieved by means of the purchase of products.

In this way, myths of racialized beauty work to articulate or link race with compulsory consumption of beautification products and to disarticulate or disconnect it from its political, social, historical, and transnational components.

Reception studies (Duke, 2000; Duke & Kreshel, 1998; Frazer, 1987) indicate that girls are not passive cultural dupes. They do not unquestioningly accept the constructions of femininity and beauty advanced by teen magazines. Yet little is known about how girls respond to constructions of race in these magazines, as well as in other media, particularly in relation to their own notions of femininity, beauty, and sexuality. This study points to an urgent need for audience research to learn more about how girls negotiate these texts in the context of the vital and powerful racial and cultural currents in contemporary youth culture.

This analysis also points to an imperative to uncover strategies for reframing beauty in terms of its sociopolitical linkages and implications for race in its expressions in youth culture. With this in mind, further analysis of a variety of youth cultural texts is called for in order to understand more about the media environment in which concepts of beauty and femininity are circulated among contemporary youth. More mainstream consumer teen magazines, as well as alternative periodicals, should be studied for their presentations of race and beauty. New magazines such as *LatinGirl*, targeted specifically to Latina girls, may contain different or more progressive representations of multiracial beauty; in addition, girls may be taking cues from nonmainstream media sources such as 'zines (self-published), independent Web sites, and musical performers whose engagements of themes of race and beauty diverge from mainstream teen magazines' unyielding discourse of assimilation and homogenization through consumerism.

Note

1. There is some debate about the terms *semiotics* versus *semiology* in the literature. Saussure originally used the term *semiology*, and as Roland Barthes points out in his foreword to *The Fashion System* (1983), the term at its inception was not specifically linked with linguistics, as it later came to be. Barthes (1983) sees semiology as a broader and more encompassing term that takes "the form of a discovery, or more precisely of an exploration" (p. ix). But in *Media Semiotics: An Introduction*, Jonathan Bignell (1997) uses the terms interchangeably and in fact prefers *semiotics* in reference to media analysis. Following Bignell, I have opted for the term *semiotics* in this chapter.

Questions for Discussion

1. How is beauty tied to race and class?

2. Why does the author consider semiotics to be a feminist research methodology?

3. What are the main critiques of semiotics? How does the author respond to them?

4. In terms of semiotics, what is a "myth"? Can beauty be seen as a myth, by this definition? Explain your answer.

5. What does the author mean by "the politics of difference"?

Accessing Additional Information

"Editorial: Feminism and Semiotics," article by Barbara Godard: http://www .newcastle.edu.au/discipline/fine-art/theory/analysis/semiotic.htm

Semiotic Analysis of Images: http://www.newcastle.edu.au/discipline/fine-art/ theory/analysis/semiotic.htm

"Semiotics, An Introduction," online paper by Donald J. Cunningham (Indiana University) and Gary D. Shank (University of Northern Illinois): http://www .indiana.edu/~educp550/shtcrs.html

Semiotics and Advertising, Web site by Tom Streeter at the University of Vermont: http://www.uvm.edu/%7Etstreete/semiotics_and_ads/

Semiotics for Beginners, Web site by Daniel Chandler at the University of Wales: http://www.aber.ac.uk/media/Documents/S4B/semiotic.html

Semiotics, Web site by Martin Ryder at the University of Colorado at Denver: http://www.carbon.cudenver.edu/~mryder/itc_data/semiotics.html

20

The Social Construction of Leadership and Its Implications for Women in Mass Communication

Linda Aldoory, University of Maryland

Leadership has been studied by hundreds of scholars in management, business, psychology, education, and organizational communication. According to Pavitt, Whitchurch, McClurg, and Petersen (1995), "More than 7,500 studies relevant to leadership have appeared in the social science literature" (p. 243). This considerable body of knowledge is filled with varying perspectives and theories that help explain leadership styles, skills, and potential gender differences.

In mass communication, however, there have been few attempts to examine what leadership means and even fewer efforts to understand what it means for women in the field.[1] In general, the defining group for conceptualizing leadership, in mass communication as well as in other organizational contexts, has been White men (Parker, 2001). Also, in mass communication, leadership has typically focused on political leadership and media leadership; research in these areas does little to help explain how leadership is constructed and practiced by women in mass communication or how members make meaning of female leaders.[2] The increasing number of women in leadership roles in mass communication education, media production, public relations, and advertising makes it necessary for mass communication scholars to study what leadership means and how leadership is enacted.

To begin to close this knowledge gap, current perspectives on leadership, gender, and communication are brought together here. The purpose of this chapter is to examine the research related to women in leadership in mass communication and to better understand what leadership means for women in the field. Overall, recent studies show how leadership is socially constructed, dependent on relationships between leaders and members. Communication plays a central role in developing these relationships, which are gendered and raced and impact the effectiveness of individual leaders. I conclude the chapter with implications of this social constructionist approach for women in mass communication.

Leadership Defined

Leadership has most often been defined in terms of guidance, direction, or empowerment given to other people to reach a goal (Bennis, 1989; Murray, 1995; Sims & Lorenzi, 1992; Thompson, 2000). Astin and Leland (1991) defined leadership as an empowering, participatory activity aimed at bringing about change in an organization or social system to improve members' lives (p. 7). A new trend is to define leadership as a relationship: Leadership is dependent on the quality and type of relationship between leader and member(s). Parker (2001) defined leadership as a "localized, negotiated process of mutual influence that would theoretically accommodate multiple viewpoints and diverse situational challenges" (p. 43).

This relational definition suggests that leadership is a social construction (Fairhurst, 2000). According to Smircich and Morgan (1982), leadership can be described as follows:

> The process whereby one or more individuals succeed in attempting to frame and define the reality of others. . . . Leadership [is] . . . a result of the constructions and actions of both leaders and led. It involves a complicity or process of negotiation through which certain individuals, implicitly or explicitly, surrender their power to define the nature of their experience to others. (p. 258)

Parker (2001) added that members come to expect leaders to look, act, and think in ways that are consistent with their socially constructed meanings of leadership. The meanings given to leaders are rooted in cultural norms and values and have high symbolic importance (Rost, 1991).

Leadership Theory

Most current leadership theory is not grounded in a social constructionist perspective; rather, popular theory is based on a rational approach whereby scholars have attempted to discover and predict a typical or "average" style used by people or groups to guide their leadership efforts. According to McWhinney (1997), style is made up of the "normal behaviors" that follow from the worldview one maintains (p. 184). Scholars have distinguished between transactional and transformational leadership, two leadership styles that have been set up as a dualism—a leader is either authoritarian or participative, and one style is considered better than the other in different contexts.

Transactional leadership is authoritarian and task oriented; it is based on a materialist exchange relationship between leaders and members. Characteristics of individuals who engage in transactional leadership include certainty, clear direction, personal oversight, and perceptions of just treatment (Cruz, Henningsen, & Smith, 1999; Lowe, Kroeck, & Sivasubramaniam, 1996). For members, only lower-order material and psychic needs are satisfied. Research has shown that this style is not effective in increasing job satisfaction (Gardner & Cleavenger, 1998; Lowe et al., 1996). Transactional leadership articulates and establishes the positions held by the leader, who excludes other positions (McWhinney, 1997). In other words, transactional leadership is one-way rather than two-way and does not take into consideration other opinions or perspectives. Studies indicate that leaders are effective using transactional style only in stable, predictable environments in which member activity can be charted and compared against prior performance records (Lowe et al., 1996).

In contrast to transactional leadership, *transformational leaders* are participative, while communicating a vision and a path to achieve that vision (Avolio & Bass, 1988; Bass, 1985; Bass & Avolio, 1993; Gardner & Cleavenger, 1998). Transformational leadership, also called *charismatic leadership,* is "the art of mobilizing others to want to struggle for shared aspirations" (Kouzes & Posner, 1995, p. 30). Instead of appeasing material needs, transformational leadership addresses higher-level needs for self-actualization and therefore motivates members to perform beyond expectations (Holladay & Coombs, 1993, 1994; Shamir, House, & Arthur, 1993). Characteristics of transformational leaders include risk taking, high expectations, emphasis on collective identity, and vision (Ehrhart & Klein, 2001).

This type of leader creates a sense of shared meaning for members that reflects the leader's vision. Transformational leadership is often prescribed as the most effective style for today's turbulent and constantly changing organizational environments (Farmer, Slater, & Wright, 1998; McWhinney, 1997).

Recently, some scholars have turned to more situational explanations of leadership because differences have been found in the relationships between leaders and members that go against a typical or "average" leadership style. *Situational leadership theory* explains how leaders change their styles to fit the situation and therefore may sometimes be autocratic and sometimes participatory (Casimir, 2001; Graeff, 1997; Grunig, 1992; Lord, Brown, Harvey, & Hall, 2001). In particular, some research has shown that transformational and transactional leadership styles do not generalize across cultures (Jung & Avolio, 1999; Parker, 2001). Jung and Avolio (1999), for example, examined how leadership styles were perceived among White and Asian research participants. They found that the same leadership style was perceived differently and had different effects on motivation and performance for White individuals than for Asian individuals. In this sense, leadership can be seen more as a social construction than as a reality that exists apart from cultural and social norms.

One situational leadership theory is known as *leader-member exchange* (LMX). The basic premise of LMX is that leaders form different types of relationships with different members through an exchange of valued resources; members, in turn, evaluate their relationships with leaders based on the degree of emotional support and intrinsic rewards they receive (Schriesheim, Castro, & Cogliser, 1999; Sparrowe & Liden, 1997). Instead of a static, "average" leadership style, leaders enact different LMXs that vary in quality and type (Fairhurst & Chandler, 1989). For example, mature relationships develop when there is mutual trust, internalization of common goals, and mutual interpersonal influence beyond that which accompanies a formal position (Fairhurst, 1993; Mueller & Lee, 2002). These relationships are transformational because members move beyond self-interests. Low LMX is characterized by formal authority, low trust and support, role-bound relations, and few rewards.

Communication researchers have examined the usefulness of LMX to better understand the social construction of leadership and the role of communication in leader-member relationships. Authors have argued that leaders ultimately construct what has been called *out-group members* and *in-group members* (Yrle, Hartman, & Galle, 2002). In-group members receive greater latitude in performance quality and greater decision-making input, and out-group members are made to adhere to more traditional performance evaluations and subordinate roles (Yrle et al., 2002). In turn, perceptions of leaders by these members differ, such that in-group members make meaning of leadership as positive and out-group members connect low job satisfaction to poor leadership qualities. The quality of LMX also positively affects a member's perceived communication satisfaction in other interpersonal groups and organizational contexts (Mueller & Lee, 2002).

Gender and Leadership

In general, researchers have not found statistically significant differences in leader behaviors or leader effectiveness based on gender (Eagly & Johnson, 1990; Knott & Natalle, 1997; Powell, 1993; Thompson, 2000; van Engen, vanderLeeden, & Willemsen, 2001; Wilkins & Andersen, 1991). However, there have been documented differences in perception and evaluation of leadership according to gender (Eagly, Makhijani, & Klonsky, 1992; Yammarino, Dubinsky, Comer, & Jolson, 1997). Studies have found that both male and female members and supervisors rate women leaders higher on transformational characteristics and lower on transactional characteristics (Bass, Avolio, & Atwater, 1996; Carless, 1998; Maher, 1997). Research has also revealed that women leaders are perceived to be less effective than male leaders and that male followers have a stronger tendency to devalue female leaders (Eagly, Karau, & Makhijani, 1995). It may be that male leaders devalue transformational leadership and therefore devalue women whom they perceive as transformational leaders. Eagly et al. (1995) also found that male and female leaders were rated equally when they portrayed stereotypical attributes: Men displayed masculine attributes (e.g., directness, authoritarian tone), and women illustrated less masculine characteristics.

With regard to women of color, stereotypes guided by White, middle-class norms have constrained women's abilities to lead effectively. Some authors have shown, for example, how African American women's leadership communication is socially constructed to be deviant, negative, and devalued by members (Lubiano, 1992; Nkomo, 1988; Parker, 2001; Parker & Ogilvie, 1996). *Directness* is often used in a pejorative sense to describe African American female leaders' communication behavior. Directness conflicts with the social norms of feminine communication being nondirective and noncontrol oriented (Hecht, Ribeau, & Roberts, 1989; Shuter & Turner, 1997). When women of color enact roles that are inconsistent with race and gender norms, they are perceived as less effective leaders. This supports the notion that leadership is socially constructed, in its tendency to fluctuate with race as well as with gender stereotypes and norms.

The research on gender and leadership illustrates the contextualized nature of relationships between leader and members. Women are ascribed characteristics consistent with transformational leadership; in other words, women should be nurturing, participative, and supportive in their leadership styles. Women leaders are perceived as more effective if they enact these characteristics. However, when a relationship is between male followers and female leaders, the meaning of leadership is different than when the relationship is female-only. Male followers have rated female leaders more negatively than they rated male leaders. Parker (2001) argued that the current models for leadership and gender are grounded within perspectives that privilege White, middle-class cultural norms and values and "are reinforced through gender symbolism that operates as the universal depiction of men and women across cultural and class boundaries" (p. 51).

Women Communicating Leadership

The studies on female leaders' use of communication have supported the premise that leadership is socially constructed, contingent on context, and relational (Fairhurst, 1993; LeClair, 1989; Lee, 1999; Parker, 2001; Parker & Ogilvie, 1996; Wilkins & Andersen, 1991). For example, Parker (2001) examined African American women executives' leadership communication within majority White male-dominated organizations in the United States. She characterized the women's communication in five ways: (1) interactive; (2) empowering, through challenging members to produce results; (3) open; (4) participative, in decision making through debate, autonomy, and information gathering; and (5) boundary spanning. Her findings challenged the stereotype that women are transformational leaders who do not attempt control-oriented leadership. For Parker's (2001) participants,

> Collaboration is worked out at the intersections of control and empowerment, where control is (re)defined as interactive and personal rather than as competitive and distant, and is viewed as a necessary strategy for managing their positions as Black women leaders within dominant-culture organizations. (p. 42)

Specifically in mass communication, two studies examined leadership in public relations, a field that has transformed itself from a male-dominant to a female-dominant profession (Aldoory, 1998; Aldoory & Toth, 2004a). The feminization of public relations has changed the profession in several ways, one of which is the meaning of leadership and the way women leaders are perceived. In one study (Aldoory, 1998), in-depth interviews were conducted with female leaders in public relations to explore their different leadership styles and use of language. Participants illustrated a mix of two-way and one-way communication when hypothetically responding to staff. They also exhibited assertiveness, empathy, and use of logical, rather than emotional, arguments. In general, the women were situational rhetoricians, enacting different leader-member exchanges with different members.

For a second study on gendered leadership in public relations, Elizabeth Toth and I used quantitative and qualitative methods to examine gender differences in perceptions of leadership (Aldoory & Toth, 2004a). Survey findings indicated that women rated themselves lower in terms of being leaders than men did; and women more than men preferred leaders who have charisma, vision, and the ability to motivate others. In focus groups, both male and female participants preferred situational leadership that combines aspects of guidance and empowerment dependent on the situation at hand (p. 178). Focus group participants perceived women making better leaders in public relations because they more often enact socially ascribed roles of supporter, collaborator, and two-way communicator—characteristics that lend themselves to more effective public relations. However, participants also recognized that women do not yet have leadership opportunities equivalent to those of men. A glass ceiling still exists for women, keeping them from promotions and constraining their ability to lead.

Implications for Women in Mass Communication

The recent research on leadership and gender offers evidence of how leadership is socially constructed and how women are perceived differently than men in the construction of what leadership is for organizational life. Leadership is relational rather than merely unidirectional, and gender, race, culture, and status mediate the relationships between members and leaders. For example, research has shown how relationships between male followers and female leaders are different from female-only leader relationships: Men more than women devalue female leaders. Research has also indicated that women tend to devalue themselves as leaders; this may point to a valuing of masculine characteristics for leadership.

Leadership as socially constructed and gendered has several implications for women in mass communication. First, social and institutional factors have an impact on individual women's abilities to lead within their organizations and in mass communication. Second, leader effectiveness depends on building relationships with members that are based on mutual trust and collaboration. In mass communication, members include not only organizational staff but also stakeholders outside the organization, such as audiences of mass communication efforts. Third, the enactment of leadership emphasizes the role of communication for relationship building. Therefore, individuals cannot rely solely on personality or on management skills—they need to also learn communication skills to be effective leaders. Finally, in U.S. dominant culture, organizations, leader communication, and relationships are embedded within norms governed by White masculine middle-class assumptions about the meaning of leadership, gender, and race. Women in mass communication industries need to be aware of these norms and how certain belief systems affect ways of leading. In our article, Elizabeth Toth and I concluded, "Women who are moving up into management positions may need to seriously consider the complexities of enacting a feminine, a masculine, or a mixed style of leadership, depending on circumstances" (Aldoory & Toth, 2004a, p. 180).

The number of women in public relations, advertising, and related media professions and education is growing, and despite a glass ceiling, the number of leadership opportunities for women is growing as well. Therefore, the gendered nature of leadership in mass communication needs to be a focus for future research and further debate. Gender scholars in the field should begin to explore the fluid nature of leader relationships and the contextual constraints placed on certain women who attempt to lead. In addition, professional settings should be sites for changing perceptions of women in leadership. Leadership literacy training could benefit women and men in mass communication who are in leadership positions or who wish to be leaders. Leadership literacy is the ability to "read" social cues about female leadership. Cues may be embedded in conversations, in professional relationships, or in nonverbal communication. Leadership literacy training would increase our understanding of the masculine and feminine as they apply to leadership roles and characteristics. Furthermore, a leadership-literate audience of women and men in mass communication might assist in breaking down the barriers that are keeping more women from leadership positions. Both scholars and practitioners need to seriously examine leadership as it is currently constructed, the impact of leadership on women and men, and the potential for change.

Notes

1. There has been important research on leadership in which scholars have conducted rhetorical analyses of leader messages and interactions between leaders and followers (Holladay & Coombs, 1993, 1994; Lee, 2001; Mueller & Lee, 2002; Yrle, Hartman, & Galle, 2002); some of this research addresses communication of female

leaders (Fairhurst, 1993; Fairhurst & Chandler, 1989; Lee, 1999). None of these studies examined mass communication, however. This chapter refers to these works but focuses on mass communication and media industries.

2. The term *member* is used in organizational studies to refer to followers of a leader.

Questions for Discussion

1. Why is the research in mass communication on women and leadership so scant and limiting?

2. What does it mean for the individual female leader that leadership is socially constructed?

3. How can men play a role in changing the organizational dynamics that influence how women in leadership are perceived?

4. How do women of color find visibility in the rhetoric and research in leadership that has been predominantly White and male?

5. What are some examples of future studies that can help us better understand women in leadership and leadership communication in mass communication?

Accessing Additional Information

AEJMC's JLID Program, Journalism and Mass Communication Leadership Institute for Diversity: http://www.aejmc.org/jlid/index.html

Association for Women in Communications: http://www.womcom.org/index2.html

International Women's Media Foundation's Leadership Resources: http://www.iwmf.org/training/resources.php

Poynter Institute's bibliography on leadership: http://www.poynter.org/content/content_view.asp?id=1211

21

Got Theory?

Laura A. Wackwitz, Oregon State University

Lana F. Rakow, University of North Dakota

I f the U.S. dairy industry needs a national advertising campaign to convince people that milk is good for them ("Got Milk?"), consider what feminist scholars face. Who thinks theory is good for them? Who thinks feminist theory is good for them? The idea of "theory" in general is disdained by too many undergraduate students and media professionals, including some who make their way onto college faculties teaching journalism and mass communication. Feminist communication theory is even more discounted, if it is known to exist at all. We have our work cut out for us and absolutely no advertising budget to pull it off.

So, without benefit of full-page color ads in magazines and billboard displays, we need to be advocates for the value and necessity of theorizing in mass communication, specifically, feminist theorizing in and about communication. We hope to demonstrate in these pages why we—all of us, women and men of feminist and nonfeminist bent—need feminist communication theory. We need to understand what it does and what it looks like. Feminist communication theory is not just taking account of women's absence from media professions or of images of women in media content. It is not simply a feminist perspective on communication theory. Rather, feminist communication theory provides alternative ways of understanding *theory* as well as alternative ways of *theorizing* communication and media (see Rakow & Wackwitz, 2004).

Feminist communication theory, to summarize what we see as its most distinctive features and contributions, seeks a critical understanding of gender, communication, and social change. Unlike the dominant theoretical position in the study of communication, feminist communication theory is explanatory, political, polyvocal, and transformative. Its major themes, played out in the past few decades more outside the field of communication than within it, have centered on concepts of difference, voice, and representation, themes that provide a heuristic model for rethinking the structure and organization of our discipline.

While these are our readings of feminist communication theory, we recognize our own limitations in fleshing out its contours and potential. Therefore, while we take the rest of this chapter to explore our renderings of it, we invite our readers to join in by identifying themes and characteristics of feminist communication theory, extending this work, that of others in our field, and those outside of it.[1]

The Need for Theory and Theoretical Change

First, we need to show what happens when theory is not valued or acknowledged or when current or received theories are recycled and perpetuated. A study of mass communication research in 10 major journals over a 20-year period showed how infrequently researchers in our field use theory to explain their findings or make theory from their findings. Kamhawi and Weaver (2003) concluded from an analysis of published articles in nearly a 20-year period that only 39% of studies even mentioned or implied a theory. They further concluded that quantitative rather than qualitative research dominated (about 70% quantitative to 27% qualitative in the 1990s) and that the theories most frequently mentioned related to media uses and effects (p. 13). Theories of gender, gender in media, or gender and media were notable by their absence in the literature.[2]

Theorizing both media and gender is relatively commonplace outside the disciplinary boundaries of mass communication yet, ironically, is stunningly absent within those boundaries. What can explain the seemingly atheoretical nature of this field? Most scholars from the dominant paradigm ignore theory on an explicit level because they subscribe to a set of unexamined theoretical assumptions. First, they do not theorize *communication,* but rather begin with Harold Lasswell's model, presented first in his 1927 *Propaganda Technique in the World War* and made into the classic definition "Who says what to whom in what channel with what effect?" They do not theorize *reality,* but believe Walter Lippman's description of "the world outside and the pictures in our heads" from his 1922 book *Public Opinion*, justifying the role and authority of experts to accurately describe the world for those of lesser interest and ability. They do not theorize *society*, instead taking for granted structures and institutions reflected in colonialism, corporate capitalism, patriarchy, and liberal democracy. They do not theorize the *media*, instead accepting U.S. systems of ownership and control over public discourse (even if they are critical on occasion of content or method or the ownership systems of other nations). They do not theorize *identity*, relying, instead, on a notion of subjectivity born of concern for the "masses" that set the research agenda for the 20th century. Rather, they universalize humans as essentially the same except for a few add-on variations created by demographic (and psychographic) variables.

In large measure, mass communication research has substituted for theorizing. Instead of listening to and encouraging a multiplicity of voices to join and enrich the discourse of theory, theory has been overlooked in favor of quantifiable questions and balkanization of the discipline into subcategories for instructional convenience and simplistic mis-learning. Thus, we have colleges and universities that organize the study of communication into seemingly discrete components based on a variety of arbitrary factors, including levels of communication (e.g., intrapersonal, interpersonal, group, mass), lines of inquiry (e.g., speech communication versus journalism), and professional tracks (e.g., public relations, journalism, advertising, broadcasting, and cinema). Divisions in the field are further ingrained in higher education by economic and social realities that pit departments and areas against each other in the pursuit of money, resources, and prestige for one area at the expense of others. Within disciplinary programs, the tendency toward division and competition results in an artificial separation of "theory" from "practice" and "professionals" from "academics." The effect has been to create a field of mass communication almost bereft of significant theorizing but ideologically and uncritically aligned with commercial media industries and occupations.

What about the theories that are used, if used at all? Most theories in this dominant quantitative paradigm are used to explain phenomenon that occur within assumptions about society, media, and identity. They are, at best, "middle-range" theories, derived from testable propositions of observable phenomenon, as advocated by Columbia University sociologists Paul Lazarsfeld and Robert Merton since the 1940s and articulated by Merton in an essay published in 1949 (see Merton, 1968). Middle-range theorists set aside the larger social and cultural frameworks or meaning systems within which these observable phenomena occur and that the researcher assumes. They typically do not inquire into the meanings people have of their own experiences. They do not consider alternative political or economic arrangements. No wonder so little substantive progress has been made in understanding and ameliorating discrimination and oppression and how the media and mass communication perpetuate those ends. Received communication theories fail to theorize communication in its contextualized and multilayered landscape of meanings and experiences—a landscape of humanity complete with multiple sexualities; genders, races, and ethnicities; abilities; ages; classes; and geographies. Received communication "theories" are not able to provide inspiration for imagined alternatives to the ways we presently communicate—ways that tend to demean, devalue, and exclude some groups while privileging others.

The field of mass communication evidently requires infusion from other sources to bring together ideas about communication and media that have been traditionally left out—excluded from a field of theorizing that impacts real people in their daily lives. Good theory ought to help ameliorate oppression, not serve to just describe or, worse yet, reinforce it, however inadvertent that reinforcement may seem. Feminist communication theory is a theory for just such an occasion.

Questions for Theory

Feminist communication theory opens the door for new questions and new ways of looking at and interpreting the communication landscape. Thus, while received communication theory might start by answering the question "Who says what, to whom, and with what effect?" feminist communication theorists question the question as well as the answer. One might ask, for example, from what space (psychological, sociological, ideological) and with what motivation was the "who," the "what," the "whom" and a concern about "effect" generated? And are we comfortable with the result—of the theory, of the research, and of the orientation adopted by communication professionals—that the underlying motive is a kind of control or an attempt to achieve a particular kind of social order through means of communication?

Clearly, feminist communication theory encourages us to ask a variety of regularly overlooked, if not purposively ignored, questions. Here is only a sample:

- *What other models of communication might we find or imagine?* Are they inclusive and pluralistic? Do they speak to, of, and from diverse groups? Do they lead us to theorizing just or unjust worlds? Do they benefit some individuals or groups at the expense of others?

- *What effect does the theorizer have on the theory?* Can we theorize the role of communication researchers in the construction of communication theory? For example, what perspective is gained if we turn some of the most well-known theories of mass communication around to explain researchers rather than audiences? What would happen to the third-person effect (do researchers think that other people are more affected by media than they are?), the spiral of silence (are some theories increasingly silenced by the perception of the weight of opinion held by other researchers?), or agenda setting (is it true that theory doesn't tell us what to think about but actually tells us what to *think*?)?[3]

- *How might we communicate differently?* What *could* people do with media? What would happen if media professionals practiced communication as if everyone had freedom of expression, just as we profess? What if everyone was a "communication professional"? What isn't communicated, and why not? How can we theorize the unimaginable?

Theory, we hope we have demonstrated, can and should be dislodged from its current moorings, which anchor it to a particular theoretical and political effort to codify and prescribe a set of social relations (sender to receiver, subject to object, elite to mass). We can only suggest what might happen if current theories were turned on their heads. The task will require that many people engaged in communication theorizing generate the questions and possible answers that need to be taken into account. This is especially true given the great diversity of experience and thought, as well as the interests and motivations of the theorists themselves.

Gender, Communication, and Social Change

While we cannot account for all experience and thought, we find it useful to identify what feminist communication theory at a minimum needs to pay attention to if it is to move us beyond the atheoretical nature of our field. At a minimum, we need to theorize that which traditional theory has assumed or ignored: gender, communication, and social change. Regrettably, much work on women and media neglects this important step.

Theorizing Gender

The "add-women-and-stir" approach to theory that characterizes much of the field of mass communication, well intentioned as it often is and an improvement over the absence of women from theory, starts from an assumption about gender that warrants examination and reflection. The assumption is that gender is theoretically unproblematic—merely socially shaped cultural forms of two categories of biological sexes, female and male, that preexist cultural and social meanings that get added on later. Gender is presumed to be simply another demographic variable from this perspective, although extraordinarily important from a marketing point of view. Feminist communication theory, on the other hand, recognizes this binary categorization of gender *and* sex as a social and an economic construct that ought to be vigorously questioned. Binary categorization is an assumption in need of challenge. Gender itself must be theorized, not taken for granted as part of the "natural" order of things. Gender is not a static or inherent condition of humans, something we are; rather, it is an accomplishment, something we do based on available and negotiated meanings. Consequently, gender is a complex system of messy meanings, replete with inconsistencies, that human societies historically have tried to "scrub and purify" by various approaches, including systems of gender segregation, enforced by custom and law and generated/maintained by myth, and the authoritative claims promoted by science and religion. A forced binary system, understood as universalized and natural, is increasingly difficult to police and preserve, particularly in light of the insistence by minority cultural groups that gender meanings are not the same everywhere and as demonstrated by gay, lesbian, bisexual, and transgendered people that gender and sexual identity can derive from a variety of combinations (see Haynes & McKenna, 2001; Tauchert, 2002).

What becomes of the binary system when an individual's gender assignment (noted and communicated by a medical authority at birth) does not match the individual's socially expected and required sexuality, which does not match the individual's gender identity (the self-identified gender), which does not match the individual's gender presentation (the gender conveyed to others), which does not match the individual's gender attribution (the gender ascribed by others)? How far can a simple understanding of gender as the cultural shape (of masculinity and femininity) given to "naturally" occurring biological features and sexuality (of heterosexual males and females) go in answering these questions? Feminist communication theory sees gender construction as an exceptionally complex developmental dynamic. Overly simplistic pronouncements of the "Me Tarzan, you Jane" variety miss the theoretical mark completely.

Once we have made gender the subject of our theoretical inquiry, accounting for gender can be seen more clearly as a complex and multifaceted project. Gender, we conclude, can best be thought of as a meaning system experienced differently by those born in different cultural groups, in different social locations, in a particular place and time. Gender is never simply an individual's attribute. Only by understanding gender as a meaning system can we begin to understand how gender is intertwined with other meaning systems, such as race and class and age and ability and sexuality and location and privilege. Thus, the seemingly obvious question asked at birth—"Boy or girl?"—is intimately tied to all the other unasked questions, questions silently answered by assumptions about a life course already cast, if not fully scripted.

Most of the received work on women and media begins with an assumption about gender as an inherent attribute, but feminist communication theory at its best tackles gender as a fundamental part of a variety of interlocking and complex meaning systems, meaning systems grounded in ideological relationships that benefit some at the expense of the many. Those systems can be changed, however, precisely because they are meaning-based assumptions about human attribution rather than being determined by the natural order or destiny. We would be wise, therefore, to ask *how* gender systems operate and differ from each other in different times and places, *why* one particular gender system is in place rather than another, *where* meanings come from, and *what* those meanings are.

Theorizing Communication

Communication is similarly complex but deceptively simple on the surface. How we define communication—as a system of transmitted messages, as a ritualistic activity, as an imagined activity, as the construction of community, as emotion, as identity, as power, as transformation—gives shape to the theories we create to explain communication and social structures. Feminist communication theory, therefore, needs to seek out new definitions of communication in order to develop multiple understandings and interpretations of a concept that, ironically, too many in the field of communication take for granted.

This blindness to its own assumptions has led "master theorists" of our tradition to perpetuate the objectification and exclusion of communicative "others" by developing a lexicon that has entered academic and popular discourse and become part of the common parlance used to describe communication. Theory, although it may sound like something best left to a core of elite academics, thinking deep thoughts and working in paper-laden offices, impacts multiple venues as the terms and ideas of particular theories enter the consciousness of other groups. We have, for example, an international discourse among academics, audiences, and media professionals concerned with "media effects." Concern with media effects exists, not only as a tradition in research; actual laws have been enacted on the basis of the assumption that media effects exist (Wackwitz, 2002). The U.S. Supreme Court subscribes, at least in part, to a media effects mentality. Technology (like the V-chip, for example) has been developed on the basis of the assumption of media effects by legislatures, governments, parents, and schoolteachers. To protect media consumers from media effects, we have initiated "safeguards," in the form of rating systems, government censorship, and assorted restrictions, to protect a variety of audiences from the dangers of media effects. Vast amounts of advertising, special interest, medical, and political dollars are channeled every day into the media on the assumption that communication media will impact and somehow affect human cognition and behavior. Yet the vast majority of this interest in media effects is based on the assumption of a transmission (sender-receiver) model of communication—a model that lies largely unquestioned in the pursuit of media effects. To ask "What are the effects of media on people?" assumes (a) that effects exist and (b) that we can assess them. Jumping to an effects model is not necessarily the most instructive or useful model for thinking about communication either as it exists or as it might exist.

The media effects model arose from an attempt to explain and predict the behavior (and presumably the attitudes and cognitions) of "the masses" in a rapidly changing U.S. social and political landscape into the 20th century and beyond. That it continues to exist as the primary model of communication taught in introductory classes at colleges and universities is troubling. The trouble is that the received model is so central and controlling that it tends to stifle creative exploration of alternative models of communication and alternative ways of thinking about communication. If everyone agrees the world is flat, there is no reason to consider alternative conceptualizations of how things work. And those who do can be readily dismissed as crackpots or sanctioned by privileged authority for their controversial ideas: Galileo was condemned to lifelong imprisonment (which turned out to be more like what we would call "house arrest") in 1633, for advancing information that supported the debunked Copernican notion (first advanced in 1514) that the earth moved around the sun. Systems of power and judgment based in received theoretical models, whether of physics or gender or communication, tend to stifle intellectual, political, and social creativity and change. In the case of the received model of communication, it serves, by virtue of its role in economic, political, and social processes, to oppress many people and suppress voices from diverse groups. The problem is not that "media effects" are studied or theorized or considered; the problem is that the model on which media effects research is based has become so engrained in human discourse, institutions, and patterns of thought that challenges to the model and, indeed, alternative ways of conceiving of and practicing communication, are readily dismissed as unimportant, unnecessary, and even unthinkable. The center transmits; the masses receive. What needs to be theorized? one might ask. Indeed, there is much, beginning with how this "center transmits—masses receive" relationship came to be and how it is sustained by the very discipline that should be interrogating it.

Because the majority of work in mass communication on women uses a media effects model—a model that seems conducive to making an argument against media sexism—we feel the need to urge scholars to question the assumptions of the model and to consider alternatives. An effects model reifies the subject-object relationship embedded in the "Who said what, to whom, with what effect?" definition of communication. Feminist resistance to sexist media content on the basis of effects has yet to produce a change in media content. It certainly has not produced a change in media ownership, structure, or motivation (a point still relevant although made some time ago by Ferguson, 1990), nor has it led to more opportunities for voice for those excluded from media access. Note, for example, the marginal dialogue in the professional media (carried on the back pages of the press) about why media coverage of missing people disproportionately privileges stories about young, White, normatively pretty women, when young, White, normatively pretty women constitute a minority of the people who go missing. People of color go missing (3 in 10 U.S. missing persons, for example, are Black/ African American). Men go missing (over half of all U.S. missing persons are male). Unfortunately, they also go missing from the pages of the nation's press (Bauder, 2005). Clearly, it is time to ask new questions.

Theorizing Social Change

Feminists advocate for social change, and change has been difficult to accomplish. In a sense, the difficulty creates additional warrant for adopting and maintaining a focus on the relationship among communication, social change, societal structure, and the social order. Feminist communication theory starts from the assumption that deep structural change is necessary to achieve social justice and to bring voices out of silence (as problematic as that is, theoretically and practically) in order to achieve a truly participatory democracy based on dialogue and mutuality. That requires us to put the "social order" itself on the table for scrutiny. Traditional theory tends to accept the social order "as is" or as it appears to be but does so without acknowledging underlying assumptions, including those of colonialism, patriarchy, corporate capitalism, and liberal democratic theory. Feminist communication theory suggests that the "natural order of things" is not necessarily natural, nor is it necessarily as it appears to be. Received communication theory, reflecting its positivist and functionalist roots, is theory that seeks to establish social stability. Theorists in that tradition assume social and political stability is both normal and desirable, with periods of change regarded as deviations from, and minor corrective adjustments to, the norm. Feminist communication theory offers alternatives, challenges the foundations of traditional theory, and rejects oppressive stability in favor of human rights, equity, and social change. Feminist communication theory, then, is theory in pursuit of social justice. Feminist communication theory can alter the realm of theory by speaking to and from feminist spaces— spaces from which competing ideas emerge and are valued, from which cooperation brings collaboration and understanding, and from which social transformation can occur. In these and many other respects, feminist communication theory has the potential to be the theoretical position broad enough to accommodate the variety of topics and issues that are in need of study within communication.

Characteristics of Theory

One of our goals in writing this chapter is to suggest directions for thought and theorizing by communication students, practitioners, and scholars. Here, we suggest that it is useful to think about the characteristics that might be used to describe "good" theory. These are characteristics of feminist communication theory, as we see it. Can other theories measure up?

• *Explanatory:* Theories are useful because of their capacity to explain and account for phenomena. Feminist communication theory describes communicative worlds, seeking connections and disjunctures between lived experience and meanings available to explain and understand them. It offers alternative explanations for women's experiences that are derived from an understanding of gender as an ideological construction rather than as a more biological or religiously ordained attribute. Do other theories explain and account for women's experiences? Can they provide alternative accounts of the same experience? Do they explain men's experiences as men, also part of a gendered system? Can they help explain the great variety in the human condition in other times and places?

• *Political:* Radha Hegde (1998) urged us to recognize and reclaim theory as politics if we hope to understand and represent the experiences of subordination. To make sure that theories are developed and used honestly, for the collective good rather than that of privileged special interests, theorists need to be clear and forthright about their political assumptions and motivations. All theories have an ideological foundation in need of acknowledgment. Feminist communication theory rests on an ideology of feminism—an ideology rooted in the view that to change the position of women throughout a majority of the world's social systems is desirable. Can other theorists be said to be as open and self-reflexive about their political positions?

- *Polyvocal:* Theories, if they are going to account for the experiences and perspectives of all humanity, should be built from the voices of those who are theorized. Feminist communication theory is theory founded by and upon the voices of the many, not the few. We speak from a variety of personal, political, economic, racial, ethnic, sexual, physical, and geographic spaces. Whose voices are represented in other theoretical positions? Who has the authority to speak? Must it be the few, the privileged, and the powerful?

- *Transformative:* A theory that simply repeats existing social relations and conditions without deep interrogation of their assumptions is doomed to reinforce the social order, no matter how much it is in need of change. Because feminists assume change is needed, they challenge us to move beyond explanation and discovery into action and involvement. By using theory to build interpersonal and cultural coalitions and bridges through communication, feminist communication theory can be used by anyone in the service of change and transformation to a just society.

Theoretical Frameworks

While much of the field of mass communication has not been theorizing, feminists have been, but much more needs to be done in order to (a) make feminist perspectives known and available to students, media professionals, and scholars; (b) further expand feminist communication theory's potential to develop pluralistic, inclusive theories that speak to and from numerous groups; and (c) continue to improve feminist communication theory by examining our scholarship to see its values and assess its shortcomings. Adding women and stirring them into existing theory is not sufficient. Women, both real and imagined, are bearers of meaning and creators of theory. Feminists have been accounting for women in ways that other theorists have not.

Based on our reading of feminist work, we propose three concepts that can provide a new framework for understanding communication generally, and women and communication specifically. These three concepts—difference, voice, and representation—emerged from our review of feminist work in a variety of disciplines over the past three decades. We have explored these themes in more detail elsewhere (Rakow & Wackwitz, 2004), but here we briefly suggest why these concepts provide a fruitful basis for theorizing in communication.

- *Difference:* One of the most important revelations to come from feminist theorizing is the extent to which differences—assumed by contemporary "experts" and lay people alike to be rooted in biology and psychology, ordained by matter or God—are demonstrated to be cultural. From the wide variety of physical characteristics and personal attributes present or possible in humans, cultural groups create order by designing simplifying category systems that are arbitrarily assigned, socially enforced, and ultimately taken for granted. These systems can be useful or detrimental, rigid or flexible, egalitarian or stratified, or binary or multiple. To understand presumed differences between women and men, and among women, we need to theorize how and why differences are created and who benefits and who does not from a society's category systems. The complexities of identity can be understood only by accounting for the great variety of experience and perspective suggested by feminist theorists and other critical scholars.[4]

- *Voice:* Feminists have assumed that having voice is an important—even the most important—goal and strategy for rectifying subordination. Without voice, some groups and individuals are denied the ability to participate in naming, and thereby creating, the realities in which they and all of us live. Their experiences cannot be taken into account in policy making. Their condition remains defined and constrained by official meaning systems. To theorize communication fully, we need to ask why everyone does not have the means and ability to make themselves heard and to have what they say be considered in social and political life. Some restrictions may be practical/real limitations, but most are political and rooted in power. We need to ask how we can create conditions basic to democratic participation. And since experience is seldom, if ever, innocent of cultural interpretation, we need to ask what interpretations are available or not available and are contested or accepted, including feminist ones, to make meaning of the experiences brought to the table.[5]

- *Representation:* It has not been difficult for feminist scholars to criticize media representations of women. What has been more difficult is theorizing representation, which at a fundamental level must account for the connections between what is assumed to be "reality" and what are assumed to be renderings of reality, more or less accurate, in visual and literary texts. Representation, and hence a theory of media, requires a deeper understanding of meanings and artifacts. "Real" women, on television or off, for example, are both subject to definitions of *woman,* creating an interplay between imagined and embodied experiences. Ultimately, there is no essential identity lying behind our meanings for ourselves and others. Consequently, theory must account for identity, reality, and meanings in order to theorize media and representation. Before proceeding, researchers who describe media content and effects are well-advised to examine their own theoretical assumptions about the relationship between media and reality in light of feminist theory.[6]

We find the concepts of difference, voice, and representation to be useful for thinking about feminist theorizing in communication, and we offer them as an alternative, a framework for viewing what is important to be theorized. These three concepts are particularly rich because of their relationships to each other. Others will no doubt find different themes in feminist work and should offer alternative schemas to guide theory making. What might communication theory look like, for example, if we took any of the following sets of concepts as starting points: Identity, Community, Place; or Interpretation, Transformation, Being; or Body, Knowledge, Culture? Imagine what the field of communication would look like if our communication programs focused on these issues rather than on industry career tracks (e.g., advertising, journalism, public relations) or assorted levels of communication (e.g., mass, organizational, and interpersonal communication).

An Invitation

We have attempted to identify the potential for feminist communication theory, which we prefer to think of as a process requiring continuous development and multiple (r)evolutions rather than a product for testing and replication. Now what? Received methods of scholarship suggest that good theories need no advocate because they represent verified Truth. On the contrary, all successful theories have needed advocates to bring them to light. Even milk, for example, seems to need a national advertising campaign. Feminist communication theory is no different in that respect. Yet the need for advocacy is greater for theories that speak to and from nondominant groups. Because the field of communication has failed in many respects to include, account for, and speak to those other than the dominant race, gender, and class, feminist voices of communication theory are needed to provide redress, to stimulate genuinely pluralistic thinking, and to reimagine our worlds. So, we ask readers to consider what they might contribute. Got theory? Of course you do, but what kind of theory have you got? Does it explain gender, communication, and social change? Does it account for the voices of everyone? Is it sensitive to its assumptions, and does it make its politics known? Does it help us to imagine new and better worlds? If not, get feminist communication theory and help to change the world for the better.

Notes

1. For a review of the discussion of feminist theory in communication, see Ardizonni (1998), Bell, Orbe, Drummond, and Camara (2000), Darling-Wolf (2004), Fenton (2000), Kramarae (1989), Long (1989), McLaughlin (1995), Rakow (1992), Steeves (1987), Treichler and Wartella (1986), and Valdivia (1995). For an exceptionally rich overview of relevant discussions outside the field, see Essed, Goldberg, and Kobayashi (2005).

2. Another study (Stephen, 2000) identified the occurrence of feminist scholarship in communication journals over the past decades but did not differentiate between articles simply using gender as a topic and those using feminist theory, a considerable difference, as we argue here.

3. We are assuming that most of our readers will be familiar with these theories, but, if not, we refer them to theorizing by Davison (1983) on the third-person effect, Noelle-Neumann (1974) on the spiral of silence, and Cohen (1963) on agenda setting.

4. See, for example, Allen (1986), Anzaldúa (1987), Bhavnani (2001), Calhoun (1995), Essed and Goldberg (2002), Flores (1996), Haynes and McKenna (2001), Sharma and Young (2003), Snyder, Brueggemann, and Garland-Thomson (2002), Tauchert (2002), Tripp (2000), and Zandy (1990).

5. The importance and complexity of theorizing voice are suggested in Bilsky (1998), Clair (1998), Fellner (2002), Ford and Crabtree (2002), Galinda and Gonzales (1999), Mahoney (1996), Mitra and Watts (2002), Roof and Wiegman (1995), and Scott (1992).

6. We recommend feminist work such as the following: Carter and Steiner (2004), Coward (1985), de Lauretis (1987), Florence and Reynolds (1995), Hegde (1998), Kember (2003), Kitch (1997), Kuhn (1985), Mikell (1995), Mulvey (1989), van Zoonen (1994), and Walters (1995).

Questions for Discussion

1. What are some attributions or characterizations that might go along with or accompany being a "feminist communication theorist"? How might those characterizations be different for someone who self-describes as a "communication theorist"? What assumptions underlie your thinking and responses?

2. What behaviors or qualities of mind "make" someone a theorist? Are you a theorist? If you are, how so or in what respects? If you maintain that you are not a theorist, what is it that makes you nontheoretical?

3. Do you agree or disagree with the view that "a good theory" is always political in character? Why? What is your reasoning?

4. How do you see the concepts of difference, voice, and representation as discussed in this chapter operating in the media? What do the terms *difference, voice,* and *representation* mean to you? How do you see them operating in your life and the media/communication around you?

5. Given the issues raised by feminist communication/media theorists, what hope do you see for the future of communication, of media, of theory? Where do we go from here?

Accessing Additional Information

Center for Digital Discourse and Culture at Virginia Tech University, Feminist Theory Web site: http://www.cddc.vt.edu/feminism/

Stanford Encyclopedia of Philosophy, Feminist Epistemology and Philosophy of Science: http://www.plato.stanford.edu/entries/feminism-epistemology/

The University of Iowa, Women's Studies Resources, "Feminist Theory," compiled and edited by Karla Tonella: http://bailiwick.lib.uiowa.edu/wstudies/theory.html

University of Maryland, Women's Studies Database: http://www.mith2.umd.edu/WomensStudies/OtherWebSites/theory.html

University of Wisconsin System, Women's Studies Librarian's Office, "Feminist Theory": http://www.library.wisc.edu/libraries/WomensStudies/core/crfemthe.htm

PART VI

Where Do We Go From Here?

22

Our Conclusion

Gender Values Remain, Inequity Resurges, and Globalization Brings New Challenges

Pamela J. Creedon, The University of Iowa

Judith Cramer, St. John's University

Neither of the first two editions of *Women in Mass Communication* had a concluding chapter. In this third edition, we added one to summarize what has not changed over these 16 years and to provide a forecast for the future.

The title of the first edition included a subtitle: *Challenging Gender Values.* Authors in that 1989 edition predicted dramatic changes for women in the various mass communication professions. We also argued that a dramatic increase in the number of women entering mass communication careers had the potential to change the dominant (male) value system in the industry.

The second edition of the book in 1994 did not include the subtitle because—based on some preliminary data—most authors found more equity and less discrimination based on gender. However, several authors in the second edition expressed concerns about successful women who were adopting the dominant value system rather than challenging it as they rose through the management ladder. The introduction to the second edition concluded,

> The power of a critical mass of women and people of color in journalism and mass communication will not come from numbers alone, but from the conscious commitment. . . . that will challenge the values of the mass communication enterprise in which women—and men—must take responsibility for the meanings they create and for those they omit. (Creedon, 1993, p. 20)

In this third edition, 10 authors from the first two editions contributed (8 from the first and 2 more from the second). One of the most striking—and disturbing—findings was that veteran and first-time contributors alike were remarkably less optimistic about positive change than in the second edition. The hope that gender would be a differentiating factor and effect change in traditional work routines and values was gone. The hope that gender would challenge discriminatory practices had all but evaporated. After 16 years, authors in this third edition show how the pendulum has swung back to pre–Title IX, pre-affirmative-action days. Studies using "sex" as the demographic variable have reappeared; gender appears to have lost its explanatory power.

Throughout this edition, authors argued that many women entering the mass communication professions have bought into or simply accepted the gendered value system without changing it—a system that the authors in the 1989 and 1994 editions challenged in every chapter. Authors found that feminism, women's liberation, and equal rights have been dismissed as passé by many women in the generation now entering the various mass communication professions.

As this volume documents in chapter after chapter, the hierarchical male value system has not changed during the 16 years from the first to this third edition. Instead, the gendered value system has been toned down, made more palatable, and sold to women and minorities as "the way the world works" if you want to get ahead.

What about the women who have made it to the top of major media organizations and broken through the "glass ceiling"? What about Martha Stewart and Oprah Winfrey, you ask? Or Mary Junck, chairman, president, and chief executive officer of Lee Enterprises, the fourth-largest newspaper company in the country in terms of dailies owned and the seventh largest in terms of total daily circulation.

Yes, we can point to some high-profile success stories, but our book examines the overall status of women and female minorities in journalism and mass communication after 16 years. Below is a summary of the dismal news reported by authors in the third edition:

- *Radio and television:* Deregulation has increased the number of stations, but consolidated station ownership has decreased opportunities in management for women and minorities. In broadcasting, especially television, women and people of color achieved a degree of success between 1984 and 2005. But the steps have been slower than desired, and many are aggressively advocating the inclusion of more voices and more diverse perspectives.

- *Newspapers:* Studies have shown that the "glass ceiling" remains firmly in place. While more women have entered journalism for three decades, they are concentrated at the lower rungs of the employment ladder and in middle management. About one third of all journalists are women, a figure that has remained unchanged since 1982. And even though for the first time more women than men work in newsrooms, salary discrepancies remain.

- *Magazines:* A major national survey comparing male and female salaries in magazine journalism disappeared in 2003 and reappeared in 2004, with salary disparities ranging from $35,000 to $185,000 for executive editors. The survey did not use any controls for experience, circulation, and so forth that would have made it possible to compare data over the past two decades. "Eventually, everything will be equal," is a concluding quote from an industry executive in this chapter.

- *Advertising:* The emphasis has shifted from reaching the largest possible audience to targeting "specific audiences," which is code for "consumers with money." The chapter concludes that the glass ceiling in advertising management consists of a "very dense layer of White men."

- *Online journalism:* This field didn't exist in any meaningful way as a career option when the second edition was written, so we assumed it would be the beneficiary of more than 20 years of struggles for equity. The chapter concludes: Online journalism "mirrors the gendered hierarchies of predecessors."

- *Public relations:* Women make up two thirds of all public relations professionals, but they still are paid less and promoted less often than men. Women in public relations face barriers that existed in 1989, which serve to subordinate their roles and their potential contributions to the profession.

In 1988, the "New Majority" study, which formed the basis for a chapter in the first edition, speculated about what would happen when women became the majority in newsrooms. The report used the term "pink-collar ghetto" to describe this "new majority." It created a firestorm.

The original intent was to raise concerns about what "feminization" had meant in numerous communication occupational categories: lower salaries, lower prestige, and a male exodus. The report resulted in "scare" headlines and mobilized some editors—notably women editors—to attack the author, the research, and the findings.

The New Majority report author, who in this edition details the turmoil she has endured, quickly learned that "some people seem unable to deal rationally with the fact that gender differences have long had an impact on our field." It was the unvarnished truth, but it was too honest for many to hear. After 16 years, it is hard to find any other rationale for the male exodus from our schools and colleges of journalism and mass communication, as well as for the resurgence of inequity as more women enter the mass communication business.

In this edition, we explore the male exodus at the scholastic level, too. Today, more high school girls than boys work on student media and enroll in high school journalism courses. Students are twice as likely to have a woman as a newspaper adviser, and more often than not, the advising assignment is given to teachers without any experience in journalism.

Issues in mass communication today are not only about gender equity and sex or racial discrimination. As one author pointed out, mass communication faces "new challenges concerning the definition of news, newsroom structure, and journalistic practices." It has been more than a decade since the second edition, and rapid changes in technology, increased demands to work longer for the same pay, coupled with eroding family-friendly practices, have made mass communication less and less attractive as a professional occupation for women—and men.

New Concerns

Yes, and men. One of the new threads woven throughout chapters in this edition is the paucity of males entering the mass communication professions and mass communication education. As several chapters document, the influx of women over the past two decades has actually depressed entry-level salaries for men and women in mass communication occupations.

In this edition, some authors found that the depressed salaries, coupled with an increased workload due in part to "time-saving technology," have resulted in male flight to other occupations and educational fields. A concern for women raised in several chapters was burnout. Increased opportunity in the workplace over the past 16 years has not been accompanied by lessened expectations for women in home and family. "You can have it all" meant the kids and housework, too.

Leadership theory, a new chapter in the book, describes research showing that women devalue themselves as leaders. Another chapter explores how the "add-women-and-stir" research approach has turned gender into a demographic variable, instead of a polyvocal "social and economic construct."

Authors found that some advances for women in media employment and leadership have fueled ideologically driven culture wars. Patriarchal family values, paternalistic governmental systems, and discriminatory religious systems are resurging. As one author described it, women have taken "three steps forward and two steps back" in the mass communication workplace.

For an increasing number of media organizations, the business side or the bottom line is the top priority. Health communication, a relatively new occupational field in communication, provides a stark example. Today, both the International Communication Association and the National Association have health communication divisions, and 54.5% and 65.6% of their membership respectively, is female. But health communication is not about a change in values; it is market-driven practice where profit most often is the top priority.

It would be easy—and justified, we think—to conclude the third edition of *Women and Mass Communication* without much hope for change in the future. After 16 years of analysis and three books, we continue to find that media organizations use gendered stereotypes, discriminate in employment, and depress women's salaries.

The More Things Change, The More They Get Worse . . .

Where do we go from here? We have been making our case for change based on equity, fairness, and opportunity by trying to make others see the world from our perspective. Over time, the perspectives of many contributors in this book have evolved. The first edition, in 1989, advocated equal opportunity and equality within the existing system and values (liberal feminism). The second edition, in 1994, advocated reforming the existing system and values (reformist feminism). Most contributors to our third edition advocate transformative feminism.

Several recent changes in law and policy provide evidence that some transformation is under way. Tragically, it appears to be in the complete opposite direction from what we have worked toward for three decades or more.

Freedom of Expression: First Amendment rights for high school students were limited in 1988 by a U.S. Supreme Court decision (*Hazelwood*), and in February 2006, the U.S. Supreme Court declined to hear an appeal of a case involving Governor's State University in Illinois (*Hosty v. Carter*), effectively extending the *Hazelwood* decision to college journalists (Student Press Law Center, 2006). Their First Amendment freedoms were curtailed when on June 20, 2005, the 7th U.S. Circuit Court of Appeals decided that the 1988 Supreme Court *Hazelwood* decision, which allowed censorship for "legitimate educational reasons" at the high school level, could extend to college and university campuses.

Two of the three student newspaper editors involved in the Governor's State case are women, and they are suing the dean of their college, who is female. Today, significantly more high school girls than boys work on student media and enroll in journalism courses. High school students are twice as likely to have a woman as a newspaper adviser.

Title IX: Title IX of the Education Amendments of 1972 is a federal statute created to prohibit sex discrimination in education programs that receive federal funding. Nearly every educational institution receives some form of federal funds and has been required to comply with Title IX for 33 years.

On March 17, 2005, without any notice or public input, the U.S. Department of Education issued a Title IX "clarification." According to the "clarification," compliance with Title IX can be shown by sending each female student in a school an e-mail survey asking whether she has the interest and ability to play sports. If for any reason the student does not reply, the school may interpret this as lack of interest.

Affirmative Action: Affirmative action policies that have provided women and minorities greater access to higher education also are under attack. Two 2003 U.S. Supreme Court decisions involving cases from the University of Michigan have raised concerns—and confusion.

On June 23, 2003, in a 5-to-4 decision, the Supreme Court upheld the University of Michigan Law School admissions policy, which uses student body diversity as an admission criterion, as constitutional *(Grutter v. Bollinger).* However, the Court, in a 6-to-3 decision, ruled that Michigan's undergraduate admissions policy, which considered diversity as a criterion, was not constitutional *(Gratz v. Bollinger).* The court's rationale was that the "undergraduate admissions policy was not narrowly tailored to advance an interest in diversity because it was not sufficiently flexible and did not provide enough individualized consideration of applicants to the University."

Some legal scholars have argued that the decisions reaffirm diversity as an admissions criterion. Others have ridiculed the court's "split the difference" decisions, which struck down an undergraduate admissions point system but upheld the Michigan law school's plan to admit a "critical mass" of minority students. The effect, however, has been for some—perhaps many— universities to abandon or begin to dismantle affirmative action programs.

A possible ray of hope: A transformation movement is afoot that may have potential to effect meaningful change. In 2003, the first National Conference for Media Reform attracted 1,700 media activists. More than 2,500 media activists, educators, and concerned citizens attended the second conference in 2005. Conference topics included media monopolies, affordable and unfettered Internet access, strategies for funding independent journalism, and censorship at the Corporation for Public Broadcasting. Recently, it was announced that the conference will be held annually.

While this movement to challenge the status quo in media organizations provides hope for change, the challenge to address inequities for women, sexual, and racial minorities in mass communication is now global.

The Gender Values Challenge Is Now Global

The first edition of *Women in Mass Communication* served to advance discussion and much-needed research to expose assumptions embedded in the mass communication system. The second edition called for a critical mass of women and people of color in journalism and mass communication to challenge the underlying values of the mass communication system.

Most authors in our third edition agree to a varying extent that women and minorities have more career options at the entry level and some increased flexibility with regard to family issues. Yet this progress is virtually meaningless.

Women are entering jobs in mass communication where the pay is declining, while the demands are greater. Media ownership is consolidating and converging. Newspaper circulation has declined precipitously. Television news is homogenizing under fewer and fewer owners, while the number of local news viewers declines.

The future of the entire mass communication industry is in question. Is "mass" communication no longer possible because of audience fragmentation? Can newspapers combine paid circulation (print version) with unpaid readership (online versions) to increase advertising rates? Where is the 18- to 35-year-old market going for news and information? How will "blogs" change journalism as we know it?

After a decade and a half, wealth, religion and patriarchy have resurfaced as controlling influences on the status of women in mass communication. Assimilation (reform and liberal feminism) has not brought about the transformation of values that so many of us had hoped for in 1989 and 1994. Even more critically, the battlefield for change is now global.

If we hope for transformation, we must take responsibility for moving our agenda for change forward. Women—and men—in mass communication with feminist values are more vital now than ever.

Accessing Additional Information

American Political Science Association: http://www.apsanet.org/content_5270.cfm

The Civil Rights Project, Harvard University: http://www.civilrightsproject .harvard.edu/policy/legal_docs/MIReaffirming.php

National Conference on Media Reform: http://www.freepress.net/conference/

Save Title IX: http://www.savetitleix.com/

Student Press Law Center: http://www.splc.org

The White House Project: http://www.thewhitehouseproject.org/v2/about/index .html

References

Adherents.com. (2005, August). *Major religions of the world ranked by number of adherents.* Retrieved August 24, 2005, from http://www.adherents.com/Religions_By_Adherents.html

Agence France Presse. (2005, August 18). *Five U.S. church leaders arrested in China; others tortured: Rights group.* Retrieved August 22, 2005, from www.nexis.com

Aldoory. L. (1998). The language of leadership for female public relations professionals. *Journal of Public Relations Research, 10,* 73–101.

Aldoory, L., & Toth, E. L. (2001). Two feminists, six opinions: The complexities of feminism in communication scholarship today. In W. B. Gudykunst (Ed.), *Communication yearbook, 24* (pp. 345–361). Thousand Oaks, CA: Sage.

Aldoory, L., & Toth, E. L. (2002). Gender discrepancies in a gendered profession: A developing theory for public relations. *Journal of Public Relations Research, 14*(2), 103–126.

Aldoory, L., & Toth, E. L. (2003). *A (re)conceived feminist paradigm for public relations scholarship: The case of organization-public relationships.* Paper presented at the AEJMC national conference, Kansas City.

Aldoory, L., & Toth, E. (2004a). Leadership and gender in public relations: Perceived effectiveness of transformational and transactional leadership styles. *Journal of Public Relations Research, 16,* 157–183.

Aldoory, L., & Toth, E. L. (2004b). Unpublished data.

Alexander, S. (1988). A woman undone. *Ms., 17*(3), 40–45.

Alfermann, D. (1996). Geschlechterrollen und geschlechtstypisches Verhalten [Gender roles and gender specific behaviour]. Stuttgart, Berlin, Köln, Germany: Kohlhammer.

Allen, A. L. (2000). Symposium: Cyberspace and privacy: A new legal paradigm? Gender and privacy in cyberspace. *Stanford Law Review, 52,* 1175–1198.

Allen, D. (1989). From opportunity to strategy: Women contribute to the communication future. In R. Rush & D. Allen (Eds.), *Communications at the crossroads: The gender gap connection.* Norwood, NJ: Ablex.

Allen, D. (1998, October 22). *150 years since Seneca Falls: Women's organizations, reform and journalism.* Paper presented at the Annual Conference of the American Journalism Historians Association, Louisville, KY.

Allen, P. G. (1986). *The sacred hoop: Recovering the feminine in American Indian traditions.* Boston: Beacon.

American Booksellers Ass'n v. Hudnut, 598 F. Supp. 1316 (S.D. Ind. 1984), aff'd, 771F. 2d 323 (7th Cir. 1985), aff'd, 475 U.S. 1001 (1986).

American Business Media. (2004). *About us.* Retrieved February 5, 2005, from http://www.americanbusinessmedia.com

American Obesity Association (2002). *AOA fact sheets: Women and obesity.* Retrieved July 9, 2005, from http://www.obesity.org/subs/fastfacts/obesity_women.shtml

The American Press Institute and Pew Center for Civic Journalism. (2002). *The great divide: Female leadership in U.S. newsrooms.* Reston, VA: Author.

American Society of Newspaper Editors. (1998). *ASNE Statement on newsroom diversity.* Adopted and published October 20, 1998. Retrieved January 26, 2005, from http://www.asne.org/index.cfm?id=1669

American Society of Newspaper Editors. (1999). *Newsroom census.* Retrieved June 28, 2005, from http://www.asne.org

American Society of Newspaper Editors. (2005). *Newsroom census.* Retrieved June 28, 2005, from http://www.asne.org

Amos, V., & Parmar, P. (1984). Challenging feminist imperialism. *Feminist Review, 17,* 3–19.

Andermahr, S., Lovell, T., & Wolkowitz, C. (2000). *Other: A glossary of feminist theory.* London: Arnold.

Anderson, G. R. (2005, February 16). *Clear Channel rules the world.* Retrieved June 28, 2005, from http://citypages.com/databank/26/1263/article12961.asp

Anderson, M. (2004). Ladies' night: WIN debuts award show honoring women. Does advertising need it? *Adweek, 45*(41), 26.

Andsager, J. L., & Hust, S. J. T. (2005). Differential gender orientation in public relations: Implications for career choices. *Public Relations Review, 31*(1), 85–91.

The Annenberg Public Policy Center. (2003). *The glass ceiling persists: The third annual APPC report on women leaders in communications companies.* Retrieved Dec. 12, 2004, from http://www.annenbergpublicpolicycenter.org/

The Annenberg Public Policy Center. (2004, March). *Companies with more women in corporate leadership have more women friendly packages, but women in communications companies made no progress in the past year in breaking the glass ceiling.* Retrieved August 24, 2005, from http://www.annenbergpublicpolicy center.org/

Anzaldúa. G. (1987). *Borderlands: La frontera.* San Francisco: Spinsters.

Anzaldúa, G. (1999). *Borderlands/ La frontera: The new mestiza* (2nd ed.). San Francisco: Aunt Lute Books.

Ardizonni, M. (1998). Feminist contributions to communication studies: Past and present. *Journal of Communication Inquiry, 22,* 293–316.

Arizpe, L. (1999). Freedom to create: Women's agenda for cyberspace. In W. Harcourt (Ed.), *Women@Internet: Creating new cultures in cyberspace* (pp. xii–xvii). London: Zed Books.

Arjomand, S. (2000). Islam, politics and Iran in particular. In M. Silk (Ed.), *Religion in the international news agenda*. Hartford, CT: Leonard E. Greenberg Center.

Arnold, M. (1996). A day in the life of the "average" high school journalism teacher. *Quill & Scroll, 71*(2), 10.

Arnold, M., Hendrickson, M. L., & Linton, C. C. (2003). *Women in newspapers 2003 Challenging the status quo*. Evanston, IL: Media Management Center, Northwestern University.

Arocha, Z. (1985, October 15). Women predominate in j-schools. *Washington Post*, pp. B1, B7.

Associated Press. (1977). *Associated Press stylebook and briefing on media law*. Reading. MA: Addison-Wesley.

Associated Press. (2004). *Associated Press stylebook and briefing on media*. New York: Basic Books.

Associated Press. (2005, August 31).*Vatican: China bishop died in August at 85*. Retrieved September 2, 2005, from www.nexis.com

Astin, H. S., & Leland, C. (1991). *Women of influence, women of vision: A cross-generational study of leaders and social change*. San Francisco: Jossey-Bass.

Astor, D. (2005a, March 21). Female op-ed columnists discuss why there aren't more of them. *Editor and Publisher*. Retrieved September 4, 2005, from http://editorand publisher.com

Astor, D. (2005b, April 6). NSNC prez writes about female op-ed columnists. *Editor and Publisher*. Retrieved September 4, 2005, from http://www.editorandpublisher.com

ASWM Online. (2005, February). *Mission statement*. Retrieved January 3, 2006, from http://www.awsmonline.org/frontpage.htm

Avolio, B. J., & Bass, B. M. (1988). Transformational leadership, charisma, and beyond. In J. G. Hunt, B. R. Baliga, H. P. Dachler, & C. A. Schriesheim (Eds.), *Emerging leadership vistas* (pp. 29–49). Lexington, MA: Lexington Books.

Bacon's magazine directory. (2003). Chicago: Bacon's Information, Inc.

Baer, J. A. (2002). *Women in American law: The struggle toward equality from the New Deal to the present* (3rd ed.). New York: Holmes & Meier.

Bagdikian, B. H. (2004). *The new media monopoly*. Boston: Beacon Press.

Bales, K. (1999). *Disposable people: New slavery in the global economy*. Berkeley/London: University of California Press.

Barrett, M. (1980). *Women's oppression today*. London: Verso.

Barrett, M. (1992). Word and things: Materialism and method in contemporary feminist analysis. In M. Barrett & A. Phillips (Eds.), *Destabilizing theory: Contemporary feminist debates* (pp. 201–219). Stanford, CA: Stanford University Press.

Barthes, R. (1972). *Mythologies*. (A. Lavers, Trans.). New York: Hill & Wang.

Barthes, R. (1983). *The fashion system*. (M. Ward & R. Howard, Trans.). Berkeley: University of California Press.

Bartow, A. (2000). Our data, ourselves: Privacy, propertization, and gender. *University of San Francisco Law Review, 34*, 633–704.

Bass, B. M. (1985). *Leadership and performance beyond expectations*. New York: Free Press.

Bass, B. M., & Avolio, B. J. (1993). Transformational leadership: A response to critiques. In M. M. Chemers & R. Ayman (Eds.), *Leadership theory and research: Perspectives and directions* (pp. 49–80). New York: Academic.

Bass, B. M., Avolio, B. J., & Atwater, L. (1996). The transformational and transactional leadership of men and women. *Applied Psychology—An International Review, 45,* 5–34.

Bates, K. G. (1994). The color thing. *Essence, 25*(5), 79–83.

Bauder, D. (2005, August 4). *Dateline* visits missing-persons coverage. Retrieved from http://www.sfgate.com

Beasley, M. H. (1985, December 14). In defense of the "Women in Journalism" study. *Editor & Publisher,* pp. 44, 33.

Beasley, M. H., & Theus, K. (1988). *The new majority.* Lanham, MD: University Press of America.

Beck, C. S., Benitez, J. L., Edwards, A., Olson, A., Pai, A., & Torres, M. B. (2004). Enacting "health communication": The field of health communication as constructed through publication in scholarly journals. *Health Communication, 16,* 475–492.

Becker, L. B., & Vlad, T. (2003). *Annual survey of journalism and mass communication graduates.* Retrieved February 5, 2005, from http://www.grady.uga.edu/annualsurveys

Becker, L. B., & Vlad, T. (2004, November). 2003 annual survey of JMC graduates. *AEJMC NEWS,* pp. 1, 4–7.

Becker, L., Vlad, T., Hennick-Kaminski, H., & Coffey, A. J. (2004). 2003–2004 enrollment report: Growth in field keeps up with trend. *Journalism & Mass Communication Educator, 59*(3), 278–308.

Bell, K. E., Orbe M., Drummond D., & Camara, S. K. (2000). Accepting the challenge of centralizing without essentializing: Black feminist thought and African American women's communicative experience. *Women's Studies in Communication, 23*(1), 41–62.

Bem, S. L. (1993). *The lens of gender: Transforming the debate on sexual inequality.* New Haven, CT: Yale Press.

Beneria, L. (2003). *Gender, development, and globalization.* New York: Routledge.

Bennis, W. (1989). *Why leaders can't lead.* San Francisco: Jossey-Bass.

Berkeley, K. C. (1999). *The women's liberation movement in America.* Westport, CT: Greenwood Press.

Bernstein, A. (2002). Is it time for a victory lap? Changes in the media coverage of women in sport. *International Review for the Sociology of Sport, 37*(3–4), 415–428.

Bernt, J. P., Gifford, J., Fee, F. E., & Stempel, G. H. III. (2003). How well can editors predict reader interest in news? *Newspaper Research Journal, 21*(2), 2–11.

Bezanson, R. P., Cranberg, G., & Soloski, J. (1987). *Libel law and the press: Myth and reality.* New York: Harvard University Press.

Bhattacharyya, K., Winch, P., LeBan, K., & Tien, M. (2001). *Community health worker incentives and disincentives: How they affect motivation, retention, and sustainability*. Retrieved January 17, 2005, from the Academy for Education Development Web site: http://www.aed.org/ToolsandPublications/upload/CommunityHealthWorkers.pdf

Bhavnani, K. (Ed.). (2001). *Feminism and "race."* New York: Oxford University Press.

Bignell, J. (1997). *Media semiotics: An introduction.* New York: Manchester University Press.

Billings, A. C., & Eastman, S.T. (2002). Selective representation of gender, ethnicity, and nationality in American television: Coverage of the 2000 Summer Olympics. *International Review for the Sociology of Sport, 39*(3/4), 351–370.

Billings, A. C., Halone, K. K., & Denham, B. E. (2002). "Man that was a pretty shot": An analysis of gendered broadcasting commentary surrounding the 2000 men's and women's NCAA final four basketball championships. *Mass Communication and Society, 5*(3), 569–586.

Bilsky, L. (1998). Giving voice to women: An Israeli case study. *Israel Studies, 3*(2), 47–79.

Birrell, S., & Theberge, N. (1994). Ideological control of women in sport. In M. D. Duncan & S. R. Gutherie (Eds.), Women and sport: Interdisciplinary perspectives (pp. 323–376). Champaign, IL: Human Kinetics.

Blake, K., Bodle, J. V., & Adams, A. A. (2004). A fifteen-year census of gender and journal productivity. *Journalism & Mass Communication Educator, 59*(2), 156–170.

Borden, D. L. (1997). Patterns of harm: An analysis of gender and defamation. *Communication Law and Policy, 2,* 105–141.

Borden, D. L. (1998). Reputational assault: A critical and historical analysis of gender and the law of defamation. *Journalism and Mass Communication Quarterly, 75,* 98–111.

Borden, D. L. (1999). Invisible plaintiffs: A feminist critique on the rights of private individuals in the wake of *Hustler Magazine v. Falwell. Gonzaga Law Review, 35,* 291–317.

Borod, L. (2004, May). Finally, a little more in the paycheck: Salary survey. *Folio: The Magazine for Magazine Management,* pp. 18–22.

Boughner, G. J. (1926). *Women in journalism.* New York: D. Appleton-Century.

Boulding, E. (1981). Integration into what? Reflections on development planning for women. In R. Dauber & M. Cain (Eds.), *Women and technological change in developing countries* (pp. 9–32). Boulder, CO: Westview Press.

Bourdieu, P. (1973). Cultural reproduction and social reproduction? In R. Brown (Ed.), *Knowledge, education, and cultural change* (pp. 71–112). London: Tavistock.

Bradwell v. Illinois, 83 U.S. 130 (1873).

Brandeis, L., & Warren, E. (1890). The right to privacy. *Harvard Law Review, 4,* 193–220.

Brandenburg v. Ohio, 395 U.S. 444 (1969).

Brazelton, E. M. C. (1927). *Writing and editing for women.* New York: Funk & Wagnalls.

Brookes, R. (2002). *Representing sport.* London: Oxford University Press.

Brooks, B. S., Kennedy, G., Moen, D. R., & Ranly, D. (1992). *News reporting & writing* (4th ed.). New York: St. Martin's Press.

Brown, C. (2004). *The Word in the world: Evangelical writing, publishing and reading in America, 1789–1880*. Chapel Hill: University of North Carolina Press.

Brownmiller, S. (1984). *Femininity*. New York: Linden.

Buber, M. (1958). *I and thou*. New York: Scribner Classic. (Original work published 1923)

Buddenbaum, J. (1987). Judge what their acts will justify: The religion journalism of James Gordon Bennett. *Journalism History*, 14, 54–67.

Buddenbaum, J. (1998). *Reporting news about religion: An introduction for journalists*. Ames: Iowa State University Press.

Buonanno, M. (in press). Visibility without power: Women journalists in Italy. In R. Fröhlich & S. A. Lafky (Eds.), *Women journalists in the Western world: Equal opportunities and what surveys tell us*. London: Hampton Press.

Burke, D. D. (1996). Cybersmut and the First Amendment: A call for a new obscenity standard. *Harvard Journal of Law & Technology*, 9, 87–145.

Butler, J. (1999). *Gender trouble: Feminism and the subversion of identity*. New York: Routledge.

Butler, M., & Paisley, W. (1980). *Women and the mass media: Sourcebook for research and action*. New York: Human Services Press.

Byerly, C. (1995). News, consciousness, and social participation: The role of women's feature service in world news. In A. N. Valdivia (Ed.), *Feminism, multiculturalism, and the media: Global diversities* (pp. 105–122). Thousand Oaks, CA: Sage.

Byerly, C. M. (1999). News, feminism, and the dialectics of gendered relations. In M. Meyers (Ed.), *Mediated women: Representations in popular culture* (pp. 383–403). Cresskill, NJ: Hampton Press.

Byerly, C. M. (2004a). Shifting sites: Feminist, gay, and lesbian news activism in the U.S. context. In M. de Bruin and K. Ross (Eds.), *Gender and newsroom cultures: Identities at work* (pp. 221–239). Cresskill, NJ: Hampton Press.

Byerly, C. M. (2004b). Women and the concentration of media ownership. In R. R. Rush, C. E. Oukrop, & P. J. Creedon (Eds.), *Seeking equity for women in journalism and mass communication education: A 30-year update* (pp. 245–262). Mahwah, NJ: Lawrence Erlbaum.

Byerly, C. M. (2005, November). After September 11: Formation of an oppositional discourse, *Feminist Media Studies*, pp. 281–296.

Byerly, K. (1961). *Community journalism*. Philadelphia: Chilton.

Calhoun, C. (1995). The gender closet: Lesbian disappearance under the sign "women." *Feminist Studies*, 21(1), 7–34.

Calvert, C., & Brown, J. (2000). Video voyeurism, privacy, and the Internet: Exposing peeping toms in cyberspace. *Cardozo Arts & Entertainment Law Journal*, 18, 469–568.

Campbell, B. (1997). *A brief history of Aimee Semple McPherson*. Retrieved September 12, 2005, from http://members.aol.com/xbcampbell/asmhistory.htm

Canadian Radio-Television and Telecommunications Commission. (1990). *The portrayal of gender in Canadian broadcasting: Summary report 1984–1988.* Ottawa, Canada: Author.

Carless, S. A. (1998). Gender differences in transformational leadership: An examination of superior, leader, and subordinate perspectives. *Sex Roles, 39,* 887–902.

Carter, C., & Steiner, L. (Eds.). (2004). *Critical readings: Media and gender.* Maidenhead, UK: Open University Press.

Carter, S. (2005). A mic of her own: Stations, collectives, and women's access to radio. *Journal of Radio Studies, 11*(2), 169–183.

Casimir, G. (2001). Combinative aspects of leadership style: The ordering and temporal spacing of leadership behaviors. *Leadership Quarterly, 12,* 245–279.

Catalyst. (2004). *The bottom line: Connecting corporate performance and gender diversity.* Retrieved July 20, 2005, from http://www.catalystwomen.org/bookstore/files/exe/fpexe.pdf

Catholic Agency for Overseas Development (CAFOD). (2004). *Clean up your computer: Working conditions in the electronics industry in Mexico, Thailand, and China.* London: Author.

Chambers, T. (2003). Structural changes in small markets. *Journal of Media Economics, 16*(1), 41–59.

Christmas, L. (in press). Women in the media in the UK: Progress at a snail's pace. In R. Fröhlich & S. A. Lafky (Eds.), *Women journalists in the Western world: Equal opportunities and what surveys tell us.* London: Hampton Press.

Churchill, W. (1992). *Fantasies of the master race: Literature, cinema, and the colonization of American Indians.* Monroe, ME: Common Courage Press.

Clair, R. P. (1998). *Organizing silence: A world of possibilities.* Albany: SUNY.

Clark, L. (2003). *From angels to aliens.* New York: Oxford University Press.

Clark, L. S., & Hoover, S. H. (1997). Controversy and cultural symbolism: A case study of the Reimagining event. *Critical Studies in Mass Communication, 14*(4), 310–331.

Clemons, M. (1999). JEA's 75-year history of visions, realities. *Journalism Education Association visions: Our seventy-fifth anniversary* [Calendar], pp, 1–4.

Clift, E. (1997). What did you say you do? Health communicators and where we fit in. *Journal of Health Communication, 2,* 65–67.

Cline, C. G., Toth, E. L., Turk, J. V., Walters, L. M., Johnson, N., & Smith, H. (1986). *The velvet ghetto: The impact of the increasing numbers of women in public relations and business communication.* San Francisco: IABC Research Foundation.

Coakley, J. J. (1990). *Sport in society: Issues and controversies.* St. Louis, MO: Times Mirror/Mosby.

Cohen, B. C. (1963). *The press and foreign policy.* Princeton, NJ: Princeton University Press.

Collins, P. H. (2004). *Black sexual politics: African Americans, gender, and the new racism.* New York: Routledge.

Columbia Scholastic Press Association. (2005). *Columbia Scholastic Press Association awards program.* Retrieved January 19, 2006, from http://www.columbia.edu/cu/cspa/AwardsPrograms.html

Cooper, C. (2003). What's age, race, and gender got to do with advertising? Everything! *Journal of Advertising Education, 7*(2), 17–19.

Cornell, G. (1990). The evolution of the religion beat. In B. Hubbard (Ed.), *Religion reporting facts & faith* (pp. 20–35). Sonoma, CA: Polebridge Press.

Corporation for Public Broadcasting. (2003, December). *Public broadcasting's services to minorities and diverse audiences.* Retrieved January 18, 2006, from http://cpb .org/aboutcpb/reports/diversity.html

Cortese, A. J. (1999). *Provocateur: Images of women and minorities in advertising.* Lanham, MD: Rowman & Littlefield.

Cottle, M. (1998). Turning boys into girls. *Washington Monthly, 30*(5), 32–37.

Courtney, A. E., & Whipple, T. W. (1983). *Sex stereotyping in advertising.* Lexington, MA: Lexington Books.

Covert, C. L. (1981). Journalism history and women's experience: A problem in conceptual change. *Journalism History, 8,* 2–6.

Coward, R. (1985). *Female desires: How they are sought, bought, and packaged.* New York: Grove.

Craft, S., & Wanta, W. (2004). Women in the newsroom: Influences of female editors and reporters on the news agenda. *Journalism & Mass Communication Quarterly, 81*(1), 124–138.

Craig, R. (2005). *Online journalism.* Belmont, CA: Wadsworth.

Cramer, J. A. (1994). Conversations with women sports journalists. In P. J. Creedon (Ed.), *Women, media, and sport: Challenging gender values* (pp. 159–179). Thousand Oaks, CA: Sage.

Creedon, P. J. (1989). Introduction. In P. J. Creedon (Ed.), *Women in mass communication* (pp. 1–20). Thousand Oaks, CA: Sage.

Creedon, P. J. (1994a). Women in Toyland. A look at women in American newspaper sports journalism. In P. J. Creedon (Ed.), *Women, media, and sport: Challenging gender values* (pp. 67–101). Thousand Oaks, CA: Sage.

Creedon, P.J. (1994b). Women, media, and sport: Creating and reflecting gender values. In P. J. Creedon (Ed.), *Women, media, and sport: Challenging gender values* (pp. 3–23). Thousand Oaks, CA: Sage.

Cronan, J. P. (2002). The next challenge for the First Amendment: The framework for an Internet incitement standard. *Catholic University Law Review, 51,* 425–466.

Cronin, M. M. (1995). *Godey's lady's book.* In K. L. Endres & T. L. Lueck (Eds.), *Women's periodicals in the United States: Consumer magazines* (pp. 113–117). Westport, CT: Greenwood Press.

Cropp, F., Frisby, C. M., & Mills, D. (Eds.). (2003). *Journalism across cultures.* Ames: Iowa State Press.

Cruz, M. G., Henningsen, D. D., & Smith, B. A. (1999). The impact of directive leadership on group information sampling, decisions, and perceptions of the leader. *Communication Research, 26,* 349–369.

Currie, D. (1998). *Girl talk: Adolescent magazines and their readers.* Toronto, Canada: University of Toronto Press.

Danesi, M. (1999). *Of cigarettes and high heels and other interesting things: An introduction to semiotics.* New York: St. Martin's Press.

Darling-Wolf, F. (2004). On the possibility of communicating: Feminism and social position. *Journal of Communication Inquiry, 28,* 29–46.

Dart, J. (1970, December 13). Masculine image of God being challenged. *Los Angeles Times,* pp. A-1, A-22.

Davis, L. (1997). *The swimsuit issue and sport: Hegemonic masculinity in Sports Illustrated.* Albany: SUNY Press.

Davison, W. P. (1983). The third-person effect in communication. *Public Opinion Quarterly 47,* 1–15.

de Beauvoir, S. (1952). *The second sex.* New York: Knopf.

de Beauvoir, S. (1989). *The second sex* (H. M. Parshley, Trans.). New York: Vintage Books.

de Lauretis, T. (1987). *Technologies of gender: Essays on theory, film, and fiction.* Bloomington: Indiana University Press.

Deeken, A. (2004, March 1). Teenage tasteland. *Adweek, 45*(9), p. 22. Retrieved October 28, 2004, from RDS Business & Industry Database, http://rdsweb2 .rdsinc.com/texis/rds/suite2/+MoeEJ8YemxwwwwwFqz6vqhmw9mwxFqh1odi w/full.html

Devor, H. (1989). *Gender blending: Confronting the limits of duality.* Bloomington: Indiana University Press.

Dickey, E. (1996). *History of scholastic journalism* (Lecture 2, Distance education course J535). Publications Advising, College of Journalism and Mass Communications, University of South Carolina.

Dickman, S. (1985, October 15). Women the "new majority" in journalism schools. *Evening Sun,* p. D2.

Dines, G., & Humez, J. (Eds.). (1995). *Gender, race, and class in the media: A text reader.* Thousand Oaks, CA: Sage.

Ditthavong, K. A. (1996). Paving the way for women on the information superhighway: Curbing sexism, not freedoms. *American University Journal of Gender & Law, 4,* 455–510.

Donato, K. M. (1990). Keepers of the corporate image: Women in public relations. In B. F. Reskin & P. A. Roos (Eds.), *Job queues, gender queues: Explaining women's inroads into males' occupations* (pp. 129–144). Philadelphia: Temple University Press.

Dorer, J. (in press). Status quo and development of the professional situation of women in Austrian journalism: An overview. In R. Fröhlich & S. A. Lafky (Eds.), *Women journalists in the Western world: Equal opportunities and what surveys tell us.* London: Hampton Press.

Dow Jones Newspaper Fund/Gallup Survey. (1988, January). *Final tabulation of 1983 journalism graduates.* Princeton, NJ: Author.

Dowling, C. (2000). *The frailty myth: Women approaching physical equality.* New York: Random House.

Dozier, D. M., Grunig, L. A., & Grunig, J. E. (1995). *Manager's guide to excellence in public relations and communication management.* Mahwah, NJ: Lawrence Erlbaum.

Dreschel, R. E. (1985). Intentional infliction of emotional distress: New tort liability for mass media. *Dickinson Law Review, 89,* 339–361.

Driscoll, C. (2002). *Girls: Feminine adolescence in popular culture and cultural theory.* New York: Columbia University Press.

Duffy, M., & Gotcher, M. (1995). Crucial advice on how to get the guy: The rhetorical vision of power and seduction in the teen magazine *YM. Journal of Communication Inquiry 20,* 32–48.

Duke, L. L. (2000). Black in a blonde world: Race and girls' interpretations of the feminine ideal in teen magazines. *Journalism and Mass Communication Quarterly, 77*(2), 367–392.

Duke, L. L., & Kreshel, P. J. (1998). Negotiating femininity: Girls in early adolescence read teen magazines. *Journal of Communication Inquiry, 22*(1), 48–71.

Duncan, M. C., & Messner, M. A. (1998). The media image of sports and gender. In L. A. Wenner (Ed.), *MediaSport* (pp. 170–185). London: Routledge.

Duncan, M. C., Messner, M., & Williams, L. (Ed.). (1991). *Coverage of women's sport in four daily newspapers.* Los Angeles: Amateur Athletic Foundation of Los Angeles.

Durham, M. G. (1999). Girls, media, and the negotiation of sexuality: A study of race, class and gender in adolescent peer groups. *Journalism and Mass Communication Quarterly 76,* 193 216.

Dvorak, J. (1989). Ann Christine Heintz. *Quill & Scroll, 63*(4),10–12.

Dvorak, J. (1998). *Status of journalism and news media in the nation's secondary schools, 1991, 1998.* Retrieved November 18, 2004, from the Indiana University High School Journalism Institute Web site http://www.journalism.indiana.edu/hsji/research/1.html

Dvorak, J. (2005). Benedict embraced life with style. *NEWSwire, 31*(1), 1.

Dyer, R. (1997). *White.* New York and London: Routledge.

Eagly, A. H., & Johnson, B. T. (1990). Gender and leadership style: A meta-analysis. *Psychological Bulletin, 108,* 233–256.

Eagly, A. H., Karau, S. J., & Makhijani, M. G. (1995). Gender and the effectiveness of leaders: A meta-analysis. *Psychological Reports, 117,* 125–145.

Eagly, A. H., Makhijani, M. G., & Klonsky, B. G. (1992). Gender and the evaluation of leaders: A meta-analysis. *Psychological Reports, 111,* 3–22.

Earnest, W. J. (2002). Between law and love: Christianity, politics, and sexual citizenship. In D. Claussen (Ed.), *Sex, religion, media* (pp. 197–213). New York: Rowman & Littlefield.

Eastman, S. T., & Billings, A. C. (2001). Biased voices of sports: Racial and gender stereotyping in college basketball announcing. *Howard Journal of Communication, 12*(4), 183–201.

Eco, U. (1976). *A theory of semiotics.* Bloomington: Indiana University Press.

Edgar, T., & Hyde, J. N. (2005). An alumni-based evaluation of graduate training in health communication: Results of a survey on careers, salaries, competencies, and emerging trends. *Journal of Health Communication, 10,* 5–25.

Ehrhart, M. G., & Klein, K. J. (2001). Predicting followers' preferences for charismatic leadership: The influence of follower values and personality. *Leadership Quarterly, 12,* 153–180.

Eichenberger, B. (2004, June). Diversity efforts are still lacking. *Associated Press Sports Editors' Newsletter.* Retrieved August 4, 2005, from http://apse.dallasnews.com/jun2004/2eichenbergerr.html

Eisenstein, Z. R. (Ed.). (1979). *Capitalist patriarchy and the case for socialist feminism.* New York: Monthly Review Press.

Elizondo, V. (2005). The Virgin of Guadalupe as cultural icon. In C. Badaracco (Ed.), *Quoting God* (pp. 201–208). Waco, TX: Baylor University Press.

Elmore, C. (2003, Fall). Two steps forward and one step back: Coverage of women journalists in *Editor & Publisher* 1978 through 1988. *American Journalism, 20,* pp. 33–54.

Engels, F. (1985). *The origin of the family, private property, and the state.* New York: Penguin Books. (Original work published 1884)

Eskenazi, G. (2003). *A sportswriter's life: From the desk of a New York Times reporter.* Columbia: University of Missouri Press.

Essed, P., & Goldberg, D. T. (Eds.). (2002). *Race critical theories.* Malden, MA: Blackwell.

Essed, P., Goldberg, D. T., & Kobayashi, A. (Eds.). (2005). *A companion to gender studies.* Malden, MA: Blackwell.

Etling, L. (2002, June). An uphill climb. *Associated Press Sports Editors' Newsletter.* Retrieved August 4, 2005, from http://apse.dallasnews.com/jun2002/5-7etling.html

Fairhurst, G. T. (1993). The leader-member exchange patterns of women leaders in industry: A discourse analysis. *Communication Monographs, 60,* 321–351.

Fairhurst, G. T. (2000). Dualisms in leadership research. In F. M. Jablin & L. L. Putnam (Eds.), *The new handbook of organizational communication* (pp. 379–439). Thousand Oaks, CA: Sage.

Fairhurst, G. T., & Chandler, T. A. (1989). Social structure in leader-member interaction. *Communication Monographs, 56,* 215–239.

Falk, E., & Grizard, E. (2003a). *The glass ceiling persists: The 3rd annual APPC report on women leaders in communication companies.* The Annenberg Public Policy Center, University of Pennsylvania. Retrieved March 4, 2005, from http://www.annenbergpublicpolicycenter.org/

Falk, E., & Grizard, E. (2003b). *Women in communications companies made no progress in past year in breaking the glass ceiling.* The Annenberg Public Policy Center, University of Pennsylvania. Retrieved October 16, 2004, from http://www.annenbergpublicpolicycenter.org

Farmer, B. A., Slater, J. W., & Wright, K. S. (1998). The role of communication in achieving shared vision under new organizational leadership. *Journal of Public Relations Research, 10,* 219–235.

Fanon, F. (1967). *Black skin, White masks.* New York: Grove Weidenfeld.

Fausto-Sterling, A. (1985). *Myths of gender: Biological theories about men and women.* New York: Basic Books.

Federal Communications Commission. (2001, January). *Review of the radio industry, 2000.* Retrieved January 20, 2005, from http://www.fcc.gov/ml/policy/radio/html

Federal Communications Commission. (2004, November 3). *Broadcast station totals.* Retrieved January 20, 2005, from http://www.fcc.gov/mbaudio/totals/bt040930 .html

Fedler, F. (1989). *Reporting for the print media.* New York: Harcourt Brace Jovanovich. (Also published 1973, 1979, 1984, 1993, 1997, 2005, some with different coauthors)

Fellner, A. M. (2002). *Articulating selves: Contemporary Chicana self-representation.* Vienna, Austria: Braumuller.

Fenton, N. (2000). The problematics of postmodernism for feminist media studies. *Media, Culture, & Society, 22,* 723–741.

Ferguson, M. (1990). Images of power and the feminist fallacy. *Critical Studies in Mass Communication, 7,* 215–230.

Fineman, M. A. (1992). Feminist theory in law: The difference it makes. *Columbia Journal of Gender and Law, 2,* 1–23.

Finnegan, J. L., & Viswanath, K. (1990). Health and communication: Medical and public health . . . influences on the research agenda. In E. B. Ray & L. Donohew (Eds.), *Communication and health: A systems perspective* (pp. 9–26). Hillsdale, NJ: Lawrence Erlbaum.

Fisher, H. (1999). *The first sex.* New York: Random House.

Fiske, J. (1993). *Introduction to communication studies* (2nd ed.). London and New York: Routledge.

Florence, P., & Reynolds, D. (Eds.). (1995). *Feminist subjects, multi-media: Cultural methodologies.* New York: Manchester University Press.

Flores, L. (1996). Creating discursive space through a rhetoric of difference: Chicana feminists craft a homeland. *Quarterly Journal of Speech, 82,* 142–156.

Folio Staff. (2001, August). Editorial salary survey 2001. *Folio: The Magazine for Magazine Management,* pp. 33–39.

Folio Staff. (2002, July). Editorial salary survey 2002. *Folio: The Magazine for Magazine Management,* pp. 33–40.

Ford, L. A., & Crabtree, R. D. (2002). Telling, re-telling, and talking about telling: Disclosure and/as surviving incest. *Women's Studies in Communication, 25*(1), 53–87.

Forer, L. G. (1987). *A chilling effect: The mounting threat of libel and invasion of privacy actions to the First Amendment.* New York: Norton.

Former JEA president receives Freedom Forum award (1995). *JEA NewsWire, 22*(2), 1.

Foss, K. A., Foss, S. K., & Griffin, C. L. (1999). *Feminist rhetorical theories.* Thousand Oaks, CA: Sage.

Foushee, H. Jr. (2002). Cult sex: The mass media reporting of sexual issues surrounding new religious movements. In D. Claussen (Ed.), *Sex, religion, media* (pp. 153–170). Lanham, MD: Rowman & Littlefield.

Fowler, K., Celebuski, C., Edgar, T., Kroger, F., & Ratzan, S. C. (1999). An assessment of the health communication job market across multiple types of organizations. *Journal of Health Communication, 4,* 327–342.

Fraser, N., & Nicholson, L. J. (1990). Social criticism without philosophy: An encounter between feminism and postmodernism. In L. J. Nicholson (Ed.), *Feminism/postmodernism* (pp. 19–38). New York: Routledge.

Fratrik, M. (2001). *State of the radio industry: Ownership and consolidation, 2001.* BIA Financial Network. Chantilly, VA: BIA Research Publications.

Frazer, E. (1987). Teenage girls reading *Jackie. Media, Culture, & Society, 9,* 407–25.

Free to be me. (1997, May 22). *Women's Wear Daily, Generation Y Supplement 6.* Retrieved on October 28, 2004, from RDS Business &Industry Database, http://rdsweb2.rdsinc.com/texis/rds/suite2/+uoe9U8YemxwwwwwFqz6vqhmw9mwxFqh1odiw/full.html

FreePress.org. (2005). Retrieved March 11, 2005, from the FreePress.org Web site, http://www.freepress.net/conference/

Freimuth, V. S., Edgar, T., & Fitzpatrick, M. A. (1993). The role of communication in health promotion. *Communication Research, 20,* 509–516.

Freimuth, V. S., & Quinn, S. C. (2004, December). The contributions of health communication to eliminating health disparities. *American Journal of Public Health, 94,* pp. 2053–2055.

Friedan, B. (1963). *The feminine mystique.* New York: Dell.

Friedan, B. (1997). *The feminine mystique.* New York: Norton. (Original work published 1963)

Frisby, C. M. (2003). The changing faces of advertising: Minority images and the media. In F. Cropp, C. M. Frisby, & D. Mills (Eds.), *Journalism across cultures* (pp. 185–201). Ames: Iowa State Press.

Fröhlich, R. (2004). Feminine and feminist values in communication professions: Exceptional skills and expertise or "friendliness trap?" In M. de Bruin & K. Ross (Eds.), *Gender and newsroom cultures: Identities at work* (pp. 65–77). Cresskill, NJ: Hampton Press.

Fröhlich, R., & Holtz-Bacha (in press). Women in German journalism: Where do all the women go? In R. Fröhlich & S. A. Lafky (Eds.), *Women journalists in the Western world: Equal opportunities and what surveys tell us.* London: Hampton Press.

Fröhlich, R., & Lafky, S. A. (Eds.). (in press). *Women journalists in the Western world: Equal opportunities and what surveys tell us.* London: Hampton Press.

Fry, H., & Wine, G. (1999). *Hayden Fry: A high porch picnic.* Champaign, IL: Sports Publications.

Gaines, J. (1989). Dead ringer: Jacqueline Onassis and the look-alike. *South Atlantic Quarterly, 88,* 461–486.

Gallagher, M. (1981). *Unequal opportunities. The case of women and the media.* Paris: UNESCO.

Gallagher, M. (1992). Women and men in the media. *Communication Research Trends, 12*(1), 1–36.

Gallagher, M. (1995a). *Employment patterns in European broadcasting: Prospects for equality in the 1990s.* Brussels, Belgium: European Commission.

Gallagher, M. (1995b). *An unfinished story: Gender patterns in media employment* (Reports and Papers on Mass Communication, 110). Paris: UNESCO.

Gallagher, M. (1999). The Global Media Monitoring Project: Women's networking for research and action. In K. Nordenstenge & M. Griffin (Eds.), *International media monitoring* (pp. 199–217). Cresskill, NJ: Hampton Press.

Gallagher, M. (2000). *From Mexico to Beijing—and beyond: Covering women in the world's news.* New York: UNIFEM.

Gallagher, M. (2001). *Gender setting: New agendas for media monitoring and advocacy.* London: Zed Books.

Gallagher, M. (2002, November 12–15). *Women, media and democratic society: In pursuit of rights and freedoms.* Paper presented at the UN Division for the Advancement of Women (DAW) Expert Group Meeting on Women and the Media, Beirut, Lebanon (doc. EGM/MEDIA/2002/BP.I).

Gallagher, M. (in press). At the millennium. Shifting patterns in gender, culture and journalism. In R. Fröhlich & S. A. Lafky (Eds.), *Women journalists in the Western world: Equal opportunities and what surveys tell us.* London: Hampton Press.

Galinda, D. L., & Maria D. G. (Eds.). (1999). *Speaking Chicana: Voice, power, and identity.* Tucson: University of Arizona Press.

Gandy, O. (1998). *Communication and race: A structural perspective.* Thousand Oaks, CA: Sage.

Gardner, W. L., & Cleavenger, D. (1998). The impression management strategies associated with transformational leadership at the world-class level. *Management Communication Quarterly, 12,* 3–41.

Garner, A., Sterk, H. M., & Adams, S. (1998). Narrative analysis of sexual etiquette and teenage magazines. *Journal of Communication, 48*(4), 59–78.

Garrison, B. (1990). *Professional news writing.* Hillsdale, NJ: Lawrence Erlbaum.

Garrison, B., & Sabljak, M. (1993). *Sports reporting.* Ames: Iowa State University Press.

George, J. J. (2002). *Lack of news coverage for women's athletics: A questionable practice of newspaper priorities.* Women's Sports Foundation. Retrieved August 4, 2005, from http://www.womenssportsfoundation.org/cgi-bin/iowa/issues/media/article.html?record=807

Gerbner, G. (1972). Violence in television drama: Trends and symbolic functions. In G. Comstock & E. A. Rubinstein (Eds.), *Media content and control, television, and social behavior* (Vol. 1, pp. 28–187). Washington, DC: Government Printing Office.

Gertz v. Robert Welch, Inc., 418 U.S. 373 (1974).

Gesenway, D. (2001, November 20). Reasons for sex-specific and gender-specific study of health topics. *Annals of Internal Medicine, 135,* pp. 935–938.

Gibbons, S. (June 3, 2005). *Multi-media tune-out: Ignoring female expertise.* Oakland, CA: Robert C. Maynard Institute for Journalism Education.

Gilligan, C. (1982). *In a different voice: Psychological theory and women's development.* Cambridge, MA: Harvard University Press.

Gilwald, A. (1994). Women, democracy, and the media in South Africa. *Media Development, 2*(1), 27–32.

Glascock, J. (2003). Gender, race, and aggression in newer TV networks' prime-time programming. *Communication Quarterly 51*(1), 90–100.

Goffman, E. (1979). *Gender advertisements.* Cambridge, MA: Harvard University Press.

Golding, P., & Murdock, G. (1991). Culture, communication, and political economy. In J. Curran & M. Gurevitch (Eds.), *Mass media and society.* London: Edward Arnold.

Gonzalez, J., & Torres, J. (2004). *How long must we wait? The fight for racial and ethnic equality in the American news media.* Oakland, CA: Robert C. Maynard Institute for Journalism Education.

Graeff, C. L. (1997). Evolution of situational leadership theory: A critical review. *Leadership Quarterly, 8,* 153–170.

Granderson, L. Z. (2005, October 26). Outside the arc. *ESPN The Magazine.* Retrieved November 27, 2005, from http://sports.espn.go.com/wnba/news/story?id=2203853

Green, J., & Silk, M. (2004). Gendering the religion gap. *Religion in the News, 7*(1), 11–13.

Gross, L. (1994). What is wrong with this picture: Lesbian women and gay men on television. In R. J. Ringer (Ed.), *Queer words, queer images: Communication and the construction of homosexuality* (pp. 143–156). New York: New York University Press.

Gross, L. (1995). Out of the mainstream: Sexual minorities and the mass media. In G. Dines & J. M. Humez (Eds.), *Gender, race, and class in media* (pp. 61–70). Thousand Oaks, CA: Sage.

Grunig, J. E. (with Dozier, D. M., Ehling, W. P., Grunig, L. A., Repper, F. C., & White, J.). (Eds.). (1992). *Excellence in public relations and communication management.* Hillsdale, NJ: Lawrence Erlbaum.

Grunig, J. E., & Hunt, T. (1984). *Managing public relations.* New York: Holt, Rinehart & Winston.

Grunig, L. A., Grunig, J. E., & Dozier, D. M. (2002). *Excellent public relations and effective organizations: A study of communication management in three countries.* Mahwah, NJ: Lawrence Erlbaum.

Grunig, L.A., Toth, E. L., & Hon, L. C. (2000). Feminist values in public relations. *Journal of Public Relations Research, 12*(1), 49–68.

Grunig, L. A., Toth, E. L., & Hon, L. C. (2001). *Women in public relations: How gender influences practice.* New York: Guilford Press.

Grunig, L. S. (1989). The "glass ceiling" effect on mass communication students. In P. J. Creedon (Ed.), *Women in mass communication: Challenging gender values* (pp. 125–147). Newbury Park: Sage.

Hackett, R. (2000). Religious freedom and religion conflict in Africa. In M. Silk (Ed.), *Religion in the international news agenda* (pp. 102–119). Hartford, CT: Leonard E. Greenberg Center.

Hall, S. (1980). Encoding/decoding. In *Culture, media, language: Working papers 1972–79* (pp. 128–138). London: Hutchinson.

Hall, S., Held, D., & McGrew, T. (Eds.). (1992). *Modernity and its futures*. London: The Open University.

Hamada, B. I. (1999). The initial effects of the Internet on a Muslim society. *Journal of Development Communication, 6*(2), 50–57.

Hantzis, D. M., & Lehr, V. (1994). Whose desire? Lesbian (non)sexuality and television's perpetuation of hetero/sexism. In J. R. Ringer (Ed.), *Queer words, queer images: Communication and the construction of homosexuality* (pp. 107–121). New York and London: New York University Press.

Harcourt, W. (1999). *Women@Internet: Creating new cultures in cyberspace*. London: Zed Books.

Hardin, M. (2005). Stopped at the gate: Women's sports, "reader interest," and decision making by editors. *Journalism & Mass Communication Quarterly, 82*(1), 62–77.

Harding, S. (1991). *Whose science? Whose knowledge? Thinking from women's lives*. Ithaca, NY: Cornell University Press.

Harris, A. P. (1990). Race and essentialism in feminist legal theory. *Stanford Law Review, 42,* 581–616.

Haynes, F., & McKenna, T. (Eds.). (2001). *Unseen genders: Beyond the binaries*. New York: Peter Lang.

HealthCOMM–Schools. (n.d.). Retrieved February 5, 2005, from http://www.sla.purdue.edu/healthcomm

Hearst Corporation. (2005). *Corporate biographies: Cathleen Black*. Retrieved February 5, 2005, from http://www.hearstcorp.com/biographies/corp_bio_black.html

Heath, C. (1992). Structural changes in Kenya's broadcasting system: A manifestation of presidential authoritarianism. *Gazette, 37,* 37–51.

Hecht, M., Ribeau, S., & Roberts, J. K. (1989). An Afro-American perspective on interethnic communication. *Communication Monographs, 56,* 385–410.

Hegde, R. S. (1998). A view from elsewhere: Locating difference and the politics of representation from a transnational feminist perspective. *Communication Theory, 8,* 271–297.

Hemlinger, M. A., & Linton, C. C. (2001). *How much progress has been made? Women in newspapers*. Evanston, IL: Media Management Center, Northwestern University.

Hemlinger, M. A., & Linton, C. C. (2002). *Still fighting an uphill battle: Women in newspapers*. Evanston, IL: Media Management Center, Northwestern University.

Henley, N. (1977). *Body politics. Power, sex, and nonverbal communication*. Englewood Cliffs: Prentice Hall.

Herman, E., & Chomsky, N. (1988). *Manufacturing consent: A political economy of the mass media*. New York: Pantheon.

Herzberg, J. (1947). *Late city edition*. New York: Holt.

Hessischer Rundfunk (Hession Broadcasting). (1987–2004). *Berichte über die Aus- und Fortbildung im öffentlich rechtlichen Rundfunk der Bundesrepublik Deutschland* (ARD/ZDF) [Reports on education and further education at the public broadcasting organizations of the Federal Republic of Germany (ARD/ZDF)]. Frankfurt an Main, Germany: Author.

Heyman, S. J. (2003). Symposium: Law and cultural conflict: Ideological conflict and the First Amendment. *Chicago-Kent Law Review, 78,* 531–618.

Hill, M. E. (2002). Skin color and the perception of attractiveness among African Americans: Does gender make a difference? *Social Psychology Quarterly 65*(1), 77–91.

Hoffman, B. (1998). Pink collar ghetto. In W. Mankiller, G. Mink, M. Navarro, B. Smith, & G. Steinem (Eds.), *The reader's companion to U.S. women's history* (pp. 450–451). Boston: Houghton Mifflin.

Hohenberg, J. (1978). *The professional journalist.* Chicago: Holt, Rinehart & Winston. (Also published 1960, 1973, 1983)

Holladay, S. J., & Coombs, W. T. (1993). Communicating visions: An exploration of the role of delivery in the creation of leader charisma. *Management Communication Quarterly, 6,* 405–427.

Holladay, S. J., & Coombs, W. T. (1994). Speaking of visions and visions being spoken. *Management Communication Quarterly, 8,* 165–188.

Horrigan, M. W. (2004, February). Employment projections to 2012: Concepts and context. *Monthly Labor Review,* pp. 3–22.

hooks, b. (1993). *Black looks: Race and representation.* Boston: South End Press.

hooks, b. (1997). *Cultural criticism and transformation* [Film produced and directed by Sut Jhally]. Northampton, MA: Media Education Foundation.

Hoover, S. (1997). Media and the construction of the religious public sphere. In S. Hoover, & Lundby, K. (Eds.), *Rethinking media, religion, & culture* (p. 2117–132). Thousand Oaks, CA: Sage.

Hoover, S., & Lundby, K. (1997). *Rethinking media, religion, and culture.* Thousand Oaks, CA: Sage.

Hosty v. Carter Information Page, Student Press Law Center (2006, March). Retrieved March 26, 2006 from (http://www.splc.org/legalresearch.asp?id=49).

Hoyt v. Florida, 368 U.S. 57 (1961).

Huffman, S., Tuggle, C. A., & Rosengard, D. S. (2004). How campus media cover sports: The gender-equity issue, one generation later. *Mass Communication & Society, 7*(4), 475–489.

Huntemann, N. (1999). Corporate interference: The commercialization and concentration of radio post the 1996 Telecommunications Act. *Journal of Communication Inquiry, 23*(4), 390–407.

Husni, S. (2005). *New titles.* Retrieved February 5, 2005, from http://www.mrmagazine.com/titles.html

Hustler Magazine v. Falwell, 485 U.S. 46 (1988).

Hyde, G. M. (1952). *Newspaper reporting.* Englewood Cliffs, NJ: Prentice Hall.

Inbaraj, S. (2005, May 25). Amnesty says violence against women is widespread. *Inter Press Service.* Retrieved August 22, 2005, from www.nexis.com

Indianapolis General Ordinance No. 35, 16–3(q)(1)-(6) (1984).

International Christian Concern. (2004, August). *Asia: India.* Retrieved August 22, 2005, from http://www.persecution.org/Countries/india.html

International Federation of Journalists. (Ed.). (2001). *Equality and quality: Setting standards for women in journalism. IFJ survey on the status of women journalists* (prepared by B. Peters). Brussels: IFJ. Retrieved January 5, 2006, from http://www.ifj.org/pdfs/ws.pdf

International Federation of Journalists. (2004). *International women's day: Prime time to put women in the media picture says IFJ.* Retrieved March 8, 2004, from http://www.ifj.org/default.asp?Index=2280&Language=EN

International Labour Office. (1996). *Statistics on occupational wages and hours of work and on food prices.* Geneva, Switzerland: Author.

International Labour Office. (2004). *The future of work and quality in the information society: The media, culture, graphical sector.* (Report for discussion at the Tripartite Meeting). Geneva, Switzerland: Author.

International Women's Media Foundation. (1996, 1998, 2001). *Leading in a different language: Will women change the news media?* Washington, DC: Author.

International Women's Media Foundation. (1999). *Women journalists of color: Present without power.* Retrieved July 20, 2005, from http://www.iwmf.org

Irigaray, L. (1993). *Je, tu, nous.* London: Routledge.

Isber, C. C., & Cantor, M. (1975). *The report of the taskforce on women in public broadcasting.* Washington, DC: Corporation for Public Broadcasting.

Isis International. (1999). *Changing lenses: Women's perspectives on media.* Manila, Philippines: Author.

Izard, R. (1982). *Reporting the citizens' news.* New York: Holt, Rinehart & Winston.

Jamieson, K. H., & Campbell, K. K. (2001). *The interplay of influence: News, advertising, politics, and the mass media.* Belmont, CA: Wadsworth.

Jenkins, S. (1996). *Men will be boys: The modern woman explains football and other amusing rituals.* New York: Doubleday.

Jenkins, S. (2005, October 1). Tickled pink by Iowa's locker room. *Washington Post*, E1.

Jerry Falwell talks about his first time (1983, November). *Hustler Magazine*, p. 20.

Jigna, D. (2004). *Beyond Bollywood: The cultural politics of South Asian diasporic film.* New York and London: Routledge.

John S. and James L. Knight Foundation. (2005). *Future of the First Amendment: What American's high school students think about their freedoms.* D. Yalof & K. Dautrich, principal investigators. Miami, FL: John S. and James L. Knight Foundation.

Johnson, S. (1995). *The gentleman and lady's town and country magazine.* In K. L. Endres & T. L. Lueck (Eds.), *Women's periodicals in the United States: Consumer magazines* (pp. 96–107). Westport, CT: Greenwood Press.

Johnson, S., & Prijatel, P. (2000). *Magazine publishing.* Lincolnwood, IL: NTC Contemporary.

Joseph, A. (2004). Southern Africa strikes a blow for gender equality at the gender and media summit. *Media Report to Women, 32*(4), 1–3.

Journalism.com. (2004). *State of the news media 2004: An annual report on American journalism.* Retrieved January 13, 2005, from http://www.stateofthenewsmedia.org/index.asp

Journalism.org. (2005). *The state of the news media: An annual report on American journalism.* Retrieved May 23, 2005, from http://www.stateofthemedia.org/2005/printable_radio_intro.asp

Jung, D. I., & Avolio, B. J. (1999). Effects of leadership style and followers' cultural orientation on performance in group and individual task conditions. *Academy of Management Journal, 42,* 208–218.

Kamhawi, R., & Weaver, D. (2003). Mass communication research trends from 1980 to 1999. *Journalism and Mass Communication Quarterly 80*(2), 7–27.

Kane, M. J., & Greendorfer, S. L. (1994). The media's role in accommodating and resisting stereotyped images of women in sport. In P. J. Creedon (Ed.), *Women, media, and sport* (p. 3–27). Thousand Oaks, CA: Sage.

Kantrowitz, B. (2005, October 23). When women lead. *Newsweek,* p. 46.

Kar, S. B., Pascual, C. A., & Chickering, K. L. (1999). Empowerment of women for health promotion: A meta-analysis. *Social Science & Medicine, 49,* 1431–1460.

Karmasin, M. (1996). *Journalismus. Beruf ohne Moral? Journalistisches Berufshandeln in Österreich* [Journalism: Profession without morality? Journalistic professional behavior in Austria]. Vienna, Austria: Linde.

Kaufman, M. (2003). Covering women's sports: Fair play? In A. Aamidor (Ed.), *Real sports reporting* (pp. xxx). Bloomington: Indiana University Press.

Keeton, W. P. (Ed.). (1984). *Prosser and Keeton on the law of torts* (5th ed.). St. Paul, MN: West.

Kember, S. (2003). *Cyberfeminism and artificial life.* London: Routledge.

Kern-Foxworth, M. (1994). *Aunt Jemima, Uncle Ben, and Rastus: Blacks in advertising, yesterday, today, and tomorrow.* Westport, CT: Greenwood Press.

Kern-Foxworth, M. (2003). Women: Representations in advertising. In *The advertising age encyclopedia of advertising* (Vol. 3, pp. 1660–1668). New York: Fitzroy Dearborn.

Kilbourne, J. (1999). *Deadly persuasion: Why women and girls must fight the addictive power of advertising.* New York: Free Press.

Kinnick, K. N. (1998). Gender bias in newspaper profiles of 1996 athletes: A content analysis of five major dailies. *Women's Studies in Communication, 21*(2), 212–237.

Kishwar, M., & Vanita, R. (1984). (Eds.). *In search of answers: Indian women's voices from Manushi.* London: Zed Books.

Kitch, C. (1997). Changing theoretical perspectives on women's media images. The emergence of patterns in a new area of historical scholarship. *Journalism and Mass Communication Quarterly, 74,* 477–489.

Kline & Company. (2005). *Cosmetics and toiletries USA 2004.* Retrieved March 11, 2005, from http://www.klinegroup.com/brochures/cia4c/brochure.pdf

Knapp, G. F. (1939). *The boys' book of journalism.* New York: Dodd, Mead.

Knott, K. B., & Natalle, E. J. (1997). Sex differences, organizational level, and superiors' evaluation of managerial leadership. *Management Communication Quarterly, 10,* 523–540.

Kreps, G. L., Bonaguro, E. W., & Query, J. L. Jr. (1998). The history and development of the field of health communication. In L. Jackson & B. Duffy (Eds.),

Health communication research: A guide to developments and directions (pp. 1–15). Westport, CT: Greenwood Press.

Kouzes, J. M., & Posner, B. Z. (1995). *The leadership challenge: How to keep getting extraordinary things done in organizations.* San Francisco: Jossey-Bass.

Kramarae, C. (1989). Feminist theories of communication. In E. Barnouw (Ed.), *International encyclopedia of communications* (Vol. 2, pp. 156–160). New York: Oxford University Press.

Kuhn, A. (1985). *The power of the image: Essays on representation and sexuality.* Boston: Routledge & Kegan Paul.

Lachover, E. (in press). Women journalists in the Israeli press. In R. Fröhlich & S. A. Lafky (Eds.), *Women journalists in the Western world: Equal opportunities and what surveys tell us.* London: Hampton Press.

Lafky, S. (1991). Women journalists. In D. H. Weaver & G. C. Wilhoit (Eds.), *The American journalist: A portrait of U.S. news people and their work* (with contributions by L. A. Bergen, D. G. Drew, & S. A. Lafky) (2nd ed., pp. 160–181). Bloomington: Indiana University Press.

Lakoff, R. T., & Scherr, R. L. (1984). *Face value: The politics of beauty.* Boston: Routledge.

Lavie, A. (2004). Organizational factors in the radio news room. Cause for hope or despair? In M. de Bruin & K. Ross (Eds.), *Gender and newsroom cultures: Identities at work* (pp. 119–142). Cresskill, NJ: Hampton Press.

Lealand, G. (1994). *A national survey of New Zealand journalists, 1994.* Wellington, New Zealand: New Zealand Journalists Training Organisation.

Leath V. M., & Lumpkin, A. (1992). An analysis of sportswomen on the covers and in the feature articles of *Women's Sports and Fitness* magazine, 1975–1989. *Journal of Sport and Social Issues, 16,* 121–126.

LeClair, D. (1989). Research on women as managerial leaders: Review and critique. *Women & Language, 12,* 31–37.

Lee, J. (1999). Leader-member exchange, gender, and members' communication expectations with leaders. *Communication Quarterly, 47,* 415–430.

Lee, J. (2001). Leader-member exchange, perceived organizational justice, and cooperative communication. *Management Communication Quarterly, 14,* 574–587.

Lee, M. (2004). UNESCO's conceptualization of women and telecommunications 1970–2000. *Gazette, 66*(6), 533–552.

Lee, R. G., & Garvin, T. (2003). Moving from information transfer to information exchange in health and health care. *Social Science & Medicine, 56,* 449–464.

Leets, L. (2001). Responses to Internet hate sites: Is speech too free in cyberspace? *Communication Law & Policy, 6,* 287–317.

Leiss, W., Kline, S., & Jhally, S. (1990). *Social communication in advertising: Persons, products and images of well-being* (2nd ed.). Scarborough: Nelson Canada.

Leland, J. (2005, September 18). Under din of abortion debate, an experience shared quietly. *New York Times,* p. 1.

Lemish, D., Liebes, T., & Seidman, V. (2001). Gendered media meaning and use. In S. Livingstone & M. Bovill (Eds.), *Young people and the new media environment: A European comparative study* (pp. 263–282). Hillsdale, NJ: Lawrence Erlbaum.

Lent, J. A. (1999). *Women and mass communications in the 1990's: An international annotated bibliography.* Westport, CT: Greenwood Press.

Lim, L. (1981). Women's work in multinational electronics factories. In R. Dauber & M. Cain (Eds.), *Women and technological change in developing countries* (pp. 181–191). Boulder, CO: Westview Press.

Littlejohn, S. W. (1992). *Theories of human communication* (4th ed.). Belmont, CA: Wadsworth.

Lockwood, N. R. (2005, June). Workplace diversity, leveraging the power of difference for competitive advantage. *Research Quarterly.* Society for Human Resource Management. Retrieved September 21, 2005, from http://www.shrm .org/research/quarterly/2005/0605RQuart_essay.asp

Löfgren Nilsson, M. (1993). *Klimat och kön* [Climate and gender]. Göteborg, Sweden: Göteborg University, Department of Journalism and Mass Communication.

Long, E. (1989). Feminism and cultural studies. *Critical Studies in Mass Communication, 6,* 427–435.

Lorber, J., & Moore, L. J. (2002). *Gender and the social construction of illness* (2nd ed.). Walnut Creek, CA: AltaMira.

Lord, R. G., Brown, D. J., Harvey, J. L., & Hall, R. J. (2001). Contextual constraints on prototype generation and their multilevel consequences for leadership perceptions. *Leadership Quarterly, 12,* 311–339.

Love, B., & Angelo, J. (1985, July). 1985 editorial salary survey. *Folio: The Magazine for Magazine Management,* pp. 69–84.

Lowe, K. B., Kroeck, K. G., & Sivasubramaniam, N. (1996). Effectiveness correlates of transformational and transactional leadership: A meta-analytic review of the MLQ literature. *Leadership Quarterly, 7,* 385–425.

Lubiano, W. (1992). Black ladies, welfare queens, and state minstrels: Ideological war by narrative means. In T. Morrison (Ed.), *Race-ing justice, engendering power: Essays on Anita Hill, Clarence Thomas, and the construction of social reality* (pp. 323–361). New York: Pantheon.

Luthra, R. (1991). Contraceptive social marketing in the third world: A case of multiple transfer. *Gazette, 47,* 159–176.

Lynggard, T. (2002, July 21–26). *Gender representations in the Nordic news media.* Paper presented at Women's Worlds 2002, 8th International Interdisciplinary Congress on Women, Makarere University, Kampala, Uganda, 2002. Retrieved January 16, 2006, from http://www.nikk.uio.no/publikasjoner/andre/artiklar_ utlatanden/tl_mediaww_e.html

Lyon, K. (2005, January 19). *Fellow Russian deserts Kuznetsova.* Retrieved January 13, 2006, from http://www.smh.com.au,news/Tennis/Fellow-Russian-deserts-Kuznetsova/2005/01/18/1105810920479.html

Macdonald, M. (1995). *Representing women: Myths of femininity in the popular media*. London: Edward Arnold.

MacKinnon, C. A. (1985). Pornography, civil rights, and speech. *Harvard Civil Rights–Civil Liberties Law Review, 20*, 1–70.

MacKinnon, C. A. (1987). *Feminism unmodified: Discourses on life and law*. Cambridge, MA: Harvard University Press.

Magazine Publishers of America. (1997). *The magazine handbook*. New York: Author.

Magazine Publishers of America. (2004). *The magazine handbook*. New York: Author.

Magazine Publishers of America. (2005). *Circulation trends and magazine handbook*. Retrieved February 5, 2005, from http://www.magazine.org/Circulation/circulation_trends_and_magazine_handbook

Magruder, C. (1936). Mental and emotional disturbance in the law of torts. *Harvard Law Review, 49*, 1033–1053.

Maher, K. J. (1997). Gender-related stereotypes of transformational and transactional leadership. *Sex Roles, 37*, 209–225.

Mahoney, M. A. (1996). The problem of silence in feminist psychology. *Feminist Studies, 22*, 603–625.

Mandel, S. (Ed.). (1962). *Modern journalism*. New York. Pitman.

Martin, M. (1991). *'Hello, central?' Gender, technology, and culture in the formation of telephone systems*. Montreal and Kingston, Canada: McGill-Queen's University Press.

Martin, M., & Gentry, J. W. (1997). Stuck in the model trap: The effects of beautiful models in ads on female pre-adolescents and adolescents. *Journal of Advertising 26*(2), 19–33.

Marty, M. (1986). *Modern American religion: Vol. 1. The irony of it all: 1893–1989*. Chicago: University of Chicago Press.

Marzolf, M. (1977). *Up from the footnote: A history of women journalists*. New York: Hastings House.

Mason, D. (1995). *God in the news ghetto: Religion news from 1944–1989*. Doctoral dissertation, Ohio University.

Mason, D. (1996). Survey of RNA members. *RNA 1996 Conference Program* (pp. 21–25). Westerville, OH: Religion Newswriters Association.

Matsuda, M. (1989). When the first quail calls: Multiple consciousness as jurisprudential method. *Women's Rights Law Reporter, 11*, 7–10.

Mattelart, A., Delcourt, X., & Mattelart, M. (1984). *International image markets* (D. Buxton, Trans.). London: Comedian Publishing.

Mattelart, M. (1986). Women and the culture industries. In R. Collins, J. Curran, N. Garnham, P. Scannell, P. Schlesinger, & C. Sparks (Eds.), *Media, culture, and society: A critical reader* (pp. 63–81). Newbury Park, CA: Sage.

Matthews, K. (2004). *Evaluating entertainment education: A case study of "Things We Do for Love."* Unpublished master's thesis, University of Oregon.

Mavity, N. (1930). *The modern newspaper*. New York: Henry Holt.

Maxwell, A. (2003). Women: Careers in advertising. In *The Advertising Age encyclopedia of advertising* (Vol. 3, pp. 1655–1660). New York: Fitzroy Dearborn.

McAdams, K. C., Beasley, M. H., & Zandberg, I. (2004). Women graduates (and men too) express reservations about journalism education. In R. R. Rush, C. E. Oukrop, & P. J. Creedon (Eds.), *Seeking equality for women in journalism and mass communication education: A 30-year update* (pp. 315–330). Mahwah, NJ: Lawrence Erlbaum.

McCall, L. (1992). Does gender fit? Bourdieu, feminism, and conception of social order. *Theory and Society, 21,* 837–867.

McChesney, R. W. (1999). *Rich media, poor democracy.* Urbana and Chicago: University of Illinois Press.

McChesney, R. W. (2004). The escalating war against corporate media, *Monthly Review, 55*(10), 1–29.

McCloud, S. (2004). *Making the American religious fringe: Exotics, subversives, and journalists 1955–1993.* Chapel Hill: University of North Carolina Press.

McCracken, E. (1993). *Decoding women's magazines: From Mademoiselle to Ms.* New York: St. Martin's Press.

McKay, J., Messner, M. A., & Sabo, D. (Eds.). (2000). *Masculinities, gender relations, and sport.* Thousand Oaks, CA: Sage.

McLaren, P. (1993). Border disputes: Multicultural narrative, identity formation, and critical pedagogy in postmodern America. In D. McLaughlin & W. G. Tierney (Eds.), *Naming silenced lives: Personal narratives and the process of educational change* (pp. 192–224). New York: Routledge.

McLaughlin, L. (1995). Feminist communication scholarship and the woman's question in the academy. *Communication Theory, 5,* 144–161.

McRobbie, A. (1983). Jackie: An ideology of adolescent femininity. In E. Wartella, D. C. Whitney, & S. Windahl (Eds.), *Mass communication review yearbook* (Vol. 4, pp. 251–271). Beverly Hills, CA: Sage.

McWhinney, W. (1997). *Paths of change: Strategic choices for organizations and society.* Thousand Oaks, CA: Sage.

Meacham, J. (2004). Holy profits! *Revenue, 1*(3), 68–73.

MediaWatch. (1995). *Global Media Monitoring Project: Women's participation in the news.* Toronto, Canada: Author.

Meehan, E. R., & Riordan, E. (Eds.). (2002). *Sex and money: Feminism and political economy in the media.* Minneapolis: University of Minnesota Press.

Melin-Higgins, M., & Djerf Pierre, M. (1998, July). *Networking in newsrooms: Journalist and gender cultures.* Paper presented to the 21st General Assembly and Scientific Conference of the International Association for Media and Communication Research, Glasgow, Scotland.

Memmi, A. (1965). *The colonizer and the colonized.* Boston: Beacon Press.

Mencher, M. (2003). *News reporting and writing.* New York: McGraw-Hill. (Also published 1977, 1981, 1984, 1987, 1991, 1994, 1997)

Merton, R. K. (1968). *Social theory and social structure.* New York: Free Press. (Original work published 1949)

Messner, M. A., Duncan, M. C., & Cooky, C. (2003). Silence, sports bras, and wrestling porn: Women in televised sports news and highlights shows. *Journal of Sport and Social Issues, 27*(1), 38–51.

Metz, W. (1977). *Newswriting.* Englewood Cliffs, NJ: Prentice Hall. (Also published 1991)

Metzler, K. (1986). *Newsgathering.* Englewood Cliffs, NJ: Prentice Hall.

Mikell, G. (1995). African feminism: Toward a new politics of representation. *Feminist Studies, 21,* 405–424.

Miller, C. (1997). Study dispels '80s stereotypes of women. In S. Biagi & M. Kern-Foxworth (Eds.), *Facing difference: Race, gender, and mass media* (pp. 221–222). Thousand Oaks, CA: Pine Forge Press.

Miller, M. C. (2002, January 7). *What's wrong with this picture?* Retrieved January 6, 2006, from http://www.thenation.com/special/bigten.html

Miller, S. H. (1985, November 23). Was "pink collar" ghetto study deliberate sensationalism? *Editor & Publisher,* pp. 52, 32–33.

Miller v. California, 413 U.S. 15 (1973).

Millett, K. (1969). *Sexual politics.* New York: Touchstone.

Minow, M. (1987). The Supreme Court 1986 term: Foreword: Justice engendered. *Harvard Law Review, 101,* 10–95.

Mitchell, C. (2004). "Dangerously feminine"? Theory and praxis of women's alternative radio. In K. Ross & C. Byerly (Eds.), *Women and media: International perspectives* (pp. 157–184). Malden, MA: Blackwell.

Mitchell v. Rochester Ry. Co., 151 N.Y. 107, 45 N.E. 354 (1896).

Mitra, A., & Watts, E. (2002). Theorizing cyberspace: The idea of voice applied to the Internet discourse. *New Media & Society, 4,* 479–498.

Moghadam, V. (1996). Feminist networks north and south: DAWN, WIDE and WLUML. *Journal of International Communication, 3*(1), 111–126.

Mohanty, C. T. (1988). Under Western eyes: Feminist scholarship and colonial discourses. In C. T. Mohanty, A. Russo, & L. Torres (Eds.), *Third world women and the politics of feminism* (pp. 51–80). Bloomington: Indiana University Press.

Money, J. (1995). *Gendermaps: Social constructionism, feminism, and sexosophical history.* New York: Continuum.

Moores, S. (1993). *Interpreting audiences.* Thousand Oaks, CA: Sage.

Morris, N., & Waisbord, S. (2001). (Eds.). *Media and globalization: Why the state matters.* Boulder, CO: Roman & Littlefield.

Moseley, B. (2000, August). Folio's 2000 editorial salary survey. *Folio: The Magazine for Magazine Management,* pp. 37–42.

MRI Teenmark. (1999). *Teen People* demographics. Available from *Teen People,* Time & Life Building, 1271 Avenue of the Americas, New York, NY 10020.

Mueller, B. H., & Lee, J. (2002). Leader-member exchange and organizational communication satisfaction in multiple contexts. *Journal of Business Communication, 39,* 220–244.

Muller v. Oregon, 208 U.S. 412 (1908).

Mulvey, L. (1989). *Visual and other pleasures.* Bloomington: Indiana University Press.

Murray, A. F. (1995). Why think about leadership? *Women of Power, 24,* 16–17.

National Association of Broadcasters radio marketing guide & fact book for advertisers, 2003–2004. (2003). Retrieved June 16, 2005, from http://www.nab.org/irc/virtual/faqs.asp

National Directory of Magazines. (2004). New York: Oxbridge Communications.

National Telecommunications and Information Administration (NTIA). (1998). *Minority commercial broadcast ownership in the United States, August 1997–August 1998.* Retrieved January 18, 2005, from www.ntia.doc.gov

Neal, R. M. (1939). *Editing the small city daily.* Englewood Cliffs, NJ: Prentice Hall.

Nellessen, T. L., & Brady, R. M. (2000, May). May I speak with the DJ? *American Communication Journal.* Retrieved January 18, 2005, from http://acjournal.org/holdings/v013/Iss3/articles/nell.html

Nelson, J. (1974). *Captive voices: High school journalism in America.* New York: Schocken Books.

Nelson, M. B. (1994). *The stronger women get, the more men love football: Sexism and the American culture of sports.* New York: Harcourt Brace.

Neverla, I., & Kanzleiter, G. (1984). *Journalistinnen: Frauen in einem Männerberuf* [Female journalists: Women in a male profession]. Frankfurt an Main, New York: Campus.

Neveu, E. (in press). Women journalists, gendered genres, and the renewal of the French press. In R. Fröhlich & S. A. Lafky (Eds.), *Women journalists in the Western world: Equal opportunities and what surveys tell us.* London: Hampton Press.

Neville, B. (1995). Anti-pornography legislation as content discrimination under R. A. V. *Kansas Journal of Law & Public Policy, 5,* 121–130.

New York Times v. Sullivan, 376 U.S. 254 (1964).

Nielsen/NetRatings. (2005). *Newspaper Web site data for July 2005.* Retrieved January 25, 2006, from http://www.naa.org/nadbase/Top_100_Newspaper_Web_Sites.pdf

Nkomo, S. M. (1988). The emperor has no clothes: Rewriting race in organizations. *Academy of Management Review, 17,* 487–513.

Noelle-Neumann, E. (1974). The spiral of silence: A theory of public opinion. *Journal of Communication, 24,* 43–51.

Nord, D. (2004). *Faith in reading: Religious publishing and the birth of mass media in America.* New York: Oxford University.

Nordin, K. (1975). *Consensus religion: National newspaper coverage of religious life in America, 1849–1960.* Doctoral dissertation, University of Michigan.

Norsigian, J., Diskin, V., Doress-Worters, P., Pincus, J., Sanford, W., & Swenson, N. (1999). The Boston Women's Health Book Collective and *Our Bodies, Ourselves:* A brief history and reflection. *Journal of the American Women's Medical Association, 54,* 35–39.

N.Y. Sess. Laws, 1903, ch. 132, §§1–2.

O'Connor, C. (2004, December 5). Our lady of Guadalupe immaculate icon symbols of piety on pop-culture decorations, La Virgen has many faces. *Denver Post,* p. L1.

Oickle, D. (2005). *Reliable nutrition information*. Retrieved March 21, 2005, from http://www.healthunit.org/nutrition/nutrition_month_2005/Reliable_Nutrition Info.pdf

Olin, C. H. (1906). *Journalism*. Philadelphia: Penn Publishing.

Ordman, V. L., & Zillman, D. (1994). Women sports reporters: Have they caught up? *Journal of Sport & Social Issues, X*, 66–75.

Ortner, S. (1996). *Making gender: The politics and erotics of culture*. Boston: Beacon.

Papper, B. (2000). Women and minorities survey. *RTNDA/F Research*. Retrieved January 22, 2006, from http://www.rtnda.org/research/womin2000.shtml

Papper, B. (2002, July/August). 2002 Women and minorities survey. *RTNDA Communicator*. Retrieved July 22, 2004, from http://www.rtnda.org/research/womin.shtml

Papper, B. (2003, July/August). Women and minorities: One step forward and two steps back. *RTNDA Communicator*. Retrieved July 22, 2004, from http://www.rtnda.org/research/womin.shtml

Papper, B. (2004, July/August). Recovering lost ground: Minorities gain ground and women make management strides in radio and TV newsrooms in 2004. *RTNDA Communicator*. Retrieved January 14, 2005, from http://www.RTNDA.org/diversity

Papper, B., & Gerhard, M. (2000). *2000 Radio and television salary survey*. *RTNDA/F Research*. Retrieved July 22, 2004, from http://rtnda.org/research/salaries00.shtml

Papper, B., & Gerhard, M. (2002). *2001 Radio and television salary survey*. *RTNDA/F Research*. Retrieved July 22, 2004, from http://www.rtnda.org/research/salaries.html

Parameswaran, R. (2002). Local culture in global media: Excavating colonial and material discourses in *National Geographic*. *Communication Theory, 12*(3), 287–314.

Parameswaran, R. (2004). Global queens, national celebrities: Tales of feminine triumph in post-liberalization India. *Critical Studies in Media Communication, 21*(4), 346–370.

Parker, P. S. (2001). African American women executives' leadership communication within dominant-culture organizations. *Management Communication Quarterly, 15*, 42–83.

Parker, P. S., & Ogilvie, D. T. (1996). Gender, culture, and leadership: Toward a culturally distinct model of African-American women executives' leadership strategies. *Leadership Quarterly, 7*, 189–214.

Parr, K. (1997, May 30). Editors of teen magazines slug it out for their piece of the Generation Y pie. *Women's Wear Daily, 173*, p. 101. Retrieved October 28, 2004, from SRDS Business & Industry Database, http://rdsweb2.rdsinc.com/texis/rds/suite2/+uoe9U8YemxwwwwwFqz6vqhmw9mwxFqh1odiw/full.html

Pavitt, C., Whitchurch, G. G., McClurg, H., & Petersen, N. (1995). Melding the objective and subjective sides of leadership: Communication and social judgments in decision-making groups. *Communication Monographs, 62*, 243–264.

Pedersen, P. M. (2002). Investigating interscholastic equity on the sports page: A content analysis of high school athletics' newspaper articles. *Sociology of Sport Journal, 19,* 419–432.

Pedersen, P. M., Whisenant, W. A., & Schneider, R. G. (2003). Using a content analysis to examine the gendering of sports newspaper personnel and their coverage. *Journal of Sport Management, 17,* 376–393.

Peirce, K. (1990). A feminist theoretical perspective on the socialization of teenage girls through *Seventeen* magazine. *Sex Roles, 23,* 491–500.

Peirce, K. (1993). Socialization of teenage girls through teen-age magazine fiction: The making of a new woman or an old lady? *Sex Roles, 29,* 59–68.

Peterson, P. V. (1980, January). J-school enrollments reach record 71,594. *Journalism Educator, 34,* pp. 3–9.

Picariello, M. L., Greenberg, D. N., & Pillemer, D. B. (1990). Children's sex-related stereotyping of colors. *Child Development, 61,* 1453–1460.

Piotrow, P. T., Rimon, J. G. II, Merritt, A. P., & Saffitz, G. (2003). *Advancing health communication: The PCS experience in the field* (Johns Hopkins Bloomberg School of Public Health Center for Communication Programs Publication 103). Retrieved January 17, 2005, from http://www.jhuccp.org/pubs/cp/103/103.pdf

Poole, E. (2002). *Reporting Islam: Media representations of British Muslims.* London: I. B. Tauris.

Porter, B., & Ferris, T. (1988). *The practice of journalism.* Englewood Cliffs, NJ: Prentice Hall.

Porter, P. W., & Luxon, N. N. (1935). *The reporter and the news.* New York: D. Appleton-Century.

Posnock, S. T. (2004, March). The real women of *Playboy. Folio: The Magazine for Magazine Management,* pp. 40–44.

Powell, G. N. (1988). *Women and men in management.* Newbury Park, CA: Sage.

Powell, G. N. (1993). *Women and men in management* (2nd ed.). Newbury Park, CA: Sage.

Project for Excellence in Journalism. (1998, March 6). *Changing definitions of news.* Retrieved July 6, 2005, from http://www.journalism.org/resources/research/reports/definitions/studied.asp

Project for Excellence in Journalism. (2005, May 23). *The gender gap: Women are still missing as sources for journalists.* Washington, DC: Author.

Project for Excellence in Journalism and the Princeton Survey Research Associates. (2005, August). *Box scores and bylines: A snapshot of the newspaper sports page.* Princeton, NJ: Author.

Pruitt, L. R. (2003). On the chastity of women all property in the world depends: Injury from sexual slander in the nineteenth century. *Indiana Law Journal, 78,* 965–1018.

Quindlen, A. (2001). Introduction. In B. Friedan, *The feminine mystique.* New York: Norton. (Original work published 1963)

Radio-Television News Directors Association (RTNDA) Research. (2000). *2000 women & minorities survey.* Retrieved January 16, 2005, from http://rtnda.org/research/womin2000.html

Rainie, L., & Horrigan, J. (2004). *A decade of adoption: How the Internet has woven itself into American life.* Pew Internet and American Life Project Report. Retrieved July 1, 2005, from http://www.pewinternet.org/PPF/r/148/report_display.asp

Rainie, L., & Horrigan, J. (2005). *Internet activity.* Pew Internet & American Life Project Tracking Survey. Retrieved July 1, 2005, from http://www.pewinternet.org/trends/Internet_Activities_5.18.05.htm

Rakow, L. F. (1989a). A bridge to the future: Re-visioning gender in communication. In P. J. Creedon (Ed.), *Women in mass communication. Challenging gender values* (pp. 299–312). Newbury Park, CA: Sage.

Rakow, L. F. (1989b). From the feminization of public relations to the promise of feminism. In E. L. Toth & C. G. Cline (Eds.), *Beyond the velvet ghetto* (pp. 287–298). San Francisco: IABC Research Foundation.

Rakow, L. F. (1992). The field reconsidered. In L. F. Rakow (Ed.), *Women making meaning* (pp. 3–17). New York: Routledge.

Rakow, L. F., & Wackwitz, L. A. (Eds.). (2004). *Feminist communication theory: Selections in context.* Thousand Oaks, CA: Sage.

Ransaw, T., & Borchard, G. (2005, August). *Sisters of the spirit: Women journalists of the A.M.E. church.* Paper presented at the meeting of the Association for Education in Journalism and Mass Communication, San Antonio, TX.

Rayne, M. (1974). *What can a woman do?* Salem, NH: Arno Press (Original work published 1893)

The Readership Institute. (2004). *Reaching new readers: Revolution, not evolution.* Retrieved June 28, 2005, from http://www.readership.org/new_readers/data/overview.pdf

Reed v. Reed, 404 U.S. 71 (1971).

Rendall, S., & Butterworth, D. (2004, June). *How public is public radio? A study of NPR's (National Public Radio) guest list.* Fairness and Accuracy in Reporting (FAIR). Retrieved May 10, 2005, from http://www.thirdworldtraveler.com/BroadcastMedia/HowPublic PublicRadio.html

Reno v. ACLU, 521 U.S. 844 (1997).

Reskin, B. F., & Roos, P. A. (Eds.). (1990). *Job queues, gender queues: Explaining women's inroads into males' occupations.* Philadelphia: Temple University Press.

Restatement (Second) of Torts, Section 46:1 (1965).

Rhodes, J. (1995). The visibility of race and media history. In G. Dines & J. Humez (Eds.), *Gender, race, and class in media: A text reader* (pp. 33–42). Thousand Oaks, CA: Sage.

Ricchiardi, S., & Young, V. (1991). *Women on deadline.* Ames: Iowa State University Press.

Rich, A. (1979). When we dead awaken: Writing as re-vision. In A. Rich (Ed.), *On lies, secrets and silence* (pp. 33–49). New York: Norton.

Rich, C. (2005). *Writing and reporting the news.* Belmont, CA: Wadsworth. (Also published 1994, 1997, 2000, 2003, 2004)

Richardson, L. N. (1966). *A history of early American magazines 1741–1789.* New York: Octagon Books.

Riordan, E. (2004). The woman warrior: A feminist political economic analysis of *Crouching Tiger, Hidden Dragon*. In K. Ross & C. M. Byerly (Eds.), *Women and media: International perspectives* (pp. 81–104). Malden, MA: Blackwell.

Rios, D. L. (2003). Diversity in communication education: The "D" word is all about including others. *Journal of Advertising Education, 7*(2), 15–16.

Roberson v. Rochester Folding Box Co., 171 N.Y. 538 (1902).

Robinson, G. J., & Saint-Jean, A. (1997). *Women's participation in the Canadian news media: Progress since the 1970s*. Montreal, Canada: McGill University, Université de Sherbrooke.

Robinson, L. (2005, November 24). The hoopster and the actor. *Gay & Lesbian Times*. Retrieved November 27, 2005, from http://www.gaylesbiantimes.com

Rodriguez, R. (2005). View from the new desk. In C. Badaracco (Ed.), *Quoting God* (pp. 209–210). Waco, TX: Baylor University Press

Roof, J., & Wiegman, R. (Eds.). (1995). *Who can speak? Authority and critical identity*. Urbana: University of Illinois Press.

Rosen, J. (2005, April 17). The unregulated offensive. *New York Times Magazine*, p. 44.

Ross, K. (2001). Women at work: Journalism as an en-gendered practice. *Journalism Studies, 2*(4), 531–544.

Ross, K., & Byerly, C. M. (2004). *Women and media: International perspectives*. Malden, MA: Blackwell.

Rost, J. C. (1991). *Leadership for the twenty-first century*. Westport, CT: Praeger.

Rubin, H. (1993, February 15). Teen idol. *Folio*, p. 48.

Ruddick, S. (1989). *Maternal thinking: Toward a politics of peace*. Boston: Beacon Press.

Russell, K., Wilson, M., & Hall, R. (1993). *The color complex*. New York: Anchor.

Russo, V. (1987). *The celluloid closet: Homosexuality in the movies* (2nd ed.). New York: Harper & Row.

Ryan, M., & Tankard, J. W. (2005). *Writing for print and digital media*. New York: McGraw-Hill.

Sabo, D., & Grant, C. H. B. (2005, June). *Limitations of the department of education's online survey method for measuring athletic interest and ability on U.S.A. campuses*. Buffalo, NY: Center for Research on Physical Activity, Sport & Health, D'Youville College.

Said, E. (1978). *Orientalism*. New York: Random House.

Said, E. (1981). *Covering Islam: How the media and the experts determine how we see the rest of the world*. New York: Pantheon.

Salwen, M. B., & Wood, N. (1994). Depictions of female athletes on sports illustrated covers, 1957–1989. *Journal of Sport Behavior, 17*(2), 98–108.

Sapiro, V. (1994). *Women in American society* (3rd ed.). Mountain View, CA: Mayfield.

Saussure, F. de. (1974). *Course in general linguistics*. London: Fontana.

Scott, J. W. (1992). Experience. In J. Butler & J. W. Scott (Eds.), *Feminists theorize the political* (pp. 22–40). New York: Routledge.

Scott, W. (2005, November 13). Personality parade. *Parade Magazine,* p. 2.

Schiller, H. I. (1971). *Mass communications and American empire.* Boston: Beacon Press.

Schiller, H. I. (1981). *Who knows: Information in the age of the fortune 500.* Norwood, NJ: Ablex.

Schneider, B., Schönbach, K., & Stürzebecher, D. (1993). Westdeutsche Journalisten im Vergleich: jung, professionell und mit Spaß an der Arbeit [West German journalists: Young, professional, and with fun at work]. *Publizistik, 38*(1), 5–30.

Schriesheim, C. A., Castro, S. L., & Cogliser, C. C. (1999). Leader-member exchange (LMX) research: A comprehensive review of theory, measurement, and data-analytic practices. *Leadership Quarterly, 10,* 63–113.

Schwarzenbach, S. A., & Smith, P. (2003). *Women and the United States Constitution: History, interpretation, and practice.* New York: Columbia University Press.

Seager, J. (2003). *The Penguin atlas of women in the world.* London: Penguin.

Seale, C. (2002). *Media & health.* London: Sage.

Seib, P., & Fitzpatrick, K. (1995). *Public relations ethics.* Fort Worth, TX: Harcourt Brace College Publishers.

Seiter, E. (1993). Semiotics, structuralism, and television. In R. C. Allen (Ed.), *Channels of discourse, reassembled* (pp. 31–66). Chapel Hill: University of North Carolina Press.

Seitz, D. C. (1916). *Training for the newspaper trade.* Philadelphia: Lippincott.

Sha, B. L. (2001). The feminization of public relations: Contributing to a more ethical practice. In E. L. Toth & L. Aldoory (Eds.), *The gender challenge to media: Diverse voices from the field* (pp. 153–177). Cresskill, NJ: Hampton Press.

Shamir, B., House, R. J., & Arthur, M. B. (1993). The motivational effects of charismatic leadership: A self-concept based theory. *Organization Science, 4,* 577–594.

Sharma, A., & Young, K. (Eds.). (2003). *Her voice, her truth: Women speak on world religions.* Boulder, CO: Westview.

Shepard, A. (1995, December). The media get religion. *American Journalism Review,* 19–25.

Shevin, C., & Erickson, J. (2002, August 31). *U.S. women shine at the Olympics, thanks to Title IX.* Retrieved November 30, 2005, from http:www.now.org .issues/title_ix/0831040lympics.html

Shifflett, B., & Revelle, R. (1994). Gender equity in sports media coverage: A review of the NCAA News. *Journal of Sport and Social Issues, 18*(2), 144–150.

Shuman, E. L. (1899). *The art and practice of journalism.* Chicago: Stevans & Handy.

Shuman, E. L. (1903). *Practical journalism.* New York: D. Appleton-Century.

Shuter, R., & Turner, L. H. (1997). African American and European American women in the workplace: Perceptions of workplace communication. *Management Communication Quarterly, 11,* 74–96.

Siew, S., & Kim, W. L. (1996). Do new communication technologies improve the status of women? *Media Asia, 23*(2), 74–78.

Silk, M. (1995). *Unsecular media: Making news of religion in America.* Champaign: University of Illinois Press.

Silk, M. (Ed.). (2000). *Religion on the international news agenda*. Hartford, CT: Leonard E. Greenberg Center.

Sims, H. P. Jr., & Lorenzi, P. (1992). *The new leadership paradigm*. Newbury Park, CA: Sage.

Singer, J. B. (2004). Who are these guys? The online challenge to the notion of journalistic professionalism. *Journalism: Theory, Practice, and Criticism, 4*(2), 139–163.

Siver, K. (1999). McPhillips leads fight for student expression. *Journalism Education Association visions: Our seventy-fifth anniversary* [Calendar], p. 13.

Sivulka, J. (1998). *Soap, sex, and cigarettes: A cultural history of American advertising*. Belmont, CA: Wadsworth.

Skwar, D. (1999, August). Women's sports gain the spotlight. *Associated Press Sports Editors' Newsletter*. Retrieved August 4, 2005, from http://apse.dallasnews.com/aug1999/14skwar.html

Sloan, W. (2000). *Media and religion in American history*. Northport, AL: Vision Press.

Smircich, L., & Morgan, G. (1982). Leadership and the management of meaning. *Journal of Applied Behavioral Science, 18,* 257–273.

Smith, C., Fredin, E., & Nardone, C. A. F. (1993). Television: The nature of sex discrimination in local television news shops. In P. Creedon (Ed.), *Women in mass communication* (2nd ed., pp. 172–181). Newbury Park, CA: Sage.

Smith, M. (1993). Feminist media and cultural politics. Gender and mass communication in a global context. In P. Creedon (Ed.), *Women in mass communication* (2nd ed., pp. 61–83). Newbury Park, CA: Sage.

Smythe, D. (1960). On the political economy of communication. *Journalism Quarterly, 37*(3), 461–470.

Smythe, D. (2000). On the audience commodity and its work. In M. G. Durham & D. M. Kellner (Eds.), *Media and cultural studies: Keyworks* (pp. 253–279). Malden, MA: Blackwell.

Snyder, S. L., Brueggermann, B. J., & Garland-Thomson, R. (Eds.). (2002). *Disability studies: Enabling the humanities*. New York: Modern Language Association of America.

Sparrowe, R. T., & Liden, R. C. (1997). Process and structure in leader-member exchange. *Academy of Management Review, 22,* 522–552.

Spears, G., & Seydegart, K. (2001). *Who makes the news? Global media monitoring project 2000*. London: World Association for Christian Communication.

Spender, D. (1982). *Invisible women*. London: Writers and Readers Publishing Cooperative.

Spitzer, M. (1990). *Justifying minority preferences in broadcasting* (Social Science Working Paper No. 718). Pasadena: California Institute of Technology.

Spivak, G. C. (1988). Can the subaltern speak? In C. Nelson & L. Grossberg (Eds.), *Marxism and the interpretation of culture* (pp. 271–313). Urbana: University of Illinois Press.

Spivak, G. C. (1999). *A critique of postcolonial reason: Toward a history of the vanishing present*. Cambridge, MA: Harvard University Press.

Splichal, S., & Sparks, C. (1994). *Journalists for the 21st century*. Norwood, NJ: Ablex.

SRDS Business Publication Advertising Source; SRDS Consumer Magazine Advertising Source. (2004). Des Plaines, IL: Standard Rate and Data Service.

Sreberny-Mohammadi, A. (1996). International feminisms: Engendering debate in international communications. *Journal of International Communication, 3*(1), 1–4.

Standard Periodical Directory. (2004). New York: Oxbridge Communications.

Steeves, H. L. (1987). Feminist theories and media studies. *Critical Studies in Mass Communication, 4*, 93–135.

Steeves, H. L. (1993). Gender and mass communication in a global context. In P. Creedon (Ed.), Women in mass communication (2nd ed., pp. 32–60). Newbury Park, CA: Sage.

Steeves, H. L. (2004). Trends in feminist scholarship in journalism and communication: Finding common ground between scholars and activists globally. In R. Rush, C. Oukrop, & P. Creedon (Eds.), *Seeking equity for women in journalism and mass communication education: A 30-year update* (pp. 289–312). Mahwah, NJ: Lawrence Erlbaum.

Steeves, H. L., & Wasko, J. (2002). Feminist theory and political economy: Toward a friendly alliance. In E. Meehan & E. Riordan (Eds.), *Sex and money: Intersections of feminism and political economy in media* (pp. 16–29). Minneapolis: University of Minnesota Press.

Steiner, L. (1996, Fall). Sex, lives, and auto/biography. *American Journalism*, pp. 206–211.

Stephen, T. (2000). Concept analysis of gender, feminist, and women's studies research in the communication literature. *Communication Monographs, 67*, 193–214.

Stone, C. (1986, January 22). Women are still being dumped on. *Philadelphia Daily News*, p. 36.

Stone, V. A. (1976, October). Surveys show younger women becoming news directors. RTNDA *Communicator*, pp. 10–12.

Stone, V. A. (1988, October). Women gaining as news directors. *RTNDA Communicator* (p. 21).

Stone, V. A. (1991). *The women of radio news*. Retrieved May 10, 2005, from http://www.missouri.edu/~jourvs/radiowom.html

Stone, V. A. (1992a, August). Little change for minorities and women. *RTNDA Communicator*, p. 26.

Stone, V.A. (1992b, January). Women and men as news directors. *RTNDA Communicator*, pp. 143–144.

Stone, V. A. (2000). *Race, gender, and radio news careers*. Retrieved May 10, 2005, from http://www.missouri.edu/jourvs/raracemf.html

Stone, V. A. (2005, May). *National public radio search for women and Blacks heard on NPR 1994–2004*. Retrieved January 16, 2006, from http://www.proglibserv/LIBRARY/BASIS/NPRTLP/WWW/segment_report/edw?W=SUBJ+PH

Stone, V. A., & Dell, B. (1972, August). More women in news broadcasting according to RTNDA survey. *RTNDA Communicator*, p. 4.

Stout, D., & Buddenbaum, J. (2003). Media, religion, and "framing." *Journal of Media and Religion, 2*(1), 1–3.

Stovall, J. G. (2006). *Writing for the mass media.* Boston: Pearson Education. (Also published 2002)

Strossen, N. (1996). Hate speech and pornography: Do we have to choose between freedom of speech and equality? *Case Western Reserve Law Review, 46,* 449–478.

Sullivan, M. (2005, March). Making a difference in the newsroom. *American Editor,* p. 11. (American Society of Newspaper Editors)

Tannen, M. (2004, October 10). Jingo belle. *New York Times Magazine,* p. 60.

Tauchert, A. (2002). Fuzzy gender: Between female-embodiment, transgender and intersex. *Journal of Gender Studies, 11*(1), 29–38.

Theberge, N., & Cronk, A. (1986). Work routines in newspaper sports departments and the coverage of women's sports. *Sociology of Sport, 3*(3), 195–203.

Thiel, S. (2004). Shifting identities, creating new paradigms: Analyzing the narratives of women online journalists. *Feminist Media Studies, 4*(1), 21–35.

Thompson, L. (2004). *Gender, title, and salary discrimination in the magazine publishing industry, 1994–2004.* Unpublished manuscript.

Thompson, M. D. (2000). Gender, leadership orientation, and effectiveness: Testing the theoretical models of Bolman & Deal and Quinn. *Sex Roles, 42,* 969–992.

Time v. Firestone, 424 U.S. 448 (1976).

Time Warner. (2005). *Senior management: Ann S. Moore.* Retrieved February 5, 2005, from http://www.timewarner.com/corp/management/executives_by_business/time_inc/bio/moore_ann.html

Toth, E. L. (2001). How feminist theory advanced the practice of public relations. In R. L. Heath (Ed.), *The handbook of public relations* (pp. 237–246). Thousand Oaks, CA: Sage.

Toth, E. L., & Aldoory, L. (Eds.). (2001). *The gender challenge to media: Diverse voices from the field.* Cresskill, NJ: Hampton Press.

Toth, E. L., & Cline, C. G. (1989). *Beyond the velvet ghetto.* San Francisco: IABC Research Foundation.

Toth, E. L., & Grunig, L. A. (1993). The missing story of women in public relations. *Journal of Public Relations Research, 5,* 153–175.

Toth, E. L., Serini, S. A, Wright, D. K., & Emig, A. G. (1995). Unpublished research data.

Toth, E. L., Serini, S. A., Wright, D. K., & Emig, A. G. (1998). Trends of public relations roles: 1990–1995. *Public Relations Review, 24,* 145–163.

Trager, R., & Obata, Y. (2004). Obscenity decisions in the Japanese and United States Supreme Courts: Cultural values in interpreting free speech. *U.C. Davis Journal of International Law & Policy, 10,* 247–275.

Traudt, P. J. (2005). *Media, audiences, effects: An introduction to the study of media content and audience analysis.* Boston: Pearson.

Treichler, P. A., & Wartella, E. (1986). Interventions: Feminist theory and communication studies. *Communication, 9*(1), 2–18.

Tripp, M. (2000). Rethinking difference: Comparative perspectives from Africa. *Signs, 25,* 649–675.

Tronto, J. (1993). *Moral boundaries: A political argument for an ethic of care.* New York: Routledge.

Tuchman, G. (1978). Introduction: The symbolic annihilation of women by the mass media. In G. Tuchman, A. K. Daniels, & J. Benét (Eds.), *Hearth & home: Images of women in the mass media* (pp. 3–38). New York: Oxford University Press.

Twitchell, J. B. (1996). *AdCultUSA: The triumph of advertising in American culture.* New York: Columbia University Press.

Ulrich's Periodicals Directory. (2005). New Providence, NJ: Bowker.

United Nations. (1995). *The world's women 1995: Trends and statistics.* New York: Author.

United Nations. (1996). *The United Nations and the advancement of women, 1945–1996.* New York: Author.

United Nations Development Fund for Women (UNIFEM). (2002). *Progress of the world's women 2002: Gender equality and the millennium development goals.* New York: Author.

United Nations Development Programme (UNDP). (2001). *Human development report, 2001: Making new technologies work for human development.* New York: Oxford University Press.

United Nations Development Programme (UNDP). (2004). *Human development report, 2004: Cultural liberty in today's diverse world.* New York: Author.

United Nations Educational, Scientific, and Cultural Organization (UNESCO). (1985). *Communication in the service of women: A report on action and research programs, 1980–1985.* Paris: Author.

United Nations Educational, Scientific, and Cultural Organization (UNESCO). (1989). *World communication report.* Paris: Author.

U.S. Bureau of Labor Statistics. (2002). *Table 11: Employed persons by detailed occupation and sex.* Retrieved February 5, 2005, from http://www.bls.gov/cps/wlf-databook.htm

U.S. Bureau of Labor Statistics. (2004). *Table 18: Employed persons by detailed industry, sex, race, and Hispanic or Latino ethnicity.* Retrieved February 5, 2005, from http://www.bls.gov/cps/wlf-databook.htm

U.S. Bureau of Labor Statistics. (2005). *Women in the labor force: A databook.* Retrieved January 25, 2005, from http://www.bls.gov/wlf-databook.htm

U.S. Department of Labor, Women's Bureau. (2002, November). *Facts on working women.* Retrieved May 10, 2005, from www.dol.gov/wb/factsheets/wb002.htm

U.S. Equal Employment Opportunity Commission. (2005). Retrieved June 9, 2005, from http://www.eeoc.gov/stats/jobpat/2002/us.html

Valdivia, A. (1995). Feminist media studies in a global setting: Beyond binary contradictions and into multicultural spectrums. In A. N. Valdivia (Ed.), *Feminism, multiculturalism, and the media: Global diversities* (pp. 7–29). Thousand Oaks, CA: Sage.

Valdivia, A. N. (Ed.). (1995). *Feminism, multiculturalism, and the media.* Thousand Oaks, CA: Sage.

Valentin, I. (1997, August). Title IX: A brief history: 25 years of Title IX. *WEEA Equity Resource Center Digest.* (Report from the U.S. Department of Education)

Valys, S. (1992, August). *Interviews with women working at consumer and business magazines.* Unpublished manuscript.

van Engen, M. L., vanderLeeden, R., & Willemsen, T. M. (2001). Gender, context, and leadership styles: A field study. *Journal of Occupational and Organizational Psychology, 74,* 581–598.

van Zoonen, L. (1991). A tyranny of intimacy? Women, femininity, and television news. In C. Sparks & P. Dahlgren (Eds.), *Communication and citizenship: Journalism and the public sphere in the new media age* (pp. 217–235). London: Routledge.

van Zoonen, L. (1994). *Feminist media studies.* Thousand Oaks, CA: Sage.

van Zoonen, L. (1998). One of the girls? The changing gender of journalism. In C. Carter, G. Branston, & S. Allen (Eds.), *News, gender, and power* (pp. 33–46). New York and London: Routledge.

Victorian Railways Commissioners v. Coultas, 13 App. Cas. 222 (1888).

Vincent, J., Imwold, C., Johnson, J. T., & Massey, D. (2003). Newspaper coverage of female athletes competing in selected sports in the 1996 Centennial Olympic Games: The more things change, the more things stay the same. *Women in Sport and Physical Activity Journal, 12*(1), 1–18.

Wackwitz, L. (2002). Burger on *Miller:* Obscene effects and the filth of a nation. *Journal of Communication, 52,* 196–210.

Waisbord, S., & Morris, N. (2001). Introduction: Rethinking media globalization and state power. In N. Morris & S. Waisbord (Eds.), *Media and globalization: Why the state matters* (pp. vii–xvi). Boulder, CO: Roman & Littlefield.

Walby, S. (1986). *Patriarchy at work: Patriarchal and capitalist relations in employment.* Minneapolis: University of Minnesota Press.

Walby, S. (1997). *Gendered transformations.* London: Routledge.

Walker, M. (2001). Engineering identities. *British Journal of Sociology of Education, 22*(75), 15–30.

Walters, S. D. (1995). *Material girls: Making sense of feminist cultural theory.* Berkeley: University of California Press.

Warner, F. (1997). Imperfect picture: Advertisers have long struggled to adjust to women's changing roles at work and home. They still often miss. In S. Biagi & M. Kern-Foxworth (Eds.), *Facing difference: Race, gender, and mass media* (pp. 223–224). Thousand Oaks, CA: Pine Forge Press.

Warren, C. (1951). *Modern news reporting.* New York: Harper & Brothers. (Also published 1929, 1959).

Washington, J. (2004, April 2). Bonnie's back where she's best: Fuller takes *Star* glossy in a bid to steal *People*'s audience. *National Post* (Canada), p. PM12.

Wasko, J. (2000). Political economy of film. In R. Stam & T. Miller (Eds.), *Film and theory: An anthology* (pp. 221–233). Malden, MA: Blackwell.

Waterman, P. (1993). Hidden from herstory: Women, feminism, and new global solidarity. *Economic and Political Weekly, XXVIII*(44), WS-83–WS-100.

Weaver, D. H., Beam, R., Brownlee, B., Voakes, P. S., & Wilhoit, G. C. (2003a). *The American journalist in the 21st century.* Bloomington: School of Journalism, Indiana University.

Weaver, D. H., Beam, R., Brownlee, B., Voakes, P. S, & Wilhoit, G. C. (2003b, April 10). *The face and mind of the American journalist.* Retrieved January 1, 2005, from http://www.poynter.org/content/content_view.asp?id=28235

Weaver, D. H., & Wilhoit, C G. (Eds.). (1996). *The American journalist in the 1990s: U.S. news people at the end of an era.* Mahwah, NJ: Lawrence Erlbaum.

Weischenberg, S., Keuneke, S., Löffelholz, M., & Scholl, A. (1994). *Frauen im Journalismus: Gutachten über die Geschlechterverhältnisse bei den Medien in Deutschland im Auftrag der Industriegewerkschaft Medien* [Women in journalism: Report upon gender representation in the media in Germany by order of the media union]. Stuttgart, Germany: IG Medien (dju/SWJV).

Weldon, M. (2004, April 21). No news in newsroom census: Gender gap persists. *WOMEN'SNEWS.* Retrieved 2005, February 12, from http: www.womenenews.com/article.cfm/dyn/aid/1797

Wetterer, A. (1994). Rhetorische Präsenz—faktische Marginalität: Zur Situation von Wissenschaftlerinnen in Zeiten der Frauenförderung [Rhetorical presence—actual marginality: The situation of female scientists in times of affirmative action plans]. *Zeitschrift für Frauenforschung* (1/2), 93–110.

Whipple, T. W., & Courtney, A. E. (1985). Female role portrayals in advertising and communication effectiveness: A review. *Journal of Advertising, 14,* 4–8, 17.

Whitaker, W. R., Ramsey, J. E., & Smith, R. D. (2000). *Media writing.* New York: Longman.

White, H. (2005). *Verité reveals the ten deadly sins of overseas factories.* Retrieved March 9, 2005, from http://www.manufacturingnews.com/news/editorials/white.html

Wilkins, B. M., & Andersen, P. A. (1991). Gender differences and similarities in management communication: A meta-analysis. *Management Communication Quarterly, 5,* 6–35.

Wilkins, K. (1999). Development discourse on gender and communication in strategies for social change. *Journal of Communication, 49*(1), 46–68.

Wilkinson v. Downton, 2 Q.B. 57 (1897).

Willard, B. E. (2005). Feminist interventions in biomedical discourse: An analysis of the rhetoric of integrative medicine. *Women's Studies in Communication, 28,* 115–148.

Williams, W., & Martin, F. L. (1911). *The practice of journalism.* Columbia, MO: E.W. Stephens.

Wilson, C. C. II, Gutiérrez, F., & Chao, L. M. (2003). *Racism, sexism, and the media* (3rd ed.). Thousand Oaks, CA: Sage.

Wolf, N. (1991). *The beauty myth: How images of beauty are used against women.* New York: William Morrow.

Wolseley, R. E., & Campbell, L. (1943). *Exploring journalism.* Englewood Cliffs, NJ: Prentice Hall. (Also published 1949, 1957)

Women in broadcasting. (1987, March 4). *Variety*, p. 110.

Women's Environment and Development Organization (WEDO). (2005). *Beijing betrayed*. New York: Author.

Women's Institute for Freedom of the Press. (2005). *Directory of women's media, 2005 edition*. Retrieved January 6, 2006, from http://www.wifp.org/DWM/periodicals.html

WomensRadio. (2005a). *Radio general sales manager gender analysis* (Biz Wiz/Career Paths). Retrieved May 10, 2005, from http://www.womensradio.com/bizwiz/careerpaths/Radio gender.htm

WomensRadio. (2005b.). *Radio GM's not faring well* (Biz Wiz/Career Paths). Retrieved May 10, 2005, from http://www.womensradio.com/

WomensRadio. (2005c). *WomensRadio announces a call for talent*. Retrieved June 20, 2005, from http://www.womensradio.com/

Women's Sports Foundation. (2003). *Title IX and race in intercollegiate sport*. East Meadow, NY: Author.

Wood, J. T. (1994). *Gendered lives: Communication, gender, and culture*. Belmont, CA: Wadsworth.

Wright, D. K., Grunig, L. A., Springston, J. K., & Toth, E. L. (1991). *Under the glass ceiling: An analysis of gender issues in American public relations*. New York: PRSA Foundation.

Wright, E. (1993). *RNS reporting 60 years of religious news service*. Nashville, TN: United Methodist Reporter.

Yammarino, F. J., Dubinsky, A. J., Comer, L. B., & Jolson, M. A. (1997). Women and transformational and contingent reward leadership: A multiple-levels-of-analysis perspective. *Academy of Management Journal, 40*, 205–222.

Young, R. F., & Kahana, E. (1993). Gender, recovery from late-life heart attack and medical care. *Women & Health, 20*, 11–31.

Yrle, A. C., Hartman, S., & Galle, W. P. (2002). An investigation of relationships between communication style and leader-member exchange. *Journal of Communication Management, 6*, 257–268.

Zandy, J. (Ed.). (1990). *Calling home: Working-class women's writings*. New Brunswick, NJ: Rutgers University Press.

Zilliacus-Tikkanen, H. (in press). Women journalists and the gender gap in Finland's news culture. In R. Fröhlich & S. A. Lafky (Eds.), *Women journalists in the Western world: Equal opportunities and what surveys tell us*. London: Hampton Press.

Author Index

Subject Index

About the Editors

Pamela J. Creedon, director of the School of Journalism and Mass Communication at The University of Iowa, previously directed the J-MC program at Kent State University for 7 years and was a faculty member at The Ohio State University for 10 years. An accredited business communicator (ABC), she spent 15 years as an editor and public relations practitioner before entering academe. Currently president of the Association of Schools of Journalism and Mass Communication, with 190 member colleges and universities in the United States, Canada, and eight other countries, she is a member of the Hearst Foundation Journalism Awards Advisory Board. She serves on the editorial boards of *Public Relations Review* and the *Journal of Public Relations Research.* She has edited two books published by Sage, *Women in Mass Communication* and *Women, Media, and Sport,* and coedited *Seeking Equity for Women in Journalism and Mass Communication,* by Erlbaum. She is a member of the International Advisory Board of the College of Communication and Media Sciences at Zayed University, in the United Arab Emirates. She earned her MA in journalism from the University of Oregon and her BA from Mount Union College.

Judith Cramer is an associate professor of Mass Communications, Journalism, TV, & Film Studies at St. John's University. She previously taught at Buffalo State College–SUNY and Long Island University. She spent 15 years as a news and sports reporter, news director, talk show host and producer, and station manager in commercial and public radio in New England, Ohio, and New York. She has written several articles and authored chapters in *Women in Mass Communication* and *Women, Media, and Sport,* published by Sage, and *Seeking Equity for Women in Journalism and Mass Communication,* by Erlbaum. She was a fellow in the Journalism and Mass Communication Leadership Institute for Diversity program, is a past member of the executive committee of the Association for Education in Journalism and Mass Communication (AEJMC), and currently serves on the editorial board of the Professional Studies Review, an interdisciplinary journal exclusively devoted to the needs and interests of those working in career-oriented fields. She earned her PhD in mass communication and cultural studies from The Union Institute and University, in Ohio; her MA in applied communication from the University of Hartford, in Connecticut; and her BS in sports information/journalism from Keene State College, in New Hampshire.

About the Contributors

Linda Aldoory, PhD, is an associate professor of communication and affiliate associate professor of women's studies at the University of Maryland College Park. In 2005, she became editor of the *Journal of Public Relations Research.* Her research on leadership includes two articles published in 2004 and 1998 in the *Journal of Public Relations Research.* She coedited the book *The Gender Challenge to Media: Diverse Voices From the Field;* she has an article in *Journal of Communication,* titled "A (Re)Conceived Feminist Paradigm for Public Relations: A Case for Substantial Improvement"; and she has an upcoming book chapter in *Mass Media and Society* (4th ed.), coauthored with Dr. Shawn Parry-Giles, on "Intersectionality in Feminist Media Research: Studies of Media Production, Representation, and Reception." She received her doctorate from Syracuse University and her master's degree from the University of Texas at Austin.

Julie L. Andsager is an associate professor in the School of Journalism and Mass Communication at The University of Iowa, with a secondary appointment in the Department of Community and Behavioral Health. Her research centers on media framing and message processing about gender, particularly regarding health issues and public opinion. Her research has appeared in *Communication Research, Journal of Communication, Health Communication, Women & Health,* and *Journalism & Mass Communication Quarterly,* among other journals. She is an associate editor for *Journalism & Mass Communication Quarterly* and serves on the Association for Education in Journalism and Mass Communication's Standing Committee for Research. She won the AEJMC Krieghbaum Under-40 Award for research, teaching, and public service in 2003. She received her PhD from the University of Tennessee.

Maurine H. Beasley is a professor at the Philip Merrill College of Journalism at the University of Maryland, College Park. She is the author/editor/coeditor of eight books, dealing mainly with the experience of women in journalism and journalism education. A graduate of the University of Missouri, Columbia, and the holder of a master's degree from Columbia University, she has a PhD in American Civilization from George Washington University. She is a former national president of both the AEJMC and the American Journalism Historians Association.

Diane L. Borden is professor and interim director of the School of Communication at San Diego State University. She teaches graduate seminars in mass communication law and theory as well as undergraduate courses in journalism. She holds a BA in technical journalism from Colorado State University, an MA in communication from Stanford University, and a PhD in communications from the University of Washington. She came to academe after a lengthy career as an editor and publisher in a variety of media markets. She has a keen interest in how the mass media and other cultural institutions, such as the judicial system, historically have constructed social reality, particularly images of women and minorities. Her research frequently focuses on the intersection of communication, gender, and the law. Her legal scholarship has been published in several refereed journals, and she is involved in a number of ongoing research projects, including a study of gender and cyberlibel.

Candace Perkins Bowen taught journalism and English and advised a high school newspaper for more than 20 years in Illinois and Virginia before she joined the School of Journalism and Mass Communication at Kent State University in 1995. She now directs its Scholastic Media Program, running two statewide press associations. As liaison to the College of Education, she works with those seeking Ohio Integrated Language Arts licensure and teaches Media Writing. She has served as vice head and head of AEJMC's Scholastic Journalism Division and received its Journalism Educator Award in 2005. She was also vice head and head of the Council of Affiliates. A former president of the Journalism Education Association and the 1989 Dow Jones Newspaper Fund High School Journalism Teacher of the Year, she has focused recently on showing how journalism fulfills curricular standards for English. She coauthored the 2002 book *Applying NCTE/IRA Standards in Classroom Journalism Projects.*

Carolyn M. Byerly is an associate professor, Department of Journalism, at Howard University, Washington, D.C., where she serves on the graduate faculty in Mass Communication and Media Studies and in the interdisciplinary Women's Studies Program. She teaches courses in mass communication theory, research methods, media effects, and political communication. Her research areas are political economy of media, media and social movements, and mass communication theory and methods, all of these with regard to gender, race, culture, and sexual orientation. She is the coauthor (with Karen Ross) of *Women and Media: A Critical Introduction* (Blackwell, 2006) and the coeditor (with Karen Ross) of *Women and Media: International Perspectives* (Blackwell, 2004). Among her articles and book chapters are "After September 11: Formation of an Oppositional Dialogue" (*Feminist Media Studies,* Fall 2005), and "Women and the Concentration of Media Ownership," in R. R. Rush, C. Oukrup, and P. Creedon (Eds.), *Women in Journalism and Mass Communication* (Erlbaum, 2004).

Carolyn Garrett Cline, former associate professor of journalism at the University of Southern California, earned her PhD and MA from Indiana University. She earned her BS from Boston University's School of Public Communication in journalism. Cline was principal investigator of the IABC *Velvet Ghetto* studies of the increasing numbers of women in public relations.

Jannette L. Dates has spent the past 24 years at Howard University, serving as a faculty member in the Department of Radio, Television, and Film, associate dean, and currently dean of the School of Communications. She has been a frequent speaker and panelist on national television and radio programs, where she has discussed images of African Americans in the mass media. She served as a fellow at the Freedom Forum Media Studies Center at Columbia University in 1992. She coedited the book *Split Image: African Americans in the Mass Media,* authoring 6 of the 10 chapters. Her work with AEJMC includes 20 years of service on task forces, committees, and panels. She served as president from 2003–2004.

Meenakshi Gigi Durham is an associate professor in The University of Iowa School of Journalism and Mass Communication. Her work centers on media and the politics of the body, with an emphasis on gender, sexuality, race, and youth cultures. She has published widely on representations of women in fashion and beauty magazines and on adolescents, media, and gender. She is the coeditor (with Douglas Kellner) of the book *Media and Cultural Studies: KeyWorks* (Blackwell, 2001; second edition, 2005). She is currently writing a book on adolescent girls and the media. She teaches courses in gender and media and magazine writing. She received The University of Iowa J-School's SPJ Outstanding Faculty Member award in 2003. Before coming to Iowa in the fall of 2000, she taught at the University of Texas at Austin, where she was the recipient of an honorable mention for the campuswide Gilbert Teaching Excellence Award in Women's and Gender Studies.

Romy Fröhlich is a full professor at Ludwig-Maximilians-University Munich (Germany) and president of the German Communication Association (DGPuK). She received her MA in mass communication and journalism

(University Munich) and her PhD in mass communication and journalism (University for Music and Theatre Hannover HMT). She has been a scientific employee/assistant professor at the Institute for Communication Research at the HMT and visiting scholar at the School of Journalism, The Ohio State University. From 1998 until 2000, she was a full professor at Ruhr-University Bochum. Since 1998, she has been member of the associate editorial board of the scientific journal *Feminist Media Studies* (Routledge) and head of the educational division of the German Public Relations Association (DPRG). Her professional experience includes the following positions: senior consultant at Kroehl Identity Consultants (PR-Agency), Frankfurt; research assistant at GFK-Market Research-Company, Nürnberg; and scientific assistant at the Press and Information Department, Munich Fair and Exhibition Association (MMG). Her major research and teaching interests are public relations, women in mass communication, journalism education, news content/content analysis, and e-learning.

Sammye Johnson is a professor in the Department of Communication at Trinity University in San Antonio, Texas, where she holds the Carlos Augustus de Lozano Chair in Journalism. Prior to joining the faculty at Trinity, Johnson was an award-winning magazine editor and writer for more than a decade. She continues to freelance, publishing more than 350 magazine articles and receiving 18 writing awards. Her research focuses on magazine content and history, particularly the depiction of women on covers and editorial pages. Her work has been published in the top refereed journals in the journalism and mass communication field. In addition to contributing 13 chapters to books about magazine publishing, she is the coauthor of *Magazine Publishing* and *The Magazine From Cover to Cover*. Johnson received the BS degree in journalism, cum laude, and the MS degree in journalism, summa cum laude, from Northwestern University, Medill School of Journalism.

Maria B. Marron is professor and chair of the Department of Journalism at Central Michigan University (CMU). She holds a doctorate in journalism/mass communication from Ohio University; a master's degree in journalism from The Ohio State University; a bachelor's degree in English, Latin, and French; and a postgraduate diploma in education from University College Dublin, Ireland. She has worked in journalism and public relations in Ireland and in journalism in the United States. Before assuming her current position at CMU, she served in administrative capacities at University College Dublin, Ireland, and at Zayed University, Dubai, United Arab Emirates. She has taught at The Ohio State University, Texas State University–San Marcos, and CMU. Her research interests include investigative journalism, with a specific emphasis on the British Isles, ethics, law, and international communication.

Debra L. Mason is an award-winning journalist and executive director of the Religion Newswriters Association (RNA), the world's only membership association for journalists reporting on religion in the mainstream media. In that position, she directs RNA's training programs and tool development, including overseeing the group's annual meeting, Web site, contests, and weekly Internet news resource service, ReligionLink. Under her leadership, RNA and its foundation have developed resources reaching more than 5,000 journalists each week. She coedited *Readings in Religion as News* (Iowa State University Press) and has written and spoken widely about religion in the U.S. news media. She holds master's degrees from the Medill School of Journalism and Trinity Lutheran Seminary, and has a PhD in mass communication from Ohio University. Before working for RNA full-time, she was an associate professor of journalism at Otterbein College in suburban Columbus, Ohio.

Nancy Mitchell is an associate professor and head of the Advertising Sequence in the College of Journalism and Mass Communications at the University of Nebraska–Lincoln, where she has taught since 1990. Previously, she taught at West Texas A&M. She has 15 years of professional media experience as a copywriter and designer. Her research focuses on effective communication with underrepresented groups, and she has delivered numerous speeches on images of women in advertising. She earned her undergraduate degree at Northwestern, master's at West Texas A&M, and PhD at the University of Nebraska.

June O. Nicholson is an associate professor in the School of Mass Communications at Virginia Commonwealth University in Richmond, Virginia, and teaches in the journalism program. She is a former reporter for newspapers in North Carolina and Virginia, and covered state government in Virginia for a decade. She has written about diversity in journalism and journalism education and is the lead editor for a forthcoming book about women in contemporary journalism to be published by the University of Illinois Press. She also is the codeveloper of a newsroom-training curriculum on covering multicultural communities offered by the Society of Professional Journalists (SPJ). She has headed SPJ's Journalism Education Committee since 2000. She holds a master's degree in public affairs journalism from The American University in Washington, D.C., and a bachelor's degree in journalism from the University of North Carolina at Chapel Hill.

Lana F. Rakow is a professor of communication and the director of the Center for Community Engagement at the University of North Dakota. She earned her PhD degree from the University of Illinois, Champaign–Urbana. She is the author or editor of four books, including *Feminist Communication*

Theory (Sage, 2004), with Laura Wackwitz, along with a number of other publications on gender and communication. She also has interests in theory and research, the history of communication technologies, reforming higher education, and communication in communities. She recently served as president of the North Dakota Professional Communicators and served 6 years on the Accrediting Council on Education in Journalism and Mass Communications. She has conducted several major studies resulting in special reports, including one on the concerns of women faculty and staff at the University of North Dakota and the future of communication professionals in North Dakota.

Roseanna M. Smith is an MA candidate in Athletic Administration at The University of Iowa (UI) and is the Coaching Director for Iowa City Kickers Soccer Club. Smith worked for *The Daily Iowan,* the UI's student newspaper, for 4 years, where she received a full tuition scholarship. The Davenport, Iowa, native graduated with a BA in journalism and sports studies in May of 2004. She worked as a reporter for the *Quad-City Times* and interned for the *Des Moines Register,* the *Sporting News,* and the *Columbus Dispatch.*

H. Leslie Steeves is professor and director of Graduate Studies and Research at the School of Journalism and Communication, University of Oregon, where she has taught since 1987. Her PhD is in Mass Communications from the University of Wisconsin–Madison. Her research focuses on two areas and their intersection: women's roles and representations in mass media, and communications in developing countries, especially sub-Saharan Africa. She has published a number of articles in these areas, as well as a book: *Gender Violence and the Press: The St. Kizito Story* (Ohio University Monographs in International Studies, 1997). She also is coauthor (with Srinivas Melkote) of *Communication for Development in the Third World: Theory and Practice for Empowerment,* 2nd edition (Sage, 2001). She has had two Fulbright grants for teaching and research in Africa and directs an annual study abroad program in Ghana.

Linda Steiner is an associate professor at Rutgers University, in New Brunswick, New Jersey. She earned her PhD at the University of Illinois at Urbana. Her most recent books are the coedited *Critical Readings: Gender and Media* and the coauthored *Women and Journalism.* Besides her book chapters, she has published articles in, among others, *Journalism & Mass Communication Quarterly; Journalism Studies; Journalism: Theory, Practice, Criticism; American Journalism;* and *Journalism History.* She is author of "Conceptions of Gender in Reporting Textbooks, 1890–1990" and coauthor of *And Baby Makes Two: Motherhood Without Marriage.* She is currently editor of Critical Studies in Media Communication and serves on the editorial boards of seven scholarly journals.

Shayla Thiel Stern is an assistant professor in the Department of Communication at DePaul University. She received a PhD in Mass Communication from The University of Iowa and an MA in Communication, Culture, and Technology from Georgetown University. Previously, she worked as "Music & Nightlife" editor for WashingtonPost.com, Affiliate Sales Manager at Cars.com, Television and Careers Correspondent for CNN.com, Community Content Manager for Edmunds.com, Content Manager for Recommender, Inc., and editor of the *Journal of Communication Inquiry,* and she has been a contributor to the *Washington Post, Britannica,* the *Chronicle of Higher Education,* and other publications. She has published academic articles in *Feminist Media Studies* and the *Journal of Electronic Publishing,* as well as a book titled *Girl Wide Web: Girls, the Internet, and the Negotiation of Identity.* Her book *Instant Identity: Adolescent Girls Articulating Gender in the World of Instant Messaging* will be published by Peter Lang Publishing in 2006.

Elizabeth L. Toth, PhD, is a full professor in the Department of Communication of the University of Maryland, College Park. She has coauthored *Women and Public Relations: How Gender Influences Practice; The Velvet Ghetto: The Increasing Numbers of Women in Public Relations; Beyond the Velvet Ghetto;* and the Public Relations Society of America *Glass Ceiling* studies. She coedited *The Gender Challenge to Media: Diverse Voices From the Field.* She has published more than 80 articles, book chapters, book reviews, trade publications, and convention papers. Her research has appeared in the *Journal of Public Relations Research, Public Relations Review, Journalism and Mass Communication Educator,* and *Communication Yearbook.* Toth edited the *Journal of Public Relations Research* between 1995 and 2001. In 2001, she became coeditor of *Journalism Studies,* a new international scholarly journal. In 2005, she received a $10,000 grant from the Public Relations Society of America to continue research on gender issues and public relations.

Laura A. Wackwitz is a feminist scholar, teacher, and digital documentarian, with particular interest in issues of communication, media, and social justice. She earned a PhD from the Grady College of Journalism and Mass Communication at the University of Georgia. Her work has been published in a variety of outlets, including *Women's Studies International Forum, Journal of Communication,* and *Free Speech Yearbook.* She and Lana F. Rakow have coauthored a number of pieces together, including *Feminist*

Communication Theory (2004). She has also produced several ethnographic-style documentaries on community mental health services, including one on the use of crisis respite homes for rural mental health care and another on an intervention program for youth with both mental health and juvenile justice issues.